Athenian Culture and Society

Athenian
Culture
and Society

T. B. L. Webster

Professor Emeritus, Stanford University,
Formerly Professor of Greek,
University College London

UNIVERSITY OF CALIFORNIA PRESS
Berkeley and Los Angeles 1973

University of California Press
Berkeley and Los Angeles, California

ISBN: 0-520-02323-4
Library of Congress Catalog Card Number: 72-87197

Preface

When this book was first proposed to me, I felt doubtful of my competence to undertake it. But over some fifty years of studying Greek I have come into contact with a good deal of the evidence, and particularly in the years after World War II with Michael Polanyi in Manchester and with A. H. M. Jones and my other colleagues in University College London, I was much concerned with this sort of problem. Still more, my teaching in Stanford has convinced me that the relation between culture and society is a very live issue in the modern world. My doubts, of course, remain, and I can only say that I have tried to state simply such evidence as I know and to draw a very few tentative conclusions at the end. I have been very greatly encouraged and helped by my colleague, William Berg III, who has read my manuscript and saved me from many imprecisions and errors (for the mistakes that remain he is in no way responsible).

Stanford T. B. L. Webster

Contents

The Illustrations

THE PLATES

Acknowledgment

The author and the publisher would like to thank the following
for the illustrations appearing in this book: Alinari for fig. 6;
Alison Frantz for figs 3, 4, 11 and 13-18; the German Archaeological Institute, Athens, for figs 1-2; the Sopprintendenza,
Ferrara, for fig. 9; the Trustees of the British Museum for fig.
10; the Louvre for figs 5, 7 and 8; the Metropolitan Museum,
New York, for figs 19-20; the Villa Giulia Museum, Rome, for
fig. 12; the Narodowi Museum, Warsaw, for fig. 21.

1 *Introduction*

All four terms of my title need defining. It is convenient to concentrate this study on a single place, and Athens has a better
right than any other ancient Greek city to be the place. It is
tenable also that the greatest flowering of Greek culture took
place in Athens roughly between the time of the Persian wars,
490-80 B.C., and the accession of Alexander the Great in 336.
When we think of ancient Greek culture we think primarily of
Periclean democracy, the Parthenon, the tragedy of Sophocles,
the comedy of Aristophanes, the philosophy of Plato and Aristotle,
and all of these belong to Athens and fall within this time-
span.

Other Greek states had different forms of government, notably the oligarchy of birth in Sparta with the whole conception
of life that this entailed and the military tyranny in Syracuse
at the beginning and middle of the period: these will only
concern us in so far as they affected the Athenians and influenced
either their ideas or their practical politics. Other Greek states
produced outstanding thinkers, poets, and artists, and these
obviously concern us; most of them either visited Athens or were
visited by Athenians, and so find a natural place in this study.

I am, however, using Athenian both as a geographical and
as a chronological term, and the chronological use also needs
defining. The Persian wars make a good starting-date because
the main achievement comes after them, but the origins of this
achievement have to be sought further back. Something must be
said, therefore, at least in outline, about the sixth century as

the background to the politics, drama, art, and philosophy of the fifth.

We may have to go further back to Homer and the Mycenaean age. If one were trying to write about modern culture and society, one would, I think, be faced with a dilemma: one would have to admit that both the Graeco-Roman and the Hebrew traditions were strong elements in our culture, but one would have also to ask whether the best and most progressive elements in our society owe or should owe anything to those traditions at all. Behind classical Greek civilisation stands the brilliant culture of the Minoan-Mycenaean world surviving both in the epics of Homer and in Greek religious practices; we shall have to ask what was the effect of this tradition on classical Athens.

Culture contains a static element and a dynamic element. The static element is tradition, which continues moderately unchanged. The dynamic side of culture is the growing points, the ceaseless changes to new forms. In the modern world we think of science and technology as dynamic, and we may even speak of two cultures with the implication that there is no communication between the adherents of one and the adherents of the other. The dynamic culture contains mathematics and science and technology and what depends on them, most obviously warfare, communications, and medicine, to a lesser degree music, architecture, and art. But here the dichotomy breaks down because music, architecture and art belong to the other culture. Architecture, art, and music are more open (architecture indeed must be open) to the new technology than poetry or philosophy, but the influence of technology is only one kind of change, although it is dominant today. Technology may provide the creator in any side of culture with new materials; the other kind of change may be defined very roughly as the new view that the creator has of his task. This is the dynamic element as opposed to the static element of continuing in the traditional forms.

The relation between static and dynamic differs very much in different times and different places. Technology has run away with us and is to a greater or less extent affecting the other arts and sciences, most obviously, as I have said, communications and warfare; politics, law, and religion are largely static. In ancient

Athens, to take a superficial and preliminary view, technology was comparatively static; so were warfare, communications, architecture, athletics, and religion. The dynamic elements were philosophy, mathematics, anthropology, geography, medicine, history, poetry, music, sculpture, painting, politics, and law.

I have not given a definition of culture, but the last two paragraphs give some idea of what activities must be included in its range. Not all of them are equally important and selection, which in any case would be necessary, is also imposed by the very varying amounts of evidence available in the ancient world. In all of them there is a part for the expert and a part for the non-expert: the priest and the worshipper, the doctor and the patient, the general and the common soldier, the dramatist and his audience, the writer and the reader. It is the non-expert element which brings in society so that a rough definition of Athenian culture would be those kinds of expertise which are accepted by Athenian society.

Athenian society is the whole body of people living in Attica. They are male and female, old and young, rich and poor, citizens and foreigner, free and enslaved. If we look at these pairs today, the slave is in the technical sense non-existent, and we see little cultural distinction between male and female or between citizen and foreigner, but we have learnt that there is a generation gap and the gulf between the rich and the poor is only too obvious. We have to keep these pairs in mind when we examine the organisation of Athenian society for private and for public life. In particular we want to know where in society the experts are found and where in society the non-experts are found: what is the social status of poet, artist, and philosopher, and what is the social range of their audiences.

The title is Athenian Culture and Society. This 'and' might be the kind of 'and' which links 'bacon and egg', which implies that they are entirely distinct and heterogeneous subjects only united on a plate at certain times of day. But other pairs like 'governors and governed' suggest quite a different sort of relationship: it is true that the two are heterogeneous, but neither of the two can exist without the other: governors must have people to govern, and the governed are only so called because they have

3

governors. Undoubtedly the 'and' of our title is of the second kind: neither poet nor philosopher nor artist can exist without their audience, but when one considers the tiny audiences who understand the modern poet or scholar or scientist, they scarcely seem to be part of society in any normal sense of the word, and high culture and society look as heterogeneous as bacon and egg.

To try to record the relationship between Athenian culture and society is the chief purpose of this book. Particularly we should like to know what elements in society encouraged the dynamic growth of culture in so many directions. There are many questions to which some sort of answer must be attempted. One has been mentioned already: the size of the audience. How were the audiences constituted for the different branches of Athenian culture? Was there anything corresponding to the modern research institute or learned society at one end of the scale or to the television audience at the other?

Two other questions immediately arise if one looks at the modern world. The first is closely connected with the tiny audiences of the scholar and scientist. He is so specialised that only his closest colleagues can understand him, and yet it seems that the great advances in science and scholarship have come from cross-fertilisation from another branch. What evidence have we either for the problem or for the answer in the ancient world?

The second question is the pace with which new ideas are generally received. For the last century at any rate every new idea in music and art has been greeted with violent opposition and has taken a very long time to permeate society. It is certainly deplorable, but it is not lethal, that many would still prefer to listen to Brahms rather than Britten. It is far more dangerous that every new political idea has met with the embattled opposition of the establishment and has only won its way by violence.

These are some of the questions, and I have now to plot the course. First the main features of Athenian culture must be described with the emphasis on those fields in which a rapid advance was made, since it is here that the problems of isolation, cross-fertilisation, acceptance, and opposition are likely to appear. The next few chapters will be concerned primarily with

Athenian society. We have to consider the size and nature of the country, the ease of communication between different parts of Attica and Athens, the nature of the city itself, and its religious, political, legal, and commercial centres. We have to consider the population, the numbers of citizens, foreigners, and slaves, and the distribution of wealth. We have to consider family life, social life, and the meeting places for private and public occasions.

Before passing to the arts and sciences, which are our chief concern, we have to try and see the adult Athenian, who creates them or uses them, as a person; he has had a certain kind of education, mental and physical (and it may be right for the ancient Athenian to regard national service as an extension of education), he has views about the gods and performs religious duties, he plays a part in politics, he serves as juryman and arbitrator and pleads his own case in lawsuits.

Religion, politics, and the law inevitably raise the kind of questions which will concern us with the arts and sciences. Traditional religion occupies a great deal of Athenian life and may be a stabilising force. Yet it may also be manipulated by politicians and its assumptions may be contradicted by philosophers and scientists. But how many people are affected and how much is left undisturbed? Political and legal theory and practice will be close together if the response of society to the changes in theory is quick. We shall have to ask who the leading figures were, who were their friends in other walks of life, how did they treat their audiences and what sort of opposition did they meet. Litigation played so large a part in Athenian life that it is not wholly unexpected that legal argument provided some of the terminology for philosophical and scientific argument.

Of the arts fine pottery plays a unique role in Athenian life and in our knowledge of Athenian life. The pottery industry is the only industry which we know in any detail; we can say something about the scale of the industry, about the number of potters and painters employed, about the size of the workshops, about the home and overseas markets. What is more important is that we know something about the social status of the potter-painters and of their patrons, and we can see that fine pottery specially commissioned for aristocratic symposia was occasionally used for political propaganda.

We can then turn to the architects, sculptors, and painters. Here we are concerned not so much with their art but with their lives and their friends, their patrons, their assistants, the technical treatises that they wrote or inspired, the criticism that they evoked and their reaction to it.

Poetry can be divided into dramatic poetry and non-dramatic poetry. Non-dramatic poetry leads us into the world of international athletes, for whom elaborate victor-odes were written and performed, particularly in the first half of the fifth century. There was also a large amount of choral poetry written and performed in honour of the gods, particularly the dithyrambs, which were performed by competing choruses of men and boys from the ten Athenian tribes in honour of Dionysos. Then there was the poetry performed solo by the great kithara players, also often in competition at religious festivals. These poets were also musicians, and music has its own history, technical literature, and criticism. Outside these again were the reciters, the rhapsodes, who had their own range of poetry and also expounded their recitations to large audiences. Finally the symposion had its own poetry as well as excerpts from epic, choral lyric, and drama.

The audiences of the dramatic poets, both tragic and comic, consisted of the whole body of Athenian citizens, resident aliens, and visitors from abroad, and the performers at any one festival amounted to something in the neighbourhood of two hundred. This was mass entertainment, and therefore, quite apart from its quality as drama, tells us a great deal about culture and society. We can see over a long period, from the early fifth century to the late fourth, how tragic and comic poets reacted to the changes in society and how the changing society reacted to tragedy and comedy. We can also see the dramatists as purveyors of ideas, religious, moral, political, philosophical, and scientific, and it is a reasonable assumption that these ideas cannot have been wholly unintelligible or wholly unwelcome to these mass audiences since the dramatists were after all competing for a prize.

6

It is much more difficult to see what the methods of dissemination were for doctors, historians, scientists, and philosophers. We shall have to put together what information can be found about books and the book trade, recitations and discussions in private houses, public lectures, discussions in Athenian meeting places, and actual schools for medicine and philosophy. Drama again provides a corrective because drama shows that a good many of the ideas of scientists and philosophers could be put across to mass audiences.

At the end of this survey it should at least be possible to formulate the relation between Athenian culture and society more clearly and to suggest some of the factors which may have been responsible for the astonishingly rapid advance of culture.

The subject is large and complicated, and I shall be told that the argument is hard to follow. In fact I have not tried to present an argument. I have tried to suggest the facts that seem to me relevant and to give a simplified picture in the conclusion. I know that to some of my readers the material is unfamiliar, and for them particularly the grouping by genres—politics, art, drama, etc.—seemed preferable to an analysis of culture and society in which each side of the opposition contained all the heterogeneous elements. The boundary between culture and society is so fluid that I could not keep culture out of Chapters 3-5, where I was trying to give some picture of the Athenian as a social being, before entering the areas where culture and society obviously interact: houses inevitably lead on to symposia, children being educated to educational theory, religious practices to theology.

In Chapters 6-13, where I am concerned with the interrelation of culture and society in different areas—politics, drama, art, etc.—I have tried to shape the chapters, where possible, as a progression through three stages. The first stage is an account of society in this aspect. How large were the audiences and what range of Athenians knew the practitioners and their works? What was the social status of the practitioners and, where relevant, who were their patrons? The second stage is an account of the aims and achievements of the practitioners and such changes in their aims as can be observed in the period under

7

review. The third stage is concerned with reactions. How far did practice give rise to informed criticism and new theory? And, most important of all, how far did advances in one field affect practitioners in another field? I think a case can be made that legal argument influenced the form of prose, that doctors influenced historians, and that mathematicians influenced philosophers. From this mass of evidence emerges a picture of a small, competitive but open and viable society which reacted very quickly to cultural change. The new ideas probably came largely from the wealthy and well-born, but they spread through society widely and quickly. This meant that society made a very real demand on the thinker, writer, or artist that he should be intelligible. So the new idea is put out in a simple form; it can be reformulated to include more of the complexities of reality; but when the form gets too complicated, it is discarded, and a new simple form is offered instead. The Greek genius may oversimplify, but it is always intelligible.

Two minor points may conclude this introduction. I have, I hope, introduced the main figures, politicians, writers, and artists, adequately in the text. But just because the permeability of society is an important part of the subject, a number of minor figures pass across the stage; it will generally be clear who and what they are. But their dates and professions can be found at once by reference to the index of names and places.

The second point is proper names. I have not attempted to be consistent. I have used the Greek form unless the person or place is so well known in the Latin spelling that the Greek form seems absurd: I cannot bring myself to write Thoukudides or Platon. One convention in tragedy-titles I have found extremely useful: where the play is preserved, I use the Latin form, e.g. *Hercules Furens*, but where the play only survives in fragments I use the Greek form.

2 *The Greek Achievement*

Achievement is essentially the achievement of something new, and this implies a starting point which is old. Achievement is also something done, and this implies tools and materials with which to do it. Before trying to describe the Greek achievement something must be said of the starting point, and something must be said of Greek technology.

Behind classical Athens lay the brilliant Minoan-Mycenaean civilisation, then the so-called dark ages, then in the latter part of the eighth century the poetry of Homer and Hesiod, then the archaic period in which lie the beginnings of the Greek achievement. I call the preceding civilisation Minoan-Mycenaean, because the two are so interwoven that for our purpose it is unprofitable to try and distinguish them clearly. It is enough to know that the Minoan civilisation of Crete was not Greek and was wide open to influences from Egypt and the Near East, and that the Mycenaeans were in contact with the Minoans from the seventeenth century B.C., so that there was a gradual take-over of ideas and technical procedures. But the Mycenaeans, as was finally proved by the decipherment of the Linear B tablets in 1952 by Michael Ventris, were Greeks, and their civilisation, however much they owed directly, or indirectly through the Minoans, to Egypt and the Near East, was a Greek civilisation.[1]

Mycenaean civilisation collapsed in the twelfth century, whether from natural disaster, emigration, Northern invasion, or a mixture of the three. The effect of the four hundred years or more, the dark ages, which separate Homer and Hesiod from the

9

Mycenaeans, is that the past appears as a heroic age when men were far greater than the men of the present, and when Greece united in great enterprises. Mycenaean palace civilisation was gone for ever, and the small Greek states gradually changed from clusters of habitation round the nobles' houses to the classical city-state which centred on the Agora, the commercial and official area.[2] The new spiritual element, which to judge from the pottery started to appear a little before 1000 (*fig. 1*), was an intense belief in the power of human reason to reduce a disorderly world to manageable and precise shapes, a belief which finds another expression in the very unmysterious Homeric view of the gods and the way in which they should be treated.[3]

From the Mycenaeans the classical Greeks derived their heroic mythology, their divine mythology, and their religion. The channels of descent through the dark ages were of various kinds. The stories grew gradually during the Mycenaean age round the great Mycenaean centres like Mycenae, Argos, Pylos, Thebes, Iolkos, Athens. They were handed down by generations of oral poets, some of whom went to Ionia, and this line ended with Homer and his immediate successors, while the mainland line ended with Hesiod and his successors; it is probably wrong to think of the two lines as distinct, and there may have been interconnections all the time.[4]

It is not easy to be certain where there was actual continuity of cult between Mycenaean and classical Greece. It has been shown clearly for the island of Keos; according to Athenian tradition the Athenian Acropolis was never sacked and the archaeological tradition seems to confirm this; continuity is highly probable in Eleusis and probable in Delos and Delphi. Caution may very well have led us to underrate this continuity, and a recent study has suggested that, in Attica particularly, both funerary customs and material objects survived, and that the figure-style of Attic geometric art is based on Mycenaean painting. Probably also some Mycenaean tombs had an unbroken tradition of cult, and certainly some hero-cults were started in the eighth century at Mycenaean tombs in Attica.[5]

The heritage of the past comes to the classical Athenian in different guises. In religious customs the tradition is continuous, and the classical Athenian felt that he was performing services that were old and venerable. But when he looked at the mythology of the gods and heroes, Homer and Hesiod interposed themselves between him and Mycenaean civilisation. They were his education when he was young; when he grew up he heard them recited at festivals; the tragic poets took their subject matter from them; they were discussed by the philosophers; the first Greek historian modelled himself on Homer. We shall have to return to this influence again and again, and it is a very strong traditional force.[6] These are some of the components: first the vision of Mycenaean gods and heroes as brilliant and strong, which, because they were Greek, gave all subsequent Greeks a feeling of optimism about being Greek, and (what we have largely lost since the nineteenth century) a set of religious and legendary paradigms for looking at their own culture and society. Second I should put the idea of a grand system (and here it is relevant to compare the great Attic geometric vases of the same period, *fig. 2*): a great deal of material about an enormous number of heroes is superbly organised into a complicated narrative with all sorts of checks and balances in the *Iliad* and the *Odyssey*, and an enormous numbers of gods and descendants of gods are organised into an immense and meaningful family tree in Hesiod's *Theogony*. These were examples which showed Herodotos the possibility of organising his history and Aeschylus the possibility of writing a connected trilogy.

Two minor elements, similes and personifications, should be mentioned here because they played such an important part in later Greek thought. Long similes are the creation of our Homer and not part of the old epic tradition. The long simile is a picture from the everyday life of the poet's audience to illustrate the situation in the heroic past which the poet wants them to appreciate. 'But not even so could the Trojans put the Achaeans to flight but they held on, just as a careful craftswoman holds the scales: she holds the balance and makes the wool equal in either pan, as she draws the balance up, that she may win a poor pittance for her children. Even so their battle was strained equally.' The poet wants to bring home this moment of crisis in a long ago battle, when the Greeks were just holding a Trojan break-through. The lines of battle are taut like the strings holding the scale-pans, they quiver as the pans quiver with the addition of a little more wool; the military operation is desperately important, just as the woman's work means life or starvation for her children. This use of a working model to explain the unknown is something new, but is essentially similar to the working models provided a century and a half later by the scientist to explain the workings of the universe.[7]

By personification I mean the attribution to something not a human being, of a quality or qualities normally associated with a human being. In Homer the range of personification includes inanimate things, 'the ruthless stone' and the spears that 'yearn to taste flesh', natural phenomena such as the 'Sun, son of Hyperion' or 'rosy-fingered Dawn', and invisible forces which affect either the human body (like Death or his brother Sleep) or the human mind (such as Prayers and Justice, the daughters of Zeus) or human life generally, like Fate or Nemesis. In Hesiod's *Theogony*, 901f., Zeus and Themis (Right), the daughter of Earth and Heaven, have three children, Good Order, Justice, and Peace, who are identified with the Seasons; thus the new moral and political order in the city-state is based on the old physical order of the universe. Personification is not only a method of understanding and speaking about the dark things and forces which surround early man, but it is also a method of showing their relationship to each other and an impressive way of arguing about them; and so it remains.[8]

Beside this brief account of the mental equipment behind the classical Athenians, some account must also be given of their material means, their technology. By modern standards it was of course extremely backward, and there was no technological revolution like ours which shook society through and through and left it doubtful of survival. Many of the techniques were old but underwent considerable refinement, which made great artistic development possible. Thus the essential techniques of glazed pottery were discovered in the Mycenaean age but were developed to produce the superb Attic red-figured pottery of our period. The technique of stone-carving was borrowed from Egypt in the seventh century, when Greeks became rich enough to have stone temples and stone statues, and was gradually developed to the stage that we see in the Parthenon and its sculpture.[9]

Early Greek bronze statuettes were cast solid, and in the seventh century larger figures were made by hammering thin bronze-plates over a wooden core, but before the end of the sixth century large statues were being cast in Athens by the lost-wax process. It was this that made possible the free sculpture of the classical period like Myron's Discobolus, and in the fifth and fourth century the great sculptors worked in bronze rather than in marble; when they worked in marble they made a clay model first, as they would for bronze, and used a method of pointing to reproduce the clay model in marble.[10]

The use of precisely cast bronze for gear-wheels is a subject about which we should like to know much more. Large cog-wheels have been found at the oracle of the dead in Epirus and were probably used for showing apparitions to the drugged worshippers; technically this shows no essential advance over the *deus ex machina* of the fifth-century Athenian theatre. Much more interesting is the reconstruction of a machine for foretelling the position of the stars. It is a wooden box in which a most complicated set of bronze gears transmits the motion put in by a handle at the side to a number of dials mounted on the front and back. By following the instructions, which are inscribed on bronze plates, the position at any future date of the sun, moon, planets, and fixed stars can be read off on the dials. This machine was found in a wreck of a ship which sank early in the first century B.C. The beautifully executed reduction gearing and epicyclic gearing implies a long line of ancestors. The so-called globe of Archimedes, which was made in the late third century, must have worked on the same principle however the actual information was displayed: a single turning movement was developed to show the motions of the sun, the moon, the five planets, and their various courses. In the fourth century the complicated theories of Plato, Eudoxos, and Aristotle about the motions of the stars and their relations to each other perhaps imply that they already knew such machines, and Plato's account of the whorls on the spindle of Ananke in the tenth book of the *Republic* may also suggest gearing. The spindle is only introduced because fate

13

spins; the picture of the heavens consists of eight concentric hemispheres each bearing its own heavenly body or bodies. The inside one, the eighth, goes fastest, then the seventh, sixth, and fifth at the same slower speed, then the fourth, which appears to be going in reverse, then the third and then the second, the outside one is in fact going in reverse.[11]

Other changes which can reasonably be reckoned as technological had a much wider effect on society. In the second half of the eighth century hoplite armour was introduced, bronze helmet, bronze breastplate, bronze-faced shield, bronze greaves, and heavy thrusting spear. The main fighting force consisted of a bronze line of middle-class citizens, advancing in line so as to protect each other, and thereby attaining a very definite status and consciousness of their own. In Athens they probably amounted to rather less than half of the male citizens liable for military service, so that they were a considerable and distinctive class.[12]

Between the time of Homer and the fifth century Athens had ceased to be a self-supporting agricultural community and had become an imperialist power dependent on imported grain. The switch from corn to olive oil and wine for export and the development of first black-figured and then red-figured pottery, which was also exported, did not depend on anything new in technology, but three new inventions, none of them Athenian, were essential to the whole development. The invention of the ram and later the invention of the powerful and fast trireme gave the Athenians a navy which could protect their commerce and control their empire. In 483 Themistokles persuaded the Athenians to use the surplus from the silver-mines at Laureion on building a powerful fleet, and it was this fleet which defeated the Persians three years later and then policed the Aegean for the Athenian empire.[13]

The third crucial invention, which may have been Lydian rather than Greek, was the invention of coinage. This was not only the lubricant which made the whole commercial expansion of the Greeks possible, but the Athenians, who had a plentiful supply of silver in their own country, found silver coin a very valuable form of export in its own right, particularly to countries which were not interested in their other products.[14]

If the creation of the hoplite army already extended political power outside the aristocracy, the creation of the commercial imperialist state heralded a much wider extension of power; the navy and the new crafts were manned not only by the entire citizen body but also by resident aliens and slaves, so that society had to change so as to reflect to some extent the demands even of the last two.

A fourth invention, the invention of writing, was perhaps as important in its effects as the invention of coinage. The adaptation of Phoenician script to Greek has been much discussed, and it is not even certain that the earlier Mycenaean script had been entirely forgotten. Our earliest piece of Attic writing is a prize inscription on an Athenian jug of about 740, and the first practice alphabets that survive come from the Agora and date before the end of the eighth century.[15]

The use of writing for commerce and for official documents need hardly be mentioned. In Athens the laws of Drakon were inscribed in the late seventh century, and from that time onwards an enormous number of official transactions were recorded in full on stone. From about 700 we have inscribed dedications and epitaphs, and from the late seventh century the mythological scenes on Attic vases commonly have the names of the figures written against them.

The first object of writing is to record—the law is such and such, the contract carried these stipulations, so and so is buried here, these painted figures are Odysseus and Ajax. The earliest references to writing all connect it with 'memory' and not with dissemination. This is the old Eastern use of writing. Eastern epics were recorded so that reciters could recite them, and we must suppose that in the eighth century Homer and Hesiod were recorded so that the rhapsodes could recite them. The introduction of writing for the purpose of recording has of itself no necessary effect on the style or content of poetry. There is no analogy between the introduction of writing into Greece in the ninth to eighth century B.C. and the introduction of writing into Yugoslavia or the West of Ireland in the twentieth century A.D.; literacy today brings with it printing and the whole range of modern culture, and this kills the traditional oral culture. The

Phoenicians had nothing comparably lethal to give the Homeric Greeks.

Perhaps it is easiest to phrase it in this way: multiple copies were unknown in early Greece. The early Greeks read where there was no other way of knowing the record accurately: they had to read the laws, the treaty, or the epitaph, but poetry they expected to hear, whether recited or sung or, in our period, acted. (The first poems composed for the eye rather than for the ear are the third-century poems of Simmias of Rhodes, poems composed so that the written lines make the shape of an axe or an egg, which can only be appreciated by the eye.) Greeks expected to hear, not to read, epic, lyric, and drama. This was the natural method of dissemination, and other authors also used it. The festival at which the epic or the lyric poet performed could also accommodate the philosopher who wrote in verse, like Xenophanes, Parmenides, and Empedokles, or the display speech of the sophist or the orator. In the fourth century Plato puts his philosophy into dialogues and Isokrates writes his political pamphlets as speeches; but dialogue and speech were the survival of a traditional form when the reality was a written book, like the early automobiles, which preserved the form of the stage coach but had an engine where the horses should have been.

Writing was introduced to record in a single copy. Its great advantage was that it could record what was difficult to remember, e.g. laws, as well as what was easy to remember, e.g. Homer. So writing made it possible for the philosopher to record his philosophy, the doctor to record his cases, the artist to record his views on his art, and the orator to record his speeches. Similarly, I think, writing made it possible for the lyric poet to record long poems in complicated metre. That epic could be composed orally is clear, and accurate oral transmission for a period is certainly possible; but it is very difficult to believe that, for instance, Stesichoros could have composed his *Geryoneis* without the aid of writing; the song was more than 1,300 lines long and consisted of triads of strophe, antistrophe, and epode; the triads were identical metrically, and the nine-line strophe corresponded to the nine-line antistrophe, but the eight-line epode had its own metrical pattern. In the early fifth century we know that Pindar could send his odes to be performed abroad, and these must have been written. But the answer to the question, 'What was the effect of writing on poetry?' seems to me to be that it immensely aided the composition of long poems consisting of stanzas of complicated metre.[16]

We hear a certain amount about the single copy. Herakleitos dedicated his book in a temple, Protagoras read his book aloud in the house of Euripides; on a late fifth-century vase the writer of a satyr-play holds his manuscript during a rehearsal, and on an early fourth-century grave relief a comic poet has the manuscript of his play in his hand. But we want to know about dissemination. The single copy can of course last beyond the life of the author: the philosopher or the doctor can hand the copy on to his pupils, and we are told that Euphorion, son of Aeschylus, produced his father's plays after his death.[17]

Isokrates in the early fourth century is the first author who tells us that he distributed his own books, but the practice may well have been earlier. From about 490 books begin to appear on Athenian vases. With very few exceptions the scenes are schools and music schools; where a text is inscribed, it is a poetic text, and where there are titles, they are titles of poems. Muses also hold scrolls, and these are surely poetic texts. The schoolmasters and the musicians must somehow have been able to get texts for themselves, and their method was probably to find someone who had a text and copy it. Euripides is said to have had books in a cave on Salamis and to have lent Socrates a text of Herakleitos. One can only suppose that some Ionian had made a copy of the text that Herakleitos deposited in the temple and brought it to Athens where Euripides made a further copy for himself. But late in the fifth century the comic poet Eupolis speaks of a part of the Agora where books were on sale. This implies at least that someone must have had the enterprise to pick up texts whenever he could get them and knew that he could resell them to people like Euripides or his younger contemporary Euthydemos 'who collected many writings of the poets and of the most famous of the sophists'.[18]

Three different stories about the philosopher-scientist Anaxagoras illustrate how difficult it is to be precise about this subject. First, Socrates heard someone reading from a book of Anaxagoras and then read it for himself; it would be nice to suppose that the someone was Euripides, but in any case this is evidently a private text. Secondly, Plutarch, after describing Nikias' terror at an eclipse of the moon during the Sicilian expedition, says that Anaxagoras was the first to put into writing his views of how the moon was eclipsed 'but he was not an old master nor was his theory well-known, but it was still secret and accepted by a few, with caution rather than with assurance'. Anaxagoras died twelve years before the Sicilian expedition, and this is how Plutarch, writing much later, accounts for Nikias' ignorance. He implies, probably rightly, that religious opposition could impede the circulation of a scientific theory. Thirdly, Plato makes Socrates' accusers say that he taught that the sun was a stone and the moon earth and Socrates answer: 'Are the young so illiterate that they do not know that the books of Anaxagoras are full of these theories, and do they learn from me what they can buy for at most a drachma from the orchestra?' It has been suggested that this means that they could buy a seat in the theatre and hear quotations of Anaxagoras in tragedy or comedy, but that would never have been so phrased. The orchestra must be the name of the part of the Agora where books were sold, perhaps deriving from a disused dancing place (*orchestra*). The price seems low, but the book may have been quite short. In any case not too much reliance can be placed on a law-court argument. The argument is viable if any philosophical text can be bought in the Agora in 399 for something like a drachma. In the same way when Aristophanes says in the *Frogs*, produced in 405, that there is no danger of the spectators missing the subtle points of the contest between Aeschylus and Euripides, because 'they are mobilised, and each learns the points from his book', the joke would only be telling if a book on tragedy was in fact available in at least more than one copy.[19]

The introduction of alphabetic writing had therefore two effects. The first was that it became possible to record the unmemorable, the law, the complicated poem, the technical treatise. The second, which only became effective in the later fifth century, was to ensure a limited circulation. In the fourth century the book-trade is probably as important as the lecture or the recital as a means of dissemination.

It is true that technology did not have the devastating effect on ancient Greece that modern technology has had and will have on our society, but the changes in the technique of land and sea-warfare, the invention of coinage and the introduction of writing, were necessary conditions for the political and intellectual development of classical Athens. These with the older but still highly efficient technology of carpentry, pottery, stone-carving, metal-working and textiles provided the material means. Religion was largely traditional. Homer and Hesiod pictured a glorious past but also provided tools that could be used for new thought.

The rest of this chapter is a brief sketch of the Greek achievement. Here I am not concerned with the relation of culture to society but simply with a statement of what the Greeks achieved in those areas in which they achieved most. It will be least confusing if I take them in the same order as in the later chapters where they will be discussed in detail. The order will be politics and law, artists, poets and musicians, writers of tragedy and comedy, geographers, doctors, and historians, mathematicians and philosophers.

We need not go further back than the early sixth century because Solon's reforms were the first steps on the road to Periclean Athens and beyond. The production of olive oil for export and the production of fine pottery, which could also be exported, and the production of fine silver for exchange and export had considerable political consequences. Foreign craftsmen were attracted to Athens, and had to be given some sort of security; a resident alien or 'metic' registered with a citizen patron, who could go to law for him if necessary. Slaves also were an essential part of the labour force in industry, in the silver-mines, and on the sea; the conception of hiring slaves out to the state or to another master for employment meant that the slave also had to have some reward and some security. But at the beginning the more obvious need was to give positive political rights to the ordinary citizen whose poverty rated him below the hoplite class, the heavy-armed citizen army. All citizens now had the right to take part in the assembly and to serve on juries, but the magistracies were restricted to the hoplite class and the two classes (the '500 bushel' men and the knights) who were wealthier than they. Nevertheless serving on the juries and voting in the assembly was a very real check against exploitation.[20]

After Solon the tyrant Peisistratos and his sons continued the commercial, literary and artistic development of Athens. When they were driven out, a further step forward in democracy was taken in 510 by Kleisthenes. The political unit now became the deme or village; the demes were grouped into thirty trittyes, ten in and near Athens, ten on the coast, and ten inland; the trittyes were grouped into ten tribes (phylai) in such a way that each tribe had one city trittys, one coastal trittys, and one inland trittys. The tribes chose the new Council of Five Hundred and elected the ten Strategoi, who really directed policy. The mixed local basis of the tribes was meant to counteract the overwhelming local influence of the aristocratic families, and Kleisthenes also introduced ostracism, which made it possible to exile, without loss of property, a prominent politician for ten years. Further moves lessening the influence of the rich were the opening of the chief civil magistracy, the nine archons, to the hoplite class in 457 (they had previously come from the top two property classes, but from 487 were chosen by lot from a slate of five hundred put forward by the demes: this was a first attempt to broaden the basis of the archonship), payment for jury service about the same date, and payment for service in the Assembly early in the fourth century. These last two reforms made it possible for the poor citizen to give his time to state service. In the later years of the Peloponnesian war the democracy survived both the brief oligarchic revolution of 411 and the more serious rule of the Thirty Tyrants in 404.[21]

The working of democracy will concern us later, and side by side with the practice we shall have to study the theory, as we know it from a few texts in the fifth century and from Isokrates, Aristotle, and Plato in the fourth. Much less need be said about law. The law of homicide was already inscribed for all to see in the seventh century, and Solon's laws were written on wooden tablets. From then we can assume that all laws were inscribed and posted. There are two interesting developments: the first is the discussion of *nomos*, the new democratic word for law. The new meaning has to be distinguished from the much wider meaning of custom, convention; law has to be distinguished from executive decree; international law has to be distinguished from national law; and a sanction has to be found which is acceptable to a society which no longer accepts its laws as a divine dispensation.[22]

The second development is the development of the art of rhetoric as a technique for writing the sort of speech which a client can deliver successfully before a large Athenian jury. The speeches of the Athenian orators, besides giving us a great deal of information about Athenian everyday life, show over about a century the different kinds of argument which may sway jurymen, as well as the different kinds of prose style to which they can be expected to listen.[23]

We can now turn to the fine arts. Architecture is far the most traditional of Greek arts and therefore the least interesting. There are plenty of refinements of detail in the fifth century but no new principles of construction. On the other hand the siting of buildings on the Athenian Acropolis, when it was rebuilt after the Persian war, was carefully considered and brilliantly solved. The whole project was immensely expensive and had great political and social implications, political because the tribute from the allies was used and this aroused the strongest conservative opposition, social because a great deal of employment was provided for citizens, resident aliens (*metics*), and slaves. During the fifth century also the grid town-plan was invented by Hippodamos of Miletos and applied in Miletos, in the Peiraeus, the harbour town of Athens, and in Thourioi, the colony sent out to South Italy in 442.[24]

Sculpture and painting were much more revolutionary. The fundamental assumptions of representational art were changed. To understand the assumptions of Greek art up to the time of the Persian wars, it is easiest to start with them at their most uncompromising, as they appear in Attic geometric painting of the late eighth century (*fig. 2*). Individualism is suppressed. Men and women alike consist of profile head, triangular body, profile legs. Sex is not always shown, but usually female breasts are indicated. Towards the end of the century the face is illuminated by a frontal eye, males are distinguished by jutting beard and females by long hair and hatched skirts. A figure may stand, sit, kneel, fight, or lie down, but whatever his posture both arms and legs can be seen, and the head remains in profile and the body frontal. Similarly the rowers on the far side of a ship are shown above the rowers on the near side, and the two wheels of a chariot are shown on the same scale side by side. This is a carefully thought-out convention, and the assumption must be that the man, the ship, and the chariot are in some sense real and must therefore have all their parts (even if they are not visible) in order to function. They are not so much a painted man, ship, or chariot as a man of paint, a ship of paint, or a chariot of paint. Two early words for statue, *andrias* 'mannikin' and *kolossos* 'substitute', may be regarded as expressions of this assumption.[25]

The extreme forms of this convention, the rotation of a lying man so that both arms and legs can be seen, the drawing of chariot-wheels side by side, and the representation of the further oarsmen above the nearer oarsmen, have been discarded by the end of the eighth century, and this is the first move towards representation. In the seventh century bodies may be painted in profile but frontal bodies are still very common; eyes are frontal in profile heads (the rare seventh and sixth-century frontal heads are probably inspired by masks); legs are profile. Stone statues are four-square; they combine a fully profile view with a fully frontal view; they either stand at attention or march forward.[26]

From the middle of the sixth century there is a move towards representation, which shows itself piecemeal in the treatment of chariots, shields, folds, furniture, and eyes, and it is this which eventually takes Greek art right out of the context of contemporary Egyptian and Assyrian art. The speeding chariot first caused the late geometric artist to leave out the second wheel; the wheeling chariot excited the black-figure artists of the second half of the sixth century. The crucial moment of turning was shown by contrasting profile charioteer and passenger with frontal chariot-body and wheels, and with four horses in profile but with the heads of the inner pair frontal. By 525 the wheels,

1 Protogeometric amphora, 900 BC (Kerameikos Museum)

2 Geometric amphora, 740 BC (Athens, National Museum)

3 Marble kouros, Aristo-
dikos, 500 BC (Athens,
National Museum)

4 Bronze, 350/40 BC (Athens, National Museum
15118)
Hermes(?)

both in painting and on reliefs, had become elliptical. In early battles the whole circle of the shield is seen; then it is represented from the side; then from about 540 the artists edge towards a convincing three-quarter view. The representation of folds also starts about the middle of the sixth century, particularly the system of stacked folds at the bottom of the chiton or himation, which is more and more elaborately treated so as to give an impression of depth (*fig. 11*). It is a curious fact that from the middle of the sixth century the inscribed name beside the painted figure sometimes is put in the genitive instead of the nominative: does this mean that the painter now feels that he is making a representation of Achilles instead of making an Achilles?[27]

A decisive step forward, which occurred in painting before the end of the sixth century and in sculpture in the first twenty years of the fifth, was to abandon the parade stance of the standing figure. From now on the head may bend and turn, the legs are differentiated as stiff leg and free leg, the upward thrust of the stiff leg is communicated to the body and the reaction to it is revealed in the musculature or the folds, if the figure is draped. This is a revolution, and the results are worked out in our period. The artist moves from the archaic figure, which is a generalised timeless aggregate of beautiful parts, to the classical figure, which is an organic whole informed by a personality (*figs 3, 4*). In one direction the development culminates in individual portraiture, in another in the individual scene with special effects of atmosphere and light. The immediate problem which the new stance forces on the sculptor and the painter is the representation of the third dimension. The archaic figure has a side-view and a front-view; now they have to be combined, and the end is the figure which is composed in three-dimensional space so that its volume must be appreciated, the achievement of Lysippos in the time of Alexander. (Technically, as noted above, hollow casting in bronze made the new free sculpture, which started at the time of the Persian wars, possible.)[28]

For the painter two small and obvious points have been mentioned already, the treatment of the eye and the treatment of furniture. The pupil of the full-face eye in the profile face by the end of the sixth century has been moved to the inner end of the eye, then the lines that make the inner corner are pulled apart, the whole eye is shortened, and the pupil is contracted until by soon after 450 a convincing formula for the profile eye is achieved. Gradually from about 470 artists begin to show the further legs of chairs and tables, and occasionally they show the underside of a stool. Similarly in the common scene of pouring a libation the jug is sometimes foreshortened so that it is possible to look into its neck, and cups held by drinkers are also occasionally fore-shortened. The new free poses of standing and seated figures involve foreshortening of individual limbs and three-quarter faces; frontal faces are much more common than in the archaic period.[29]

All this means that bits of the picture are represented in depth. A more striking attempt to set figures in three-dimensional space can be seen on some vases, notably the Niobid painter's 'Argonaut' krater (*fig. 5*), from about 460, which illustrate for us the description of the frescoes by the great painters Polygnotos of Thasos and Mikon of Athens. Here the base line is abandoned, and the figures are set on a system of wavy lines representing ridges one behind the other. This again is partial: it did not bring with it any diminution of scale in the figures at the back of the picture and it could only be used for scenes set in open country.[30]

The Greek for perspective is *skenographia*, which means scene-painting. I think that we can assume that some time about 430 the panels on either side of the central door of the theatre were painted with perspective buildings for a revival of Aeschylus by the Samian painter Agatharchos. (To avoid misapprehension let it be stated here that it is probable that at any one time the theatre had one set of tragic scenery, one set of satyric scenery, and one set of comic scenery, and that they went on being used until they wore out.) Perspective buildings—shrines, temples, and palaces—appear in the background of Greek vase-paintings from about the same time. There has been much discussion as to when, or whether at all, the Greeks discovered the use of a single vanishing point in which all lines of recession should meet; in any case the date would seem not to have been earlier than the second century B.C. The original connection of perspective with scenery may have been important for the subsequent development. What we know of Greek painting down to the third century suggests that they always massed their figures, even the crowded battle-scene of the Alexander mosaic (*fig. 6*), on a shallow stage with a backdrop behind it.[31]

The other component of three-dimensional painting is shading. It appears soon after the Persian wars on shields, cauldrons, and rocks, and rather later on folds. The first cast shadow appears about 430 and the first shading on male bodies about the end of the fifth century, when Pliny dates Apollodoros, who was known as the 'shade-painter'. Some strange restraint withheld shading from female bodies until about 330, and the discovery of unitary lighting was even later. Here too as with perspective the final step was not taken in the classical period, but the remarkable thing is how far Greek painters managed to go in the fifth and fourth centuries, when they started with the rigid conventions of the archaic period.[32]

We must turn now to poetry, and there is indeed a link between one development in poetry and the new figure-sculpture of the classical period. The link is the victorious athlete. It was for statues of victorious athletes that the new conception of the male figure was invented, and for the celebration of their victories a new kind of choral poem was composed. The athlete who was victorious in the great international competitions had international fame and was honoured through his life in his home town. From the late sixth century his victory was celebrated with an elaborate choral hymn praising him and the illustrious family to which he belonged. We can appreciate the words and the metre. The metre, which regulated the steps of the choral dance, is our only clue to the music, but it is a valid clue to the rhythm of the music. We can also see that the new metrical complexity, which we call the periodic style, appeared very quickly in other types of song, choral hymns to the gods, choral songs of consolation for the survivors of the dead, and the songs sung at a symposion. The reason is presumably that the singers in all these cases might be the same or in any case had had the same musical education. We are apt to think of choral lyric poetry and solo lyric poetry as firmly divided because the Alexandrians so divided their poets for cataloguing in the library, but the division has no other basis; poet-musicians, like Melanippides and

Timotheos, who we think of as singing solo to the lyre in the competitions for kitharodes, are the direct successors of Pindar, who we think of primarily as writing victor-odes to be performed by a chorus.[33]

Metre is our only clue to what we know from ancient authors to have been a very fast evolution of music through the course of the fifth century, an evolution which evoked a great deal of theory and criticism. What we can see of this evolution is something like this. Pindar used the periodic style either in repeating stanzas of the same metrical shape or in repeating triads, which had metrically identical strophe and antistrophe and variant epode. In his later odes the triads tend to be longer and the individual periods within the stanza tend to be longer so that the metrical musical structure is in fact more complicated before it repeats. Melanippides, who was a younger contemporary of Pindar, wrote prologues to his songs which had no strophic correspondence, and when we come to Timotheos in the last quarter of the fifth century (and he is the only one of these later lyric poets of whom a long fragment survives) we find no strophic correspondence at all; it is very difficult to describe the metrical structure because it is so extraordinarily free. It would probably be true to say that the dominant metre is iambic, but the iambics come in many different lengths and they are interspersed with many other metres, sometimes in single lines, sometimes in short runs so that they are easier to appreciate. What is clear, is that we have an extraordinary freedom of rhythmical structure, compared to which the most elaborate systems of Pindar appear orderly as well as repetitive. This development in the use of rhythm is as much as we can see of a musical revolution which was evidently as startling as the revolution in sculpture and painting.[34]

This metrical-musical development is also reflected in the lyric parts of tragedy and comedy. The creation of drama and its development through our period to a form of social comedy which echoes down the ages through Plautus, Shakespeare, Sheridan to Eliot is one of the most remarkable Athenian achievements. Tragedy was introduced into the festival of Dionysos by Thespis in 534. Before that we have various kinds of costumed choruses which could be absorbed in drama, men representing fertility spirits (satyrs?), nymphs (maenads), knights, Titans, dolphin-riders, birds. In some cults also, including that of Dionysos, the priest or priestess impersonated the god by wearing the god's mask. Probably also costumed choruses sang at the tombs of Mycenaean heroes buried in the Athenian Agora. What Thespis did, I believe, was to combine a prologue and a messenger speech spoken by a character with the choral songs sung by the existing costumed choruses. It seems to me likely that two kinds of story were in the repertoire very early. One is the Resistance story, of which the Pentheus story is the obvious example, and this sets the rhythm for serious tragedy. The other is the Release story, in which the Earth goddess is released in the spring; the best known example is the binding of Hera by Hephaistos and her subsequent release, after a number of unsuccessful attempts, when Hephaistos is brought back by Dionysos; the essential of this story, transposed to the human level, is the overcoming of a number of obstacles in reaching a joyous termination, which is usually accompanied by marriage; this is the rhythm of comedy and satyr play but also of the kind of tragedy which has a happy ending.[35]

But it must be made entirely clear that we know nothing certain about drama before Aeschylus, and it may very well be that Aeschylus, whom we can only see in the last sixteen years of his long life, constituted a new beginning. The addition of the second actor made dialogue scenes possible and increased the possible number of characters that the dramatist could include in the play; before the end of Aeschylus's life a third actor was added, increasing the possibilities still more. If it is right to suppose that the earliest tragedy was played with the Old Temple of Dionysos as a background, the move to the existing theatre in the early fifth century had two results: the wooden stage-building could represent a palace or a cave as well as a temple, and the new auditorium could seat as many of the population as were available and eligible, in safety if not in comfort. The form with its alternation of spoken, recitative, and lyric was based on the traditional form derived from Thespis, but much extended and elaborated. To later Greek critics Aeschylus seemed to have used all the resources of the Greek stage, language, music, and spectacle to 'knock out' his audiences. Here was a view of Homeric heroes (and except in the *Persae*, which was uniquely based on contemporary experience, tragic audiences always had the epic as a standard of reference) caught in a web of past history and present compulsion, whose decisions subjected them to the inevitable working out of the law of Zeus with long-term consequences sometimes only solved by a cosmic crisis.[36]

Sophocles, who was thirty years younger than Aeschylus, accepted the Aeschylean divine framework but shifted the emphasis from the framework itself to the characters, and as far as we can see from the seven surviving plays, asked what sort of people acting under what stimuli and in what environment would make the old stories come true. His is a very conscious art with an eye firmly fixed on the effect to be produced in the audience by every speech and every song, and to this end he trained his actors and his chorus.[37]

Euripides, who was twelve years younger than Sophocles, must have seen Aeschylus' *Oresteia* when he was twenty-five. If one can judge by the string of murderesses and adulteresses which he produced from 455 to 428, he was captivated by the Aeschylean Klytaimestra but completely changed the formula. He asked what would these characters be like and how would they act if this was a contemporary Athenian situation. Unlike Sophocles and even more than Aeschylus, he was wide open to influences from the contemporary world. This shows itself partly in his modern characterisation, partly in the modern views that his characters express (sometimes in defiance of the mythological situation), partly in the influence of modern music on his choruses and particularly on the long lyric solos and duets which he gives to his actors, but also, I think, in his acceptance of the validity of two other views of the world—the mythological view of the epic, to which he returns most frequently in his choruses, and the religious view of the ordinary believer, whose cults he normally validates in the epilogue speech made by a god or goddess. The fascination of Euripidean tragedy, particularly late Euripidean tragedy, is partly its ability to move through these different views, seemingly unaware when they are mutually exclusive. Where different views may be valid, all views are uncertain, and humans, particularly elderly humans, are apt to bungle; what remains are some clear values, chiefly friendship and loyalty and the heroism of the young.[38]

Aeschylus, Sophocles, and Euripides all produced on an average every other year. The earliest surviving Aeschylus was produced in 472, four years before Sophocles' first production; Aeschylus died in 456, one year before Euripides' first production. This means that, in so far as we can be said to know these three, we can be said to know a third of the total production of tragedies from 472 to 405. Our knowledge of the three, particularly of Sophocles, is very imperfect, but it is probably fair to say that further discoveries, if we are lucky enough to make any, are more likely to extend our knowledge than to alter it fundamentally. The position with comedy is entirely different. There we have eleven plays of Aristophanes produced between 425 and 388 and seven plays of Menander in various stages of preservation from the end of the fourth century. For the early fifth century and the period from 388 to 320 we have nothing but fragments, few of them more than ten lines long.

Comedy starts from the same matrix as tragedy, pre-dramatic costumed choral dances, and the tradition of these dances is evidently alive in the fifth century since we still find in Kratinos a chorus of Titans and in Aristophanes a chorus of Knights and a chorus of Birds, and the costume of the ordinary male chorus and the actors representing male characters has been plausibly derived from the pre-dramatic choruses of men representing fertility spirits and their phallic leader. It is also probable that the formal structure which is so marked in early Aristophanic comedy derives from the formal structure of pre-comedy. The simplest form of this is (a) sung strophe, (b) recitative in a long metre, (c) sung antistrophe, (d) recitative, in the same metre and with the same number of lines as b. The change from pre-comedy to comedy may have come when iambic dialogue scenes, imitating tragedy, were put on either side of this formal structure. However we reconstruct the history, it seems likely that comedy inherited from pre-comedy a shape of theme which led through conflict to rejoicing, a phantasy world in which the impossible was natural, a tendency to obscenity because it was in origin a fertility rite, and a licence to criticise any and every kind of established value.[39]

It is this amalgam which we find in Aristophanes. He starts with a phantastic idea, which is realised against considerable opposition; then its consequences are shown and the play ends in rejoicing. The language ranges from lyric poetry to the bawdiness of the gutter. His peculiar interest for us is the intimate knowledge of poetry, rhetoric, science, and philosophy that he assumes in his audience.[40]

After Aristophanes we have only fragments of comedy for seventy years. They do however help us to assess how far the critical function of comedy continues through the fourth century, and they also show that some of the themes of social comedy were beginning to appear long before Menander.

Menander strictly belongs outside our period but for several reasons must be mentioned briefly. In the first place he wrote for a different audience. The franchise was restricted in 322 and again in 318. This would presumably not exclude the disfranchised citizens from buying theatre tickets, but it rather looks as if the allowance of money (*theorikon*), which during the fourth century had enabled them to buy theatre tickets, was abolished at the same time. The obscene elements in comic costume are dropped so that the characters look like ordinary Athenians, bawdy jokes vanish, political criticism is reduced to a minimum; instead we have a very elegant social comedy portraying the lives of middle to upper class Athenians. It is New Comedy for the new Hellenistic society.[41]

Comedy and to a lesser extent tragedy are our best guide to the ordinary Athenian's knowledge of science and philosophy in the fifth century. I am using these words to cover medicine, mathematics, and history, as well as the subjects more ordinarily included under science and philosophy. In sketching the development, we have to remember the legacy of Homer and Hesiod and the geometric age. From there comes the idea of grouping things together into a system, the idea of reducing complex shapes to simple geometrical figures, the use of working models to explain the unknown, the use of personification, and an old Eastern idea that the world arose from personified water. The three Milesian philosophers, who between them covered rather more than the first half of the sixth century, all show this legacy. All think of the world as arising from a single ensoulled element, for which Thales chose water (but his *hydor* is less obviously personal than Homer's Okeanos). All used comparisons to explain the process. Anaximander, Thales' successor, constructed a geometrical universe and a geometrical map of the world.[42]

The third of the Milesians made his original element air, and spoke of 'breath and air containing the whole universe just as our psyche controls us'. We have here for the first time the conception of a world soul and of an individual soul controlling us. It opens the way to a new view of god as primarily wise, instead of primarily strong, and a new view of man, if his soul, which is by Homeric usage the part of him which survives death, also controls him. This was the way that the philosophers who belong to the second half of the sixth century took, Pythagoras, Xenophanes, and Herakleitos. They are very much concerned with the wisdom of god and the wisdom of man.[43]

With them also we see for the first time a new problem, what kind of knowledge can we have of the unknown? This is less obvious in Pythagoras, who is the earliest of the three but he provides one of the possible solutions. Thales was a practical geometer. Anaximander's universe had geometrical proportions. Pythagoras was a mathematician on a much larger scale. It is true that we only know him from later reports, but it seems certain that he left Ionia to found an ascetic ruling community in South Italy, that he believed in the transmigration of souls, that he discovered that the chief musical intervals can be expressed in simple numerical ratios between the first four integers, that he invented the theorem that is called by his name, and that he held that in some sense things were numbers.[44]

However much nonsense the last view may have given rise to, it did also contain the very fruitful idea of a numerical relationship between things and raised the question whether other forms of argument could be given the same kind of certainty as mathematical argument. It is this question that begins to appear in Xenophanes and Herakleitos, who tend to cast their arguments in the form of a mathematical proportion and are much concerned with the contrast between knowledge and opinion. This leads on to the dualism of Parmenides and Zeno in the early fifth century, followed by Melissos in the mid-fifth century and by the two-world system of Plato in the fourth. All through our period, although we can say very little that is useful about the mathematicians, we have to be aware of the existence of mathematical argument as having a kind of certainty to which other thinkers would like to attain and for which they strive, if only by adopting some of the terminology. And mathematics invades quite alien spheres like architecture and sculpture so that the chief dimensions of a building or a figure can be expressed as a multiple of one of its parts.[45]

But Anaximander's map of the world as a circle with the ever-flowing Ocean as circumference and with the east-west diameter formed by the Black Sea and the Mediterranean and the north-south diameter formed by the Danube and the Nile invited elaboration. As the Homeric similes already show, the Ionians were naturally observant, and Ionia with its contacts with Lydia and Persia in Asia and with the Thracians in the North and the Scythians on the shores of the Black Sea was a good place for observation. Hekataios of Miletos, who wrote in the last third of the sixth century and lived on to take part in the Ionian revolt at the beginning of the fifth, wrote a sort of world guide-book in which he recorded his own observations and the observations of others about men and animals in the world as far as he knew it. He also recorded Greek genealogies, so that he combined history and geography.[46]

The fifth century inherits both this anthropological strain of thought and the mathematical strain which has been already described. What is new and is no doubt partly occasioned by Athenian democracy and the ease of communication in a Mediterranean made safe by the Athenian fleet, is the extension of cosmogonies to cover the growth of human civilisation down to the present condition of mankind. This is clearest in the myth told by Protagoras in Plato's dialogue *Protagoras*. Earlier echoes of this show that by and large Plato is reporting Protagoras truly.

In the myth Protagoras proceeds from the creation of the universe on a principle of balance, so that, for instance, the strong animal has few offspring and the weak animal is prolific, to the growth of human civilisation on a principle of differentiation of skills but universality of the political virtues of Justice and Modesty. The whole is based on the 'foresight of the Divine', which, although Protagoras admits to ignorance about the gods, he regards as a reasonable conjecture from the observable facts, reasonable enough as a basis for the making of constitutions and the teaching of civic virtue. Similarly, though without the practical extension into public life, his older contemporary Anaxagoras and his younger contemporary Demokritos seem to have appended an account of the growth of civilisation to their accounts of the origin of the universe.[47]

Protagoras is not the only practical political teacher who is based on a more general philosophy. The rhetorician Gorgias is the pupil of the philosopher Empedokles and the brother of a distinguished doctor. The sophist Prodikos seems to have been trying to give the precision of mathematical terminology to ethical argument by insisting that each word should have a special meaning. Socrates started in natural science before turning to political virtue and its definition.[48]

But this is also true of the Greek doctors. Hand in hand with accurate and detailed observation of the symptoms of the particular case went general theory based either on a Pythagorean 'harmony' or on the equation of soul with air, going back to Anaximenes, or on an Anoxagorean theory of opposites like 'the hot' and 'the cold'.[49]

The same is true finally of the historians, Herodotos and Thucydides. They are of course extremely different. Herodotos is very strongly influenced by Homer. His work is an epic with a main line of story punctuated by numerous digressions, which are brought in where they illustrate the story. It is a moral story: he starts with the 'crime' that Kroisos committed against the Greeks, and he ends with the release of the Greek cities from Persian rule. But the peoples who make up the Persian Empire are described as a geographer would describe them, and both in the first book and in the last book he writes like a doctor when he describes the interaction of climate and institutions as responsible for character.[50]

Thucydides' framework is the framework of the earlier Greek annalists. But he starts with a brief history of Greece from the earliest times down to the beginning of the Peloponnesian war, which in its earlier stages could perfectly well be fitted into or on to the philosophers' accounts of the basis of civilisation and is a fascinating construct from the evidence of literary tradition, archaeology, and survivals both Greek and non-Greek. This establishes the basic drives of lust for power and fear of the powerful as the determining forces in history, and his account of the Peloponnesian war is so arranged as to show them in operation. The language in which he describes these drives, particularly in the speeches which are an essential part of his demonstration, is the language of the more philosophical doctors.[51]

The beginnings of this many-sided Greek achievement lie well before the fifth century. In the fourth century specialisation begins to set in in many areas of activity and thought. Cross-fertilisation certainly has something to do with the Greek achievement, and we shall have to consider how far this is aided by the organisation of Athenian society.

3 *Attica and its Population*

Attica is a peninsula about fifty miles long from Phyle in the North to Sounion in the South, and about fifty miles wide from Salamis in the West to Rhamnous in the East. Beyond the borders to the West were the often hostile states of Boeotia and Megara. From the Akropolis of Athens itself one can see south five miles to the sea and on every other side five to ten miles away the mountain masses of Aigaleos, Parnes, Pentelikon, and Hymettos. To us it appears rugged and barren, but a fourth-century Athenian describes its advantages: the climate is very mild so that the fruit comes very early and ceases very late, the sea is very productive of fish, there is abundance of marble for buildings, statues, and export, and there is a rich vein of silver. Athens may be called the centre of the world because the land route from the north and the sea-routes from the East, West, and South pass through it. It has good, safe harbours, and provides merchants with desirable return cargoes or with silver, which will always fetch more than its price abroad. Athens in peace is a focus for trade, for artists, poets, and intellectuals, and for the tourist industry.[1]

This is a picture of Athens and Attica in the middle of the fourth century in a moment of calm after the Peloponnesian war and the troubles that succeeded it, and before the Macedonian menace of Philip and Alexander swamped the Greek world. It shows a commercial and intellectual centre based on a supporting countryside with the silver mines as the key to the economy. The scale from the modern point of view is tiny, but that had

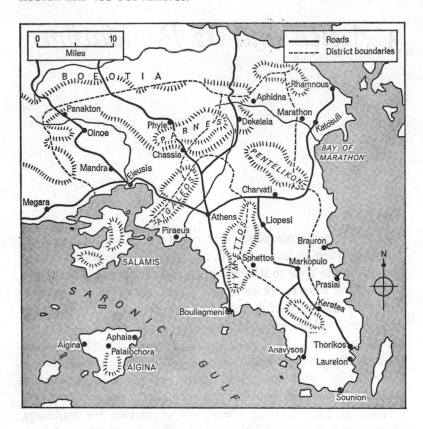

Map of Attica in the fifth and fourth centuries B.C.

its own advantages. The Athenians had none of our modern means of communication, but they did not need them. The sailing ship could carry their cargoes with sufficient speed across the Mediterranean, and their warships had the necessary extra speed provided by their oarsmen. Pack-animals were sufficient for heavy transport on land, with carts for some purposes. Most people travelled on foot. Most of Attica was within fifteen miles of Athens, only Rhamnous in the extreme north-east and Sounion in the extreme south-west is over twenty miles. The Athenians were sturdy and walked fast, and it is clear from comedy that they thought nothing of these distances.[2]

36

Another kind of communication, which was solved by the smallness of the country and by the smallness of the population, is what may be termed political communication. In the modern democracy the mass of the citizens is only consulted at election times, and the day-to-day administration is done by representatives; every communicational medium is used to keep the representatives in touch with their constituents between election times and to activate the constituents effectively at election times. But in Athens all the citizens who were not on active service or otherwise engaged could walk in to the routine meetings of the Assembly, which governed Athens and its empire. The routine meetings took place on forty days in the year, and special meetings could be summoned at other times.

Attica was a tiny country but very varied, and it is worth looking for a moment at some of the communities outside Athens itself which had a strong individuality.[3] In the early fifth century the more commodious harbour of Peiraieus superseded the older harbour of Phaleron as the port of Athens; it had three harbours instead of one, and good dockyards and warehouses. As an international port, it naturally had a number of foreign cults, and a number of resident aliens lived there. During the fifth century Peiraieus was given a grid town-plan in spite of its hilly configuration, an aqueduct, and an exceptionally large warehouse for the imported corn. This was a thriving industrial and commercial community.

Some seven miles further along the coast to the west was Eleusis, a great religious centre. The cult of Demeter and Persephone went back to Mycenaean times. The Athenians had a double pride in Eleusis: first, they claimed that from here Demeter and Persephone had sent out Triptolemos to teach agriculture to the world; secondly, they celebrated here every year the secret rites of the Greater Mysteries, which gave initiates a hope of immortality. The Sacred Way, along which the procession went from Athens to Eleusis during the celebration of the Mysteries, was lined with tombs of famous men, shrines of local heroes, and temples of the gods.

Ten miles north-west of Eleusis was the fort of Phyle, guarding the Boeotian border. This was wild rugged country with a

37

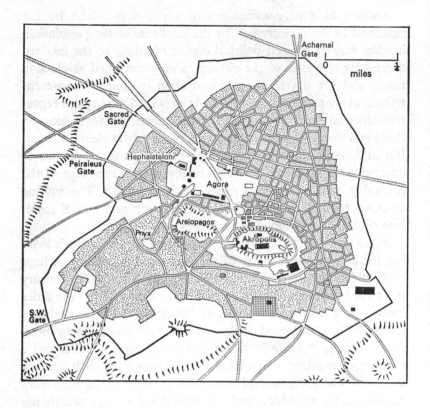

Map of Athens in the fifth and fourth centuries B.C.

famous but almost inaccessible cave of Pan and the Nymphs, country where the farmer had to work very hard to get any living from the soil, as Menander describes in the *Dyskolos*. Further to the east in the foothills of Parnes was the deme of Acharnai. This was a large deme with land rich in olive trees, which provided a large number of hoplites for the Athenian army. It had cults of Apollo, Athena, Dionysos, and Herakles, and a Mycenaean tomb which received worship from the eighth century onwards; we do not know what name was given to the hero. In the far south-east, behind Cape Sounion were the silver mines of Laureion, which, as has been said, were a major factor in the Athenian economy. The state leased the mines to private contractors, who worked them by slaves. One such contractor hired a thousand slaves from the conservative politician Nikias, the disastrous general of the Sicilian expedition; he paid Nikias sixty drachmai a year for each slave, and sixty drachmai was probably not much below the purchase price of a slave used in the silver mines.

This is enough to give some idea of the variety of places in Attica. Peiraieus, Eleusis, and Acharnai were large and important demes. Most of the 170, of which a third was in the city itself, were tiny. But they all had their local administration and they all had at least one cult. In Roman times Pausanias, listing the more interesting cult-places that he saw outside the city, mentions at least seventy.

The industrial, political, legal, and religious area of the city itself is very small. The inner city consists of the Akropolis with the Pnyx (where the Assembly met) and the Areiopagos to the west and the Agora just north of the Areiopagos; the Agora is bounded on the west by the ridge of the Kolonos Agoraios, from which the temple of Hephaistos dominates the potters' quarter to the north and the bronzeworkers' and stonecutters' quarter to the south. The Agora measures about 200 metres from east to west and about 250 metres from north to south. The Pnyx is about 300 metres from its south-west corner, and its south-east corner joins on to the foot of the Akropolis. The levelled top of the Akropolis is about 300 metres long. Into this inner city a great deal of the religious, industrial, commercial, legal, and political life of Athens was jammed, and except for the top and steep sides of the Akropolis private houses were fitted into this area too wherever they would go.[4]

The City Walls run about 400 metres west of the Agora and south and east of the Akropolis, but they embrace a considerably larger area to the north-east and the south-west of the inner city. The north-eastern gate is about 700 metres from the Agora, and the south-western gate is about 700 metres from the Pnyx. The whole area within the City Walls is 2,150,000 square metres, or rather less than a square mile. It has been estimated that in the classical period thirty per cent of this area was unoccupied, fourteen per cent made up the Agora, public places (like the Pnyx), the Akropolis and other shrines, and the rest (fifty-six per cent) private-houses and streets. The 12,000 square metres of private-housing and streets is broken down into 6,000 houses, each with six inhabitants, giving a city population of 36,000.[5]

Such figures cannot, of course, be accurate. Modern Athens has effaced most of the traces of private housing. What remains of classical housing in the city has been found round the Pnyx (which is said to have got its name from the housing density), on the north and west slopes of the Areiopagos, in the Agora, under the west end of the Akropolis on the south side, and along the Street of Tripods on the north side of the Akropolis.

The figure of 6,000 houses is reached by taking 200 square metres as a mean between the larger Areiopagos houses of 240-290 square metres and the smaller Areiopagos houses of 90-120 square metres. But it must be remembered that private houses in this estimate include workshops, because there is a good deal of evidence that in the normal Greek house built round a courtyard a craft could be pursued in one of the groundfloor rooms (sometimes with its own door on to the street) or in a shed in the courtyard.[6]

The city of Athens was not neatly planned in rectangles like the Peiraieus, but except for the Akropolis, which was reserved for religious buildings, and the partial reservation of the Agora for shops, law-courts, and public buildings, was a jumble of narrow streets with houses, private or partly industrial, and shrines closely huddled together. To return once more to the theme of communication, in such a crowded city news spread fast, and one could not help knowing what one's neighbour was doing.

The figure of 36,000 for the population of the city including slaves must be put against a figure for the whole of Attica. Unfortunately it is extremely difficult to get at a reliable figure. The figures for 317 B.C. seem to give 1,000 in the first two property classes, 8,000 in the hoplite class, 12,000 in the lowest property class of citizens, 10,000 resident aliens—a total of 31,000 adult males. There is some evidence that the fifth-century figure was higher, something more like 52,000. This is probably the figure that we should set against the estimate of 6,000 houses for the city. The area of Peiraieus was half as large again as the area of Athens, and probably eighty per cent was given up to housing (and industry), so that it may well have had 12,000 houses. This would leave something in the neighbourhood of 13,000 in the late fourth century and 34,000 in the fifth century for the rest of Attica. We should of course assume a large concentration round the walls of Athens itself, round Peiraieus, and round Eleusis, but even so it is probably right to think of the Athenians as largely living in the country rather than the city.[7]

The figure so far given is for adult males. It is suggested that women and children should be reckoned at three per adult male giving a total of 124,000 in the late fourth century and 208,000 in the fifth. This leaves slaves; the figure given for 317 is 400,000 and another fourth-century figure probably for 338, is 'more than 150,000'. A modern estimate for 317, based on the figures for imported wheat, is 20,000. The discrepancy is enormous, and the highest figure must be wrong. If we take 30,000 as a convenient round figure for households, the 338 estimate gives five slaves per household. The modern estimate gives one slave to two-thirds of the households and none to the rest. I do not know how sound the wheat figures are. How many adult males were serving overseas at this time and so feeding off the country? Is the figure for women and children both an overestimate of the number of persons and an overestimate of the amount of wheat needed to feed them? The figure of 20,000 is brought into connection with Thucydides' statement that when the Spartans fortified Dekeleia, some ten miles north of Acharnai, more than 20,000 slaves deserted to the Spartans, most of them tradesmen, and this in turn is connected with a statement in Xenophon that at the time of Dekeleia many more than 10,000 slaves were working in the silver mines at Laureion. Dekeleia is more than 30 miles from Laureion, and there is no evidence as to how many of the 20,000 deserters came from the silver mines. In fact the figure is useless except in so far as it shows that 20,000 tradesmen was an uncomfortably large number to lose.[8]

We can look at some individual slave-holdings. Nikias had 1,000 slaves in the silver mines in the years before Dekeleia. We know a little about the people who were sold up after the Mutilation of the Hermai in 416: a metic in the Peiraieus had sixteen slaves, another man had four slaves, two others at least five. In 404 Lysias and his brother had 120 slaves, in their shield-factory and household. In the fourth century Demosthenes' father had over fifty slaves in his household and knife factory.[9] At the other end of the scale there were no doubt many Athenians without slaves, but we very seldom hear of them. The thirty men depicted in Theophrastos' characters are not very high in the social scale, but two-thirds of them are expressly stated to have one or more household slaves. The heroes of Aristophanic comedy all have their slaves, usually more than one. In Menander the social scale is rather higher, and the New Comedy household usually has two male slaves, a nurse, and at least one maid for the wife.[10] It is perhaps more important to try and get the flavour of this than to arrive at an accurate computation. Granted that the figure of slaves per household runs from 1,000 to 0, and accepting the average figure for a household as six, that six may be made up of one adult male, three women and children, and two slaves. This would give a slave-figure of 62,000 in 317 and 104,000 in the fifth century, and a total population of 186,000 in 317 and 312,000 in the fifth century. This at least gives some idea of the scale of Athenian society.

We can say something of the range and distribution of wealth in Athenian society. It is easiest to take the figures for 317 and discuss the citizens first. The 12,000 in the lowest class (thetes) were assessed at less than 2,000 drachmai. To get some idea of the range here, we should perhaps remember wages. In the fourth century half-a-drachma was the subsistence allowance paid for attendance at the Assembly or as a juror; an unskilled labourer got one and a half drachmai, and a skilled labourer two drachmai a day (this was double the fifth-century rate). We can suppose then that 180 drachmai was a minimum income. At the other end of the scale a man with just under 2,000 drachmai might own five industrial slaves, who would together bring him in about 300 drachmai, so that here the range is not very great. In fact the man with five slaves would need considerable public service to bring his income up to that of a well-employed labourer.

Alternatively, of course, the man with just under 2,000 drachmai might have a holding of about four acres with house and stock, but it is impossible to measure his income on that.[11]

Above the lowest class of citizens come the 8,000 in the hoplite class and the 1,000 in the two highest property classes (the knights and the 500-bushel men). It has been reasonably reckoned from the figures for the war-tax on property that 3,000 of them were assessed at 2,000-2,5000 drachmai. Above this level are the 6,000 who were liable to war-tax and the majority of them must have been assessed at 2,500-3,000 drachmai. This would mean that something like ninety per cent of the citizens were in the income range 180-480 drachmai.[12]

It is only in the top 1,200, who were responsible for fitting out and manning triremes and performing other state services, like producing dramatic choruses, and within them in the top 300, who were responsible for collecting the war-tax, that the really rich men were found. It is interesting to look at some of these fortunes, particularly where we can see how they were composed. In the mid-fourth century one of the clients of the speech-writer Isaios had land at Phlya worth 6,000 drachmai, houses in Athens worth 2,000 and 1,300 drachmai, three female slaves and furniture worth 1,300 drachmai and an unknown number of slaves out on hire, perhaps rather over 12,000 drachmai in all, representing an income of getting on for 2,000 drachmai. The spread of property reminds us of two of the men sold up after the Mutilation of the Hermai; one of them had estates in two coastal demes and two inland demes, and the other owned land east of the city walls and in Mounichia near Phaleron. In the fifth century, prices were lower than at the end of the fourth. We have already mentioned the politician Nikias and his 1,000 slaves in the silver mines who brought him in 60,000 drachmai a year. They were only a small part of his capital; he was reputed to possess 600,000 drachmai but what he actually left his son was 84,000 drachmai. It is difficult to make sense of these figures. We know more detail about another 84,000 drachmai fortune, the fortune of Demosthenes' father, who died in 377. This can be tabulated:

Property	Value	Revenue
2 workshops		
32 knife-makers	16,000 dr.	3,000 dr.
20 couch-makers	4,000	1,200
Loans	6,000	700
Raw materials	15,000	
House	3,000	
Furniture etc.	10,000	
Cash	8,000	
Nautical loans	7,000	? 900
On deposit	4,600	? 570
Sundry loans	6,000	? 750
Total	(84,000)	?7,120

The total figure for property is given by Demosthenes, but he gives no figures for the income on nautical loans, money on deposit, and sundry small loans. Demosthenes gives no figures for the two workshops, and it is therefore probably right to assume that they were included in the house. Demosthenes' father was a very rich man, and his estate gives us some idea of the property of the top 300 citizens in the fourth century.[13]

For resident aliens we have no comparable method of showing the distribution of incomes, but we can quote instances which show the range. In 317 there were 10,000 resident aliens, and they were not allowed to own land, which is the big distinction between them and citizens. We do however hear of agricultural labourers (as well as bakers, donkey-drivers, nut-sellers), and they were presumably paid at the normal unskilled rate. Much higher on the scale was the metic Kephisodoros in the Peiraieus, whose property, when he was sold up, consisted of four female slaves and twelve male slaves; they would represent a capital of about 3,000 drachmai and probably brought him in at least 500 drachmai a year. Also in the Peiraieus was the house of Kephalos, which provided the scene for Plato's *Republic*. Kephalos was a Syracusan invited to Athens by Pericles. He lived there thirty years and bequeathed his shield-factory to his sons, Lysias, Polemarchos, and Euthydemos. Polemarchos was put to death by the Thirty Tyrants in 404, because they wanted to get their hands on the family fortune. A good deal of detail comes out in Lysias' prosecution of Eratosthenes, one of the Thirty. In 404 the brothers had three houses. The shield-factory was attached to Lysias' house, and employed, as we have said, 120 slaves; the stock-in-trade was 700 shields; and Lysias had in his safe the equivalent of 31,200 drachmai and four silver libation bowls. The slaves would have been worth about 24,000 drachmai and and would have brought in about 5,000 drachmai, and these are the low fifth-century prices. The family was clearly very rich, and one understands Lysias' claim that he had performed all public services and paid all war-taxes.[14]

The banker Pasion, who died in 370, had a very large fortune indeed. He had 120,000 drachmai in land, a shield factory bringing in 6,000 drachmai (perhaps 100 slaves worth 20,000 drachmai), a bank with 66,000 drachmai bringing in 10,000 drachmai, and private loans to the extent of 234,000 drachmai. What is so interesting about Pasion is that he started as a slave and was then liberated by his banker-masters, probably in the late fifth century, so that he then had metic status. Finally he was made a citizen of the deme Acharnai for his services to the state; he had given Athens 1,000 shields and five triremes. When he became too old and blind to make the five-mile journey from the Peiraieus to the city, he let out the shield-factory and bank to his own former slave Phormion, who was now a metic. When he died, his will provided that Phormion should marry his wife with a dowry of 12,000 drachmai and a house worth 10,000 drachmai, and should be guardian of his two sons.[15]

This is a remarkable success story, and presumably had few parallels, but at least Phormion carried on the tradition. Three fifth-century figures should be mentioned here, because they were all sons of slaves. This is obviously mentioned to prejudice their cases in the law-court speeches from which we know them, but this does not mean that it was in itself untrue. Nikomachos is accused in a speech of Lysias of not having rendered an account of his office, and it is said that his father was a public slave and he was far higher than the normal age when he was accepted on the phratry-register (as a citizen). His job was producing a new copy of the laws of Solon, and the charge is that he caused great difficulties to legal and religious business because he took so long about it; he sounds like an overconscientious lawyer's clerk. Agoratos also was accused in a speech of Lysias; he was an informer under the Thirty Tyrants and had so brought about the death of a relative of the prosecutor; his father and his father's masters are named. The most interesting is Hyperbolos. In a fragment of the orator Andokides he is called a barbarian lampmaker, whose father is still working as a slave in the mint. In 424 he had made a proposal in the Assembly that 100 triremes should be sent to Carthage; in 423 he had made 'more than many talents by wickedness', which presumably refers to prosecutions of the rich rather than lampmaking; in 421 he is said to be the most prominent democratic politician; shortly before the Sicilian expedition he was ostracised by the combined efforts of Nikias and Alkibiades, and he was murdered while in exile.[16]

Hyperbolos was a lampmaker, and lamps were turned on the potter's wheel and decorated with the same beautiful black-glaze as Athenian fine pottery. Sometimes the same shop made lamps and pots (Hyperbolos is called a potter by Eupolis). Several of the Athenian potter-painters have names that suggest that they were foreigners and possibly slaves: the Lydian and Amasis in the mid-sixth century, Douris and Brygos in the early fifth. Brygos in particular sounds like a name given to a Thracian slave. He had an extremely successful workshop, and made a dedication to Athena on the Akropolis. It is certainly possible that he bought his freedom. The whole question of the status of potter-painters will concern us later.[17]

Occasionally slaves were freed for services to the state or services to their master or in their master's will. More often they bought their freedom. An industrial slave was paid the wages of his craft. The sculptors and stonemasons of the Erechtheion were citizens, metics, and slaves; they worked side by side and were all paid a drachma a day. Citizens, metics, and slaves worked side by side in the silver mines and were paid the same wage. If we take the fifth-century wage for a skilled craftsman, a drachma a day, we can suggest how long it might take to buy freedom: the slave would have to pay one-sixth to his master and two-sixths for food. He would therefore have a maximum of half-a-drachma a day to save towards his purchase price. Prices varied enormously: Xenophon in the fourth century gives a range from 50 to 1,000 drachmai, but then notes that Nikias bought an overseer of mines for 6,000 drachmai. More useful perhaps are the auction lists to which we have referred before. There the average price is 174 drachmai and the highest 360 for a Carian goldsmith. On our calculation it would take him two years to save his purchase price. The Athenian slave was in quite a different position from the ancient slave elsewhere and from more modern slaves. On the job he was indistinguishable from the metic or the citizen: as a fifth-century political tract puts it, 'the common citizens are no better in clothing or appearance than the slaves and the metics'. The slave had the same legal protection as the metic, and he had his chance of buying freedom. The reason for this whole situation is implied in the same tract. Athens needed labour for the building programme, occasionally in the armed forces, and in the mines. These were outside the normal house-industry situation, where probably a good and profitable slave, like Pasion, was freed by his master. There had to be two incentives: an incentive for the rich master like Nikias to hire out his slaves, and an incentive to the slave to work when outside his master's control.[18]

Politically it may be right to think of citizens, metics, and slaves as three different grades. But economically, and therefore to a considerable extent socially, they ran parallel. Metics and slaves were certainly found in quantity in the same income range which covered ninety per cent of the citizens, the unskilled and skilled labourers. In the range above this we should probably find very few slaves, because slaves who were so successful would have bought or been given their freedom, but we should find plenty of metics, both resident aliens and freed slaves, as well as citizens. And just as we find metics, slaves, and poor citizens working together on the land or at the more skilled labour of carving the columns of the Erechtheion, so at the beginning of Plato's *Republic* we find Polemarchos, the son of the rich Syracusan metic, Kephalos, inviting Socrates (who had hoplite-census), Nikeratos, the son of the very rich Nikias, and Glaukon and Adeimantos, the brothers of the aristocratic Plato (who is more responsible than anyone else for our perverted aristocratic view of Athenian society), to spend the evening in his father's house.

There can be little doubt of cross-communication both between rich citizens and metics and between poor citizens, metics, and slaves. The question which we shall have to keep in mind is whether there was communication between the small number of very rich and the rest, or was culture the private preserve of the very rich? Let us note first two institutions which made for the spread of culture. One was the *theorikon*, or allowance of a third-of-a-drachma, made to Athenian citizens out of surplus revenue so that they could attend festivals. As far as we know, the festivals for which it was used were the City Dionysia and the Greater Panathenaia. But these were the great cultural festivals, the Dionysia with dithyramb, tragedy, and comedy, and the Panathenaia with games and competitions in music. While the *theorikon* provided the audiences, the choral performers were provided by the liturgies, for which the 1,200 richest men were responsible. One of Lysias' rich clients says that he spent four times as much as he needed to spend on liturgies; in the first year after he came of age, he produced tragedy and a men's chorus, in the next year he produced pyrrhic dancers and a men's chorus; these together cost 10,800 drachmai. In the next year he only spent 300 drachmai on a dithyrambic chorus, but in that year and for the next six he spent a total of 36,000 drachmai on keeping a trireme at sea and also twice paid war-tax amounting to 7,000 drachmai. When he came back, he spent 1,200 drachmai on the torch race at the Prometheia and 1,500 on a boy's chorus and in the next year 1,600 on a comedy and 700 on pyrrhicists. He was obviously extremely rich, and his figures may be exaggerated. It looks as if a very rich man might be required or volunteer to perform two liturgies a year. A number of them clearly put more money into it than was necessary. All the performances were competitive, and they wanted to win, and apart from this it was a way of making themselves known as patriotic citizens, and this reputation might be extremely useful both politically and when avoiding condemnation, but they were in fact also spreading culture in two ways, to the audiences, who came to see a well-produced show, and more intensively to the performers. The performers, who were ordinary citizens, made up a considerable number. We know most about the City Dionysia, which probably also employed most; there each year ten choruses of fifty men and ten choruses of fifty boys sang dithyrambs, three choruses of fifteen men sang tragedy and satyr-play, and five choruses of twenty-four men sang comedy, a total of 1,165.[19]

Religious festivals like the City Dionysia are a rather special case of the mingling of all kinds of people to enjoy culture, and we shall continually have to return to them later. The very crowding of Athens, particularly in the Agora, made meeting certain. We have to think of the Agora as a square with shops, public buildings, legal buildings, shrines, monuments, and private houses, all jumbled together. A large part of the square could be cleared for ostracism or for the Panathenaic procession, possibly also for part of the Panathenaic games. In this part most of the retail trade and banking was done in temporary booths, huts, and stands. But it is clear that people gathered round the traders to talk as well as to buy. The barbershop was then, as now, particularly popular, and it was to a barbershop in the Peiraieus that the news of the Sicilian expedition was brought by a sailor who had just landed.[20]

When the Sicilian expedition was being planned, Plutarch speaks of the young men in the palaistra and the old men in the workshops sketching maps of Sicily as they talked about it. This does not mean the old craftsmen but the visitors to workshops, who stayed on to gossip. A particular case of such a workshop (usually as we have said, a room or rooms in a private house) was the house of Simon the cobbler at the edge of the Agora. He was visited by both Pericles and Socrates, and took notes of Socrates' conversations which he published later as a book of dialogues. Then there was the saddler's, where the young Euthydemos, who had collected many writings of the poets and the sophists and hoped for a political career, used to go and have discussions with Socrates, presumably in the hearing of the saddler.[21]

Among the public buildings of the Agora were the Stoai. They were open buildings which apart from their official uses were excellent meeting places sheltered from the heat or the cold. Three were built in the Agora in the fifth century, the Stoa of Herms, which was especially the resort of young cavalrymen (they rated among the richest members of the population) and was probably used as a rehearsal place for choruses; the Stoa Poikile, which was sometimes used for trials and arbitrations and got its name from the magnificent pictures on its walls (to which we shall have to return); and the Stoa of Zeus, which was decorated with pictures in the mid-fourth century. The older Royal Stoa, held the offices of the King Archon and was also sometimes used for trials. There were convenient places in which people could walk and talk, and in two of them contemplate first-rate patriotic art while they did it.[22]

The young men, according to Plutarch, discussed the Sicilian expedition in the palaistra. Three kinds of establishment to a certain extent overlap. The palaistrai were, as far as we know, privately owned training establishments with arrangements for all kinds of athletics, dressing rooms where one could sit and talk, and washing arrangements. The gymnasia were possibly in origin meant for military training, and the three known in classical Athens were all connected with shrines outside the walls, the Academy with the hero Akademos in the north-west, the Lykeion with Apollo in the east, and Kynosarges with Herakles in the south-east. The general lay-out was the same as in the palaistrai. The baths only had washing arrangements; two of Isaios' clients owned baths; one in the Peiraieus was worth 30,000 drachmai and was called Serangeion after the tunnel deity in whose caves it was built.[23]

All three kinds of establishment were admirable for sitting about and talking, but certain distinctions can be drawn between them. Nobody ever speaks of a serious discussion in the baths, and they were despised as a place were the young wasted time. The distinguished fourth-century general and statesman Phokion, who was a pupil of Plato, prided himself on having never used a public bath. The palaistrai were possibly the most aristocratic of the three, and it was probably here that the great trainers like Melesias trained athletes for the international festivals. Socrates went and talked to the young men both in the palaistrai and in the gymnasia; so did other sophists. There is a tradition that Kynosarges was used by citizens of doubtful legitimacy, and that Themistokles, who had a foreign mother, tried to persuade the well-born to come and exercise there. The discussions in the other two gymnasia led straight on to the great philosophical schools, because Plato taught in and near the Academy and Aristotle in the Lykeion.[24]

Two difficult passages in the fifth-century political tract already mentioned say something about athletics in the Periclean democracy. The first runs : 'those who practise athletics and music have been dissolved by the demos, which knows that it cannot practise these things'. I think that the author, who is certainly an aristocrat, is simply making capital out of two famous ostracisms, Thucydides, son of Melesias, the famous trainer of international athletes, and Damon, the great musician. He goes on : 'but in liturgies they realise that the rich perform the liturgies and the demos receive the money. The demos is prepared to receive the money for singing and running and dancing and sailing in ships, in order that they may have it and the rich become poorer.' One thinks naturally of Lysias' client and especially of the money that he spent on dancers of the pyrrhic (a war-dance) and the relay torch-race. Where did he train the teams of his fellow-tribesmen? Probably he hired trainers in the private palaistrai. The other passage in the tract is this : 'gymnasia and washing-places and dressing rooms are partly private for the rich, but the demos builds itself many palaistrai, dressing rooms, washrooms, and the masses get more use out of them than the few and the rich'. The baths are not relevant here because we do not know of their having athletic facilities. Nor, however do we hear either of private gymnasia or of public palaistrai. It may be that our knowledge is deficient, but it is possible that we should not press the terminology of the tract too hard, and that the contrast is between the private palaistrai and the gymnasia, which, because they were attached to a shrine, could be increased or renovated by a public decree. It would be here that the poorer citizen exercised when they were not being trained at the expense of a team manager like Lysias' client.[25]

The author of the tract thinks of the rich on one side of a

divide and the poor on the other, but if our interpretation is correct there was a possibility of mingling both in the three gymnasia, which, even he admits, were also used by the rich, and in the palaistrai, when the poor were paid to compete in one of the great festivals. A fringe benefit of athletics was to listen to the sophists talking in the changing rooms.

Finally we come to the house and family. A great deal of the Athenian's day was spent outside, on his land, in the Agora, on official business in the deme, and in the city. Only the self-employed craftsman spent much of the day in his own house, and that was his workshop. Houses differed greatly in size. At one end of the scale the house of Simon the cobbler had a courtyard 21 by 18 feet, containing his workshop, and perhaps three additional rooms. At the other end of the scale is the magnificent house of Kallias, son of Hipponikos, in the Peiraieus, which was the scene of Plato's *Protagoras*. It had an entrance corridor with a porter's lodge and then a large courtyard with a colonnade on either side. In one of these Protagoras was walking up and down talking, with Kallias, Paralos the son of Pericles, and Charmides on one side of him, three others on the other side, and a row of disciples behind them. In the colonnade on the other side Hippias was seated on a chair with three Athenians and a number of foreigners, and in a refurbished storeroom Prodikos was lying wrapped up on a couch with four Athenians and some others sitting on the adjacent couches, listening to him.[27]

Kallias was extremely rich and liked entertaining sophists, and his house was specially arranged for this purpose. But a courtyard is normal, and it is the link between the street and the men's dining room (*andron*), which was the largest room in the men's quarters, and the loom room (*histeon*), which was the chief room of the women's quarters. For us much in the status of Greek women seems alien. Marriages were arranged by the fathers of the bride and the bridegroom. The woman brought with her her dowry and her trousseau; control of this property passed to her husband on marriage, but he was always responsible for it to her family, and if she left him, he had to return it. She was responsible for the children in their early years and for the female slaves in the household. She was responsible for the spinning and weaving, which provided the clothes and other textiles for the family, and she was responsible for normal provision of food. She had some religious duties in the household and could take part in women's festivals in the city. She could go to market or visit her friends, accompanied by her maid.[28] By twentieth-century urban standards her life was terribly restricted; it appears less so by country standards or by nineteenth-century standards. The wife's chief contact with the outside world was certainly through her husband and her sons. But she had her own world of household management, and in her weaving at least could be an artist in her way. She had her religious duties and these took her into the world of men. The comedy situation where the boy falls in love with the girl, because he sees her in a religious procession, was presumably drawn from real life, and it was up to the boy to persuade his father to arrange the marriage. An arranged marriage might also be a love-match; Nikeratos, son of Nikias, according to Xenophon, was in love with his wife, and she with him.[29]

It may be right to suppose a general change in the attitude of men to women in the fifth century. On the literary side the plays of Euripides show a much less restricted view of women than the plays of Sophocles, and the *Lysistrata*, *Thesmophoriazusae*, and *Ecclesiazusae* of Aristophanes give women a very positive part, which shows their good qualities as well as their bad qualities. Greek vases with scenes of women and men or of women alone are comparatively rare in the sixth century but become more and more common in the fifth. They were probably mostly bought by men, whether as presents to women or for use in their own symposia, so that what they show is a change of taste in men. Many of the women on Greek vases are, of course, hetairai, but many of them are the respectable wives and daughters of citizens. It is perhaps significant that we cannot always tell the difference between them.[30]

Hetairai (I prefer to keep the ancient name to avoid the modern associations of prostitute) might be slaves and might be metics, and metics included both emancipated slaves and foreigners. One of Isaios' rich clients had a freedwoman who managed an apartment house in the Peiraieus for him and kept 'girls'. This probably was not uncommon. Very often the girls were trained as musicians; they played for the religious choruses of free women, and supplied both music and sex at the male symposia. At Kallias' symposion the guests are entertained by a Syracusan slave and his troupe, which consists of a flute-girl, a girl trick-dancer, and a boy lyrist and dancer.[31]

The most famous of the foreigners was Aspasia, but we hear of plenty more in comedy, particularly in the fourth century, and one gets the impression that they were like the grandes cocottes of Edwardian Paris. Aspasia came from Miletos. It is difficult to know how many of the stories told about her derived from the jokes of Old Comedy. She was said to have had numerous lovers and to have kept a number of 'girls'; also to have been highly educated in politics and rhetoric and to have been visited by Socrates. What is certain is that Pericles fell in love with her, married off his wife to someone else, and lived with her. He finally persuaded the Athenians to accept his son by Aspasia as a citizen.[32]

Until 451 the children of an Athenian who married a foreigner or a freed woman were legitimate; in that year Pericles got a law passed restricting the citizenship to the children of two citizen parents. After that a certain number of special exceptions were made, of which Pericles' son by Aspasia was one. Probably in fact a number of Athenians did have children by foreigners or freedwomen, and their children were accepted as citizens. But there could always be legal trouble, and there are several cases in the orators which turn on the citizenship of the mother. In comedy the problem was always solved by having the girl finally recognised as a citizen. Athenian society was permissive as nineteenth-century society was permissive. A husband might have an affair with the housemaid or have a mistress outside, provided he kept it reasonably quiet, but Alkibiades' wife divorced him because he continually associated with hetairai. What an Athenian wife did not tolerate was a mistress under her roof.[33]

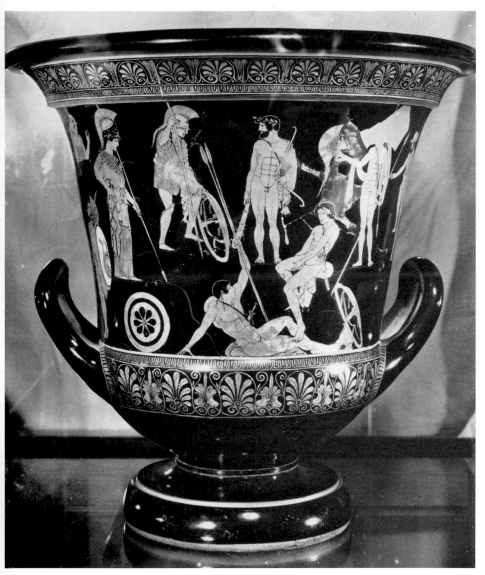

5 Red-figure kalyx krater, Niobid painter, 460–50 BC (Louvre G 341)
Athena, Herakles, and heroes

6 Alexander mosaic, original 330/20 BC (Naples, Museo Nazionale)

Many of the hetairai were trained musicians and so they brought poetry and music to the symposion. The symposion was the chief cultural event that took place in the ordinary private house. Kallias in Xenophon's account had eight guests at his symposion and then they were joined by Philippos the Jester. After the tables had been removed and they had sung a paian, the Syracusan troupe arrived. They provide the entertainment but there are intervals of semi-serious discussion, and once Socrates began a song. The *andron* of Kallias probably had ten couches, which is the number that Xenophon mentions elsewhere. The house of Agathon, the tragic poet, which is the scene of Plato's symposion is smaller. He has six guests, and when Alkibiades arrives late, he sits at the foot of Socrates' couch, as we often see hetairai sitting in the symposia on Attic vases. In this symposion the whole entertainment consists of speeches by the guests in praise of Love, ending with Socrates' highly philosophic speech. Agathon's dining room evidently had seven couches.[34]

Any symposion to which Socrates went was likely to bog down in philosophical discussion, but Xenophon and Plato would not have chosen symposia as the scene for Socrates' operations unless philosophical discussions were known to take place in symposia. We need not suppose that such discussions were necessarily limited to the circle of Kallias, who had a weakness for sophists, or Agathon, who was similarly inclined, as his appearance listening to Prodikos in Plato's *Protagoras* shows. The paian sung in Kallias' symposion was standard practice, and was presumably a hymn to one of the gods which was known to the guests. Other entertainment provided by the guests we know partly from surviving texts of symposion poetry, partly from allusions in comedy, and to a small extent from pictures on vases. The surviving texts run from Archilochos and Alkaios in the seventh century through Anakreon in the sixth, Simonides and the collection of Attic drinking-songs (skolia), Pindar, and Bacchylides from the late sixth and early fifth, to Aristotle's praise of Hermias in the fourth century. Many of them are hymns to the gods and could be sung as paians in the symposion. The rest are very varied in content:

political abuse and praise, praise of the host, love-songs, philosophical discussion.[35]

That the early songs are not irrelevant to the symposia of classical Athens is proved by the allusions in comedy. They also show that kinds of poetry which had nothing to do with the symposion could be performed in the symposion. In Aristophane's *Banqueters*, which was produced in 427, the father asks his son to sing a drinking-song of Alkaios or Anakreon. In the *Clouds*, which was produced in 423, the father asked the son to sing a victor-ode of Simonides or recite a speech from Aeschylus, but the son insisted on reciting from a recent play of Euripides. One was therefore expected not only to know the poetry of the last three centuries but also victor-odes and tragedy, which had nothing to do with symposia.[36]

We should, of course, like to know what range of people had symposia with this kind of intelligent entertainment. Kallias' guests and Agathon's guests clearly belong to the top stratum of Athenian society. But if we are right in supposing that Kallias had a ten-couch *andron* and Agathon had a seven-couch *andron*, their dining rooms were no bigger than the dining rooms of the two houses on the Areiopagos, which may have been the houses of fairly well-to-do people but certainly not of people who lived on the scale of Kallias. The prominence of the *andron* in all preserved houses suggests that the symposion was a very important feature in Greek life. And the hero of Aristophanes' *Clouds*, who demanded Simonides or Aeschylus, was a fairly poor farmer, although he had married above him. Aristophanes had no reason to give him tastes which would seem absurd in a poor farmer. One other Attic symposion is relevant here; it is painted on a mixing bowl of about 510. The party consists of Theodemos, a flute-girl called Suko, the vase-painter Smikros, and a rather older man called Ekphantides, who may be the grandfather of the fifth-century comic poet of the same name; Ekphantides is singing the beginning of a hymn to Apollo, which has plausibly been connected with Anakreon. Here then is a vase-painter, a skilled workman, taking part in a symposion at which good poetry is sung.[37]

We can, of course, assume that the songs and discussions of the symposion were known to the whole household. The slaves who served the guests, and among the slaves would be the *paidagogos* of the children, told their fellow-slaves, and the host told his wife and children. The symposion is one more instance which adds to the evidence collected in this chapter that Athenian society gave opportunity for the spread of culture between rich and poor, citizen and foreigner, male and female, free and slave.

4 *Education*

The symposion, the choruses, in which Athenians danced and sang at religious festivals, the dramatic performances in the theatre, the law-courts, and the Assembly were, of course, part of Athenian education in the wider sense. In this chapter we are concerned with education in the narrower sense of formal instruction. And we can narrow the subject still further. Most ancient discussions of education and most modern histories of Greek education see education as aimed at the attainment of *arete*, the kind of excellence which enables the recipient to lead the good life in the Greek city-state; so the worried fathers in Plato's *Laches* want to know what learning or training will make their sons as excellent as possible. This search for an ideal education is, of course, an important part of Greek civilisation particularly in the fourth century, but it is largely irrelevant to our question: what in Greek education made the Greeks create and accept their particular form of civilisation?[1]

Another problem which bulks large in modern discussions of Greek education is the part played by the separation of the sexes. Greek males were, particularly in the richer families, separated from females at an early age (but the Greeks did not, as far as we know, have boarding schools) and lived a great deal of their adult daytime lives away from their wives and daughters, and the girls who were trained as musicians were trained with other girls and not with boys. Teaching is impossible without a strong personal attraction between the teacher and the taught, and this may always in any society erupt into actual physical

58

intercourse, but it makes no difference to the quality of the teaching whether the attraction is heterosexual or homosexual or both, as in a modern mixed school.[2]

It is possible to give a fairly adequate account of Athenian education, but it is very much more difficult to discover how restricted a privilege it was. Plato in the *Protagoras* gives a general account of Athenian education, which may be summarised as an introduction. As soon as the child understands speech, nurse and mother and *paidagogos* and the father himself struggle to make him as good as possible. Later when they send him to school, they instruct the masters to care for discipline more than for reading and lyre-playing. The children are compelled to read and learn the poems of good poets, in which there are many admonishments and many praises of the good men of long ago, so that they may copy them. When they learn to play the lyre, they are taught the lyric poems of other good poets so that, by making the rhythm and harmony their own, they may become more civilised and better in speech and action. They also go to the physical trainer (*paidotribes*) so that their bodies may become subservient to their minds. The sons of the richest are the earliest to go to school and the latest to leave school.[3]

The first stage is common to all families and to children of both sexes. The old woman, who may have been the wife's nurse before, and the male slave, the *paidagogos*, who later took the son to school, were certainly not restricted to the rich. What they and the parents taught, in addition to behaviour and physical instruction, can be deduced from the discussion of education in the *Republic*. Plato says there that nurses and mothers must be persuaded to tell the children the right 'myths'. From what follows it is clear that the myths which were told to children come from the general range of Greek mythology, and we can assume that all Greek children were told stories about gods and heroes very early. This kind of instruction in the home continued for the girls and for all children whose fathers could not afford to send them to school.[4]

Reading and writing were taught in school by the *grammatistes*, but those children who did not go to school must have learnt them at home. Reading was a necessity from the time that laws began to be posted, and, quite apart from the existence of eighth-century inscriptions, practice-alphabets survive from the beginning of the seventh century. One of the earliest is scratched on a loom-weight, but this does not necessarily mean that it was written by a woman. Evidence can be quoted for illiteracy—nonsense inscriptions and misspelt inscriptions on vases, the man who had to ask Aristeides to write his name on an ostrakon, characters in comedy who do not know how to read or have difficulty in reading—, but universal schooling today has left plenty of illiterates and many more bad spellers. In the classical period the large number of inscribed public notices and the number of vases with exquisitely written inscriptions, which were meant to be read, argues for a rather high degree of literacy.[5]

If the *Protagoras* is taken literally, it does not mean that the poor did not go to school, but that they went to school later and for a shorter time than the rich; in fact that it was a question how much parents could afford. Aristophanes' picture of the boys walking through the streets in a body to the local school does not sound as if education was on a very small scale. In the early fifth century in Chios the roof fell in on a boys' writing school, and only one out of 120 boys escaped. Aristophanes implies some sort of local official organisation, and this is supported by the fact that when the Athenians were evacuated to Troizene at the time of the Persian War, the city of Troizene put up money to hire them schoolmasters. The natural local unit is the deme, and a pile of school slates has in fact been found from what must have been a deme school near Plato's Academy. The word which Aristophanes uses for 'local' is a word which has the technical meaning of city-demes as distinct from country-demes. If the 170 Athenian demes each had its school on the scale of the school at Chios, this would give more than 17,000 Athenian boys in school at any one time. Is this a conceivable figure? The only figure that we can put against it is the figure for those with hoplite census and over who were called up for military training at the age of eighteen in the later fourth century; that figure is 500. If 500 is the draft figure for these 9,000 adult citizens, we can assume a proportionate figure of 670 for the 12,000 adult citizens below the hoplite census and 550 for the 10,000 resident aliens, making a total of 1,720 eighteen year olds. This makes nonsense of the 17,000 figure since it is most unlikely that all citizens and resident aliens had nearly ten years' schooling. If, however, the richest ten per cent of citizens and metics had ten years' schooling and the rest had an average of two years' schooling, then the school population would be 4,820 and the average deme school would have twenty-eight pupils.[6]

These figures do not have any pretence to accuracy, but they do suggest that the Athenian schools catered for far more than the very rich. The pictures of schools on vases add a little further evidence. First, one special instance. The vase-painter Euthymides is painted by his colleague Phintias as he sits with his lyre waiting to accompany the singing of the boy Tlempolemos, who is being instructed by the bearded Smikythos. Tlempolemos is not a common name so that, given the presence of Euthymides, it is natural to connect the boy with the older Tlempolemos, who made lip-cups about 550. This is a school scene, and the interest for us is the presence of a boy and a youth connected with the pottery industry, who were surely not in the top ten per cent of rich Athenians. Euthymides' father was a sculptor but not a famous sculptor: he himself was certainly painting vases at this time. It looks as if he took the afternoon off to accompany a young friend who was still in school.[7]

School-scenes are not uncommon on red-figured vases. They show boys with writing-cases, tablets, or rolls, boys playing or singing to the flute or lyre; often, particularly on cups, these scenes are associated with athletic scenes, showing that reading, writing, music, and athletics belong together as education, as we have seen already in Plato. The only figure that can be given is obtained by counting the school-scenes in Beazley's *Attic Red-figure Vase-painters*. The number for the fifth century is 100. This is not a large number compared with something like 1,400 vases with athletic scenes over the same period, but when we remember that these surviving and attributed school-scenes are a tiny percentage of the number of school-scenes actually painted, the number seems too large to be accounted for by the special commissions of the very rich. The two ways of detecting special commissions in these vases are first a prefired name, which shows that the vase was a present (normally the name is written alone with *kalos*; the Euthymides vase is a special case) and secondly in the writing or music scenes the book-rolls are sometimes given a title or inscribed with the words of a poem. Counting the Euthymides vase, there are only fifteen of these specially commissioned vases. The rest of the school-scenes show no signs of having been made to a special order, and their number rather suggests that the market was not restricted to the very rich.[8]

The vases also tell us a little about the curriculum. From the *Protagoras* it appears that the poems learnt in the writing school were partly didactic and partly epic and in the music school lyric. So on the vases we find inscribed rolls with a didactic title (the *Cheironeia* ascribed to Hesiod), a presumably epic title (the *Companions of Herakles*), words from a didactic poem ascribed to Linos or Mousaios, words from an epic about the Trojan War and words from a choral lyric. When Plato in the *Republic* gives instances of poetry which is unsuitable for the education of young soldiers, he is presumably thinking of what was actually being taught in the schools: he names Homer and Hesiod, and most of his instances come from Homer but a few from Aeschylus. Two other stories show the dominance of Homer. One is the account given by Nikeratos, son of Nikias: 'My father, considering how I should become a good man, made me learn the whole of Homer, and now I can recite the whole of the *Iliad* and the *Odyssey*.' The other is the story of Alkibiades finding a writing master who claimed that he had a text of Homer that he had emended himself: 'Do you teach writing when you can emend Homer? Why are you not teaching the young men?' Alkibiades says that he should move from elementary to secondary education, but at the secondary level the text is still Homer.[9]

The common assumption of the old men in the *Laches*, of the *Protagoras*, of the *Republic*, of Nikeratos, and of Aristophanes in the *Clouds* is that the purpose of school education is to become a good man, and a good man is very near to meaning a good soldier. Good poetry provides moral sentiments and good examples; music was believed to be character-building, and athletics produced bodies which obeyed the dictates of the mind. Of course for a state like Athens, which was in a more or less constant state of war with its neighbours, the production of adequate soldiers was of supreme importance. But ancient wars though frequent were limited, and Athens did produce a very remarkable civilisation. Did the schools make no contribution?

At first sight Aristophanes seems to offer a way out with his contrast between the Old Education and the New Education in the *Clouds*. But, whereas the Old Education is the education of the schools with a very strong emphasis on conventional and traditional morality, the New Education is not an education in the same sense; it is not a new school programme for boys but simply an attack on the values presupposed by the Old Education, and in so far as it proposes instead the techniques of sophistic argument it is aimed at young men at the top end of or beyond the school range who could take lessons from the sophists.[10]

If we ask realistically what did the schools achieve, we may wonder whether the ordinary schoolmaster turned high-spirited boys into such paragons of discipline as Aristophanes and Plato require; their ideals sound depressingly like propaganda for the English public school. What the literary and musical education clearly could achieve was to fit them to recite and sing in the symposion, when they came to that stage, and to take their part in the various boys' choruses which sang in honour of the gods. And the physical training fitted them for boys' athletics and later for men's athletics, and by way of general physical endurance and dexterity for war.

The schools certainly did provide an acquaintance with the epic, didactic, and lyric poetry of the Greeks, and lyric poetry involved also acquaintance with music and dance. This is not to be underrated. Homer may not provide a quick answer to the practical problems of life, as Nikias appeared to think, but Homer is superb poetry and encourages a sympathetic understanding of a very wide range of people, which is a valuable possession. And lyric poems like Simonides' 'It is difficult for a man to be truly good' challenged the whole value-system of the aristocrat. There were two other advantages in this traditional literary and musical education. Just because it was traditional, its pupils had a common frame of reference: the old stories gave models for thought and behaviour which everyone recognised. Secondly, it is tenable that Greek art, literature, and thought, in spite of its revolutionary advances, was always traditional, and that the advances were possible and acceptable because the traditional starting point was clear.[11]

But when all this has been said, we cannot look to the schools for the source of the Athenian's inventiveness or his receptivity; these qualities must have been developed, as in the older English universities, in spite of the instruction. One remembers rather the child Pheidippides in Aristophanes making houses, carving ships, and constructing waggons of leather, which his father quotes as evidence of his suitability for higher education, or one remembers the young Demosthenes getting his first sight of a trial because his *paidagogos* knew the janitors of the law-courts. The intriguing slave of comedy, who tricks money out of his old master to get his young master a girl, is no doubt exaggerated, but an experienced slave could produce a great deal of information for an inquisitive boy, and I should suspect that boys got far more education from *paidagogos* and parents, from walks in the Agora, from the cobbler, from the barber-shop, and from life on the farm than from school.[12]

What we should now call technical education and higher education must also be considered. Technical education was essentially an apprentice system. Xenophon says that, when one sends a boy to learn a craft, one should have a written agreement as to what he shall know when he has finished the course. It is not clear whether the 'boy' is a son or a slave, and possibly it does not matter very much, as presumably the arrangements would be the same in either case. Perhaps one might quote here as an interesting instance a man called Hieron. He was brought up in the house of Nikias (and this sounds as if he was a slave). Nikias had him taught at the writing and music school, and he was then adopted by a man called Dionysios, but he served as a sort of public relations officer to Nikias.[13]

In the whole range of what the Greeks called *technai*, which covered e.g. artists, doctors, and bankers, as well as what we should call craftsmen, various arrangements for training were possible. The master might take a fee for a pupil, either free man or slave, and train him so that he could practise on his own. But if the master wanted a successor, he might either train his own son or some other member of his family or buy a slave and train him. Taking fees from pupils is the common practice of the sophists, to which we shall return, but we also hear that the fourth-century Sikyonian painter Pamphilos taught no one for less than 6,000 drachmai, which puts him in the same class. We have already noted the succession in the banking industry: the two owners of the bank bought Pasion as a slave and trained him. In due course he became so efficient that he either bought or was given his freedom and finally succeeded his masters, and then the same process was repeated with Phormion, who succeeded Pasion.[14]

Many *technai* were hereditary, and the workshop passed from father to son. We can trace one pottery workshop for something like a hundred years by its names. Ergotimos signs fine pots about 570, he has a son Eucheiros, and a grandson whose name we do not know; this takes the succession down to the end of the sixth century, and then about 480 we find another Eucheiros, probably the great grandson of Ergotimos. I suspect that another family can be connected with the same workshop. Contemporary with Ergotimos was the potter-painter Nearchos, and he had two sons, Tleson and Ergoteles; the name Ergoteles is so like Ergotimos that it is tempting to suppose that Nearchos married the sister of Ergotimos and gave his son a name like her brother; the names Nearchos and Tleson recur in the last decade of the sixth century: it is possible that these are not the original holders of the names but that they represent a younger generation, contemporary with the grandson of Ergotimos. As a contrast to this, another pottery workshop, producing mostly cups, small vases and moulded vases through the fifth century, shows no signs of family relationships, as far as we can see; the names are Brygos and Syriskos in the first quarter of the fifth century, Sotades in the second quarter, Epigenes and Aison (who signs as painter), in the third quarter, and possibly we should add Meidias, Erginos, the younger Phintias, and the painter Aristophanes in the fourth quarter. The only two of these names that we can say anything about are Phintias and Brygos. Phintias is extremely likely to be the descendant of the potter-painter Phintias of the late sixth century. If that is so, this is presumably also a family workshop, although the names do not reveal it. Brygos, as we have said, was probably a slave and was successful enough to make a dedication on the Akropolis, which suggests that he bought his freedom. The difference between the pottery industry and the shield-factory which Kephalos passed on to his sons is that there the owner is merely an owner, but in the pottery industry we believe that he was also a craftsman, although he may not have practised much in the later years of his life.

What interests us and what we shall have to look out for when we consider some of these *technai* in greater detail is where the new ideas come in. If we look at pottery or sculpture, we should probably say that they come in with new men. Brygos, Sotades, Epigenes, Meidias, and the painters who worked with them (some of them were probably identical with them, but they do not sign their names as painters) represent the successive infusions of new ideas into a traditional workshop. In the sculpture of the Parthenon, which took about fifteen years to complete, the hands of old-fashioned, up-to-date, and forward-looking sculptors have been recognised. This suggests a number of ideas which may be applicable mutatis mutandis to quite different *technai* such as poetry, oratory, and medicine. First, the training was limited and technical; when the pupil had learnt the technique, he applied it in his own way. Secondly, communications were good; sculptors, bronzeworkers, terracotta-makers, and potters were crowded together at the West end of the Agora and across in the neighbouring Kerameikos; and Athens was in fact a small place. Thirdly, the masters of workshops themselves encouraged new ideas, and this implies that their patrons did too. This is really the most important point, since it is the receptivity of the patron that sets the pace.

We should perhaps include in technical education the training of girls (and indeed boys) for entertainment. Little is known about this. One pattern is the troupe in Xenophon's *Symposium*. A Syracusan slave has a flute-girl, a boy lyrist and dancer, and a girl trick-dancer. At the beginning the girl plays the flute and the boy plays the lyre; probably this is neither solo playing nor a duet but song to flute or lyre; later he sings to his lyre, while the girl plays a flute-accompaniment. The trick-dancer dances with hoops and then does acrobatics over a ring stuck with swords, and later she proposes to do acrobatics on a potter's wheel. Finally she dances Ariadne to the boy's Dionysos while the flautist accompanies them. The troupe performs for money. The Syracusan is called their dancing-master, and they are called his slaves. He is called *anthropos*, which should mean slave, but if he owns them it is perhaps slightly more likely that he is a freedman. Such dancers and acrobats are frequently shown on Attic vases. Sometimes a man, like the Syracusan, and sometimes an older woman is shown playing the flute for them. Often young men look on, and they are presumably going to hire them for the symposion. On one vase with several tumblers and dancing-girls the woman playing the flute is called Elpinike. She is presumably the famous Elpinike, the sister of the aristocratic leader Kimon. To own a number of girls who can perform at the symposion is perhaps better than to own a number of girls to let out for prostitution, like Lysias' client or the freedwoman in pseudo-Demosthenes' speech against Neaira. If a girl was hired to play the flute or lyre in an aristocratic symposion she would have to be a good musician, which meant also knowing the range of songs which were in demand. It would therefore be worth the while of an Elpinike or her male equivalent to pay the best music-masters to train their girls. And the girls did not only play at the symposion but also at women's festivals, so that they were indirectly a means of educating the free women in music.[15]

Higher education in anything like the modern sense only began in the fifth century, and then haphazardly. A clear distinction can be drawn between the fifth century and the fourth. In the fifth century the sophists and Socrates had in the main no fixed location for teaching, but in the fourth century Plato and Isokrates both had their schools, which were followed later by others. Here I am only concerned with education in the formal sense so that I think it is reasonable to exclude philosophers like Anaxagoras and Parmenides, although they were both in Athens for a shorter or longer time, since no one speaks of their giving formal instruction. The mathematician Theodoros of Cyrene was also in Athens but had only a single pupil, Theaitetos. Parmenides also had a single pupil, Zeno. This master-single pupil relationship seems to me rather to belong to technical education.[16]

More will be said about the ideas of all these men elsewhere. At the moment the questions are, what caused this new phenomenon in the Greek world, what was taught, and who were the pupils? It was not simply an Athenian phenomenon because none of the sophists except Socrates and Antiphon of Rhamnous was Athenian, and we know that many of them taught elsewhere too. I include Socrates among the sophists because, although according to Plato he did not take fees and although he seems to have proceeded almost entirely by interrogation, he did have a recognisable circle of disciples and he was concerned with political life.

Concern with political life is the common concern of all the sophists. Protagoras of Abdera in the north, Gorgias of Leontinoi in Sicily, and Antiphon were born in the decade after 490, Socrates, Prodikos of Keos and Hippias of Elis in the decade after 470. Most of what we know about all these men's activity in Athens dates from a little before 430 and later. But Protagoras was certainly in Athens before 444, and may even have been in Athens as early as 460. What characterises the whole period from 460 in Athens is the bitterness of political strife between the aristocrats and the democrats, and the concern of the aristocrats with their fading position is sufficient reason for the rise of the sophists. This was not only an Athenian problem. Gorgias came from Sicily, and was in his youth when the Syracusans replaced tyranny by democracy. We are told that the many lawsuits on claims for land gave rise to the art of rhetoric. The technique of argument and the technique of speaking are never very far from the sophists' preoccupations.

Much of our information about the sophists comes from Plato, and in particular the settings of some dialogues show us where sophists could be met. Often it is the private house of a rich man. We have noticed that Socrates met Protagoras, Prodikos, and Hippias in the house of Kallias. Similarly Socrates met Gorgias at the house of the rich Kallikles and Thrasymachos at the house of the rich Kephalos. Socrates himself belonged to the hoplite class, but everyone else at these meetings belonged to the richest class. Outside these Plato gives two meetings with minor sophists. Euthydemos and his brother Dionysodoros give their demonstration of eristics in the dressing room of the Lykeion gymnasion before a great crowd, partly the disciples of the two sophists and partly the lovers of Kleinias. A gymnasion is clearly a suitable place for a sophist to be heard and the crowd is likely to be more mixed than in the private house of a rich man. The other minor sophist is Mikkos, who is said to be a comrade and admirer of Socrates; he teaches in a newly built palaistra, but we do not hear any more about him, and again the probability is that he is beginning.[18]

The great foreign sophists were already famous by the time that they appeared in Kallias' house. There they are surrounded by their foreign pupils and their Athenian admirers. Protagoras has collected his pupils in the various cities which he has visited, and they go on tour with the master. They pay him a fee just as they would pay a fee to Hippokrates to be taught medicine or to Pheidias to become a sculptor. We have already seen parallels in technical education; the painter Pamphilos charged 6,000 drachmai in the fourth century, and Protagoras charged 10,000 drachmai in the fifth century, when the drachma was worth considerably more. These sophists had however to become known. The method was to get themselves appointed to represent their native city on some delegation, and attract attention in the city to which they had been sent by the brilliance of their public presentation of their state business, and then go on to give lectures and thereby attract private pupils, who followed them round. The pupils must always have been the very rich, but the tour did at least cause them to meet the very rich in other cities, rather as the athletes met at international games.[19]

The games where the international athletes met were in fact one of the places where the sophists performed, and the audience consisted of the delegates from the cities; the delegates from democratically governed cities would not be only the very rich. When a sophist arrived in a city, he presented his own city's business to the Assembly or the Council of the city that he was visiting, and here again in a democratic city a wide range of citizens would have a chance of hearing him and could at least assess his eloquence, even if the subject matter precluded much display of erudition. Then he gave his lectures. Prodikos had a fifty-drachma lecture; this was the price that he charged for seats, because when he gave cheaper lectures he used to wake up the audience when they nodded with a bit of the fifty-drachma lecture. Hippias presumably charged the same sort of prices if he made 2,000 drachmai at quite a small town in Sicily.[20]

These were not the sort of prices that any but the rich could pay. But Socrates heard Hippias describing his display at Olympia 'at the tables', i.e. in the part of the Agora where the bankers set up their tables. Socrates himself was, of course, continually in the Agora. He visited Simon the cobbler and met Euthydemos at the saddler's. The *Euthyphro* is set by the Royal Stoa. This broadcasting of wisdom is what we expect from Socrates, although Plato is at pains to provide him only with the richest and most eligible young men as an audience. It is more interesting to hear of Hippias in the Agora. Again we are reminded how small Athens was. Although the sophists aimed their instruction at the rich and powerful, they were seen and to a small extent heard by a much wider section of society, and their ideas filtered through by a number of indirect channels.[21]

The aim of the rich in seeking education by the sophists was to be effective in political life when the control of political life was passing more and more into the hands of the majority. They needed to be able to argue successfully in the political assemblies and in the courts (except in so far as they employed speech-writers). Rhetoric in one or another of its departments is found in all the curricula: theory of argument and the beginnings of grammar in Protagoras, argument and style in Gorgias, Antiphon is probably to be identified with the speech-writer, Prodikos was searching for correctness in terminology, Hippias besides giving display speeches invented a system of mnemonics, and the whole point of Socrates' interrogations was to arrive at tenable definitions.

But they did or were capable of doing much more than fulfilling this practical aim. Protagoras started with a theory of how the universe was constituted and from this he developed a theory of human culture and from this again a theory of politics, which could be realised by the right use of rhetoric. He was probably the most profound thinker of them all. Like him, Antiphon was a practical political theorist and developed in a very interesting way (which will concern us later) the contrast between *physis* (nature) and *nomos* (convention). Gorgias and Prodikos were both interested in the criticism of poetry, and Prodikos in addition wrote the moral parable of *The Choice of Herakles*. Hippias had an extraordinary range. He evidently had an ideal of self-sufficiency and appeared at Olympia in clothes, shoes, ring, and girdle made by himself, and with poetry and prose composed by himself. He claimed to be proficient in metre and music, in ancient history, and in mathematics and astronomy. I think it is fair to say that to be educated by the sophists was to be put in touch with the most exciting thought of the time.

Socrates, as presented in Aristophanes' *Clouds*, has the wide range of the sophists. The pupils are living in his house. They are taught astronomy, geometry, natural science, geography, grammar, metrics, methods of argument, mnemonics, and rhetoric. At first sight what we should call science seems to preponderate, but then we remember Protagoras and Hippias and wonder whether our general view of the sophists is not somewhat distorted by Plato's preoccupation with morals and politics. At any rate the *Clouds* must represent sophistic education as Aristophanes saw it in 423. It was a New Education because its aims were different from the Old Education, but the two had in fact a different age-spread. The Old Education started with children but might be continued to eighteen; the New Education scarcely started before eighteen. The Old Education was a training for the symposion, for athletics, and so for military service. The New Education was a training for success in the law-courts and the Assembly, but on the evidence of the *Clouds*, the *Protagoras* myth, and Plato's picture of Hippias it involved a wide acquaintance with modern thought in addition to technique of argument and rhetoric.[22]

How far the *Clouds* presents a true picture of Socrates will always be debated and does not greatly affect the picture of sophistic education. Three points should, I think, be made. First, in the *Phaedo* Socrates says that he was fascinated with 'physical inquiries' in his youth, and was then diverted from them by his disappointment with Anaxagoras' failure to provide in *Mind* a final cause for the workings of the universe. If Socrates really changed direction about 430, the recollection of his earlier interests could have accounted for his picture in the *Clouds*, and he could himself have said truthfully in 399 that the majority of the jurors at his trial had never heard him conversing about any of these subjects. Secondly, Xenophon, in refuting the charge that Socrates corrupted the young, nevertheless admits that the reason why Kritias and Alkibiades associated with him was that this association would make them 'most efficient in speech and action'; the Socratic technique could therefore be diverted to political purposes, and Aristophanes was not wholly untruthful in portraying him as a teacher of rhetoric. Thirdly, the use of Socrates' house as a school must surely be based on something in Athens. Most of the sophists were foreigners. Antiphon of Rhamnous is a possibility. But whether it was Socrates' house or not, a 'thinkshop' in Athens did not seem an impossibility in 423.[23]

One other Association should be mentioned here, although it belongs rather to technical education. The ancient *Life* of Sophocles tells us that Sophocles 'collected from the educated a thiasos in honour of the Muses'. 'The educated' may very well mean from the context the actors and chorusmen whom he had trained, and a case can be made for supposing that they held symposia for which vases with scenes from tragedies were specially painted. Possibly the remarks attributed to Sophocles about tragedy come from the discussions at these symposia. At least we have here a fifth-century Athenian Association in honour of the Muses which antedates Plato's Academy.[24]

There are therefore two Athenian forerunners of the Academy, the 'thinkshop' in the *Clouds* and Sophocles' Association in honour of the Muses, as well as the Pythagorean communities in South Italy, which are usually quoted in this connection. About these we know extraordinary little, but we can assume that they were societies of aristocrats who lived an ascetic life and studied a mixture of mathematics and mysticism under bonds of secrecy, and that Plato actually saw them when he visited Archytas of Tarentum on his first Sicilian journey. Plato went to South Italy in 388, and according to the account in Plato's *Seventh Letter*, which, whether it is genuine or not, seems to give a reliable account of Plato's life, the Academy was a going concern when Plato was invited to go to Sicily in 367.[25]

The Academy was one of the three famous gymnasia outside the walls of Athens. It lay about a mile northwards from the Dipylon gate close to Kolonos, the scene of Sophocles' *Oedipus Coloneus*. The olive trees were supposed to derive from the original olive on the Acropolis. In the early fifth century Kimon had given it running tracks and shady walks. It had the normal changing rooms and porticoes for a gymnasion. Plato added two things, a shrine of the Muses and a house. The shrine of the Muses made the school a religious association, like that formed by Sophocles, and this may have been some protection against prosecution for impiety. The house is described as 'a little place bought for 3,000 drachmai' (the sort of price that Lysias' rich clients paid for houses in the city, where they were presumably more expensive). Plato himself lived in the house, which passed to his successor. Instruction took place probably in the house as well as in the gymnasion. Apparently there was no payment, and we only hear of a demand for subscriptions, probably to meet the needs for common meals and symposia, under Plato's successor Speusippos.[26]

In the *Republic*, the middle books of which were written about the time that the Academy was beginning to become established, Plato gives a grandiose scheme of higher education, which has been supposed to be the programme of the Academy. This higher education must develop the intellect and not merely the senses. Therefore the first discipline is the science of numbers, which leads the mind from this apple or this pear to consider the nature of unity, the second discipline is plane geometry, the third solid geometry, the fourth astronomy, and the fifth harmonics. All these sciences lead away from the world of sight and sound to the ideal world of number, shape, and motion, and they are therefore a preparation for the culminating science of dialectic, by which it is possible to push beyond the unexamined hypotheses of these abstract sciences to the first principle, the Idea of the Good or the Purpose of the Universe. From this practical ethics and politics can be derived, and the philosophers go on to hold office in their cities. The timetable provides for them to study the preliminary sciences from age twenty to thirty, dialectic from thirty to thirty-five, and then to hold office for fifteen years. At the age of fifty the best of them are to return to philosophy for the rest of their lives, making occasional excursions into practical politics for the sake of their cities and to train their successors.[27]

Let us compare this with what we know otherwise about the Academy. The programme is an ideal and could not be rigid practice. But some did come to the Academy very young, Aristotle from Stageira at seventeen and Theophrastos from Eresos before he was twenty-three. At the other end Plato stayed on until he died, and his excursion into practical politics in Syracuse was made at the age of sixty; his successors Speusippos and Xenokrates were very senior in the Academy when they succeeded and also took a part in practical politics. Perhaps the most striking fact about the Academy which comes out of such lists as we have is the large number of non-Athenians: to quote the obvious examples in addition to Aristotle and Theophrastos, Dion came from Syracuse, Herakleides came from the Propontis, Menedemos came from Pyrrha, Philip came from Opous. The Athenians are all distinguished and all took a major part in practical politics. Chabrias, who was a distinguished general, Phokion, both general and politician, Hypereides the orator, Lykourgos, who restored the morale and the finances of Athens after the defeat by Philip of Macedon. Most of the non-Athenians also played a part in politics: Dion's involvement in the politics of Syracuse is well known, and he took a number of other Academicians with him, Aristonymos was sent by the Academy to make a new constitution for the Arcadians; Aristotle and Eudoxos made laws for their native cities. The general line was probably an adaptation of Plato's ideals to the local situation, anti-tyrant on the one side and anti-democratic on the other, and an intelligent conservative framework of laws, which repressed excesses of all kinds. The image of the Academician was of a man incorruptible, traditional, beautifully dressed, and slightly ineffective. Popular in any real sense the Academy can hardly have been; but general lectures were given in the gymnasion, and Plato's dialogues were a running commentary on what was going on; in the fourth century the circulation of books was considerably wider than in the fifth.[28]

How far, in the sense of the *Republic*, political practice was derived from political theory and political theory from a view of the universe based on higher mathematics, is unclear, but there is no doubt that political activity and scientific activity were going on in the same not very large community; some, like Aristotle and Eudoxos, practised both, and everyone must have known what was going on. In one direction the Academy points towards universities and research institutes, and this direction was taken by Aristotle when he returned to Athens and set up the Peripatetic school in the Lykeion. But there are also signs of the Academy giving a more practical and more humanist training in the later years of Plato's life; certainly Aristotle was lecturing in the Academy on rhetoric and literary criticism before he left Athens in 347, and I suspect that the distinguished rhetorician and tragedian Theodektes came over to the Academy from Isokrates' school sometime after 360.[29]

Isokrates was the son of a wealthy flute-maker and had been taught in his youth by Prodikos and Gorgias. He lost his patrimony during the Peloponnesian War and set up his school, probably in his own house, near the Lykeion about 393. Like the sophists he charged for his courses, and if the story of Demosthenes being refused when he offered 1,000 drachmai for a fifth of the course is true, the course had to be taken complete. He himself speaks with scorn of those who charge 3,000 or 4,000 drachmai for their courses, but his quarrel is evidently with their pretensions rather than with their fees. He speaks of his pupils spending three or four years with him and coming from Sicily and the

Black Sea to hear him. This was a rich man's course, and what we know of the pupils, the general Timotheos, the rhetorical tragedian Theodektes and the historians Ephoros and Theopompos, supports this. It was quite small and probably did not contain more than four or five pupils at any one time.[30]

Isokrates carefully distinguishes himself from the teachers of rhetoric on one side and Plato on the other. The teachers of rhetoric, although their courses are not so expensive, make enormous promises and do not consider either the native ability or inability of their pupils or the demands of the particular occasion; it is strongly implied that what they do is simply to make their pupils learn off their own speeches. On the other side he sees a line linking Empedokles, Parmenides, and Gorgias to the present-day practitioners of philosophical debate (eristic) and mathematics. He is kinder to these in the later speech, *On the exchange* (xv), of 353 than in the earlier speech, *Against the sophists* (xiii), of 391; in the later speech at least the reference must be to Plato and the Academy, as the established school in Athens which taught higher mathematics and philosophical argument, and I think the kindlier tone, which echoes or is echoed by Plato's reference to Isokrates in the *Phaedrus*, reflects Isokrates' awareness of the new trend in the Academy, as well as his own confidence. But he still sees these studies as entirely unpractical but a useful form of mental gymnastics, which should be abandoned at the end of adolescence.[31]

What he offers instead is something that is nearer to practical politics than Plato, and is, he claims, a better training than the rhetoricians give. The training he describes as first continued practice in what he calls the forms of speech (these are primarily the parts of an oration, prologue, narration, proof, conclusion), then practice in stringing these parts together into a complete speech, in order that being firmly based in this his pupils may come nearer in imagination to the actual occasions which they will have to meet. 'The choice of the right forms for each event, their intermixture with each other and arrangement in proper order, moreover the seizing of the opportunity and the suitable embellishment of the speech with arguments and the rhythmical and artistic employment of language, these things need much practice and are tasks for a courageous and adventurous soul.'[32]

The subjects which are to be chosen for practice orations should be 'broad, noble, moral treatments of foreign affairs'. This is in fact an adequate description of Isokrates' own speeches (or perhaps, as they were not spoken, they might better be described as political journalism). He describes himself as standing aside from the hurlyburly of practical politics and considering the grand strategy. His outlook is conservative but more liberal than Plato's, and his strategy does change with the changing realities of the fourth century. A passage in the very late *Panathenaicus* (XII) gives a picture of him at work with his school. After a flamboyant praise of Athens he adds an epilogue: 'I was correcting the speech, which had been written out up to this point, with three or four of my students. When we had gone through it, it seemed to us good and only to need an ending, but I decided to summon one of my former students who had lived in an oligarchy with a strong pro-Lacedaemonian bias, so that, if any false statement had escaped us, he might see it and point it out.' There then follows a long fencing-match between the pro-Lacedaemonian and the aged Isokrates, which Isokrates wins; but after three days he becomes exceedingly unhappy about his victory and summons a full meeting of all his former students in Athens to advise him whether to publish the speech or not. The speech was read to the meeting with enormous applause, and then the pro-Lacedaemonian gives his opinion that the speech should be published with a full account of the debates, which in fact happened. Probably this process of communal editing was the normal practice of the school (one would like to know whether Plato's dialogues were similarly edited in the Academy), and this was the main way in which, besides the training in rhetorical practice, the students absorbed Isokrates' grand political strategy. A rather wider public was reached by the publication of the speeches.

The entry to the two schools of higher education was in practice restricted to the rich, but they were both of them international in the sense that a large number of the students were non-Athenians (the Academy even included a Persian). Their aims were very different. Isokrates can be given the credit for inventing the idea of serious political journalism and a suitably pompous style for conveying the views of the establishment. The less practical Academy probably had more practical effect both by its law-giving activities, which were copied in the Hellenistic age, and in its institution of organised research.

5 *Religion*

Two impressions arise from a cursory review of Athenian religion, first its pervasiveness and secondly its inadequacy from the point of view of the believing Christian. It is not only that the idea of a god dying to save mankind and rising again is lacking; it is also that the consequences of this idea for the individual and for society and for culture are absent. We miss on the one hand the dedicated priest or layman who lives his life by his duty to god and his duty to his neighbour, and the literature that this ideal has inspired, but we miss also the pompous hierarchy of organised religion with its charitable and educational institutions and its on the whole restrictive influence on thought, literature, and art. We have to take Athenian religion on its own terms, and ask how it works in the individual, in society, and in culture. In one sense, and this is part of what I mean by the pervasiveness of Greek religion, most classical Greek poetry is religious because it was performed at a religious festival or at a symposion, which is a ceremony in honour of Dionysos, and a great deal of Greek art is religious, because it was made either to decorate the temples of the gods or to be dedicated to the gods or to be used in their ceremonies. But with no established or quasi-established church the Greeks had much greater freedom to interpret their gods, even when producing religious art and literature, than we have. They had no established church and they had no bible. Homer and Hesiod are often called the Greek bible, and this is a reasonable tribute to their tremendous and abiding influence, but respect for Homer did not for a moment prevent Aeschylus and Euripides from producing a completely unhomeric picture of gods and heroes at a religious festival. Homer and Hesiod were not the Greek bible but the earliest surviving, major, and universally known, interpretations of the gods and heroes. It is probably true to say that already in the eighth century Homer and Hesiod represented a dynamic theology in contrast to a static religion.[1]

The decipherment of the Linear B tablets showed that most of the major Greek gods, including Dionysos, were being worshipped with a ritual of sacrifices and offerings in the fifteenth century B.C., so that classical Athenian religion has a history of more, probably much more, than 1,000 years behind it, and in Athens, which was never sacked, more of the old is likely to have survived than elsewhere. Two obvious changes intervene. The Mycenaean sacred, if not divine, King gave place to the Athenian King Archon, an official chosen from the whole citizen body, and the palace shrine gave place to the city temple. Although the general supervision of the older cults fell to the King Archon, who could come from the poorest class of citizens, certain priesthoods or religious offices were in the hands of old aristocratic families: the Eteoboutadai were concerned with Athena Polias, the Eumolpidai with Eleusis, the Lykomidai with Mysteries at Phlya, and the Gephyraioi with Mysteries at Aphidna. But the restricted choice of officials does not imply a restriction of worshippers, and we shall have to note where cults were open not only to citizens but also to resident aliens and even slaves.[2]

We can distinguish between city cults, deme-cults, and private religious observances. The Athenian religious calendar gives something like fifty festivals, and that includes only a very few of the deme-cults. It is from such figures that the first impression of pervasiveness comes. They can be classified roughly into festivals originating in fertility cults, festivals to win the help of powerful spirits, and festivals concerned with important stages in human life. Only a few of each kind can be mentioned, and they are chosen because they show one or more of three distinct characteristics. First, the celebrants may be resident aliens and slaves as well as citizens, and such festivals interest us because they show in another way that there were no sharp divisions in

Athenian society. Secondly, some festivals have competitions in athletics, music, choruses, or drama. Here again a considerable number of celebrants are involved and a still larger number of onlookers. Moreover in most cases the events, choral, dramatic, or athletic, were financed by the richest citizens, who, as we have said, hoped thereby to win favour for themselves: it is one instance of a phenomenon which we shall have to examine, the political manipulation of religion. The competitions themselves were religiously acceptable because no Greek doubted that the gods had the same pleasures as he had. Thirdly, some festivals come near to our modern conception of religion because they offer a hope of immortality or a sense of communion with god.

For Athens the fertility of land, animals, and women is so important that the calendar is studded with festivals based on rites designed to secure this fertility. The year started about the middle of July, but for us it is easier to see the progression by beginning in the depths of winter. At the turn of our year the Haloa, named after cultivated land, was celebrated in honour of Demeter and Kore (but Poseidon as an earth-god and Dionysos also had a part), and the Rural Dionysia was held in the demes in honour of Dionysos. In both models of sexual organs were openly displayed to secure fertility. In the Haloa women, as well as men, played a part and hetairai, as well as free women; in the Rural Dionysia, as described by Aristophanes, the whole household took part. At the same time the Lenaia was celebrated in the city. Masked dances, for which we have evidence in the sixth century, developed into regular competitions in comedy and tragedy in the fifth century. Similarly in the fourth century several of the demes had their local performances of drama, produced by rich men at the Rural Dionysia. There are two suggestions that the Lenaia gave a hope of immortality and of communion with god. First, Dionysos is summoned as 'Iakchos, giver of wealth', and the procession of the festival is managed by the supervisors of the Eleusinian Mysteries, with which Iakchos is primarily connected; the Mysteries, as we shall see, promised immortality.[3]

The second suggestion is doubtful in the sense that the evidence may be better connected with the February festival of the Anthesteria than with the January festival of the Lenaia. This has been much discussed but for our purposes the answer is unimportant. The evidence is a series of vases running from the late sixth to the late fifth century, made either for the festival itself or for symposia after the festival. They illustrate women dressed as maenads performing an ecstatic dance before a mask of Dionysos nailed to a pillar or tree, in front of which stands a table with kraters (mixing-bowls) of wine. The women's ecstatic dances put them into communion with Dionysos. The mask of Dionysos may be the mask which is worn by the man who impersonates Dionysos at the Anthesteria. The three days of the Anthesteria were called Pithoigia (jar-opening), Choes (jugs), and Chytroi (pots). On the first day the new wine was opened, and choral dithyrambs were probably sung to Dionysos. On the second day the spring return of Dionysos was celebrated: the god was brought on a wheeled ship and married Basilinna (perhaps Ariadne), whom we know to have been the wife of the King Archon. Essentially, the god of fertility marries the earth goddess and so ensures fertility (the Theogamia, celebrated in the same month, was a similar marriage of Zeus and Hera). The day ended with the drinking competition which gave it its name, the Jugs. On the third day the dead received their offerings in pots. The connection of this with the other two days is the parallelism between the death of vegetation and human death, and Dionysos was connected with the dead in many cults. Slaves as well as citizens participated in the festival on all three days.[4]

The City Dionysia in March was a comparatively modern festival introduced in the sixth century. The essential fertility ritual was the offering of phalloi to Dionysos, and the rest of the festival was a magnificent holiday in which foreigners and parolled prisoners, as well as resident aliens and citizens, shared. The main parts were the Procession with choruses sung at the shrines of various gods in the Agora, the competition of dithyrambs by choruses of fifty men and fifty boys from each of the ten tribes, the competition of tragedy, satyr play, and comedy. Three tragic poets produced each three tragedies and a satyr play, and five comic poets (at one period only three) produced each one comedy.[5]

In May the Thargelia is a festival of Apollo which combined an elaborate purification ritual with an offering of first-fruits; the rites were meant to ensure the coming harvest. There was also a tribal contest of dithyrambs. In the same month two important Athena festivals took place: the Kallynteria, in which the temple of Athena was cleaned, and the Plynteria, in which the cult statue of Athena was escorted down to Phaleron and bathed in the sea before being restored to her temple. This Athena is a fertility goddess, and her statue must be purified in preparation for the new harvest. Further fertility festivals in June, with secret use of sexual emblems, were the Arrhetophoria in honour of Athena and the Skirophoria in honour of Demeter and Kore, with whom Athena and Poseidon were also associated. The Dipolieia was a harvest festival in honour of Zeus Polieus, and after the sacrifice the meat was distributed among the demes. At another harvest festival in July, the Kronia, masters and slaves feasted together.[6]

The great festival of July was the Panathenaia. In three out of four years this consisted of a night festival of dancing and singing, a procession, a contest of dithyrambs, and a contest of pyrrhicists. In the fourth year the Great Panathenaia was celebrated with the bringing of a new robe to Athena, which had been woven by two of the girls concerned with the Arrhetophoria. Thus the connection of the old fertility cult with the new holiday festival was asserted, and the Panathenaia was a harvest festival. The robe was brought to the Akropolis in a splendid procession, in which resident aliens, freedmen, and slaves, as well as citizens, took part. Besides the pyrrhicists, there were athletic and musical contests of many different kinds, including the recitation of the *Iliad* and the *Odyssey* by relays of rhapsodes, and the prizes were black-figure amphorai of a special shape, filled with olive oil from the sacred olive trees.[7]

In August a harvest festival for Demeter and Kore in Eleusis was accompanied by games in which the victors won a prize of holy grain. In September the Greater Eleusinian Mysteries were held. They were preceded by the Lesser Mysteries in February, which were regarded as a preparation particularly for foreigners. The Greater Mysteries were an international festival to which the other Greek cities were asked to send delegates. The celebration lasted nine days and included a great procession from Athens to Eleusis, in which the sacred objects, presumably sexual symbols, which had been brought from Eleusis to Athens for this purpose, were carried back to Eleusis. What happened at the climax in Eleusis is secret. There were two stages, one for all the initiates and one for the higher grade of initiates, who were called Epoptai or viewers. What they saw beyond the sacred objects we do not know, but here certainly the symbolism of the death and resurrection of the grain was linked to the death and resurrection of the human being. Somehow they felt themselves united with the processes of the universe and sure of a better life hereafter.[8]

The Thesmophoria in October was a three-day festival to secure the fertility of women, and every deme sent two married women as delegates, but it was associated also with the first sowing and ploughing, because the secret things which had been buried at the Skirophoria were brought up and mixed with the seed-corn. Finally we may mention the Pyanopsia, a thanksgiving to Apollo for the fruit-harvest, and the Oschophoria, a thanksgiving to Dionysos for the vintage.[9]

Most of what these festivals sought to secure is secured in the modern world by other means, by science, technology, and medicine; only the desire for immortality and the desire for communion with god remain for religion to fulfil. For our present purpose we have noted a good many occasions when a wider circle than the circle of citizens is admitted to the rites as spectators and participants, and some occasions, notably the Dionysiac festivals and the Panathenaia, when great poetry and great music were performed by considerable numbers on religious occasions.[10]

A second kind of festival is designed more generally to secure the goodwill of the god or hero whom it honours. A good many of these had competitions—unspecified contests and later a torch-race at the Theseion, a torch-race on horseback at the festival of Bendis in the Peiraieus, boat-races for Poseidon at Sounion, for Ajax at Salamis, for Zeus at the Peiraieus, and for Artemis at Mounichia. The cult of Theseus at the Theseion was old, and the families who claimed that their ancestors went with Theseus to Crete administered it; the contests and the public sacrifice, which provided meat for the people, were probably instituted in the fifth century when Kimon brought Theseus' bones back from Skyros. Herakles had many cults in Attica; the best known were at the gymnasion at Kynosarges and at Marathon. The rites included a sacrifice and a meal in which the hero (in effigy?) was joined by fellow-diners (*parasitoi*) and in Kynosarges, if not elsewhere, these fellow-diners had to be illegitimate themselves or the sons of illegitimate parents in memory of Herakles' mixed ancestry.[11]

We cannot mention the many hero-cults in the demes, which were often attached to Mycenaean tombs. But one other class of festivals must be added, the festivals in honour of gods who were patrons of professions. This kind of association is found already on the Linear B tablets in the 'smiths of Potnia' and 'the slave of Artemis', who is presumably a hunter; in Hesiod the carpenter is 'the slave of Athena', and with another terminology the doctors are called 'sons of Asklepios'. It is, of course, in this tradition that Sophocles and Plato made the Muses patrons of their associations, and perhaps already in the fourth century the actors formed an association of Artists of Dionysos, which gained them considerable protection, privileges, and status. The festivals which may be included in this class are the Chalkeia, Hephaistia, Promethia, Hermaia, and Elaphebolia. The name of the Chalkeia shows that it was primarily a festival for bronze-workers, although ancient authorities say that it was originally a festival of Athena for the whole people, and it is certain that it marked the beginning of the weaving of the peplos for the Panathenaia (but the weaving also belongs to Athena as a patron of crafts). To put it in modern terms, as artists bronze-workers and potters belong to Athena, but as technologists they belong to Hephaistos and Prometheus, who both provided fire. The Hephaistia and Promethia were suitably celebrated by a torch-race but also by choruses of men and boys. Hermes was the patron of athletes, and Hermaia were celebrated in the palaistra; many vases show young men sacrificing or praying to herms, and were either dedicated to Hermes or used in a symposion by young athletes.

Elaphebolia was a festival of Artemis as the patron of hunters; hunting was sufficiently important as an aristocratic sport for this festival to give its name to the month which lasted from mid-March to mid-April.[12]

Finally a number of festivals may be associated with stages in human life. The Apatouria was the festival of the phratries, the old kinship groups; it was a three-day festival in honour of Zeus and Athena; the children were introduced at an Apatouria soon after birth and were registered at the Apatouria after their eighteenth birthday, and when they married they introduced their wives at the next Apatouria. The Brauronia may be included because it was certainly connected with marriage. In the precinct of Artemis at Brauron on the east coast of Attica young Athenian girls lived as her servants until they were married; they were called bears because, presumably before the Greeks came into Greece, Artemis was worshipped as a bear. The festival had women's races and dances, which are illustrated on many dedications in the sanctuary. Every five years a special delegation was sent to the festival from Athens, and at these special festivals rhapsodes performed. The Genesia in the same month as the Great Eleusinian Mysteries was a public festival to Earth in honour of dead ancestors. The Diasia in the same month as the Anthesteria was a public festival in honour of Zeus Meilichios, the god of the underworld who could treat the dead kindly as well as sending blessings to the living.[13]

So far I have spoken of state festivals (and more might be added) and to a lesser extent of deme festivals, which we cannot begin to appreciate. Before considering religion in private life, another side of religion, both official and unofficial, ought to be mentioned, the prediction of the future. If we want to go beyond the foresight of human intelligence, we consult the fortune-teller or the astrologer or the computer, but this has nothing to do with our ideas of the omniscience of God. For the Greeks the gods were not only omniscient but were prepared to share this knowledge with men. In its raw form this knowledge took the form of oracles, portents, omens, and dreams, which were in themselves, at least in their detailed application, unintelligible but could be interpreted by experts, and given this it was natural also to try and tap this knowledge by consulting the experts when no sign had been given. On the state level oracles were consulted before any important undertaking; unfortunately conflicting oracles or conflicting interpretations could easily be found by rival politicians, as is very obvious during the discussions about the advisability of the Sicilian expedition. On the private level people probably varied very much: Nikias kept a soothsayer in his house and apparently used him to predict what strikes were likely to be profitable in the silver mines. The fourth-century philosopher Theophrastos regards it as superstitious (which he defines as 'being cowardly when faced with the supernatural') to take every dream to the dream-interpreters, the soothsayers, and the bird-watchers, implying thereby that important dreams do need explanation. The use and misuse of prediction could, of course, be discussed at very great length; what is important from our point of view is that the Greeks were accustomed by all these kinds of prediction to have an eye open for events which needed interpretation, and this vigilance could lead to scientific interpretation as well as mantic interpretation. The two are neatly contrasted in a story of Pericles. He was brought the head of a ram with a single horn, which had been born on his farm. The seer Lampon said that the two great political rivals Pericles and Thucydides, son of Melesias, would be reduced to one and the one would be Pericles because the portent was found on his farm. The scientist Anaxagoras split the skull of the ram and showed that the single horn was due to a malformation. Shortly afterwards Thucydides was ostracised and Lampon's interpretation was accepted.[14]

State religion, except for the Eleusinian Mysteries and the maenad cult, does little to satisfy those who crave for immortality or communion with God. Probably much more of this was done by minor cults than we know. At the deme level the cults administered by the Lykomidai at Phlya and the Gephyraioi at Aphidna were certainly mysteries. Two examples of private mystery cults may be quoted. The fourth-century orator and politician Aischines was taunted by his rival Demosthenes with having helped his mother with her mystery cult in his youth, reading aloud from the sacred books, purifying the candidates for initiation, and teaching them to say 'I have escaped evil, I have found better'. And Theophrastos puts down as a mark of superstition 'when one is going to be initiated, to go every month with one's wife, or the nurse, if she is not free, and the children to the Orphic initiators'. Perhaps, we can get some idea of what this kind of personal religion could mean to a Greek from the prayer which Euripides' Hippolytos, who is taunted by his father with reading Orphic books, makes to Artemis, as he offers her a garland: 'Beloved Queen, receive this band for your golden hair from my pious hand. I alone have this privilege. I am with you and I converse with you, hearing your voice but not seeing your face. May I end my life as I have begun?'[15]

➤ Most private religion is much more material. Birth, marriage, and death were accompanied by ritual and offerings. The house had a Herm and an altar of Apollo outside, an altar of Zeus in the courtyard, and the hearth belonged to Hestia. On the farm the country gods needed propitiating, Demeter for the grain, Athena for the olives, Dionysos for the vines, Pan for the flocks, the Nymphs for the water, Zeus for the weather, Artemis for the hunt. Meat was only eaten after a sacrifice to a god, and the subsequent symposion included libations to Zeus, as well as Dionysos. Nothing was done without a prayer and a libation, and the prayer was often accompanied by a vow to make a sacrifice or dedication if the prayer was answered. The theory of this religion is neatly expressed by an early inscription: 'Telesinos dedicates this statue to you, rejoicing in which grant him to dedicate another.' He made a prayer and Athena granted it; he dedicated his statue, perhaps going beyond the specification in the hope that she may favour him further and the process may be repeated. An actual instance of such repetition can be quoted: Kallias, son of Dindymias, dedicated a marble statue to Athena on the Acropolis after he had won the boy's contest, probably at the Panathenaic festival in 482; about 450 he dedicated a bronze statue to Athena to celebrate the close of an extremely successful career in international athletics. The inscriptions recording dedications often have the words 'first fruits' or 'tithe', and here there is presumably some relationship between the profit made and the object offered: the tithe suggests that it was somewhere near a tenth. There may be a distinction between a tithe of a normal year's profits and the first fruits of a special commission or windfall, but this is not certain. Dedications differ enormously in scale. A woman dedicated an Attic perfume pot to Hera with a picture of Dionysos; she had not even bothered to look for one with a picture of Hera. But many exquisitely painted vases with prefired dedicatory inscriptions are found in Attic sanctuaries, which are certainly special commissions. Statues and reliefs were always special commissions; they also have a considerable range from miniatures to life-size and over; larger still are the elaborate monuments put up by the victors in dithyrambic contests, like the monument of Lysikrates, which still stands on the Street of the Tripods in Athens.[16]

Enough has been said to establish the pervasiveness of Greek religion. Some cults provided hopes of immortality and communion with God. None, I think, substituted for the services of the confessional or the psychiatrist; perhaps they were not necessary. What religion did provide was an insurance for all activities, but it was mostly an insurance for life on earth rather than an insurance for heaven like Christianity. Its very pervasiveness may have had a positive value. So many of men's hopes and doubts and fears must have been canalised into a beautiful drill of dance and song and ritual, performed with beautiful objects, that they may have been left freer to range in thought.

So far I have tried to say what the Athenian festivals and the private observances of the Athenian were meant to achieve, what the Athenian felt about his gods and heroes, and what may have been an effect of religion on culture. In the state festivals with competitions another element comes in; the rich man who produces the dithyramb, tragedy, or comedy, or trains the team of torch-racers or pyrrhic dancers (war dances) wants to win the competition because he will thereby also win the goodwill of the audience and this may help him politically or in the law-courts. This political element in religion shows itself in various ways, both internationally and nationally.

The great international centres of religion were Delphi and Olympia. In the late sixth century the distinguished Athenian family of the Alkmaionidai used marble in rebuilding the temple of Apollo at Delphi when they had only contracted to use lime-stone, and this was an efficient way of influencing the oracle to give responses in their interest. Alkibiades entered seven teams in the chariot race at the Olympic games and had a superbly decorated marquee erected there for entertainment; he claimed that this made foreigners appreciate the power of Athens. An interesting mixture of public display and private intercession is seen in Nikias' delegation to Delos. The Athenians used to send a chorus to sing in honour of Apollo and chose a rich man to produce it (like a tragic chorus). Nikias did this in an unusually splendid fashion: he landed his chorus on the neighbouring island of Rheneia and then led them across a specially built bridge of boats to Delos, and after the performance erected a bronze palmtree as a dedication to the god; so far all was public, but then he bought a piece of land for 10,000 drachmai from the revenues of which the Delians were to make sacrifices accompanied by prayers for the prosperity of Nikias.[17]

In Athens itself Nikias had neither the authority of Pericles nor the eloquence of the democratic Kleon but tried to win over the people by lavish and sumptuous production of choruses and torch-races. This is exactly what the political tract means when it says that the rich men are the producers and the poor are paid for singing and dancing. It is interesting to trace in a few instances the political use of religion from Kimon to Pericles. At the time of Salamis it was essential to persuade the Athenians to evacuate the city and fight with their fleet. Kimon, the young aristocratic leader, dedicated his bridle to Athena to show that this was not the time to use the cavalry. After the Persian War he beautified Athens in a number of ways, but perhaps the most important was to rebuild and decorate the Theseion and to bring back Theseus' bones from Skyros and bury them there; it is probably from this time that the public feasting and competitions at Theseus' festival date. Theseus had been made popular in the late sixth century as the hero of the new democracy, probably by the Alkmaionids, into whom Kimon had married. Now Kimon and the more conservative of the Alkmaionids were saying that they were the true Athenian democracy under the patronage of Theseus. Shortly after, Kimon was ostracised, and the radical

Alkmaionid Pericles got the power.[18]

Kimon was succeeded as the aristocratic leader by Thucydides son of Melesias, and Plutarch is quite clear that at this stage Pericles won over the votes of the people by proposing a succession of religious spectacles, banquets and processions, but he quotes a line, probably from a comedy, which describes him as 'educating the city with artistic pleasures'. This ambivalence appears also in the great building programme which produced the Hephaisteion, the Parthenon, the Propylaia, and after Pericles' death the Erechtheion and the temple of Nike (*figs 14-18*). The aristocrats said that he was 'gilding and dressing up the Akropolis like a vain woman, hanging round her neck precious stones and statues and six million drachma temples'. Pericles said that he had brought the whole city on to the payroll (and this was undoubtedly a good way of getting votes); but he also said at the beginning of the Peloponnesian war that the whole city was an education for Greece, and this surely included the new buildings on the Akropolis. We shall have to discuss the Periclean building programme in more detail later; here it is enough to say that the sculpture of the Parthenon put forward self-discipline and piety as the condition of Athena's favour to Athens. The Parthenon was therefore political manipulation of religion in two senses: it both provided full employment and put forward a political ideal.[19]

Another kind of political manipulation of religion was to charge an enemy with impiety. Details and dates of the attacks on Pericles' friends are obscure, but it seems clear that Pheidias, who made the cult statue for the Parthenon, the philosopher Anaxagoras, who was closely associated with Pericles, and Pericles' mistress Aspasia were accused. The accuser of Aspasia was the comic poet Hermippos, and probably the whole accusation was in a comedy, and not in the law-courts: it was hardly impiety to name prostitutes after the Muses and certainly not impious to keep a brothel, which were the two charges against her. The charge against Pheidias that he put portraits of himself and Pericles on the shield of Athena Parthenos is also probably due to comedy, but the accusation of embezzling gold from the statue was a real accusation. It was disproved and carried no subsequent slur, because Pheidias went on to make the cult statue of Zeus at Olympia. The charge against Anaxagoras was not believing in the gods and teaching theories about the heavenly bodies (Anaxagoras said that the sun was stone and the moon was earth), and he avoided them by leaving Athens. A similar charge was made against Protagoras, who had disclaimed all knowledge of the gods, and he was drowned in escaping; Protagoras had also associated with Pericles, but this was some seven years after Pericles' death, and it is possible that the political object of the attack was Pericles' young kinsman Alkibiades. Alkibiades himself was attacked at the time of the Sicilian expedition for being involved in the mutilation of the Herms and the profanation of the Mysteries. The accuser was Thessalos, son of Kimon, so that there is no doubt of the political motivation of the trial, even if there was here some substance in the religious charges. Finally, Socrates was accused and condemned for not believing in the gods and corrupting the youth. The first charge was largely based on comedy; the second charge was true in the sense that more than one of the young men who had associated with Socrates took part in the oligarchic government of the Thirty Tyrants. Thus either the left or the right could use a charge of impiety to attack a political rival, and the ordinary Athenian jury was ready to condemn on these grounds. The prosecution in all these trials was aiming to damage or remove a political rival; to damage Pericles by removing his friends, to remove Alkibiades by direct attack, to damage the aristocrats by putting Socrates to death. Only Pheidias was acquitted because the gold could be weighed. From what we know of the large randomly selected Athenian juries one would expect their bias to be left rather than right: they were the people who profited from Pericles' policy of full employment. If, therefore, they condemned Pericles' friends (and the flight of Anaxagoras suggests that this condemnation was regarded as a certainty), they condemned on religious rather than political grounds. Socrates they would condemn on political grounds, but according to Plato considerable prejudice was aroused against him by the picture drawn of him in Aristophanes' *Clouds* 'contemplating the sun': teaching theories about heavenly bodies had been the charge against Anaxagoras.[20]

In the trials of Anaxagoras, Protagoras, and Socrates the clash between static religion and dynamic theology became overt and dangerous. Plato in the fourth century put his Academy under the patronage of the Muses, and this may have helped him to avoid it. The conflict had always been possible, but in Athens in the fifth century the situation was explosive. To a large extent the new theology came from abroad, its proponents were associated with Pericles, whom the old families who administered the old cults distrusted politically; later the pendulum swung the other way; the old families embraced the new theology, and the political opposition came from the left. But the remarkable phenomenon is the creation alongside religion of what I have called the new theology, and that must be briefly examined. For us Homer and Hesiod are the first Greek theology; they are also the first great codification of mythology. The technological condition for the performance of epics on this scale was the invention of writing. The social condition was the wider based society of the Greek city state and the greater material riches of eighth-century Greece. The occasion was a religious festival so that Homer and Hesiod were privileged, as later Attic tragedy and comedy were privileged. The occasion was a religious festival because it was a permanent assumption of Greek religion that god enjoyed what man enjoyed. What lies behind Homer and Hesiod we can only guess. Roughly I should suppose a long period, going back into Mycenaean times, of assimilation and systematisation of stories of four main kinds: stories partly historical of the Mycenaean heroes (which became the cult myths of their shrines when they were worshipped), stories of the gods helping the heroes (which could be reused in religion to activate the god's power), stories ultimately based on fertility cults (many of them became at this late stage the love-affairs of gods and goddesses), stories borrowed, some very early and some quite recently, from the Near East.[21]

I have noted already the power of systematisation, the use of the simile as a working model of the unknown, the use of personification to identify a potency and express its relationship to other potencies, as tools bequeathed by Homer and Hesiod to later Greeks for scientific and philosophic thinking, which are for a

Greek inseparable from theology. Among the personifications I noted the personification of natural phenomena; it would perhaps be better to speak of identity of natural phenomenon and god: fire is Hephaistos, the sea which surrounds the world is Okeanos. Homer's Okeanos, like the water in Eastern cosmogonies, is the origin of all. Thales changed the name to the impersonal Hydor but kept the divinity, and the first principles of his successors, down to and including the Mind of Anaxagoras, are spoken of as divine or given the predicates of divinity. Here again both Homer and religion helped. Homer himself usually says which god is responsible for a particular action, but he often makes his characters speak of 'the god' or 'the gods', as if they knew that a divine power was responsible but not which divine power. And religious texts are often phrased, e.g. 'X dedicated this to the goddess' rather than to Athena or 'to the goddesses' rather than to Demeter and Persephone. And these Greek gods were, as is clear from their cults, multivalent, and resist the attempts of ancient and modern theologians to put them in pigeon-holes. Athena was virgin warrior, fertility goddess, and patroness of arts and crafts. Zeus was god of the sky but also god of the dead. Therefore from this angle too it was natural to have a generalised word for god beside the many names of gods and goddesses. So the first principle of the philosopher-scientists was divine, and under this seemingly religious umbrella they could develop a world-view in which more and more was attributed to natural causes. The sun became a stone and the moon became earth, and storms were due to the clashing of clouds and not to Zeus' anger with sinful men. It was only in fifth-century Athens that the incompatibility of the scientific view with the religious view became apparent.[22]

Before that another strand of theological thought must be followed. It looks as though the conception of a just god appeared in the Near East and in Greece about the same time. In Greece it was attached particularly to Zeus and Apollo. It appears in the *Iliad* and *Odyssey* and very clearly in the *Works and Days* of Hesiod. Solon proclaims it in his long elegy, and clearly means it to be the theological background of his political reforms. In Athens it appears again as the essential nerve of Aeschylus' tragedy, pronounced with all the pomp and majesty of Aeschylean language. Our knowledge of Athenian thought between Solon and Aeschylus is scanty, but when one remembers how astounding the Greek victory in the Persian wars must have been, it does not seem unlikely that the generation which fought the Persians should respond again to the belief in the justice of the gods.[23]

Homer did not feel any contradiction between the just rule of Zeus and Zeus' behaviour in imprisoning his father Kronos and raping other goddesses and mortal women. Such divine behaviour was a problem for the Persian War generation; the Aeschylean Apollo is enraged when the Furies argue that Zeus imprisoned his father, and says that fetters can be loosed; Pindar refuses to believe certain crude myths. The problem was stated already in the sixth century by Xenophanes: 'Homer and Hesiod attributed to the gods all that bring reproach and blame among men, theft, adultery, and deceiving each other'. This is part of an argument to show that man makes god in his own image, whereas the mind and structure of god is in no way like the mind and structure of man. The argument does allow a hierarchy of gods, but how Xenophanes conceived these subsidiary gods we do not know. Aeschylus clearly assimilated his Zeus to the supreme god of Xenophanes; but the criticism of Homer and Hesiod involved also a complete breach with ordinary religion. The divinity of Dionysos and Herakles depended on Zeus' adultery with Semele and Alkmene, and this according to Xenophanes was a poetic fiction. In fact, of course, the believers continued to believe, but a line of criticism had been started, which led Aeschylus, Pindar, and the early classical artists to moralise the myths which could be moralised. From that time on the responsibility for unacceptable myths is shifted to the poets, and for Plato the tragedians join Homer as the makers of stories that misrepresent the gods.[24]

Xenophanes' highest god is a first principle like Anaximenes' Air and in the fifth century Anaxagoras' Mind, which according to Plato set a mechanistic universe in motion. But such a Mind could be purposive: Protagoras attributes the balance, which he perceives in the animal kingdom as well as in the universe, to the Forethought of the divine. And Diogenes of Apollonia, who equated god, mind, and air as his first principle, said that all has been arranged as well as possible, so that it is likely that his thought is reflected in certain passages of Xenophon, where the heavenly bodies, the earth, and the animals are all designed for the welfare of man, and man's whole bodily structure is designed for his preservation. Similarly the development of civilisation may be ascribed to divine forethought rather than human skill answering to human needs. This kind of theology fitted fifth-century experience, particularly medical experience, but had little relation to the gods and beliefs of cult.[25]

More subversive still was Xenophanes' perception that different peoples made their gods in their own image, because this meant that gods were in fact man-made. Xenophanes quotes three pieces of evidence: the criminal behaviour ascribed to the gods by Homer and Hesiod, the snubnosed black gods of the Ethiopians, and the blue-eyed red-haired gods of the Thracians. The last two show the increasing geographical observations of the Greeks in the late sixth and early fifth century, of which we have already spoken. The greater the knowledge of the different customs and beliefs and institutions of different peoples the clearer it became that Greek customs were made by the Greeks and not given them by the gods. The Greek word for custom is *nomos*, and included in its meaning belief in the gods; the normal Greek word for believing in the gods means literally 'to have the gods as part of your *nomos*'. Any observation, therefore, that showed the relativity of customs could be interpreted to mean also that belief in the gods was relative. In the late sixth century, and specifically in democratic Athens, *nomos* got an additional meaning of 'law passed by the democratic assembly'; it was the new democratic word, and it rapidly became obvious that *nomos* in this sense too was man-made; the instability of decrees passed in the democratic assembly showed that *nomos* in this sense also had no divine origin or sanction. Even the time-honoured distinctions between Greek and barbarian and between citizen and slave seemed artificial, when Greek and barbarian worked side by side at the Peiraieus and citizen and slave received the same wages on the Akropolis. *Nomos* in all its applications was man-made convention; the Greeks with their genius for contrast found a polar term for it in *physis*, nature.[26]

Here we are only concerned with this contrast in so far as it effects theology. The first principle of the universe, whether it merely provided original stuff or set creation in motion or had had forethought in its operation, was part of *physis*. The problem was the gods of cult and mythology. Kritias, the leader of the Thirty Tyrants, took the extreme modern view: he regarded the gods as the invention of a wise and cunning statesman, who needed a policeman to frighten men from committing crimes which the eye of the law could not detect; lightning, storms, and thunder were said to show the anger of the gods with human transgressions. This is the final realistic interpretation of the Homeric-Hesiodic belief that Zeus punishes human crime with agricultural disaster. Kritias' conduct in politics suggests that he drew the conclusion that religion was a desirable means of keeping subjects in order, but that higher politics should be conducted by the only law visible in the natural world, the law of the jungle.[27]

Other thinkers wanted to maintain the reality of the gods or at least of some of the gods. The sophist Prodikos taught that 'those things in nature which are wholesome and nutritive for mankind have been looked upon as gods by the earliest of men and honoured accordingly'; the gods are man-made, but instead of being the invention of an authoritarian state they are the results of an early reverence for the beneficent forces in nature. He in fact modernised the very old Greek personification of natural phenomena (it is worth remembering that Mycenaean Knossos had a priestess of the winds). This provides a modern sanction for the cults of Demeter and Dionysos; they are now a part of human history. Protagoras, according to Plato, gave a rather similar account of the laws; he described them as the discovery of old and wise lawgivers, and it is therefore tempting to see the influence of Protagoras in a passage of Xenophon where Socrates says that it is the oldest and wisest of human institutions, cities and races, which most revere the gods. Similarly Protagoras' younger fellow-townsman Demokritos, the most thorough-going of the materialistic philosophers, held that 'a few of the wise men raised their hands to what we Greeks now call air, and said that Zeus holds converse about all things and it is he who knows all things, gives and takes away all things, and he is the king of all'. All these thinkers find the origin of religion in a natural human reaction, which took place in early times. Religion so based is man-made and belongs to *nomos*, that is admitted; but the fact that the essential act was done so long ago means that this *nomos* has become part of modern man's nature or *physis*, and to this extent the contrast between artificial *nomos* and real *physis* is resolved, and the resolution makes it possible for religion and natural philosophy to coexist. This battle was largely fought out in democratic Athens. How far the noise of it spread outside the circles of the sophists and their pupils is hard to know. The echoes were certainly there in tragedy and comedy for the mass audiences to pick up, and the trials for impiety suggest that the juries of ordinary citizens knew that Protagoras and Anaxagoras were not believers in the ordinary sense.[28]

Euripides with transparent honesty asserts the possible validity of all these theologies, including the belief of the ordinary man, and draws the conclusion that the reality for men is certain human values such as friendship and loyalty. Plato in the fourth century also reflects all theologies, and accepts or rejects them according to their suitability for his system. His general concern is to have a theology which justifies a moral life for the individual and the framing of laws which will encourage that moral life. In the extreme case, where he bases the stability of the ideal state on the myth of the different sorts of metals in the different classes and the god's command to maintain the status quo, he is doing what Kritias said the cunning statesman did, inventing a religious myth to establish the government. Elsewhere he rejects or accepts or adapts. The *Republic* starts with a rejection of the jungle-law position in politics, and it is this rejection which the whole book is written to justify. Moral behaviour must not be produced by promises of rewards (Homer and Hesiod) and to secure access to heaven by adherence to a mystery sect is absolutely wrong: it implies that the gods can be bribed. In discussing the education of the guardians of the ideal state, Plato modernises Xenophanes' criticism of Homer and Hesiod, bringing in the tragedians, and will only accept myths that show that god is good, is the only cause of good in the world, and is changeless. This god can be identified with the Idea of the Good and with the divine forethought of the fifth century; indeed when Plato draws a picture of the construction of the universe he owes much to the teleological passages ascribed above to Diogenes of Apollonia, and his criticism of the materialistic philosophers is chiefly that they entirely omitted this element of design.[29]

His description of the materialists shows that he associated them with the *physis-nomos* contrast in the extreme form which was adopted by Kritias. What he does himself is to stand the *physis-nomos* contrast on its head. In the contrast the material world of *physis* is real, the conceptual world of *nomos*, including the gods, is artificial. For Plato the material world is unreal because it is subject to change and decay, the conceptual world is real, and because it is real it is called *physis*. The conceptual world has superior reality because within it we can find certainty, particularly in mathematics (the relation between Parmenides, the mathematicians and Plato must be discussed in a later chapter). To over-simplify, the nearest thing to mathematical certainty in the material world is the movements of the heavenly bodies, and they are gods because they move themselves; from this we can argue back to the divinity of the planner. Plato's theology is a combination of Parmenides, the mathematicians, and teleological physics. Because the highest reality is a god with good purposes, man will realise himself best by assimilating himself to god, and the best government will be the government which imposes the laws which will most encourage him to do so.[30]

Not much is left for traditional religion. The mysteries are an attempt to bribe a way to heaven; so are many other sacrifices and prayers. When Plato mentions individual gods in the *Laws*, it is nearly always as patrons. Zeus is the patron of the state, Ares is the patron of soldiers, Hera is the patron of marriage (and receives fines from those who have not married), Athena and Hephaistos are the patrons of craftsmen, Apollo is the patron of one kind of music and of the law, Dionysos is the patron of another kind of music and of the culture of fruit (and he receives the fines if anyone picks fruit too early). This is a very old relationship between god and man, but it is only one part of the many-sided immediacy of Greek religion; perhaps Plato's citizens would be too well conditioned to need such strong medicine, but the ordinary Athenian continued to worship his gods, much as he had before.

6 *Political and Legal Life*

In the early sixth century Solon had given all the citizens the essential rights of voting in the Assembly and serving on juries. The reorganisation by Kleisthenes at the end of the century had decreased the power of the great aristocratic families. Subsequent reforms in practice opened all magistracies to all classes of citizens, and the institution of pay for service on the jury and attendance at the assembly made it possible for the poor man to leave his job and perform these functions. On the other hand the great names, Kimon, Pericles, Demosthenes are certainly not poor men, and we have to ask how far their policy dominated, and how far the poor men did in fact operate to modify their policies or actually initiate policy. The period from Kimon to Demosthenes is about a century and a half and covers the formation of the Athenian Empire, the Peloponnesian war, the formation of the Second Athenian Confederacy and its collapse, and the rise of Philip of Macedon and his son Alexander. In this long period political practice certainly changed, and this raises the further question how far and how quickly political theory corresponded to these changes. There is also another and more intimate line to consider. The politician has to persuade his audience, the plaintiff and defendant try to persuade the jury; the technique of speech-writing develops in this period, and an examination of the speeches will show what kinds of argument and what ideals appeal to an audience, and the very modes of expression that are accepted at different times as convincing.[1]

If we consider such figures as we have, we can form some idea of how far the ordinary Athenian did in fact participate in government. The curious institution of ostracism, part of Kleisthenes' reforms, by which a leading citizen was exiled for ten years, only operated if more than 6,000 votes were cast, and it is probably a fair assumption that the number was reckoned on the attendance at an important meeting of the Assembly. The number is less than a third of the 21,000 citizen body (males over twenty), but one has to remember that in war-time, and it usually was war-time, the Athenians might have had 12,000 or more serving in the army, in garrisons, in the police, in the navy, or in the merchant-marine. Or it is perhaps more useful to look at the figure from the other end. The really rich men only amounted to 1,200 so that, even if all of them were present, they would only amount to a fifth of a large Assembly meeting. We can then be confident that a representative Assembly meeting did contain a high proportion of poorer citizens, which is what the literary evidence would lead us to expect.[2]

The number of jurors empanelled for service during the year was also 6,000, so that again the number of really rich men serving on juries cannot have been more than a fifth. The evidence from the fifth century, particularly Aristophanes, suggests that it was the poor and elderly who made pocket-money serving on juries. It is difficult to place Aristophanes' old men accurately, but it would perhaps be right to place them in the lower ranges of the hoplite class and in the upper ranges of the lowest property class (*thetes*). The total number of jurors represents about a half of the total number of available citizens, which was in the neighbourhood of 12,000, since the twenty-thirty-year-olds were excluded. Demosthenes expects jurors to feel sympathy with those who paid war-tax, and this has been used as evidence that jurors were not so poor in the fourth century. But it has to be remembered that 5,000 of the 8,000 in the hoplite class were included among the payers of war-tax so that it is extremely probable that some of the jurors were eligible for war-tax. But the general picture that the juries were composed of the poor and the elderly is probably true. The numbers were too great for the rich to flood the courts to secure acquittal for their friends, and there

were extremely complicated procedures to prevent a juror switch-
ing from the court to which he had been allocated to any other
court which might have been trying a friend. Probably we should
think of the jurors as a very high proportion of the citizens over
forty-five with the rich playing rather less than their proportionate
part.[3]

The Council of 500 was chosen by lot, 50 from each tribe.
Each set of 50 served in turn as a presiding committee for a
35-36 day period. The Council convened the Assembly, arranged
its business and saw that its decrees were carried out. The
Council also scrutinised the qualifications of officials and the
allocation and use of their funds, and generally coordinated their
activities. They looked after the making of triremes and docks
and surveyed public buildings. Rents of public lands, mining
royalities, and confiscated property all came under the general
supervision of the Council. They examined the horses of the
cavalry, and they administered state-pensions. They received all
foreign delegations. Membership of the Council, as for other
offices, was for one year, but it was possible to serve a second
term. A minimum of 250 new members had to be chosen every
year, and it has been reckoned that something like a third of
the over-thirties must have had council experience. Serving on
the Council was a full time job, and it is unlikely that many of
the richest men found time to do it. Possibly the men with
Council experience were more or less coincident with the hoplite
class.[4]

Certain officers, nearly all connected with war and training,
were elected, and there was no ban on re-election. These offices
were on the whole the preserve of the rich, although certainly
in the case of the board of ten generals (*strategoi*), the preserve
was often invaded. The number of officers needed in any one
year was rather over sixty, and the number of the richest men
who became available every year on reaching the age of thirty
was a little over forty, but this figure does not tell us much because
re-election was possible.[5]

A large number of offices were allocated by lot. These included
the archons, the officials in charge of the games (elected for four
years), commissioners of sacred places, officials to perform sacri-

fices, officials in charge of the market and the corn-supply (half of these operated in Athens and half in the Peiraieus), deme judges, police-officers, five boards who worked closely with the Council (the treasurers of Athena, sellers of public properties, receivers of public monies, scrutineers of official accounts, examiners of official conduct at the end of the year of office), and guards of the dockyards and of the Akropolis. All of these acted for a single year except the officials of the games, and the same office could not be held twice. The Councillors and the guards were chosen by lot from the demes, and the demes must have known what numbers to provide. The rest were chosen by lot from the ten tribes, so many from each tribe. Only the board of ten scrutineers was chosen from existing Council members. Every year 500 Councillors and 550 guards were chosen by lot from the demes, and 277 other officials from the tribes (the officials in charge of the games elected every fourth year are not included). All of these were scrutinised by the Council before they took office so that alternatives must have been available, and in any case drawing lots only makes sense if something like twice the number are available. It is difficult to square these figures with an annual intake of about 800 men over thirty years of age. There seems to have been nothing like the Roman *cursus honorum* in Athens, and there is no reason to suppose that holding one office after another was common. On the other hand guard duty, membership of the Council, and holding one of the other offices may not have been uncommon, and a fair number of Councillors, like Demosthenes, may have served twice. If we can exclude the guards, as possibly being drawn from the under thirties and the over sixties, we can perhaps suppose an actual annual intake of 500 to replenish the Council and the offices, the gap (of 277) being filled by second term Councillors, Councillors who switched to offices and office-holders who switched to Council, and by office-holders who submitted themselves again for another office. This rate of intake would mean that something like two-thirds of the over thirties had served on the Council or held office or both. It would also mean, if we assume that the elective offices were the preserve of the top two property classes (the 500 bushel men and the knights) and the higher members of the hoplite class, that the proportion of men in the lowest property class (*thetes*) holding offices allocated by lot would probably be nearer a half than a third. However rough this estimate may be, two things seem to be clear: the large number of offices and the rapid turnover ensured that a very large number of Athenians held some political position in their lifetime (even Socrates, who prided himself on avoiding practical politics, served on the Council), and secondly, as a consequence of this, the Assembly, with which the real power lay, had a highly sophisticated membership.[6]

The rapid turnover must also have helped the system to work. On the boards of officers the membership was on a tribal basis, and the choice was made by the tribes; this meant that a new officer could, if he wanted, consult the twenty-thirty surviving members of his tribe who had held that particular office before him. He could also consult the records, and some boards had a permanent clerk, who was a state slave. The public on the other hand had the assurance of the scrutiny of qualifications before an official took office and the examination of his conduct at the end of his term, and the official could be sued at any time for corruption. Most helpful of all was probably the small scale of the operations of any one official or board, and the amount of day-to-day contact that any official had and had had with his fellow-citizens, foreigners, and slaves in the everyday life of Athenian society.

The system as described is the system which Aristotle gives in the *Constitution of Athens* and which he regards as having been fixed in its main lines with the restoration of the democracy after the rule of the Thirty Tyrants in 403. It is a considerable advance on the democracy of Kleisthenes, probably in the number of offices, certainly in the opening of the archonship to the hoplite class and in practice to the lowest property class too, and in the establishment of pay for Council, offices, jury, and Assembly, which made it possible for the poorer citizens to take time off to serve. Except for payment for the Assembly, which was introduced in the early fourth century, the rest seems to have been due to Pericles. Pericles was responsible for full democracy, and with Pericles we can commence the parallel history of theory and practice. One point should be cleared out of the way first: it is sometimes argued that full democracy was financed by the subject cities of the empire. This is demonstrably untrue in the long run because full democracy continued after the dissolution of the empire at the end of the fifth century, and payment for the Assembly was added to the bill. What the empire paid for was first protection and then freedom of the seas, and outside that perhaps for the Periclean building programme.

Before turning to the great political issues of the fifth century and to the political theories to which the debates on them gave rise, I must describe briefly how the Assembly, the ultimate political authority in democratic Athens, actually worked. It had forty regular meetings a year, four in each of the ten 35-36 day periods into which the Council's year was divided. The Council's presiding committee appointed its chairman by lot every day, and the chairman of the Assembly was the chairman appointed for the Council's presiding committee on the day when the Assembly met. The four regular meetings of the Assembly in each 35-36 day period dealt with different kinds of business. The first meeting considered whether the holders of offices were performing their work satisfactorily, problems of corn-supply and defence, proposals for political prosecutions, the list of property confiscated, the list of heiresses, and (once a year only) the desirability of holding an ostracism. At the second regular meeting anyone might ask the Assembly to consider his motion on private or public affairs. At the third and fourth regular meetings the Assembly debated three motions chosen by lot on religious affairs, three on foreign affairs, and three on secular affairs.

Outside the regular meetings special meetings could be summoned, usually at the instigation of the generals (*strategoi*) to deal with important business that had not been completed in the regular meeting or to meet an emergency. Demosthenes describes an emergency-meeting when Philip of Macedon had captured Elateia, which was uncomfortably near to Athens. The news arrived in the evening, the generals were summoned, and an emergency was declared. On the next day the presiding committee called a meeting of the Council while the people gathered for the Assembly. The Council then came to the Assembly and reported the news, and the man who brought the news gave his own account. The herald pronounced the formula 'Who wants to speak?', and, according to himself, only Demosthenes came forward and made practical proposals for dealing with the situation. Here the operative proposal is made in the Assembly; the normal rule, particularly at regular Assemblies, was that the Council had already formulated a proposal for the Assembly to debate. Such a proposal might however leave details to be decided in the Assembly and might be amended as well as accepted or rejected.

At the beginning of the *Acharnians* Aristophanes parodies a a regular meeting of the Assembly, and this tells us something about procedure. It is the third or fourth meeting of the 35-36 day period, and Aristophanes has left out the motions on religious affairs and secular affairs. His hero, an old countryman, is only interested in foreign affairs, i.e. in peace. He arrives early in the morning and complains that the people are still walking about in the Agora. On Assembly day at a certain time all the exits from the Agora were closed except the one which led to the Pnyx, and all the people were shooed in by attendants holding a ruddled rope. Finally the presiding Committee of the Council arrived, and the Herald asked who wanted to speak. Amphitheos proposed that he should be sent to Sparta to make peace, and the herald called to the police to remove him. The police were Scythian archers, slaves, probably mostly foreign, but named after their Scythian bows and costume, whose job it was to keep order at public meetings. There is, of course, comic abbreviation here. Presumably in real life Amphitheos' proposal would have been known to the Council and had been drawn by lot for that particular meeting, but in real life also an unruly or long-winded speaker might be removed by the police. After this the Herald announces the delegates from the king of Persia. These are Athenians who have been on an embassy and have come back with a Persian official, who makes promises of financial aid. The ambassadors and the official repeat their account, which in real life they would have given earlier to the Council. The official is invited by the Council to entertainment at the public expense. The third proposal is to hire at a high-rate light-armed troops from Thrace. This the old countryman baulks by announcing that he feels rain, a bad omen, and the chairman adjourns the Assembly, again a parody of real procedure. It is, of course, comedy, and the dialogue with the old countryman takes the place of the speeches and counterspeeches, the proposals and counter-proposals of real life, but it gives something of the flavour of government by public meeting in the years just after the death of Pericles.[7]

Periclean democracy grew out of the split in policy between those who saw Athens as an equal partner with Sparta in the Greek world after the Persian War and those who saw Athens as the mistress of an empire basically opposed to Sparta. On the one side was first Kimon, the son of Miltiades, the victor of Marathon, and then Thucydides, the son of the Melesias who trained international athletes, and on the other side first Themistokles and Aristeides, to whom the chief credit for the victory of Salamis must go, and then Ephialtes and finally Pericles. Kimon had a brilliant string of victories against the Persians to his credit, he was generous and beautified the Agora and the Academy, and he kept open house for his fellow demesmen, so that he was said to have restored the golden age. We must suppose that this was the policy favoured by the Council of the Areiopagos, which according to Aristotle governed Athens from 480 till 463. It was composed of ex-archons, who until 457 were drawn from the top two property classes (the '500 bushel' men and the knights). It was primarily a murder-court but had been charged by Solon with a general guardianship of the laws. Probably in the difficulties of the Persian invasion this strong board of experienced officials took over the government and kept it. Themistokles fortified Athens and made the Peiraieus the chief harbour, linked to Athens by the long walls: Aristeides organised the allies into the Delian League and assessed the tribute; this was the beginning of imperial Athens.[8]

The first attack on the Areiopagos must have been made in the late 470s, as it resulted apparently in Themistokles' ostracism late in the decade; Ephialtes was Themistokles' younger associate. Kimon then claimed that he and his friends were the true democrats by bringing back Theseus' bones from Skyros and building the Theseion and, through his brother-in-law, the Stoa Poikile. The religious counterstroke was, as we have noted, the Periclean building programme criticised by Kimon's successor, Thucydides, son of Melesias, but before that Pericles and Ephialtes had made attacks on Kimon and members of the Areiopagos in the law-courts, and in 462 persuaded the Assembly to reduce the Areiopagos to a murder-court and hand over its other powers to the council, the assembly, and the law-courts. In 461 Kimon was ostracised, and about the same time Ephialtes was murdered.[9]

Pericles and Ephialtes had used the power of the people in the law-courts and the Assembly to destroy the Areiopagos, and Pericles had introduced payment for jurors before Kimon's death in 450. The difference between Kimon's buildings and Pericles' buildings was that the former were dedications by Kimon and his friends, but the Periclean programme was financed by public money voted by the Assembly. Thucydides, son of Melesias, tried to counter this management of the Assembly by collecting his supporters in a single part of the Pnyx, so that he had them under his eye when they voted. But this mobilisation of the opposition was evidently not effective as he was ostracised in 443. From that time practically until his death in 429 Pericles dominated Athenian policy. Officially he was one of the board of ten generals; but exceptionally he was continually re-elected and so achieved continuity.[10]

Political theory is first formulated in this period. Pericles formulated his own views in the speech which he delivered in memory of those killed in the first year of the Peloponnesian War in 431. Thucydides the historian was himself present, and there is no reason to doubt that he recorded what Pericles said, even if he restyled the thoughts; it is conceivable that he had access to a text, since Pericles is said to have spoken from a written text in the law-courts. According to Pericles the essential marks of democracy are equality of justice, equality of opportunity, and social equality. The first was secured by the jury system, and it should be remembered that resident aliens and slaves had representation in law through their patrons. The third is some confirmation of what has been said about the absence of barriers in Athenian society. Equality of opportunity does not mean that every man has a right to every thing, but that the criterion for choosing people for political office is efficiency and not wealth. At the same time the diversity of occupations makes the ordinary man a good judge of policy. 'Athens is an education for Greece, and the individual Athenian has the versatility to adapt himself to the most varied forms of activity with grace.' This is the Periclean dream, and this kind of society, he says, is possible because the Athenians fear to transgress the laws, a fear which shows itself in obedience to the authorities and to the laws, particularly the criminal laws and the unwritten laws, which everyone admits it is shameful to transgress (piety towards the gods, respect towards parents, and acceptance of the rights of suppliants).[11]

What Pericles leaves out is his own position, or rather all he can say is that excellence is the criterion for office. Thucydides supplies the want in his obituary of Pericles: he had the reputation and the intellect, but he had also tremendous moral stature so that he could lead the Athenians as free men, neither giving in to their whims nor being moved by their irrational elation or depression. 'It was in theory a democracy but in fact it became the rule of the first Athenian.'[12]

A close parallel to Thucydides' account of Pericles is found in a sentence of the historian Herodotos; 'nothing could be found better than one man, the best. He would have the best intellect and would be a blameless guardian of the people.' Herodotos is recording the debate of the Persian conspirators when Dareios was made king. It is most unlikely that they would have discussed tyranny, democracy, oligarchy, and monarchy as alternative forms of government for Persia or that their discussions would have been recorded. Herodotos was in Athens during the struggle between Thucydides, son of Melesias, and Pericles, which ended in Pericles' long supremacy. This and the murder of Ephialtes are remembered when Dareios says that oligarchy causes rivalry between leading men, which gives rise to civil war, murder, and so to monarchy. Otanes praises democracy as having equality of justice, magistrates chosen by lot and subject to audit, and public discussion of state policy, which are very much the marks of

Athenian democracy. And when Megabyzos, urging oligarchy, argues that the mob is senseless and violent, but a small association of the best men will make the best policy, we can well imagine that these were the views of the Athenian aristocrats.[13]

Someone had evidently formulated the characteristics of the different forms of government, and the formulation is often repeated afterwards. It may very well have been Protagoras, whose account of Divine Forethought was used by Herodotos later in the same book. And the views expressed in the Persian debate seem to correspond with what Plato says about Protagoras. When Protagoras says that wise and good orators substitute in their cities sound for unsound views of what is right, this is a good description of Pericles. He also comes very near to the Periclean view of the sound judgment of the ordinary man in politics, when he says that the Athenians naturally accept the advice of the smith and the cobbler in public affairs because justice and respect are a part of every man's equipment, which he gains from education and finally from the laws; the laws regulate the conduct of the subjects and the rulers, and those in office are constrained by an audit, again a characteristic feature of Athenian democracy. Thus Protagoras' instruction was based on a very clear formulation and appreciation of the development and working of Periclean democracy, and if the debate in Herodotos is rightly considered to be inspired by him, also by an appreciation of the peculiar position of Pericles himself. Protagoras' account of the rise of civilisation would seem to have culminated in a description of the Athenian democracy with its multiplicity of specialist talents contrasting with a universal sense of moral and social values, which makes the ordinary man a sound judge of policy. The policy is initiated by the wise and good orator, and that is what Protagoras hoped to make his pupils.[14]

A view of democracy peculiarly like the view of the proponent of oligarchy in the Herodotean debate is found in the political tract bound up with the works of Xenophon, which also dates from the years before the Peloponnesian war: 'in every land the best part is hostile to democracy. In the mob there is the maximum of senselessness, disorder, and badness.' The author must be an Athenian aristocrat, but it is useless to guess at his identity. His tract is designed to show other Greeks, particularly Spartans, that the Athenians, having chosen the wrong course, have designed their customs and institutions quite admirably to preserve it. The wrong course is democracy, and the reason for choosing democracy is that the city's power depends on the poor men, who man and build the ships, much more than on the hoplites and the nobles and the good. (Good and bad are used by this author in a purely social sense.) Therefore all must be allowed to hold office and speak in the Assembly; slaves and resident aliens are given legal rights, and slaves can buy their freedom; athletics and musical contests are arranged for the benefit of the poor; like-minded democracies are fostered in the cities of the empire; allied lawsuits are heard in Athens to the profit of the Athenian juries; comedy is used as a weapon against the rich; the whole organisation is to preserve the freedom of the poor, and the only magistracies left to the rich are the board of generals and the commanders of the cavalry. This is a wide-ranging and not entirely well-expressed or well-argued survey. But the author sees clearly that Athens is an imperial city and the centre of Mediterranean trade. This position depends on the fleet, the merchant marine, and the commercial community, or in political terms the citizens of the poorest property class (he is thinking of the four classes when he distinguishes them from the hoplites, the nobles, and the good), the resident aliens, and the slaves. It is of course an exaggeration to rule out the hoplite class from the fleet, the merchant-marine and the commercial community, but his assumptions at least suggest that we were right in supposing a high proportion of the lowest property class in the juries and the offices elected by lot. He brings the fact that the rich held the elected offices into line with his theory by saying that the people realises that it derives more benefit from allowing the rich to hold the generalship and the cavalry offices.[15]

There was in fact a change in the generalship after Pericles' death. Till then generals and leading politicians were identical. From that time both tended to become specialised. The distinction between them is extremely clear in the fourth century, but started already in the fifth. Thucydides in his obituary of Pericles phrases it that Pericles' successors were more on a level with each other, and desiring each to be first secured the people's favour by surrendering policy to their guidance. In practice this meant that foreign policy was fought out in the Assembly instead of being debated on the proposal of the great commanders, Kimon or Pericles. Both Thucydides and Aristotle saw Kleon as the beginning of this tendency. Both, like Aristophanes, are strongly opposed to him. All three see him as originating a new kind of violent rhetoric in the Assembly. Aristophanes speaks of flattering the people, and Aristotle of corrupting the people. Aristophanes makes it very clear that Kleon also operated against his enemies through the law-courts (like Pericles and Ephialtes before him), and that the jurors loved him because he brought them so much work. He was a tanner, and Aristophanes makes the maximum out of this malodorous occupation, but there is no reason to suppose that he did not have hoplite status (and he was in fact elected general). We cannot use Kleon's speeches in Thucydides because there is no reason to suppose that his reporting was accurate; they are certainly rhetoric and dishonest rhetoric. It is a notable fact to which we shall have to return that in the year when Kleon first became prominent two famous rhetoricians were in Athens, Gorgias of Leontini and Thrasymachos of Chalkedon.[16]

We must note briefly two later revolutions before returning to theory. Both were short lived. The first was in 411 after the failure of the disastrous expedition against Sicily. The new constitution of 411 was based on an Assembly of 5,000 over thirty years of age. They were to be divided into quarters and a committee of each quarter was to form the Council and to elect the strategoi (generals) and the nine archons and the treasury officials from its own quarter of the 5,000 to serve for a year. This constitution, which Thucydides describes as the best government in his day, because it had a moderate blend of oligarchy and democracy, restricted the Assembly and the major magistracies to the top two property classes (the '500 bushel' men and the knights) and the upper half of the hoplites, and excluded at least 16,000 citizens. The government imposed by the Spartans in 404 was much narrower. The Thirty Tyrants led by Kritias based the government on 1,000 men, presumably all of the top two property classes, from whom the Council of 500 and the other magistrates were chosen. The Thirty Tyrants governed entirely in their own interest, and the democracy was only restored after a civil war of great ferocity in 403. Then Athens regained the full Periclean democracy as described by Aristotle in the *Constitution of Athens*.[17]

The brains behind the two revolutions were Antiphon and Kritias. Antiphon according to Thucydides was second to none of his Athenian contemporaries in excellence, and most fertile in ideas and in formulating his ideas; he never appeared publicly if he could help it, because his intellect made him suspect to the masses, but nobody was a more powerful aid to his friends when they were fighting in the Assembly or the courts. There is no doubt that this Antiphon was Antiphon the orator; the question which has been much debated is whether he was also Antiphon the sophist. Antiphon the sophist is noted for two views which at first sight seem opposed: he said that there was no greater evil than anarchy, but he also said that the majority of the rights laid down by law are at enmity with nature, and that in nature all men are one, both Greek and barbarian.[18]

The artificiality of law (*nomos*) and the reality of nature (*physis*) is the accepted model for political thought in the later fifth century, but it can be applied in different ways. One way is to find jungle-law, the clearest kind of behaviour in the animal world (*physis*), in politics. So pseudo-Xenophon explains the Athenian constitution in terms of the power of the working class: they have the power, and therefore Athenian institutions (*nomoi*) are framed to their advantage. This is essentially the view attributed to the sophist Thrasymachos in the first book of Plato's *Republic* where he urges that justice is the advantage of the stronger, the government, whether the government is tyranny, oligarchy, or democracy. This, as we shall see, was the model for Thucydides' sketch of early Greek history, and he carries the two essential drives, the desire of the strong to exploit the weak and the fear of exploitation in the weak, on into the history of the Peloponnesian war, particularly in Pericles' and Kleon's account of the Athenian empire, in the Athenian treatment of

Melos, and in his account of revolution in Greek states. Kritias also in the revolution of 404 exploited his power ruthlessly. He is the perfect example of the political doctrine expounded by Kallikles in Plato's *Gorgias*: 'But supposing a man is born with sufficient natural force (*physis*), he will trample underfoot our formulas and spells and charms and laws, which are all contrary to nature; our slave rebels and is revealed as our master, and then natural justice shines forth.'[19]

Given the superior reality of nature, the obvious analogy for action was the behaviour of the strong animal which exploits the weak animal. But Protagoras saw further that the strong animal had the weakness of producing few offspring and the weak animal the strength of producing many. He conceived of a balanced democracy in which the many, the rich, and the wise each played their special part, and the laws had a new sanction as the invention of old and wise lawgivers. Antiphon, if he recognised the truth that Greeks and barbarians were one in nature, can hardly have taken the jungle-law as his analogy for constitution-making. It seems to me probable that the line that he took was something like this. Laws may be artificial and nature real, but a society which has no laws, what he called anarchy, has no framework within which the individual can realise his nature. He probably saw the post-Periclean democracy much as Thucydides did, as an entirely selfish struggle between individuals, in fact as jungle-law in a jungle with no big animals. He thought he could get the framework which he desired by restricting the decision-making and the execution to the richest quarter of the citizen body, but the other three-quarters did not endure this for long.

After the much worse revolution of the Thirty Tyrants full democracy was finally restored with an amnesty between the democrats and the moderate oligarchs, which was slightly extended to include the extreme oligarchs. Technically the trial and condemnation of Socrates in 399 was not a breach of the amnesty, because the charge was impiety, but in fact it was the political trial of an alleged collaborator. On the whole, however, the restored democracy behaved with great moderation. From the speeches of the orators, particularly Lysias in the late fifth and early fourth century, some idea can be formed of practical political theory and how far the attitudes of the late fifth century continued. The restoration rested on the reality of the covenants of the amnesty, so that this was not the time to trumpet the artificiality of law, and in 403 an elaborate machinery was instituted for codifying the laws and examining them annually for possible revision: so in the fourth century three areas in the old wide sphere of *nomoi* are defined; *nomoi*, covering criminal law and constitutional law, which could only be revised by the new machinery, *Psephismata* or the day-to-day executive decrees of the Assembly, and Ancestral Customs, which include the unwritten laws of Pericles' Funeral Speech and much else of the old vague concept of *nomos*.[20]

The keywords of the restored democracy are *homonoia*, the concord between the democrats and oligarchs after the amnesty, and *nomos*. Lysias puts them together in a funeral oration delivered in 391: 'They established democracy, believing that universal freedom was the greatest kind of concord ... and that the proper human behaviour was to define justice by law and urge it by argument, and to live under the rule of law and under the instruction of argument.' A little earlier Isokrates, looking back at the revolutions of 411 and 404, had said that we have twice seen democracy destroyed by those who despised the laws. Later, Demosthenes returns again and again to the theme of the benefits provided by the laws: 'nothing can more truly be called responsible for the city's blessings and for its being a democracy and free than the laws', 'the laws express the characteristics of the constitution', 'listen to the just dealing of the law, which does not allow violence even against slaves'.[21]

In detail the optimistic view of democracy in the fourth century comes near to the view of Protagoras. The theory of balance is put very clearly by Isokrates: the people as a whole must establish the offices, audit the holders, and judge on disputed points; the rich must look after public policy as servants of the people. So in Demosthenes the people are the only sure guardian of the laws, and the people must share in the planning and the discussion and the execution of policy. 'You do not order anyone to take part in politics; but if anyone comes forward himself, you elect him, and if he succeeds he will be honoured and in this way will have superiority.' And the true statesman (like Pericles) 'often thwarts your wishes, never speaks simply to please you but always what he sees to be best'. The rich themselves claim that they serve the state by war-tax and liturgies.[22]

Against this optimistic view can be set a pessimistic view, which has much in common with the jungle theory of the fifth century. From one angle we hear of the selfish politicians, whose policies are entirely directed to making profits for themselves, who live in enormous estates, and who accept bribes to get the guilty off in lawsuits, threatening the jurors with a stoppage of pay if they do not acquit. From the other angle Isokrates claims that the city rejoices in oppressing and humbling the rich and giving authority to the poor.[23]

Except for the few quotations from Isokrates' pamphlets, the foregoing paragraphs have been based on speeches designed for large juries or for the Assembly: this is political theory as the ordinary man recognises it. In an earlier chapter I tried to show how the Academy worked as an educational institution and its practical effect on Greek politics. Here I want to point very briefly to some aspects of Plato's political theory and its modification by Aristotle. Plato was born in 427 and can only have known Socrates from the time of the Sicilian expedition to his condemnation and death in 399. What he saw in Socrates politically can be deduced from the early dialogues. First, Socrates believed that it was possible by rigorous examination to treat the soul as a doctor treats the body, and to arrive at healthy ethical views. Secondly, he pursued this aim partly by interrogating experts in the presence of aristocratic young men and partly by interrogating the aristocratic young men themselves. Thirdly, he thought that survival in Athenian public life was impossible for anyone who stood up for his ethical standards; he narrowly escaped on two occasions—as a member of the presiding committee of the Council, he tried to prevent a mass condemnation of the generals after the battle of Arginusae in 406, which was contrary to the law, and he refused to carry out an order of the Thirty to arrest one of their victims in Salamis. In the same spirit he refused to escape from prison himself after his condemnation because this would be disobedience to the law, and it was not the law but its interpreters that had condemned him.[24]

Plato started his own work disillusioned both with his kinsmen and natural associates, the Thirty, because of their crimes, and with the restored democracy, because they had put Socrates to death. At the moment both the circle of aristocratic young men, Socrates' pupils, and the rule of law, the restored democracy, seemed to have failed. The belief in the possibility of ethical and political education remained. Looking back on the fifth century (and possibly reading the obituary of Pericles in Thucydides and knowing Protagoras' account of the wise orator) Plato conceived the notion of the philosopher king. Practically this led to the disastrous attempt to educate the younger Dionysios when he became tyrant of Syracuse, but also to the longer road of education in the Academy, which we have described.[25]

In the *Republic*, after reviewing the social-contract theory and the jungle-law theory, he founds his ideal city firmly on the natural differences of men. This is essentially the old aristocratic interpretation of *physis* as breed, with the further implication that it is possible to breed men, as it is possible to breed horses. So the definition of justice at which he arrives is 'doing one's own thing and not meddling'. The ideal state consists of four breeds, which must not intermingle, rulers, soldiers, farmers, craftsmen; everyone is, according to his capacity, an expert, and his life is directed by the supreme expert, the philosopher king. Judged by the standards of this city, the existing constitutions are seen as a progressive decline. The first stage is the Cretan-Lacedaemonian or Timocracy, which suffers from choosing warriors rather than wise men as rulers; the second is oligarchy, in which the criterion is wealth: the third is democracy when the poor conquer and offices are for the most part allocated by lot; the rich are finally forced to resist and are branded as oligarchs, and the poor then find a champion who becomes a tyrant.[26]

In the later *Statesman* (or *Politicus*) the classification is changed. The ideal state with the philosopher king stands outside the series, and the rest are better or worse copies. Laws are likely to be a better copy of the ideal than day-to-day improvisations, and so the primary division is into law-abiding

and lawless. Law-abiding monarchy stands first, and he is probably thinking of the early days of the Persian Empire which
he praised in the *Laws*. Aristocracy comes next, and the imaginary
city of the *Laws* is presumably a model for 'the rule of the
best'. Law-abiding democracy comes third, and for that the *Laws*
gives the reference to Athens at the time of the Persian wars.
Democracy heads the lawless constitutions because the diffusion
of authority makes it the most endurable of them (and Plato
did after all continue to live in Athens), then oligarchy, which
is surely coloured by his experience of the Thirty Tyrants, and
finally, as before, tyranny. What distinguishes this classification
from the *Republic* is first the new emphasis on laws as an attain-
able political reality, and secondly (particularly in the *Laws*) the
obvious cross-references to history. Here we can see the research
interest of the Academy and probably the influence of Aristotle.[27]

The *Laws* themselves are the laws devised for an imaginary
new city. They cover the whole range of the citizen's activity
from the time that he is conceived to the time that he is buried.
The citizen is educated to accept absolute moral standards from
the womb. Wealth is regulated so that the minimum is the
standard holding of land and the maximum four times that
amount; hostility between the rich and poor is thus avoided in
this tiny agricultural state. Trade and industry are in the hands
of resident aliens, who are only admitted for twenty years, unless
they can make a special case for staying longer. Offices are elected
from the whole body of 5,040 citizens. There is an elected
Council of 360, and thirty-seven Guardians of the Law, who are
over fifty years old, and one of them is Minister of Education.
A final check to prevent variations in the laws, except within
very carefully considered limits, is provided by the Nocturnal
Council, part ex-officials, part philosophers, and part trainees.
This is a remarkably complete scheme for a tiny changeless
society of carefully bred and conditioned citizens.[28]

Aristotle himself based his political theory on more than 150
summaries of the constitutional histories of Greek states, of which
the *Constitution of Athens* was one. He was therefore much
more aware of what worked in practice than Plato. He can find
room in his theory both for an outstanding royal house, like the

Macedonian, and for the amateur judgment in the Athenian Assembly, Council, and law-courts. Like most fourth-century political thinkers, he saw the dangers of a sharp division between the rich and the poor, but he found a remedy in a large middle class. Only in a city with a large middle class will the relation between the citizens be the relation between members of a family (which relationship for Aristotle is the origin of city life) and not the relationship between master and slave. Where we disagree with Aristotle is where he, logically from his own point of view, restricts the citizenship to those that have leisure to be citizens in the fullest sense. He is, of course, Plato's pupil, but even his ideal state gives the individual much more opportunity than Plato does, and his acceptance of deviations, where they can be show historically to work, make him more sympathetic as a political theorist.[29]

For Athens itself another branch of activity must be discussed here. In the Assembly and in the law-courts the large audiences were persuaded by speeches to adopt or reject a policy and to give their verdict. We know a little about the speeches of Pericles and his predecessors, and we have noted a change in Kleon. We know a good deal about rhetorical theory from the mid-fifth century to Aristotle, and from the late fifth century through the fourth we have a large body of speeches composed by the Attic orators, which, whether they were actually delivered on particular occasions or not, at any rate purported to have been the speeches which were written for clients to deliver or delivered by the orators when they were themselves involved. Within this long history lines can be drawn roughly at 430, at 403 and at 360.

What little we know about the eloquence of Kimon and Pericles suggests that it depended largely on the startling image which remained in the hearers' minds. Kimon, speaking against Ephialtes at the time when Sparta needed help after an earthquake, said that Greece had been lamed and Athens had lost its yoke-mate. Pericles called the island of Aigina, which he proposed to attack, the eyesore of the Peiraieus, and on another occasion saw war sweeping down from the Peloponnese. It is this kind of effect that the comic poets had in mind when they described Pericles as using thunder and lightning, and being the only orator who left his sting in his audience. The speeches of the historian Thucydides are no use for comparison because he has written them in his own style, but within a single author the change from the methods of the earlier fifth century can be seen by comparing the debate between Kreon and Haimon in Sophocles' *Antigone*, which can be dated in 442, and the debate between Klytaimestra and Elektra in his *Electra*, which can probably be dated in 413. Haimon's speech has startling images like Pericles: the men who are opened up and found empty, the tree uprooted by the torrent, the ship capsized. The later debate is hard-hitting argument with clear disposition of prologue, narrative, successive arguments, and conclusion. The audience wants something different: it is not enough simply to enthral them with imagery, they now demand to follow the steps of the reasoning themselves if they are to be convinced.[30]

A rather similar change was taking place in the law-courts. It has been suggested that the major difference between fifth-century and fourth-century law-court speeches is a switch of emphasis from witnesses, oaths, documents, and the like to arguments based on probability and character, which are then supported by testimony if desirable; and this change has been connected with the general political degradation in Athens at the time of the Peloponnesian war. I suspect that the general moral degradation is theoretical rather than actual—Thucydides and others, as we have seen, interpreted human activity in terms of the jungle-war and we are apt to accept it—and that the real reason for the change is that the juries wanted more than the simple statement of oath or testimony; they demanded a logical reconstruction of events to enable them to understand the action and decide between the participants.[31]

In our earliest law-court-scene, the trial of Orestes in Aeschylus' *Eumenides* produced in 458, Athena dismisses the Furies' attempt to make Orestes swear an oath, as a technical trick: he admits the murder. The emphasis is certainly on Apollo's testimony, that he commanded the murder, and on the evidence of Athena's birth as proving the father more important than the mother, but Apollo's speech is well shaped, with narrative, objections and counter-objections, and appeal to the jury. In the trial of the dog in Aristophanes' *Wasps* (produced in 422) again the decisive factor is the evidence of the cheese-scraper, but here we have, in addition to narrative and defence of character, a pathetic epilogue, in which the wailing puppies are displayed to move the jury. Antiphon's speeches belong shortly after this, and the line is drawn between him and Lysias, whose earliest speech was written in 403. Antiphon still used witnesses and documents as the focus round which he organises his evidence.[32]

Rhetorical theory came largely from the West because of the number of lawsuits after the putting down of the local tyrants in 466. Aeschylus' Sicilian experience may have influenced the pleading in the *Eumenides*. It is not easy to distinguish the Sicilian Korax from his pupil Teisias, who taught Lysias. Between them they worked out the standard disposition of the speech (prologue, narration, proof, epilogue, for which then common topics could be collected for the use of orators) and the theory of probability (*eikos*), which meant primarily the reconstruction of the events as a logical sequence in tune with the character of the performers. The sophists added much, particularly Protagoras with his pairs of demonstration speeches maintaining directly opposite views, Thrasymachos with his collection of pathetic epilogues, and Gorgias (the pupil of Korax) with his poetic and rhythmical prose.[33]

Apart from the possible early Sicilian influence on Aeschylus and the probable influence of Protagoras on the debates in early Sophocles and Euripides, it is in the last quarter of the fifth century that the influence of the new rhetoric becomes obvious in Athens. Thrasymachos may have been there by 428, and Teisias and Gorgias came on an embassy in 427, the year in which Thucydides notes Kleon as introducing a new and violent kind of rhetoric in the assembly. Three years later in the *Knights* Aristophanes gives a description of the young aristocratic politician Phaiax (who later combined with Nikias and Alkibiades to get Hyperbolos ostracised) which puts together the technical terms of the new rhetoric; it can only be paraphrased: 'he is a master of the simple style and the complicated style, he can coin neat general sentiments, he is clear, he can knock out his opponents, and he is extremely good at inciting to violence'.[34]

Law-court rhetoric at this stage may be illustrated by a literal translation of a short section of a speech written by Antiphon for a client accused of murder: 'They say that he died on land and I threw a stone at his head, though I never left the boat. This they know well, but they can find no logical explanation of how the man vanished. It was clearly logical for it to happen somewhere near the harbour, first because he was drunk, secondly because he left the boat at night. For he would neither have been able to guide himself nor would there be any logical reason for anyone to take him far at night. But though he was sought for two days both inside the harbour and outside the harbour, no eyewitness appeared nor blood nor any other evidence. Nevertheless I concede their argument, providing witnesses that I did not leave the boat, but even if I did leave the boat, it was in no way logical for the man to vanish unnoticed unless he went a very long way from the sea.' Two things stand out here: the repeated use of logical (*eikos*) as a keyword—this is the new defence against witnesses whose testimony goes against the speaker—and secondly the tendency, which is much clearer in the more emotional prologue and epilogue, to cast sentences and clauses in pairs: here it can be seen in the second sentence, the end of the third sentence, the whole fourth sentence, and the latter part of the last sentence.[35]

Greeks naturally phrased things in contrasting pairs. But this was brought to a very high art by Gorgias, and Antiphon feels his influence. I suspect that this was a new startling trick, which took the place of the vivid imagery with which the old rhetoric captured its audiences. In its most extreme form the repeated pairs of sentences, clauses, or phrases had members of equal length, often contrasting with each other, and often beginning and ending with words of similar sound. The end of one sentence from the funeral oration of Gorgias will show the manner: 'servants of the unjustly suffering, chastisers of those who unjustly prosper, stubborn when expedient, temperate when suitable, by wisdom of brain checking the madness of brawn, violent to the violent, orderly to the orderly, fearless before the fearless, terrible in terrors.' This style appears to us as a magnificent display of fireworks, but we must conclude from the immense success of Gorgias on embassies and the use of what is recognisably the same style by Antiphon in the prologues and epilogues of his law-court speeches that the Athenians were deeply moved by it. Isokrates was the pupil of Gorgias and took over this style in a modified form. He gave up the extreme constriction of Gorgias' parallel and antithetic phrases, but took over the antithetic structure as the basis of a larger fabric. Isokrates loves to build his sentences in pairs with the halves connected by 'on the one hand ... on the other hand', 'not only ... but also', 'both ... and', and then he constructs further pairs of clauses or phrases within each of the paired main sentences, so that the result is a succession of balanced parts which may be of great length. This was 'the rhythmical and artistic employment of language', 'the flowery and gracious style', which he taught his pupils. It was unsuccessful in the law-courts but did very well for his leisurely and not very intellectual political pamphlets, as indeed it has echoed in serious journalism ever since.[36]

Isokrates' style can be seen in a later and rather debased form in the speeches of Lykourgos and Deinarchos in the second half of the fourth century. A much more interesting stylistic line leads from Lysias through Isaios to Demosthenes. Here there is no attempt to force every sentence into an antithetic mould, but pairing on any scale can be used whenever the author wants it for a particular effect. Sentence structure is very varied and full use is made out of the contrast between long and short sentences. I quote an example from Lysias and an example from Demosthenes. Lysias is narrating his escape on the night that the Thirty put his brother to death: 'We found there Theognis guarding the others, to whom they handed me over and left. In this position I decided to run a risk, as death was likely anyway. Calling Damnippos, I said to him, "You know me, I am come to your house, I have done nothing wrong, my money is my ruin. Help me in my plight, use your influence to save me." He promised to do this. He thought it better to speak to Theognis, for he believed that he would do anything if one gave him money. While he was talking to Theognis, as I knew the house and remembered that it had a back-door, I decided to try for safety this way, thinking that if I was not seen I should be safe, but if I was caught, I thought that, if Theognis was persuaded by Damnippos to take money, I should none the less be let off, but if not I should die just the same.' This is admirable staccato narrative, which works up to a minor climax in the last sentence. The passage recalls two words in Aristophanes' description of Phaiax, 'the simple style' and 'the complicated style'. Up to the last sentence the style is simple, but the last sentence is a complicated period in which the main sentence is 'I decided' and the circumstances, the conditions, the reasons, and even the content of the decision are all subordinated syntactically to that. This is the essential difference between the simple style and the complicated style: in the simple style a number of statements are strung together as facts of equal value, but in the complicated style a single fact is stated and the others are related to it as condition, cause, result, or attendant circumstance. It is a different way of communicating facts, which stresses the relations between them. The more emotional narrative of the burial of Lysias' brother, which follows this, is cast entirely into the complicated style. Demosthenes developed this style further. His comparison of his own past life with the past life of his political opponent Aischines, which occupies over two pages of the *Crown*, will serve as an example. He recounts his own life in a single twelve-line sentence with a number of clauses describing his boyhood, his manhood, and his public life, all hung on to a brief main sentence, 'My private life was ...'. His description of Aischines begins, 'You with your pride and scorn of others, should put alongside my life the things that have happened to you, how that as a boy ...' This sentence goes on for thirty-five lines describing Aischines' private life. Then Demosthenes takes another breath to add shorter but still complicated sentences describing Aischines' public life, and then ends staccato: 'you were a clerk, I a member of the assembly ...'.[37]

Demosthenes not only develops Lysias' style, but, as has long been recognised, from about the middle of the fourth century the whole conception of portraiture in law-court speeches has changed. In the speech against Eratosthenes, one of the Thirty, which is quoted above, Lysias concentrates on Eratosthenes' public actions, first in the earlier revolution of the Four Hundred, and then under the Thirty, but says nothing of his private life. But Demosthenes and Aischines give minute detail of private lives, whether they are speaking for themselves or for clients. This marks a further shift in what the jury wants to hear. The earliest cases rested on testimony to fact; this changed to a logical reconstruction of the action with attention to character-traits in so far as they were responsible for the action; from this there is a further shift to regarding the details of private life as expressive of the character responsible for the action.[38]

Rhetorical theory kept pace. I have already mentioned Isokrates' criticism of the earlier rhetoricians, his interest in composition and ornamental language, his insistence on the need to fit the speech to the particular occasion. I have noted also that Aristotle was lecturing on rhetoric in the Academy before Plato's death in 347. The first sign of willingness to accept rhetoric in the Academy is Plato's *Phaedrus*, soon after 360. I suspect that Aristotle had a hand in the account and criticism of late fifth-century rhetorical theorists which is there put into the mouth of Socrates. They all of them only provide the preliminaries and the materials and the combination of them into a whole the learners have to provide for themselves. The important thing to know is the different kinds of soul and the way in which the soul is affected by different kinds of words. So Aristotle in his *Rhetoric* considers the means of persuasion which belong to the art of rhetoric (he rules out oaths, documents, witnesses etc., as lying outside the art); they are first the character of the speaker, secondly the emotions of the audience, and thirdly types of argument. These are worked out in detail in the second book so that the speaker knows how to present himself and his opponent, and how to raise any emotion that he may require in his audience, as well as how to argue. The third book deals with the arrangement of the speech and with prose style. In the second half of the fourth century detailed portraiture of prosecutor and defendant is the major means of securing condemnation or acquittal.[39] Thus in this long period of over a century political theory and theory of rhetoric changed to meet the changing practice of full democracy.

7 *Potters and Patrons*

Painted pottery has a special place in Athenian life which justifies giving it a chapter on its own. The Athenian used it for his ordinary household purposes, he dedicated it to his gods, and it was buried with him in his tomb. But it was also exported all over the Greek world and beyond the Greek world to the East, to Etruria, Spain, and across the Alps. For us it is a unique source of information. It is the one export which we can trace easily and infallibly: it is breakable but the fragments survive, and it cannot be confused with any other type of pottery. It is the one industry about which we can say something in detail over a number of years. The pictures cover the whole range of mythology and daily life, and have already in this book provided us with knowledge on school-practice and cults (but there is, of course, infinitely more information to be extracted from them). The pictures are drawn by artists who range from the first-rate to the competent; they are practically our only material source for the history of Greek painting, but, as we have seen, they illustrate accurately the history of wall and easel painting as we can derive it from the ancient literary authorities. Painted pottery was made by artist-craftsmen, and the whole of Athenian society bought it. It is the relation between the potter and his patrons that particularly concerns us.[1]

The workshops were situated in the Kerameikos adjoining the west side of the Agora, so that the potters were very close to the bronze-workers, the terracotta-makers, and the stone-carvers, who worked on the edge of the Agora a little further to the south.

This was good for the interchange of ideas, and the potters made moulded vases in the form of human heads and animals, as well as pots. The workshops, as we have said, were family workshops, which can in some cases be traced through several generations; and slaves worked side by side with free men and in some cases bought or were given their freedom. Many also were resident aliens. It is difficult to form any estimate of the number of workshops or the number of men employed. Probably we should think of something like ten major workshops employing something like 200 potters and painters in any one quarter of a century between 525 and 425, with the scale tapering off considerably after that. But the boundaries between workshops were fluid, whether in the sense that at some times larger units were formed by some dominant personality, or in the sense that workmen were borrowed from one workshop by another to deal with rush orders. Similarly we are apt to think of potters and painters as distinct, and they very often were; but it is only in the rather rare case where a man signs both as potter and as painter that we can certainly identify them. There are seven of these, but more have been suspected, and many more may escape our notice; and two of the seven show very different careers: Douris signed as potter a single small early *aryballos* (oil-flask), which he also painted, and can be traced on as a painter for another thirty years; Euphronios signs as a painter about 515, and a number of excellent vases can be attributed to him on style; then soon after 500 he starts signing as a potter and runs an extremely successful establishment making chiefly cups, which were painted by ten different painters; he gave up about 470. It is obvious that a vase takes much longer to decorate than to make, and in one shop, which can be traced afrom about 475 to 425, the decoration of cups was habitually divided between two painters. But the fine painted ware, black-figure, red-figure, and white-ground, was only one of the lines produced in the normal workshop. It also produced black-glaze ware, black-glaze lamps, and undecorated kitchenware; in all of these the main work was the potter's. (Moulded ware was confined to a comparatively small number of shops and did also have painted decoration.) Of course the painters also may have had other employment; we know that they painted clay plaques for dedication, and it is perfectly possible that they also painted on wood and marble; they were so good that one is loth to assume too great a gulf between them and the great names known to later art-historians.[2]

The status of potters obviously varied enormously between the latest slave-apprentice and the master-potter. Dedications give some idea of the range—from a plate made and painted by Epiktetos at one end to a bronze statue dedicated by Andokides and Mnesiades and a very large kore dedicated by Nearchos at the other end. These three dedications are all dated in the last quarter of the sixth century. Epiktetos was probably very young, and Mnesiades was well established. We cannot tell whether Nearchos is the old potter-painter, who was already signing about 560, or a younger relative. All of them are likely to have marked a special occasion, and it is of course possible that the larger dedications celebrated the winning of a large contract like the making of the 1,300 special amphorai for holding the sacred olive oil which was given as prizes in the four-yearly Panathenaic games. But for this moment at any rate the potter was on a level with the victorious athlete or the successful general who made similar dedications. There are some other indications that the potter could stand fairly high in society. Hyperbolos 'the lampmaker' (and probably also potter), though the son of a slave, was a successful radical politician until Nikias and Alkibiades combined to get him ostracised. Euthymides, who was one of the best and most revolutionary painters in the late sixth century, was the son of a reputable sculptor, but what is more interesting is that on a red-figure hydria (fig. 7), which was probably specially painted for a symposion before a naval expedition, the painter, before firing the pot, painted a double greeting to Euthymides and to Sostratos, who appears on contemporary pictures with such famous figures as Xanthippos, the father of Pericles, and was probably the Sostratos who won a chariot race in the Pana-thenaic games early in the fifth century. Smikros, another con-temporary vase-painter, appears on a mixing-bowl by Euphronios, taking part in a symposion with Theodemos, Melas, Syko, and Ekphantides, who is probably an elder relative of the comic poet Ekphantides. Again the vase is a special commission, and, as it has on the back *Leagros kalos*, it was probably ordered by Leagros, who was elected strategos in 465. Melas provides another link with Leagros, because on another mixing-bowl by Euphronios (*fig. 8*) Leagros and Melas are shown sitting with Kephisodoros, while a young flautist, called Polykles, prepares to sing. I think that we can probably assume that Leagros and his son Glaukon, who lived in the Kerameikos, were not only patrons but friends of the painters and potters who were colleagues of the young Euphronios when he painted, and of those who worked for Euphronios when he set up an independent or semi-independent workshop. We shall have to try and assess the value of this aristocratic patronage.[3]

The purchaser could either go to the potter's workshop or go to the section of the Agora called 'pots', where presumably rough ware, black-glaze, and the more ordinary painted pottery was on sale. The purchaser might be a trader, a foreign visitor, or an Athenian. Let us try and assess what sort of influence these different kinds of purchasers (representing society) exercised on the Athenian potter. The activity of traders can be detected from the number of Athenian vases found abroad. There is a little evidence of designing for the export trade. An uninteresting but homogeneous class of early black-figure amphorai, late black-figure and early red-figure amphorai of a peculiar shape and handled ladle-cups mostly made in the same workshop, and classical red-figure plates with high stems are all found almost exclusively in Etruria, and they may represent the product of a single workshop working from about 570 to about 400 partly for the Etruscan market. But this is a tiny proportion of the Attic vases found in Etruria. The vast majority show that what the Etruscans wanted was good Attic vases, and they did not mind in the least whether they were new or secondhand. A number of the best, for instance the well-known cup by Douris with the picture of a school with a specially inscribed roll and a *kalos* name (evidently the Athenian recipient), were painted for a special Athenian occasion and can only have come to Etruria by the secondhand market (we shall have to consider later what this practice implies for the Athenian purchaser and potter). We have a few possible traces of the trader in Athens. A red-figure cup of about 450 has an owner-inscription in Etruscan put on before firing, so that the trader must have been there to instruct the potter. There are also about fifty large vases with SMI scratched on the bottom. Most of them were found in Etruria but one was found on the Acropolis, so that it looks as if SMI was a successful trader who dedicated at least one vase to Athena to insure his success. A similar scratched inscription LE occurs on the bottom of over forty large vases, both black-figure and red-figure of the late sixth century, and again seems to be a trader's mark. All of which we know the provenance were found in Etruria. The black-figure vases have also a scratched inscription giving a number of small vases with a price; the red-figure vases have a record of a number of small vases without a price. We have therefore records of the dealer's consignments, and he purchased some of his vases secondhand, since the red-figure vases include the hydria with the double greeting to Euthymides and Sostratos (*fig.* 7) and the hydria with Euthymides watching Tlempolemos recite. Outside Etruria it is worth quoting the nearly 200 classical tombs excavated in Sicily at Vassallaggi, the ancient Motyon: the men's tombs all contained an Attic red-figure mixing-bowl and wine jar or wine jug, the women's tombs all contained an Attic red-figure mixing-bowl or wine jar. Here was a ready market for stock and secondhand vases, and in all probability the vases were bought for everyday use and later put in the tombs (as in Etruria); the lyric poet Pindar expected his Sicilian friend Thrasyboulos in Akragas to use Athenian cups.[4]

Foreign visitors, as distinct from traders, can only be traced occasionally. A tomb in Taranto contained a late sixth-century Panathenaic prize-amphora and four contemporary mixing-bowls with chariot scenes. Evidently a citizen of Tarentum had visited Athens and won the chariot-race in the Panathenaic games and brought home not only his prize but four Athenian mixing-bowls for his celebrations. At Gela in Sicily the shrine of the hero-founder, Antiphamos, contained a fragment of a red-figure drinking cup with a picture of the death of the Athenian tyrant Hipparchos. The subject may have been not too uncommon on Attic pottery soon after the new statues of the tyrant-slayers were set up in the Agora after the Persian wars. It has been suggested that a Geloan, who was disaffected with the local tyrants bought it in Athens and dedicated it to his local hero. Much earlier, in the mid-sixth century, the potter-painter Exekias signed a large mixing-bowl and added another inscription in the Sikyonian alphabet 'Epainetos gave me to Charops'. At least one of the two must have been a Sikyonian, and the inscription in foreign letters was put on in Athens; subsequently the vase found its way to Etruria, presumably by the secondhand market. Earlier still, someone had an inscription added to a black-figure cup, dedicating it to Apollo, and then took it to Boeotia; this may have been either an Athenian visiting Boeotia or a Boeotian who had visited Athens. These few instances show that there was a market for discriminating foreigners, as well as traders.[5]

We can sample the ordinary Athenian market by taking one example of a sanctuary, one example of a house, and one example of a tomb. The festival of Artemis at Brauron was, as we have said, a women's festival and in particular a festival for girls before marriage. One special line of vases is found there, curious chalices decorated in a rather rough black-figure technique with women's dances and races; they may be of local manufacture, but they have been found at another Artemis sanctuary in Athens; they are certainly cult vases. Wedding-vases (clay copies of the hydriai and cauldrons used for fetching and heating the water for the bride's bath), thigh-shields for working wool, perfume vases and ointment boxes, all decorated, are suitable dedications in this sanctuary. There are also a number of cups, some of them extremely fine. The decoration is sometimes obviously connected with Artemis and her mythology, sometimes relevant because portraying women, and sometimes irrelevant, as for instance Demeter and Persephone or a maenad or a purely male symposion. Artemis was supposed to be satisfied whether the purchaser bought her a vase specially decorated for her or a stock but relevant vase or simply a stock vase.[6]

A large country house on the slope of Mount Aigaleos between Athens and Eleusis, which was occupied for a short time, roughly between 422 and 413, contained three red-figure vases (two mixing-bowls and a marriage-cauldron), about 40 black-glaze cups and smaller vases, and a much larger amount of undecorated kitchenware. The red-figure vases all have stock scenes of no particular interest, but the marriage-cauldron is considerably earlier than the other two, and was probably a wedding-present, which the owners brought with them when they occupied the house. Other houses in Athens (or the wells which contain the throw-outs of private houses) show the same sort of proportion between painted vases, black-glaze, and cooking pots. The ordinary Athenian had a few painted vases, mostly large mixing-bowls, but used black-glaze for cups, sauces, salt, and perfume because it was cheaper.[7]

Certain shapes were suitable for putting on or in tombs. The best known is the tall perfume pot (called *lekythos* by the archaeologists), particularly the kind covered with a white slip to take outline drawing. Some of these are very beautiful and certainly special commissions, but many of them are stock. Both men and women who died either before marriage or very early in marriage could be given vases of the same shapes as wedding-vases but with funeral scenes; these are not very common and mostly of high quality, and probably most of them are special commissions. As an example of an ordinary tomb in Athens the tomb of Asopodoros will serve. It is called after an *aryballos* (man's oil-flask) made and painted by Douris, which has the inscription 'Asopodoros' lekythos'. The rest of the vases in the tomb were twenty-two cheap black-figure *lekythoi* from the workshop of the Haimon painter and five black-glaze vases. Asopodoros must have been a poor man, but he had the lovely aryballos as a present from Douris or another, and it was put in his grave when he died about fifteen years later. The mourners evidently thought that numbers rather than quality counted with the gods of the underworld and so they bought twenty-two cheap lekythoi from the Haimon painter's shop rather than two really good red-figure or white-ground lekythoi. Similarly a richer burial of the late fifth century had eleven good white lekythoi of some size in the sarcophagus. The aryballos is an instance of the common practice of giving to the dead vases of other shapes than the special funeral shapes, and except for the rather rare wedding-vases mentioned above, when the ashes were put in a painted vase, non-funerary shapes like amphorai, pelikai, mixing-bowls, or hydriai had to be used. The chief principle governing the choice of decoration was probably what the dead man was believed to have liked, and often the vase must have been a precious possession like the Douris aryballos. Funerary scenes or farewells or women preparing to go to the tomb are often found on lekythoi and the special wedding-vases, but also sometimes on vases of other shapes which the potter presumably thought might be bought for tombs. Some mythological subjects were thought suitable. Dionysos with his maenads and satyrs carried the hope of a similar bliss in the other world. Apparently also gods and goddesses (or even heroes) carrying off or pursuing men or women conveyed a hope of immortality. In the case of one story we can see a transition from historical tribute to mythological paradigm. The north wind, Boreas, was summoned to damage the Persian fleet in 480, and immediately afterwards the myth that Boreas carried off the Athenian princess Oreithyia appears on vases. It may be chance that vases appear in tombs with this subject, but in the fourth century the scene appears on bronze funeral hydriai, and there it surely carries a hope of immortality.[8]

Let us sum up what we have found so far. A large number of painted vases were exported, but, except for a small line of special shapes made for Etruria, the potter did not design for export, and the really good exported vases to a considerable extent came from the secondhand market. A number of intelligent foreigners commissioned vases when they were in Athens, but they can hardly have been sufficiently numerous to change the potters' ideas. The potter designed for the Athenian market, and the Athenians needed a great many vases for cult, weddings, funerals, presents, symposia.

Special shapes for cult are extremely rare, perhaps three out of over seventy shapes would qualify. In addition to the chalices dedicated to Artemis at Brauron we have mentioned already the Panathenaic prize amphorai. The prize amphorai themselves have a shape adapted from an existing shape and progressively refined; they were always decorated in black-figure with Athena on one side and a sporting or musical event on the other. But beside them until at least the end of the fifth century runs another series, the black-figure stopping about 470 and the red-figure

7 Red-figure hydria, Pioneer Group, 515 BC (Louvre G 41)
Shoulder: chariot departing. Body: Hermes, Dionysos, Ariadne, Poseidon, Amphitrite

8 Red-figure kalyx krater, Euphronios, 515 BC (Louvre G 103)
Leagros at a concert

9 Red-figure cup, Penthesilea painter, 460–50 BC
(Ferrara)
Tondo: two knights. Surround: labours of Theseus

10 Red-figure cup, manner of Douris, 480–70 BC
(London E 51)
Woman smelling rose

11 Metope, Athenian
Treasury at Delphi,
510 BC
Herakles and hind

12 Red-figure cup,
Skythes, 515 BC (Rome,
Villa Giulia 20760)
Theseus and sow

starting before the end of the sixth century, which lack the official inscription of the prize amphorai and are often not of canonical size; in the beginning they were probably made for the symposia held after a Panathenaic victory and repeat with variations the scheme of the prize amphorai; the red-figure Panathenaics (*fig. 19*) quite often carry some allusion to some part of the festival; but many of them are decorated with mythological scenes, and we cannot say whether these were, for instance, the subject of a song at the festival or whether the connection between shape and cult no longer exists. The third of the rare instances of special cult vases is a set of late fifth-century jugs found on the Akropolis, the product of a single workshop, decorated on the neck with a fighting Athena (as on the prize Panathenaic amphorai) and with moulded breasts on the body (a very archaic element and presumably here connected with the cult); these must have been made for use in some special cult of Athena.

The shrine of the Nymph (or rather Hera as 'the bride') under the south slope of the Akropolis received very large numbers of *loutrophoroi* (wedding amphorai and hydriai) from the seventh century until the Hellenistic age; it was evidently the custom for Athenian girls to dedicate one on marriage. But they were not special shapes: they were no different from the ordinary vases of the same shape given as wedding presents and, like them, were decorated with weddings or mythological paradigms of weddings, Herakles and Hebe, or Boreas and Oreithyia (which has a different implication here). A large proportion of the pictures of women ecstatically dancing before the mask of Dionysos (perhaps at the Anthesteria) occur on a particular type of wine jar which the archaeologists call *stamnos*; it is a normal symposion vase, but these examples were probably painted for symposia occurring after the festival. Similarly the jugs (*choes*) used in the drinking competition on the second day of the festival, which are a normal form of symposion jug, are echoed in miniature form with pictures of children, which are often found in children's graves; children attended the Anthesteria when they were three years old.[9] What we have in these three cases are not special cult-shapes but ordinary shapes used in connection with particular cults.

Many vases have cult scenes, sacrifices, men or women before an altar, men or women before a herm, men or women pouring a libation. It is often clear to which god sacrifice, prayer, or libation is being made, but we cannot say that the vase is a dedication to that god unless it was found in a sanctuary. A dedicated vase may be of any shape, and the subject, as we have seen, need not be relevant. Many of the vases with cult scenes were found in places other than sanctuaries, in the wells of private houses in Greece or in tombs in Greece or overseas. The reason is simple: the performance of cult precedes a meal and a symposion, and the host chooses for the symposion vases which recall the cult performance. Some of these vases too can be identified as special commissions, chiefly because the names of living Athenians have been written against the figures before the vase was fired. One of the most interesting is a mixing-bowl (bell-krater) of about 430 with the sacrifice of a young ram. Among the participants are Aresias, one of the Thirty Tyrants, Kallias, one of the aristocrats prosecuted for mutilating the Herms just before the Sicilian expedition, and Hippokles, one of the Ten, who took over in Athens when the Thirty withdrew to Eleusis—a nest of ultra-conservative Athenians perhaps already plotting oligarchic revolution. This Athenian occasion can have meant nothing to the citizens of Capua, where the vase was found, and it must have come there by the secondhand market.[10]

Price-inscriptions scratched on the bottom of vases are extraordinarily difficult to interpret, but the range in Athens would seem to have been from upwards of three drachmai to one-twelfth of a drachma for painted vases and from one-sixth to one-hundredth of a drachma for vases only decorated with black-glaze. This means that the ordinary Athenian would afford a good painted vase for a special dedication, wedding presents, or a gift to a friend, and would have a couple of stock painted mixing-bowls, for daily use, but where he needed quantity, cups, sauce-plates, salt-cellars for the symposion, or a number of lekythoi for a grave, he bought black-glaze or the cheapest kind of painted ware. On the other hand the rich man could afford painted cups, water jugs, and wine jugs, as well as painted mixing-bowls, for the symposion and better painted lekythoi for his friend's tomb.

The number of specially commissioned vases, especially symposion vases, which have been found overseas suggests that it
was the custom to use specially painted vases once and then dis-
pose of them. A complete set for a ten-man symposion (an ordinary
size) with ten deep cups, ten shallow cups, two mixing-bowls,
two wine-jugs, two hydriai, two amphorai would cost in the
neighbourhood of forty drachmai, and that would not be an
unreasonable price for a rich man for a special occasion.[11]

Here perhaps is one clue to the swift change of style in the
drawing, which affects not only the best artists but also the
inferior artists. The pace is set by extremely intelligent patrons
buying from the best painters in quantity and frequently, and
the rest, both painters and purchasers, observe it and keep up
as best they may. It is worth looking at different kinds of subject
on specially commissioned symposion vases to see how this
operates and to observe some of the patrons. Symposion vases
naturally illustrate the symposion itself and the revel after the
symposion. We have noticed the symposion of Smikros and his
friends and the fact that the aristocratic Leagros apparently
ordered the vase. The scene itself is not new but goes back to
early black-figure. The novelty lies in the treatment and the
names. A slightly later symposion is also a special commission
because one of the drinkers has a line of song coming out of
his mouth; the other side has a very special revel, the poet
Anakreon dancing to the lyre in maenad costume. This is the
ancestor of a number of later pictures, and here we can probably
truthfully say that a special commission inspired a line of stock
vases. Perhaps the dances went on, but certainly Anakreon was
remembered, and his songs were still sung after his death.[12]

But symposion vases often had pictures of the occasion for
the symposion rather than the symposion itself or its aftermath.
Several specially commissioned symposion vases with different
types of scene have been mentioned already, the farewell hydria
for Sostratos and Euthymides (fig. 7), the school hydria with
Euthymides and Tlempolemos, the Douris school cup, Leagros
at the concert (fig. 8) when the young flautist sang of Herakles
and Antaios, the sacrifice made by the oligarchs. Of these only
the two school vases can probably be claimed as the beginning of

a line, in this case a line of school vases, of which several were special commissions. The school scenes very often share the vase with a scene representing athletics; prowess in both are celebrated at the same party; the inside of the Douris school cup has an athlete taking off his sandals. Many symposion vases have pictures of athletes, and all kinds of events are represented. In the early red-figured period scenes in the palaistra are rather more common than actual events, and many of them are shown to be special commissions either by *kalos* names or by names against the athletes. It is very possible that the fashion was started by Leagros and his friends. Leagros appears himself on a mixing-bowl by Euphronios with seven other named athletes including Polyllos. Polyllos is a most unlikely name and is probably a mis-writing for Phayllos, who came from Kroton and commanded his own ship at Salamis in 480. Phayllos appears again with ten other named athletes on a wine-cooler by Phintias; one of the others is Sostratos, of whom we have already spoken, and another is Epilykos, whose granddaughter married Pericles' son. With these vases we are very much in the aristocracy, but a mixing-bowl (bell-krater) of the late fifth century illustrates democratic athletics, as described by Pseudo-Xenophon. It was painted to celebrate the victory of the tribe Antiochis in the torch-race at the festival of Prometheus. Exceptionally the potter, who may also have been the painter, signed it with his full official name, Nikias, son of Hermokles, of Anaphlystos; Anaphlystos is a deme grouped in the Antiochis tribe, and the use of the official name perhaps means that Nikias himself was a member of the success-ful team.[13]

The young Leagros appears also in Thracian cloak, as a cavalry-man, on a cup made by Kachrylion and decorated by Euphronios. The outside has the story of Herakles and Geryon on one side and an attempt to steal Geryon's cattle from Herakles on the other. The story was told by the Sicilian lyric poet Stesichoros, who was sung at Athenian symposia. The cup, therefore, both shows Leagros in his pride and gives the kind of song sung at his symposia. A generation later another painter painted an enormous cup with two young knights, one dismounting and placing an oakwreath on an altar; conceivably one of them had won a race in the Pythian games at Delphi, as the victor there wore an oakwreath. Round this picture, inside the cup, the painter has painted the deeds of Theseus (*fig. 9*), a popular Athenian subject, to which we shall return; on the outside of the cup, one picture has been interpreted as the duel between Ajax and Hektor, and the other is the struggle between Ajax and Odysseus for the arms of Achilles. The great size of the cup, about 23 inches in diameter (the Leagros cup is less than 18 inches), the special character of the central picture, and the extra circle of pictures on the inside strongly suggest that it was a special commission and reached Etruria by the second-hand market. Possibly the two scenes with Ajax imply that the purchaser came from Ajax' island of Salamis, which was now an Athenian deme, but it may merely be that in his glory he felt himself the equal of the epic heroes. Vases with horsemen, heavy-armed cavalry, light-armed cavalry, young men in Thracian cloaks, hunters, jockeys are common from the early sixth century; but in the generation of Leagros and his son Glaukon the young knights in Thracian cloaks dominate. The cavalry were provided by the '500 bushel' men and the knights, and these subjects were always popular with them, but jockeys certainly and probably hunters and cavalrymen would have been popular with a much wider section of the population.[14]

The numbers of vases with pictures of horsemen and athletes are so considerable that they are some guide to Athenian taste at different times. It is interesting to set them against two other popular types of non-mythological picture. These are first pictures of men and women (men visiting women, men courting women, men watching women, women visiting men) and secondly pictures of women by themselves. The figures of attributed vases for the two main groups are large enough to give some indication of a change of taste. Over the period from 570 to 400 there are just under 2,500 vases with athletes and horsemen and just over 2,500 with men and women or women alone. But if we divide the period at 480, we find before that date nearly 1,500 horsemen and athletes but only 500 men and women or women alone, and after 480 under 1,000 horsemen and athletes and 2,000 men and women or women alone. The startling change occurs in the twenty-five years after the Persian War: the numbers then are 392 for men and women and 749 for women alone, together more than twice the total for the same two groups from 570 to 480. In the last two quarters of the fifth century the numbers of all attributed vases decrease, but even in the last quarter there are 254 vases with women alone as against thirty-four with men and women, ninety-eight with athletes, and seven with horsemen. Various trends are at work here, and probably more than we can now detect. In what I may term the active-male group it is the horsemen rather than the athletes who show the great decline after 480; the figures are 565 horsemen and 929 athletes before 480, and 164 horsemen and 777 athletes after 480. I suspect that the really rich men had changed in various ways: after the generation of Glaukon, son of Leagros, what they prided themselves on was neither athletics nor the cavalry but chariot-racing; it is also possible that they bought silver cups for their symposia, and these lasted, so that they no longer so often gave special commissions to the potters; and thirdly, they shared and may indeed have initiated the new interest in pictures of women. Athletics on the other hand had much more general appeal because the ordinary man took part in the various events in which teams were entered by the tribes. But much the most interesting change is the new place of women in pictures on Greek vases (fig. 10). A considerable number, and perhaps the majority, of these vases were vases meant for women's use, particularly perfume vases, and for the first time women bought or were given vases with their own occupations depicted on them. Considering the restrictions on women in Athens, they were probably more often gifts from men than purchases by the women themselves. This is suggested also by the inclusion of Erotes to show the presence of sexual love in these scenes of women's life, more and more frequently from 450 onwards. The vases reflect this shift of interest earlier than literature, but Euripides started writing tragedies about women in 455, and then later the shift of interest from athletics to sex is part of what Aristophanes was criticising in the *Clouds* of 423.[15]

Many vases have mythological subjects, and here again we can detect changes of taste. One obvious reason for choosing one subject rather than another is relevance. In the simplest sense of relevance a scene with Dionysos is relevant on a vase in which one drinks, mixes, or serves wine, or a story connected with Artemis is relevant on a vase dedicated to Artemis. Or a myth may be relevant on a symposion vase either because a lyric version is often sung in the symposion or because the symposion celebrates a recent performance of it by a singer who is a guest at the symposion. Further a myth may be relevant if it is a heroic example of what the owner of the vase is or wants to be: a very beautiful thigh-shield for working wool has Peleus struggling to win Thetis on the end, the wedding of Harmonia on one side, and the wedding of Alkestis on the other; it was obviously a specially commissioned wedding present.[16]

These reasons for choice are relatively permanent, but sometimes an entirely new story or set of stories appears, or a new treatment of an old story, and then we have to ask for a reason and if possible for a patron. One of the most striking of these is the Theseus cycle. Until about 515 the only Theseus scenes appearing in Attic art are Theseus and the Minotaur, Theseus' rape of Helen, and Theseus in the Centauromachy. Then suddenly we find Theseus' journey from Troizen to Athens, his struggles with the wild men on the way, his capture of the bull of Marathon, his defeat of the Pallantidai, his visit to Poseidon under the sea, his battle with the Amazons including his rape of Antiope, and the Amazon attack on Athens. Moreover from the beginning the artists tend to show several Theseus scenes on one vase instead of a single scene, or at most one scene on one side and one on the other, and this is a new principle of composition. Thus one of the earliest cups has Theseus and Sinis, Theseus and the Minotaur, and Theseus and Prokrustes on one side, and on the other Theseus and Skeiron, Theseus and Kerkyon, and Theseus and the bull of Marathon; the well-known struggle with the Minotaur legitimises the rest. It is surely right to suppose that a new epic on Theseus inspired these scenes. Two different patrons have been suggested, Peisistratos and Kleisthenes. Peisistratos died in 528, so that, although he may have been the inspiration of the epic, he cannot have been the inspiration of the vases. The strong argument against his son Hippias as patron, who was not expelled from the tyranny until 510, is that these scenes continued to be popular under the democracy and indeed rapidly passed into the stock-in-trade of the Athenian vase-painter, and Theseus himself was later credited with the foundation of the democracy and the invention of ostracism. But that just before the expulsion of the tyrant Kleisthenes, the organiser of the new democracy, should have commissioned symposion vases illustrating the new exploits of the Athenian hero, and so have made him the talk of the aristocratic symposia, the symbol of the new world which was coming into being, is a very attractive possibility.[17]

There is a little evidence which may point in this direction. One of the earliest vases, a cup (*fig. 12*) which has Theseus and the sow of Krommyon on one side and Theseus attacking a man (possibly Prokrustes) on the other, is inscribed *Epilykos kalos* and was therefore either a present to him or bought by him. Epilykos had connections with the Alkmaionid family, to which Kleisthenes belonged. His granddaughter, as we have said, married the Alkmaionid Pericles' son. Secondly, a very fine amphora painted about 500 has Theseus carrying off the Amazon Antiope (one of the new stories) on one side and on the other the unique representation of Kroisos the king of Lydia seated in festal garb on a funeral pyre, which is being lit by an attendant labelled 'Cheerful'. The Alkmaionids owed their wealth to a visit by Alkmaion to Kroisos, and a young Alkmaionid, who was killed about 530, was named after him. Kroisos' capital was sacked by the Persians in 546. Delphi was involved, because Kroisos had made many offerings to Apollo and had consulted the oracle before attacking Persia. Delphi put out the story, which we know from Bacchylides in 468, that Apollo carried Kroisos off from the flaming pyre and settled him in the fabulous land of the Hyperboreans. This is the story implied by our amphora with the festal robes and the attendant named Euthymos 'Cheerful'. And the Alkmaionid family are linked not only to Kroisos but also to Delphi, because they had contracted to rebuild Apollo's temple and had rebuilt it in marble instead of limestone, securing thereby Delphi's goodwill for the expulsion of the Athenian tyrants. They were a natural vehicle in Athens for the Delphic version of the end of Kroisos. They may also have been responsible for the Athenian treasury at Delphi in which the metopes (*fig. 11*) showed the new deeds of Theseus as well as the deeds of Herakles.[18]

The next moment when we can see a new treatment of the Theseus story used 'politically' on vases is in the decade 460-50, but that is so much tied in with the development of wall painting and sculpture that it is better left to the next chapter. But two rather later instances may be mentioned because they point to another kind of reason for specially commissioning symposion vases. A mixing-bowl of about 425 is decorated with two rows of pictures: the upper row has the Theseus cycle running right round the vase; the lower row has on one side satyrs taking fire from Prometheus and on the other side the dawn-goddess, Eos, pursuing the Attic hunter Kephalos, a myth which is common in the fifth century, and, like Boreas and Oreithyia, if interpreted symbolically, suitable for either a wedding present or a funerary gift. One would not normally at this late date see any necessary connection between the Theseus cycle and the Alkmaionid family, but in this case there is another possible connection; the Prometheus scene reproduces a moment in Aeschylus' satyr-play, *Prometheus Pyrkaeus*, which was produced with the *Persians* in 472, and the rich man who paid for the first production was the great Alkmaionid, Pericles. This vase may therefore have been ordered by a younger relation after Pericles' death. But the more interesting point is the connection with the production of the play. In this case we have an earlier vase from the same workshop, which reproduces one of the same satyrs but this earlier satyr is shown by his costume to be a chorusman in the satyr play. Aeschylean plays were revived in the fifth century after his death, and it seems reasonable to suppose that this earlier vase was painted for a symposion celebrating such a revival. The scene was attractive in itself and so became a stock scene for vases produced in this workshop, the same kind of development suggested for the pictures of Anacreontic dances. Then, if it was an Alkmaionid who ordered the later vase, he asked for the combination of Theseus cycle and satyr-play originally financed by Pericles.[19]

Another instance where we can very probably say that a vase or vases specially commissioned to celebrate the production of a play then inspired a long series of stock vases is a new version of Theseus' capture of the bull of Marathon. The story belongs to the Theseus cycle and is possibly even a little older. It is constantly represented from about 530, but soon after the middle of the fifth century a new version appears in which a woman, Medeia, runs away holding a jug and phiale. It has been suggested that Euripides in his *Aigeus* reversed the order of events in the epic and made Medeia first persuade Aigeus to send Theseus to capture the bull of Marathon and then, when he, unfortunately for her, succeeded, attempt to poison him. Euripides' first production was in 455 so that the series, which runs on into the fourth century, started fairly soon afterwards.[20]

Other mythological representations can be connected with performances of comedy and others again with choral lyric, particularly dithyramb (*fig. 21*). To account for the first commission of such vases it is natural to think of the celebration after the performance; in Plato's *Symposium* we are told that Agathon and his chorusmen made a victory sacrifice after his first tragedy had been successful. But the private celebrations of individual performers could also cause the production of such vases, and their private dedications. For tragedy and satyr-play vases the symposia of the Association which Sophocles made in honour of the Muses must also be remembered. When a scene originally inspired by a performance became a stock scene, we have no means of telling whether the purchaser felt the literary allusion or merely bought a pot with a mythical scene which he liked.[21]

Many other special commissions could be quoted, but these are enough to show the kind of thing that happened. A patron goes to a potter and commissions a pot or a set of pots, which are given to the best painter or painters in the shop to execute, and then, if the scenes seem likely to be popular, they continue as stock scenes, and, as the Greeks had no copyright, they were copied in other shops. This process helped the whole range of Athenian purchasers to keep up to date not only with their choice of pictures but also with the latest developments in artistic representation. The pace was set by the great painters and the aristocratic purchasers. We know the names of the purchasers partly from the names written alongside the figures in non-mythological pictures and partly from the *kalos* names, of which 150 are preserved for the period between 530 and 450. A number of these names can be identified as coming from the top ranks of Athenian society. I have mentioned Leagros and Glaukon, Sostratos, Epilykos, and Xanthippos, and later the nest of Athenian oligarchs. To these can be added Kimon's father Miltiades and Kimon's son Lakedaimonios, and of the Alkmaionid family an older and a younger Megakles, Hippokrates, Alkmaion, Euryptolemos, and Peisianax, and, outside the great families but still distinguished, Euaion, son of Aeschylus. The pottery industry shows once more the viability and adaptability of Athenian society. The pace is set by the best painters and the aristocrats, but they are followed at a very short interval by the ordinary painters and the ordinary purchasers down to the humblest.[22]

8 *Architects, Sculptors and Painters*

Examination of the pottery industry has shown various points which may be relevant also to the great arts of sculpture, architecture, and painting: a family-workshop tradition which nevertheless allows continuing innovation, a considerable range in artistic competence, a great variety in purchasers from the poorest to the richest, and the main changes probably due to the special commissions of the richest. Clearly there is a similar range both in artists and in patrons of the great arts. In architecture we have at one end the Parthenon and at the other the small private house; in sculpture we have at one end the sculpture of the Parthenon and the bronze and marble statues dedicated by the rich, a middle-range of marble grave-reliefs and dedicatory reliefs, and at the other end statuettes and reliefs in terracotta, which the poor man dedicated or placed in his tomb or had in his house; in painting the frescoes of public buildings and the internal decoration of rich man's houses are at one end and the small plaque dedicated by the poor man at the other. It is also clear that though the swift changes in style may be due to the great artists the lesser artists follow with great speed.

In this chapter we are primarily concerned with the great artists and with public art, but the links between the great artists and the lesser craftsmen may be briefly stated first, as far as we know them. Architecture was the most traditional of Greek arts, and this meant that the architect could and did leave far more to the individual craftsman than he does in the modern building. We have no evidence that he either made for himself or issued to his contractors and craftsmen any drawing of the building or its parts. He marked the building out on the ground. He issued detailed specifications about the size and number of marble-blocks to be quarried, transported, and erected on the site, and on the site he must have given instructions about the refinements, the slight irregularity of the curvature and the slight inclination of the columns, but it has been shown that they were very simple instructions, which the well-trained mason could easily carry out on his own. There may have been no one between the architect and the actual craftsmen, whom we know from the accounts of the Erechtheion (*fig. 16*), the curious building just north of the Parthenon housing a number of very ancient cults: the accounts show citizens, resident aliens, and slaves working together on the same columns for the same wage.[1]

The frieze of the Erechtheion consisted of figures of marble fixed to a background of dark grey limestone. The sculptors were paid by the figure at the same rate as the men channelling the columns, and again citizens and resident aliens were working side by side. But here they must have had, however skilled they were, a rough sketch to work to. The same must be true of the pediments, metopes, and frieze of the Parthenon. Pheidias himself was fully engaged on the colossal gold and ivory cult statue of Athena, but he probably planned the rest of the decoration, as we shall see. The architectural sculpture, particularly the frieze with its alternation of long slow groups and short quick groups, can only have been done on the basis of drawings. A large number of different hands can be detected, and it has been claimed that individual craftsmen can be traced from metopes to frieze and even to pediments. The work of other great sculptors, Alkamenes, Agorakritos, and Paionios, who are known to us by major statues, have been traced in minor reliefs, particularly the reliefs of the Nike balustrade (*fig. 17*), and even grave-reliefs. Sculpture also was a great traditional craft with no hard barrier between the great artist and the craftsman.[2]

The Erechtheion accounts also tell us of payment to resident aliens for painting ornament on the epistyle and the ceiling. We have to remember that Greek public buildings were profusely coloured, ceilings, capitals, mouldings, triglyphs, the backgrounds of metopes and pediments, and the sculpture itself, like all classical Greek sculpture. The ornament on temples is closely parallel to the ornament on contemporary vases, and it is not impossible that vase-painters sometimes carried it out; recently a connection has been pointed out between the ornament on the coffers of the Propylaia ceiling and the incised ornament which sometimes decorates the inside of Athenian cups. The colouring of sculpture one would naturally associate with humble crafts-men, but the great fourth-century sculptor Praxiteles seems to have employed the very good painter Nikias to colour his statues. Another kind of monument for which we can probably quote vase-painters, as well as big painters, as artists is the painted grave-stele, which was sometimes chosen instead of the commoner (or more commonly surviving) grave-relief. Three painted grave-stelai of the late sixth century have been placed very near or actually ascribed to the vase-painters Euthymides, Euphronios, and Skythes; later, in the fourth century, we hear of two famous painters, Aristratos and Nikias, painting grave-stelai. In painting also there seems to have been no hard and fast line between the great artists and the minor artist.[3]

The reason why we know the names of stone-carvers, sculptors, and painters who worked on the Erechtheion is that we have the annual accounts which were inscribed by the commissioners appointed by the Council and Assembly; although the original proposal came from a single man and the inspiration from Pericles, it was passed by the Council and the Assembly and the people had a right to know how their money was spent in detail. What we put together as Periclean buildings (*figs 14-17*), the Parthenon, the Erechtheion, the Propylaia (or gatehouse), and the temple of Nike on the Akropolis, and the Hephaisteion in the Agora, were all public buildings in this sense. The Akro-polis buildings formed a single great project, planned soon after 450 and completed after Pericles' death by the Erechtheion and the temple of Nike. The Hephaisteion, which was begun before the Parthenon but completed only in 416, was complementary because it looked across at the Akropolis from its hill on the west side of the Agora. It was designed to dominate the Agora, which had not long before been beautified by Kimon and adorned with the Theseion and the Stoa Poikile. In the eyes of Kimon's political successor Pericles was using the allies' money to dress Athens up like a vain woman; he himself said that the city was an education for Greece; for us the Parthenon and the Hephaisteion particularly seem to carry on the tradition of the Stoa Poikile and the Theseion. All were decorated by the greatest artists of the day, all were public buildings in the sense that they were open to the Athenian public. Were they saying anything to the Athenians, and if so, were the Kimonian buildings saying the same thing as the Periclean buildings?[4]

The Theseion was built soon after 470, and the paintings were by the Athenian artist Mikon. One side had Theseus and the Amazons, one Theseus and the Centaurs; it is not clear from Pausanias' description whether Theseus' visit to Amphitrite to recover Minos' ring and Herakles' rescue of Theseus from Hades were also included. Kimon had brought back Theseus' bones from Skyros and these pictures celebrated his exploits. Theseus was the hero of democratic Athens, and if his new prominence was originally due to the Alkmaionids, Kimon had married into the Alkmaionids. In the Theseion Kimon is asserting his claim to be the true leader of the Athenian democracy.[5]

But the battle with the Centaurs leads us into a curious and interesting sideroad. Some vases of this period present us with a new version in which the battle takes place in the house, where the marriage banquet of Peirithoos was being held, instead of in the open air. This has naturally been connected with the picture in the Theseion, especially as one of the vases has also a very striking Amazonomachy; the vases may have been commissioned for the feasts in the Theseion. But this is also the version of the West pediment of the temple of Zeus at Olympia (*fig. 13*), which was built between 470 and 457 by the people of Elis. The rest of the decoration of the temple, the metopes with the labours of Herakles and the East pediment with the preparations for the chariot race between Oinomaos and Pelops, is strictly relevant to Olympia. The best that can be said for the west pediment is that Peirithoos was a son of Zeus, and that the scene has been made more relevant by inserting another son of Zeus, Apollo, in the middle; but his only relevance to the scene is that he points the moral: modesty and discipline is better than intemperance and violence. In fact this Attic scene in its new Attic form seems to advertise Athenian patronage, and it is a curious coincidence that Mikon, who painted in the Theseion, also made a victor-statue for the Athenian athlete Kallias in Olympia sometime after his victory in 472. Kimon himself gave his sons names which echoed his policy: one was called Lakedaimonios after Sparta, and one was called Eleios after Elis. An interest in Elis and Olympia was natural enough for one who belonged by birth to the aristocratic athletes who took part in the great games. It looks as if Kimon, remembering what the Alkmaionidai had done at Delphi in the late sixth century, persuaded the Elians to accept an Athenian story and an Athenian designer for the west pediment. Perhaps also he was responsible for getting Pheidias appointed to make the gold and ivory cult-statue of Zeus for the temple. It is probable that this commission was not carried out until after the completion of the Parthenon, but the glorification of Athens at Olympia would have appealed to Pericles as much as to Kimon.[6]

Pheidias also made a group of statues at Delphi, dedicated to Apollo as a tithe from the spoils of Marathon. The group consisted of Athena, Apollo, Miltiades, the heroes of the ten tribes formed by Kleisthenes, Theseus, Kodros (who had died defending Athens against the Dorian invasion), and Phyleus (perhaps a male personification from Phyle, tribe). The only contemporary included is Kimon's father, Miltiades, and the suggestion has naturally been made that Kimon was responsible: the message to Delphi and those who visited Delphi for the Pythian games or to consult Apollo, was that Kimon was the natural leader of the Athenian democracy.[7]

Marathon was the subject of the main picture in the Stoa Poikile erected by Kimon's brother-in-law Peisianax and completed about 460. It was painted by Mikon and Panainos, the brother of Pheidias. This was a battle-picture with Miltiades again conspicuous; Theseus was rising from the ground; Athena, Herakles, who was specially worshipped at Marathon, and two local heroes were also present. Mikon also painted Theseus fighting the Amazons; it is not clear how this picture differed from

13 Olympia, Apollo from West pediment, 470/60 BC

14 Parthenon, 448/30 BC

15 Parthenon Frieze, west; slabs VII, VIII, IX, X, 442–38 BC

16 Erechtheion, south Porch, 420–10 BC

17 Temple of Nike, 420–10 BC

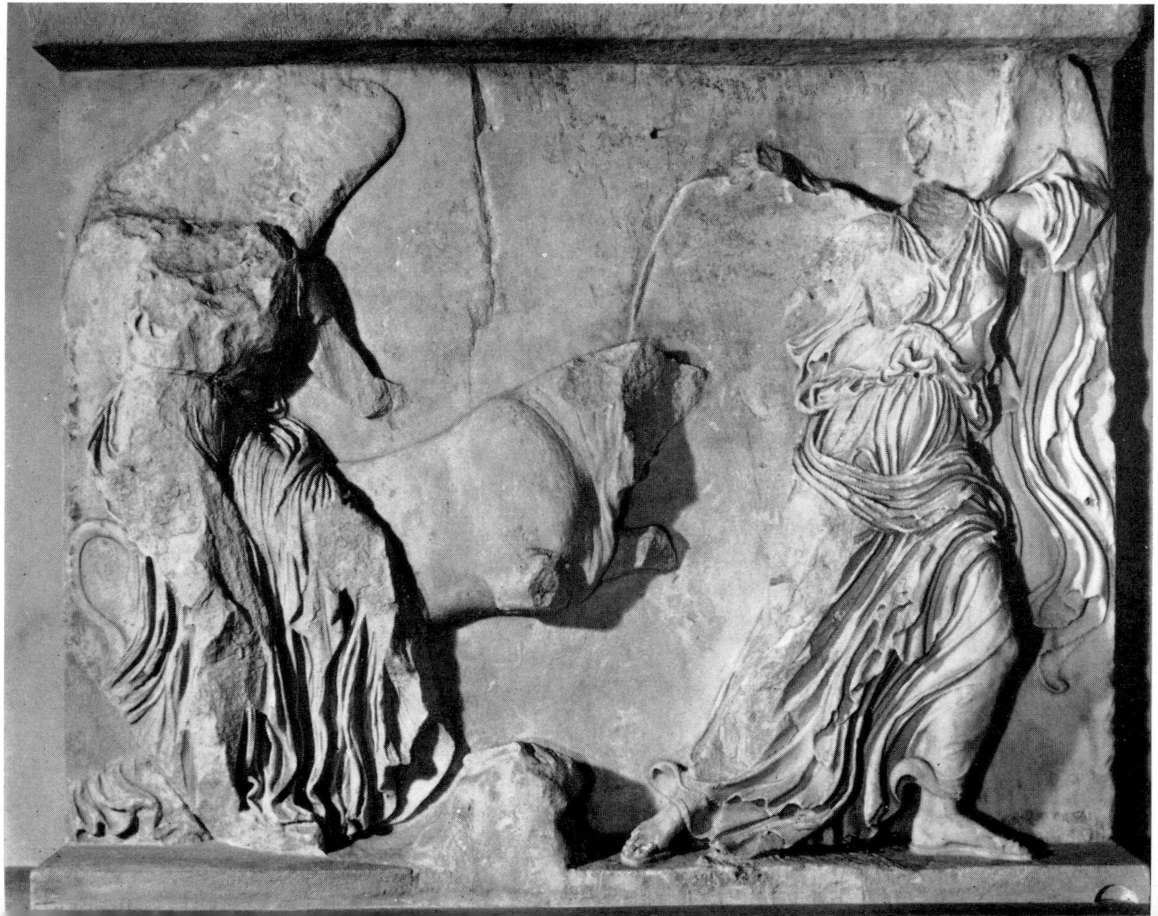

18 Nike balustrade, 410 BC Victories and bull

20 Pelike, Meidias painter, 410–400 BC (Metropolitan
Museum 37.11-23)
Herakles and Deianeira

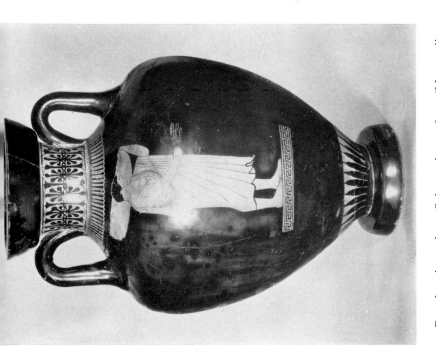

19 Panathenaic amphora, Syleus painter, 480 BC (Metropolitan
Museum 20.244)
Youth carrying tray and sprigs

21 Bell-krater, Lykaon painter, 430 BC (Warsaw 142355)
Dionysos with satyrs and maenads

the picture in the Theseion, but here it had an obvious relevance as a mythological parallel for an unsuccessful invasion of Attica by Orientals. So far all is clear, but the other two pictures are for different reasons problematical. One 'is the Greeks after the capture of Troy and the kings assembled because of the lesser Ajax attempt on Kassandra; it includes Ajax and Kassandra and other captive women'. We also hear that the painter was Polygnotos of Thasos, that he painted it for nothing (according to some, to get Athenian citizenship), and that he gave one of the Trojan captives the features of Kimon's sister Elpinike, whose lover he was said to have been. Kimon may have brought him from Thasos originally. He painted pictures in various other shrines in Athens and then went on to Delphi, where he painted the Sack of Troy and the Underworld in the Lesche of the Knidians. The parallel between the Trojan War and the Persian wars is obvious, but why choose Ajax' attempt to rape the Trojan priestess Kassandra—or rather, his trial after the attempt— which seems to have been the chief, if not the only scene in the picture in the Poikile? Several of Polygnotos' pictures in Athens, including this one, have the same subjects as tragedies by Sophocles, who was Kimon's favourite tragic poet. This rather than relevance to Marathon may have been the reason for the choice. The fourth picture, for which no artist is named, has been identified with a great occasion in legendary history rather than an unknown battle of Oinoe: the appeal of Adrastos to the Athenians to help him recover the bodies of the seven champions who had fallen in Thebes. If this attractive suggestion is right, Theseus was represented using Athenian power to help the Argives, and to use Argos as a counterbalance against Sparta in the late 460s was the new policy of Pericles. It is not impossible that here, as in the temple of Zeus at Olympia, Pericles took over an operation inspired by Kimon and used it for his own ends. At some time, and very likely now in the late 460s, the name was changed: the stoa was no longer called after Kimon's brother-in-law Peisianax but became the Stoa Poikile, the painted stoa.[8]

Pheidias, who had made the Marathon monument at Delphi for Kimon, became the leading spirit of the Periclean building programme and the sculptor of the cult-statue of the Parthenon (*fig. 14*). At first sight the decoration of the Parthenon seems to repeat the Theseion and the Stoa Poikile. The repeated themes are Theseus and the Amazons on the West metopes and on the shield of the cult-statue of Athena, Theseus and the Centaurs on the South metopes and on the sandals of the cult-statue, Trojan War on the North metopes. But the interpretation depends on the new context. The fourth set of metopes on the East front has the battle of the gods and giants, and this is repeated on the inside of Athena's shield. If the four themes are saying the same thing, they must be saying that Greek gods and heroes managed to defeat opponents who because of their confidence in their strength, numbers or wealth stepped out of their proper sphere to commit aggression, an aggression which disciplined modesty successfully withstood. And because three of these themes are repeated on the cult-statue, the words are put into Athena's mouth. The other themes are concerned with the goddess herself. On the East pediment she springs fully armed from the head of Zeus, so that, having no mother, the goddess of Athens is in a very special sense the daughter of the king of gods and men, and her birth is greeted by the assembled gods and goddesses, including the demigod Herakles. It has been noted that the gods in the southern half of the pediment have sanctuaries to the south of the Akropolis and the gods in the northern half of the pediment have sanctuaries to the north of the Akropolis; they were the Olympian gods, but they were also the gods of Athens. The west pediment represented the contest of Athena and Poseidon for the rule of Athens; Athena gave Athens the olive, and the olive oil was the foundation of Athenian commerce, and Poseidon gave her a salt water spring, symbolic of naval supremacy. This theme, the gifts that the gods gave to Athens, is picked up by the relief on the base of the cult-statue, the birth of Pandora, who in this context is Athens, the receiver of all gifts from the gods. Finally the frieze (*fig. 15*), which, exceptionally in a Doric temple, runs round the walls, has the first celebration of the Panathenaia, the service of a pious people to their goddess. The procession starts from the south-west corner, and the two lines, one running up the south side, the other across the west front and up the north side, converge on the east front; each line is received by a group of seated gods and goddesses, and between the two groups and over the door into the shrine, priest and priestess receive and fold the sacred robe for Athena. The two Greek words which sum up the message of the Parthenon are *eusebeia* (piety) and *sophrosyne* (modesty). The virtues are traditional, and no Athenian aristocrat could object to the emphasis put upon them. At this particular moment, when Athens was powerful and could have indulged in imperialist aggression, and when the full employment provided by the building programme and the fleet made the possibility of class-war a real danger, Pericles may have felt the public proclamation of these virtues desirable; essentially they are the same as the 'obedience to the authorities and to the laws, particularly the unwritten laws', which he enjoins in the Funeral Speech as the means to make the free society work.[9]

The Parthenon is a unique building in a unique position, and it is justifiable to seek a political interpretation. The Hephaisteion is primarily the temple of the craftsman population living on either side of the hill on the west of the Agora, the potters, the bronze-workers, the terracotta-makers, and the stone-carvers. It celebrates their gods, Hephaistos and Athena, whose cult-statues stand within and a myth which unites them, the birth of Erichthonios, is in relief on the base. Pediments, metopes, and frieze are shared between Herakles and Theseus, the former as a protégé of Athena long revered in Athens and Theseus as the hero of the Athenian democracy. The small friezes of the Erechtheion (*fig. 16*) and of the Nike temple (*fig. 17*) are much less imposing, and it is not even clear what they represent. The primary purpose of the Erechtheion is to house a number of very ancient cults, and the striking decoration of the Nike temple is the balustrade (*fig. 18*) with its repeating figures of Nike (Victory) and Athena.[10]

One later case of political art revives something of the Pheidian formula and something of the Pheidian style. After the battle of Mantineia in 362, in which Xenophon's son Grylos was killed after wounding the Boeotian commander Epameinondas, the Greek cities made a common peace. In Athens this was celebrated by a painting of the battle in the Stoa of Zeus in the Agora. The painter was Euphranor of the Isthmus, who was also a sculptor. He added two other pictures, the Twelve Gods (the great Olympians who receive the Panathenaic procession on the east frieze of the Parthenon) and Theseus with Demos (the Athenian people) and Democracy (personified as a woman). It seems likely that Theseus is giving Democracy to Demos as a bride. The whole set of pictures celebrates the triumph of the Athenian democracy in battle with the approval of the Olympian gods.[11]

Euphranor said that his Theseus was fed on beef whereas Parrhasios (a painter of the latest fifth century) had painted a Theseus fed on roses. What he meant can be seen by contrasting fourth-century pictures of Herakles with Herakles as he appears on vases of the late fifth century (fig. 20). Between Pheidias and Euphranor lie the beginnings of art criticism, and Euphranor's remark shows that he was conscious of the critics. The beginning of the great revolution in Greek art described in Chapter 2 was marked by another such statement by an artist: the vase-painter Euthymides wrote on one of his pictures 'as never Euphronios'; he regarded, with some exaggeration, Euphronios as rooted in the archaic conventions but himself, most justly, as in the van of the new, strong realistic art. And he expected his patron to read this and realise his claim.[12]

I suggested that the change from archaic to classical art implied a change in the artist's conception of what he was doing. He has ceased to make an Achilles (in paint or stone instead of in flesh and blood); he is now representing Achilles. The new aim involves a whole new set of conventions, which means developing new technical skills, and the new product may be differently assessed (or criticised). On the old view the head is in profile, the eye full-face, the torso frontal, the legs profile, because these are the memorable aspects of these parts and they have to be stated to give the figure its complete reality. On the new view the figure has to be an organic whole, as he appears to normal vision in a particular light. The relation of part to part and to surrounding space is now the important thing, not the equal statement of each several part in its most memorable aspect—a change analogous to the change in sentence structure discussed in relation to the orators. The figure had been a substitute for its original, often as a memorial or as an offering to the god; it is now a likeness of its original, and though it can and often does perform its old function, the change of status may raise a new question, what is the value of a likeness?[13]

Much of the change went on gradually within the old framework, but the new stance in sculpture and the move to represent depth in painting in the early fifth century were a real breakthrough, and from that time we find a new terminology, a new self-consciousness in the artist, and a statement or questioning of values. The new words for the new view which immediately come to mind are *eikon* 'likeness' and *mimesis* 'imitation'. Neither are used of visual representation before the fifth century. They are nicely linked together in Euripides' *Helen*, which was produced in 412, when Teukros sees Helen, whom he believes to have drowned with Menelaos, and says: 'I see the hated likeness (*eikon*) of the woman who destroyed us all. What a resemblance (*mimema*) you have to Helen.' Whether Euripides was really a painter or not, he knows, and expects his audience to know, the terminology and technique of modern painting. In his *Hecuba* the queen tells Agamemnon to stand off like a painter, and see her woes; painting that depends on juxtaposition of colours for its effects needs to be viewed from a distance. And in the *Oidipous* he describes the effect of the sunlight shining through leaves on the wings of the sphinx. He describes effects of colour and light just at the time when painters are concerned to portray them. The technical terms are *skenographia* for the perspective rendering of buildings (it means 'scene-painting', which implies that perspective buildings were first painted on stage sets) and *skiagraphia* both for rendering cast shadows and for plastic shading in the ordinary sense. Xenophon, describing Socrates' conversation with Parrhasios, uses *photeina* and *skoteina* for light and shade, and there must have been a further word for highlights, which come in the mid-fourth century and are called in Latin *splendor*.[14]

One sign of the self-consciousness in the artist is the writing of technical books. The Roman architectural historian Vitruvius gives a list of such treatises which include Agatharchos on *skenographia*, Iktinos on the Parthenon, and Euphranor on *symmetria*. *Symmetria* is a technical term for the commensurability of the parts of the human body (or of a building); the Argive sculptor Polykleitos had already written on this in the fifth century and embodied the result in his Achilles shouldering a spear; Euphranor varied the ideal proportions in his figures. The note on Agatharchos is worth quoting in full: 'Agatharchos made the set for an Aeschylean production at Athens and left a notebook about it. This caused Demokritos and Anaxagoras to write about the same problem, that the representations in *skenographia* might render the visual appearances of buildings and what is drawn on vertical flat walls should appear to be now receding, now projecting.' This must have been a revival of Aeschylus since the other dates for Agatharchos put him in the latter part of the fifth century; he painted the interior of Alkibiades' house, and that cannot have been before 430; on the other hand Anaxagoras left Athens in 432 or soon after. The philosophers were interested in perspective as a problem of optics rather than as a subject for art criticism, but the new set for tragedy was evidently something of an event.[15]

At the same time we meet flamboyant artistic personalities. The architect and towner-planner Hippodamos, who designed the Peiraieus, had a mass of untidy hair and wore cheap warm clothing in summer and winter; he claimed to be an authority on the physical nature of the universe and had his own theory of politics. Apollodoros, who invented *skiagraphia*, had inscribed on his works 'easier to criticise than to imitate'. The next great painter Zeuxis had his name in letters of gold on his cloak, and wrote an epigram: 'if any man says that he has reached the boundaries of our art, let him show it and defeat me. I do not think that I shall come second.' The allusion is to his older contemporary Parrhasios, who was also a flamboyant personality with a purple cloak, a white scarf round his head, and gold decoration on his stick and gold eyelets on his boots. He had written on one of his works: 'the limits of this art have been discovered and revealed by my hand. The mark is fixed and cannot be passed, but nothing done by humans escapes criticism.' The next vocal artist was Euphranor, who contrasted Parrhasios' rose-fed Theseus with his own beef-fed Theseus, and this clearly marks a reaction against the slender figures of the late fifth century.[16]

The remarks of these artists perhaps suggest the competition of rivals rather than the criticism of outsiders, and the fact that the advances made by Polygnotos, Agatharchos, Apollodoros, and Parrhasios can be read off on vases contemporary with them, and not only on vases which are supposedly special commissions, must mean that in fact this extraordinarily swift advance took the general run of Athenians with it. They certainly accepted painting and sculpture in the new style as performing its function as offering or memorial and affording pleasure to god or man. Our question is what new values did the new art imply and what did the critics say about it? It is natural for us to interpret the decoration of the Parthenon as a sermon on modesty and piety, and to invoke Pericles' description of his Athens as educating Greece to justify our opinion. Pheidias himself, we are told, said that his model for the Zeus at Olympia was a passage in the *Iliad* where Zeus nodded his assent and made great Olympos tremble. Zeus appears again in the east pediment, his son Apollo in the west pediment, and Herakles, also his son, in the metopes, so that the decoration of Olympia can also be interpreted as a sermon on Zeus and the rules by which he governs men, a very Aeschylean theme. A hundred years later Aristotle contrasts Polygnotos, who was probably slightly older than Pheidias, with Zeuxis, who was painting in the last quarter of the fifth century: 'Polygnotos was a good painter of *ethos*; Zeuxis' painting has no *ethos*.' *Ethos* in Aristotle means character and especially moral character, so that Aristotle found moral character in Polygnotos' painting and none in Zeuxis. This is not a bad description of the great solemn figures of Early Classical and Classical art, and we can credit the artists, like Aeschylus and Sophocles, with the desire to expound the ideals which they found in heroic mythology.[17]

Aristotle found this lacking in Zeuxis, and it is fair to interpret Euphranor as meaning that he found it lacking in Parrhasios

but had recaptured it himself. For the art of Zeuxis and Parrhasios, the art of the late fifth and earliest fourth century, we
have plenty of criticism in Xenophon and Plato. It does not
matter for our purposes whether the conversation which Xenophon describes ever took place or not. Socrates makes three
points in his discussion with Parrhasios. First, the painter imitates
the shape, lighting, and texture of things seen, getting their likeness with colours. Secondly, when painting an ideal figure the
painter may select features from many different models; here
Xenophon shows that he knows the story of Zeuxis using five
models for his Helen. Thirdly, Socrates maintains that the painter
can also represent moral qualities by the expressions and gestures
of his figures. Later art historians noted the beginning of varia-
tion in facial expression in Polygnotos and credited Parrhasios
with great subtlety in facial expression. Socrates thinks primarily
of moral qualities, but very often it was grief or pain that these
artists represented. Zeuxis painted a bound Marsyas and a
Menelaos bathed in tears, as he poured libations on his brother
Agamemnon's tomb; Parrhasios painted Prometheus, Philoctetes,
and Telephos, all in agony; but Xenophon is perhaps thinking of
his picture of the Athenian Demos, which showed contrasting
qualities of anger, violence, pride, and mildness, pity, self-abase-
ment. It has been suggested that this could have been done by
adopting the theatrical convention of the mask with different
expressions on the two sides of the face. The substitute for the
moral character which Aristotle found in Polygnotos' painting was
not only increased realism but realistic representation of
emotion.[18]

The art of Agatharchos, Zeuxis, and Parrhasios was the art
of Plato's youth, and his general position towards it is clear
from the *Republic*. He knows the technical terms and the procedures, and he rejects their products both on metaphysical and
on ethical grounds. What is real for Plato is the Idea, of which
the individual person or thing is a less real copy; the realistic
work of art is a copy of the individual person or thing; it is
therefore twice removed from metaphysical reality. The instance
which he chooses, a couch, 'whether one sees it from the side or
straight on or in whatever way', is, as we have seen, one of the

earliest things on which the Greek artist practises foreshortening, but it is possible also that Agatharchos painted Alkibiades' dining-room with couches and tables in perspective to make the room seem larger. In addition to producing appearances, which are only copies of copies of reality, painting appeals to an irrational part of the soul; reason applies a measuring rod to its seeming hollows and protuberances, and pronounces them flat. For Plato the irrational part of the soul is the emotional part. Plato does not here go on to attack the pictures of heroes in grief or pain, because he is only using illusionistic painting as an analogy to mimetic poetry, but what he says about emotional displays by the heroes of epic and tragedy leaves no doubt of his condemnation. And when he is discussing the education of the young soldiers the instruction to the craftsmen, who expressly include painters, to leave out from their works 'this immoral, unrestrained, unseemly element which ill becomes a free man', implies that he found plenty of it in emotional realism.[19]

It is a strange fact about late fifth-century art, which can be paralleled in drama by contrasting the decorative choruses and the realistic iambic scenes in Euripides, that Parrhasios painted a rose-fed Theseus as well as a pain-ridden Philoktetes and Zeuxis painted a rose-wreathed Eros as well as a tear-drenched Menelaos. This other decorative style we know from the vases of the Meidias painter and the reliefs of the Nike balustrade (*fig. 18*). The Meidias painter's Herakles (*fig. 20*) is thin and fine drawn, as is also the Herakles of the east pediment of the Hephaisteion. It is possible that this Herakles is inspired by Prodikos' Herakles, who chose the life of virtue instead of the life of pleasure, and that Sophocles produced Herakles like this at the end of the *Philoctetes*: 'I won immortal virtue, as you can see.' Such a Herakles, driving to Olympos with Athena, and the Hesperides, among whom he sits at ease on the Meidias painter's hydria, may well have been in Plato's mind when he wrote of the place beyond heaven in the *Phaedrus*, where the charioteer of the mortal soul catches a glimpse of Justice herself, Modesty herself, and Knowledge herself. This line of art is developed further by Praxiteles; and his smiling, young, detached figures of Aphrodite, Apollo, and Hermes are the nearest the artist can get to expressing the bliss, perfection (*fig. 4*), and detachment of the philosopher's god.[20]

The painting of the late fifth century (not Parrhasios, who was rooted in the Pheidian tradition and was an expert in plastic outlines) may have gone too far in the exploitation of colour at the expense of line. The Sikyonian painter Pamphilos, who belonged to the next generation and was probably painting from 390 onwards, switched the emphasis back to composition and outline; he is said to have introduced drawing into the schools in Sikyon and later into the rest of Greece. Sikyon became famous for good drawing, *chrestographia*. This had its influence both on the critics and on Euphranor. His art partly reflects the new clean composition of Pamphilos and partly, I think, Plato's criticism, since later art historians regarded him as the first to express the 'dignity of the heroes'. The beef-fed Theseus is an obvious example; he also made a statue of Hephaistos which did not show his lameness. And to judge from contemporary vases, this dignity was probably also achieved by increasing the scale of the figure in relation to the frame.[21]

In their turn the critics reacted more kindly to the new direction taken by the artists. In the *Republic* Plato is only concerned with the parallel between late fifth-century painting and realistic and emotional poetry, particularly tragedy. He may, however, have been aware of the emphasis on composition in Sikyonian painting by the time that he wrote the *Gorgias*; there we find the painter equated with the architect and the shipbuilder, in that he works with his eye on the form of what he is making and makes a composed and ordered whole, in which the parts are adapted to each other. This kind of criterion is never mentioned in the *Republic* but is found again in the works of Plato's later years, written after Euphranor's painting in the Stoa of Zeus, particularly the *Phaedrus* and the *Laws*. In the *Laws* Plato not only admits the pleasure which is aroused by works of art but lays down standards of criticism. The true critic must know first what the subject is; then he must know further the proportions and the composition and the colours and the shapes; then he can say whether it is beautiful, and beauty he defines in the *Philebus* as measure and proportions.[22]

Aristotle was in the Academy for the last twenty years of Plato's life, and the *Poetics* is both an answer to the literary criticism of the *Republic* and very closely connected with the literary criticism of the *Phaedrus*. So in Aristotle again we find an emphasis on organic composition and proportion, but he also introduces the new idea that there is a positive virtue in size, provided that it does not destroy the intelligibility of the picture, and here one is reminded of the large scale of the works connected with Euphranor. Aristotle, unlike Plato, finds a real value in *mimesis*; it is a fundamental and distinctive human activity and a valid first method of learning. The most accurate representations of subjects which in themselves are painful to look at give pleasure, the pleasure of recognition. If the viewer has not seen them before, the picture does not please him as a representation but because of its finish or its colour or some other reason. He introduces here yet another criterion, the painter's technique, and again he may be reacting to a contemporary development. Pausias, the pupil of Pamphilos, was a master of the comparatively new encaustic technique, the ancient equivalent of oils, and painted pictures of garlands with a great variety of flowers; he also painted Methe (the personification of intoxication) drinking out of a glass cup so that you could see her face through the cup. This is very much what Aristotle means by enjoying a picture because of its finish.[23]

Two other developments in Aristotle point forwards to the future—history of art and historical criticism. He certainly had in his mind a schematic history of art parallel to the history of literature. Polygnotos is compared to Sophocles as representing men better than ourselves, Zeuxis to new tragedy as having no ethos, and Pauson to the poets of Old Comedy as representing men worse than ourselves. In the beginning of the chapter on Problems and Solutions Aristotle says: 'As the poet uses *mimesis* like the painter and the sculptor, the subject of his *mimesis* must be one of three things; (1) the sort of thing that was or is, (2) the sort of thing that is reported or thought to have been, (3) the sort of thing that ought to be.' From the instances that he gives in poetry it is clear that he is opening the door to historical criticism, explaining Homer by the usage of Homer's time

161

as attested by survivals outside Greek lands, and the opening
sentence implies the same sort of criticism for the visual arts.
Thus at the very end of our period we can see the beginning of
Hellenistic scholarship in art history.[24]

9 *Poets and their Patrons*

Poetry has been mentioned continually in the course of this book: poetry read and sung at school, poetry recited and sung at the symposion, poetry sung and danced in cult, poetry sung and danced or only sung at the contests which accompanied the greater religious festivals, verses inscribed on dedications and on works of art. The same characteristics appear as appeared from our discussion of Athenian art—an enormous range from the humble versifier to the great poet, an audience, whether of readers or of listeners, ready to follow the latest developments, and the gradual development of criticism. But for a great deal of Greek poetry we have to add as intermediaries between the poet and the public the performers, the singers at the symposion, the choruses at the religious festivals, the reciters, soloists, choruses, and actors at the contests. At the City Dionysia every March each of the ten tribes entered in the contest of dithyrambs a chorus of fifty men and a chorus of fifty boys, each with its poet and flute-players; the three tragic poets each had three actors, a chorus of fifteen men and a flute-player; and the five comic poets each had three actors, a chorus of twenty-four and a flute-player, so that at every City Dionysia there were 1,200 performers. It follows that in every Athenian audience the number of spectators who had themselves performed was extremely high.[1]

Inscribed poetry, which was not written for speaking or singing, may be taken first, then the spoken poetry of epic, then the sung poetry of the symposion, the victor-odes, the religious

POETS AND THEIR PATRONS

festivals and contests; the mixed spoken and sung poetry of
tragedy and comedy is so important for our subject that it must
be reserved for the succeeding two chapters. I quoted in the last
chapter the proud verses which the painters, Apollodoros, Zeuxis,
and Parrhasios wrote on their pictures; there is no reason to
suppose that they did not compose them themselves. In the
sixth century the potter-painter Exekias signed a vase with an
iambic trimeter: 'Exekias was painter and my potter too.' But
the elegiac couplet stating that Polygnotos painted at his own
expense the temples of the gods and the Agora in Athens is
inscribed to Melanthios, who, like the philosopher Archelaos,
wrote poems to Kimon; it was not an inscribed poem but possibly a symposion poem. The majority of inscribed poems are
either dedications or epitaphs; I quote a very few to show the
manner. The potters Mnesiades and Andokides had the base of a
bronze statue inscribed with a single hexameter: 'Mnesiades the
potter and Andokides dedicated me.' The rest are all in elegiac
couplets. Soon after the Persian wars an Ionian Hegelochos
dedicated a statue by Kritios and Nesiotes, the sculptors who
made the group of the Tyrant-slayers in the Agora:

To the Maid, Ekphantos' father and son me dedicated,
    to Athena here, in memory of war's toils,
Hegelochos. Great share in hospitality
    and virtue has he, dwelling in this town.

An epitaph of the end of the sixth century praises that modesty
(sophrosyne), which as we saw, was later the message of the
Parthenon:

At the tomb of Antilochos, a brave and modest man,
    stranger, making offering. Death waits you too.

The public memorial for the Athenians who fell besieging
Poteidaia in the north in 432 is interesting because it expresses
the philosophical theory that the souls of the dead return to the
Upper Air:

The Air received the souls of these and Earth their bodies,
sundered at the gates of Poteidaia.
Their foes, some lie now in their graves, but others fled
and found in walls their surest hope of life.

These are a few samples of a large mass of verse, very varied in quality but always enlightening.[2]

Spoken poetry as distinct from sung poetry and drama is primarily epic. We have noted the use of epic and didactic poetry in education and the enormous reverence of the Athenian aristocrat for Homer. This was renewed every four years by the recitation of the *Iliad* and *Odyssey* by relays of rhapsodes at the Panathenaia. We have noted also the popularity of a new epic poem about Theseus, probably inspired and promoted by Kleisthenes and his family. This again we must assume was recited by rhapsodes at some festival, but we do not know what festival. The one certain picture of a rhapsode, on a vase of about 480, has the words 'So once in Tiryns' coming out of his mouth, so that the poem was probably an epic of Herakles, but again we do not know the festival. Later in the Hellenistic age rhapsodes are recorded as performing at many local festivals, and the same was probably true of our period. We know most about Ion of Ephesos, whom Plato records as having met Socrates when Ion came to Athens to compete at the Panathenaia in the latter part of the fifth century. Ion is a specialist in Homer and claims to be able not only to recite him but also to lecture on him, better than any of the other authorities. Unfortunately we are not told anything about his lectures, and the rest of the dialogue leads us to suspect that they were eulogies rather than criticism, but it does emerge from Socrates' questions that Hesiod and, less expectedly, Archolochos were also recited by rhapsodes in the fifth century. What we do get, however, and this is more important, is a picture of the engaged artist and the engaged audience. Ion says that when he has to speak anything like Andromache's lament for Hektor, his eyes are filled with tears, and when he has to recite some frightening episode like Odysseus shooting the suitors or Achilles attacking Hektor, his hair stands on end with fear and his heart leaps. And he knows that he has the same effect on the audience:

'I look down from the platform and see them weeping or with fear in their eyes and joining in the thrill of the recital.' Epic was traditional and much of it very old, but by the schools and the rhapsodes it was kept continually alive.[3]

A good deal of the poetry sung in the symposion was songs or extracts from the great lyric poets of the archaic and classical period; Alkaios, Stesichoros, Anakreon, Simonides are all known to have been sung at Athenian symposia in the fifth century. They were good old songs, probably some of them learnt in school and some of them handed down from symposion to symposion. The anonymous Attic drinking songs called *skolia* date from the late sixth to the early fifth century; they were short, usually quatrains in some fairly easy lyric metre, often political and representing the views of some great Athenian family; the song about tyrant-slayers Harmodios and Aristogeiton became something like a national anthem. The symposion tradition did not in any way prevent the introduction of new material, such as songs from Aeschylus or even speeches from Euripides, and a few new symposion songs can be quoted from the fifth century.[4]

Four poets are connected with Kimon, and what they wrote in praise of him was probably intended for the symposion. I have mentioned already Melanthios and Archelaos. The elegiac couplet which Melanthios wrote about Polygnotos may have come from a symposion poem. None of Archelaos' poetry survived, but Plutarch says that he did write poetry in praise of Kimon; he was a philosopher and is said to have taught Socrates while Socrates was still young, presumably in the late fifties. He is the rather fascinating figure of a philosopher who is also a poet and mixes with statesmen. Ion of Chios is another, a philosopher, a writer of prose 'Visits' (both his own visits abroad and the visits of foreigners to Chios) from which much of our knowledge of fifth-century personalities is derived, particularly of Themistokles, Kimon, Pericles, and Sophocles, and a writer of dithyrambs, tragedies, and symposion poetry. He disliked the boasting of Themistokles and the haughtiness and pride of Pericles, and he liked the easy grace of Kimon; Sophocles had the same easy grace; he was 'like one of the Athenian nobles'. Kimon probably brought Ion to Athens, and he stayed there for long periods before his death in 422. One of his symposion songs was, it has been suggested, sung in the joint camp of Kimon and Archidamos of Sparta when the Athenians went to help the Spartans in 463; it is in the traditional elegiac couplets and after the initial mention of the Spartan king's ancestors gives a good description of a symposion:

> All hail, our king, our saviour and our father,
>   For us the slaves who pour the wine must mix
> the mixing-bowl with silver pitchers, and another
>   set a great golden jar upon the floor.
> Pour solemn libation to Herakles, to Alkmene,
>   to Prokles, Persëids; from Zeus begin,
> let's drink, let's sport, let loose the singing through the night,
>   the dancing; and goodwill lead on the cheer.
> Whoever has a fair-faced girl to lie beside,
>   will drink more gloriously than all the rest.

The fourth poet is Sophocles, whom Kimon helped to his first tragic victory in 468. He only belongs here because he wrote an ode to the historian Herodotos in 442 and in another mentioned Archelaos, again a sign of the permeability of Athenian society. There are later elegiac poems, for instance by Kritias, which were composed for the symposion, but they do not add much to the picture. More interesting, partly as training for and partly as a reflection of the choral poetry to which we must now turn, is the continued practice of singing the great lyric poets in the symposion.[5]

The odes which were sung to celebrate the victories of athletes at the great international games deserve mention, although only four examples survive of odes which were written for Athenian victors. There must have been many more, but they are lost and their poets are unknown. We also do not know whether athletic victories at the Panathenaia and other Athenian festivals were celebrated in specially written victor-odes; certainly victories at the Panathenaia were sufficiently important to be mentioned in the victor-odes written for non-Athenians who had also won victories at the international games. Winning a victory at the Olympic games, the Pythian games, the Nemean games, or the

Isthmian games was a great event. It was celebrated by a choral ode sung at the site of the games and another usually longer choral ode sung at home, either at the victor's house or at a local shrine. The victor was afterwards given free meals in the city hall for his life. The choruses who sang the odes were the compatriots of the victor, and the song at the site of the games was presumably sung by the party who went to support the victor; the friends and supporters of the athlete could cope at short notice with the rhythms of Pindaric odes, which make us blench. The metre, and therefore the dance, of choral lyric at this time falls into two classes; one, called dactylo-epitrite, is on the whole smooth and regular, because it is made up out of standard units, which are linked together by a bridge syllable. The other is rougher and much less regular, because its units are much more varied and long syllables are left in juxtaposition without any link. It seems to have been the convention that whichever of these two classes was chosen for the song at the site, the other was chosen for the song at home.[6]

The earliest of the three victor-odes for Athenians is Pindar's Seventh *Pythian*, which was written to be sung in Delphi for the Alkmaionid Megakles, who won the chariot race in 486. It is in a difficult variety of the second class of metre but is very short and merely refers to the greatness of Athens, the Alkmaionid rebuilding of the temple of Apollo, the other victories won by the family, and ends with a tactful reference to Megakles' ostracism: 'I rejoice at your new success, but I am grieved at the envy which rewards fair deeds.' In the next year Pindar wrote a processional of five simple stanzas to celebrate the victory of Timodemos of Acharnai at Nemea (*Nemean II*): it prophesies a great future for him because his family has won many victories, and welcomes him home. Bacchylides' tenth victory-ode was written in dactylo-epitrites for an Athenian who had won a double victory at the Isthmian games; it again is quite short and describes the victory and lists the athlete's other victories, and was probably sung at the site. The fourth and latest is only a fragment, but the Olympian victor was Alkibiades and the poet was said to be Euripides. None of these is typical. They do not have the heroic myth told in brilliant style, which is the common feature of the longer victor-odes and associates the present victor with the Mycenaean past, nor the moral, which emphasises the duties as well as the privileges of aristocratic birth and the gleam of glory illuminating a victory. We have spoken of the palaistra in the late sixth century at Athens where Phayllos of Kroton trained, and we have noted that the conservative politician Thucydides was the son of the Athenian trainer Melesias. Athenian trainers are mentioned in four of Pindar's odes written for athletes from Aigina. In 483 a pankratiast is told that he has won a sweet reward for the labours of Menandros: 'the builder of athletes should be from Athens'. The other three references are to Melesias, and come in odes to wrestlers. In the two *Nemean* odes, written just before and after 480, the praise of Melesias comes in the last verse and is unshadowed: 'quick as a dolphin in the sea I would call Melesias, who held the reins of strength and hands'. But in the later *Olympian VIII*, which was written in 460, Melesias is introduced after the myth in the third verse with an apology: 'If I repeat in my song the glory that Melesias wins from the young, let envy not hit me with a jagged rock.' Envy is the word that Pindar had used to allude to the ostracism of the Athenian Megakles; here again it is political ill-will, the ill-will which Pindar may get for praising an Athenian in a song sung for an Aeginetan victor at a time when with Kimon's ostracism the new democratic Athenian policy was menacing Aigina. Melesias was now an old man and this was his thirtieth success. He deserved the praise, and it was perhaps easier to give in a song sung at Olympia, not at Aigina. These songs show something of the international society of athletes in the early fifth century, and in Pindar their code is formulated.[7]

Except for the dithyrambs, sung in honour of Dionysos, we know very little about the very large number of songs that were sung and danced by men and women at religious festivals in Attica. On the analogy of Boeotia, where we have songs written by Pindar for very varied religious occasions down to small family celebrations, they did not differ metrically and therefore were sung and danced the same way as the victor-odes. This again is evidence of the amount of musical education that the normal

Athenian, man or woman, girl or boy, managed to pick up. We know rather more about dithyrambs, but the subject has to be approached with a certain caution because the name seems to have been used as a general term for any narrative chorus, and there may also have been great variations between dithyrambs sung in Athens at the Panathenaia, City Dionysia, and Thargelia. The name may also have been given to the choruses sung in honour of Dionysos at the Anthesteria and Lenaia and to the choruses in the great Procession at the City Dionysia. The annual production must have been very considerable, since at the City Dionysia alone each of the ten tribes entered both a chorus of men and a chorus of boys for the festival. As all the twenty choruses performed in a single day, the individual dithyrambs cannot have been very long. It is therefore tempting to suppose that Bacchylides 19, which is headed 'for the Athenians' and consists of a single triad of strophe, antistrophe, and epode, of about twenty-five singing lines (the end is corrupt) was written for the City Dionysia competition. It is in a very smooth periodic metre, and traces surprisingly the birth of Dionysos from Io. Bacchylides 18 has four stanzas, each of eight singing lines, describing the arrival of Theseus from Troizene; the chorus impersonate his father Aigeus in the even stanzas and someone else, probably Aigeus' wife Medeia, in the odd stanzas (this impersonation is unique); as Theseus founded the Thargelia, it has been suggested that the Thargelia was the occasion. Pindar's two dithyrambs written for the Athenians are very different from these and from each other, though both are written in periodic metre of a much rougher kind than Bacchylides. One is an appeal to the Olympian gods to come to the Athenian Agora and hear his spring song to Dionysos and Semele; this must have been sung in the Agora, and this excludes the tribal dithyrambs of the City Dionysia because they were sung in the theatre; the other praises Athens for her part in the Persian wars; both are fragments so that nothing can be said about the length of the poems.[8]

About 450 Melanippides of Melos wrote a dithyramb on the story of Marsyas. It has been suggested that the group of Athena and Marsyas on the Akropolis by the sculptor Myron was erected in honour of Melanippides' success, and as the story of Marsyas suddenly appears on a number of vases from this time on, some special occasion is needed. Marsyas was a satyr who picked up the flute when Athena threw it away and challenged Apollo to a contest of music; Apollo won the contest and in one version of the story, which Melanippides probably adopted, Marsyas took up the lyre instead of the flute. The subject would be appropriate for a dithyramb at the Thargelia, which was a festival of Apollo. Melanippides was the precursor of a musical revolution which ran through the later fifth century: this consisted partly in an increase in the number of notes or tones that the lyre could play and partly in writing preludes which were free of strophic correspondence, the beginning of the new free metric and music. Melanippides represented this in the Marsyas dithyramb as the conquest of the flute by the lyre. A very similar theme is found in a song which I believe to have been a dithyramb sung by men dressed as satyrs carrying lyres at the Lesser Panathenaia about 425: 'the Muse has made song the queen. Let the flute dance behind. It is only a servant.' 'Song' here is the song which they sing to their own lyres; the flute is the official accompanist to the dithyramb. The vocal proponents of the new music are lyre-players and therefore say that the lyre is defeating the flute, but it might be truer to say that the lyre was copying the flute, as professional flute-players came more and more into prominence in the fifth century and on into the fourth. An early blow against the new music was struck by Sophocles, who produced his *Thamyras* before 450. Thamyras was a legendary lyre-player, who challenged the Muses to a contest of song. Sophocles evidently contrasted the wild emotional music of Thamyras with the sober music of the Muses, and Thamyras was struck blind for his presumption and broke his lyre. Melanippides was probably active as early as 480, so that at the very least one must say that Sophocles coloured his *Thamyras* with the new music: it is noticeable that Sophocles, unlike Euripides, never abandons strophic correspondence even when his actors sing laments.[9]

The one later figure in this line of whom we can form some opinion is Timotheos of Miletos, who was born about 450 and lived till at least 360. He was greeted with great hostility when he first arrived in Athens, but with the encouragement of Euripides defeated the older Phrynis, who was the successor of Melanippides, at the Panathenaia between 420 and 415 with a solo lyric to the lyre called *Persae*, of which a considerable part survives. He certainly regarded himself as a revolutionary:

> *I do not sing the old.*
> *My new songs are better.*
> *New the Zeus who reigns.*
> *Of old Kronos was king.*
> *Away with the old Muse.*

He developed further the two characteristics of Melanippides. He was the first person to use a twelve-string lyre, and he went much further in free verse. Melanippides had introduced long preludes to his dithyrambs before he began the balanced pairs of strophes and antistrophes, but the *Persae* has free verse all the way through. In our only fragments of Melanippides the metre is fairly regular dactylo-epitrite, but in the *Persae*, though the metre is predominantly iambic, the iambics are of very varied lengths and have insertions of many other rhythms. It may be that he was freer in writing solos than in writing choral poetry like dithyrambs, but on the whole in Greek lyric poetry the metric of solo and choral poetry seems to advance side by side. He matches his music and metre with an extremely bold use of language, ranging from vivid imagery to the realism of broken Greek when a Phrygian addresses his Greek captor. Contrast his description of sailors shot down by arrows:

> *Many a life they sacrificed,*
> *long-winged, bronze-faced, string-stretched.*
> *Furrow of emerald-tressed sea*
> *was reddened by naval dew,*
> *and shouts and groans held all.*

and the capture of the tongue-tied Phrygian:

> *When a captor led*
> *a dweller of rich-fleeced Kelainai,*
> *bereft of battles,*
> *iron-bladed Greek*

leads by a grasp on his hair,
weaving hands about his knees,
he begged, inweaving Greece with Asian speech,
breaking the clear seal of his mouth,
tracking Ionian tongue:
'To say to me, to you, how and what?
I'll never come again.
And now my master
led me hither here.
But never again, father,
I'll never come here again to fight,
but I'll sit still.
I to you hither, I
thither by Sardis, by Sousa,
Ekbatana dwelling.
Artemis, my great god,
by Ephesos shall guard.'[10]

The battle of Salamis which Timotheos describes was a great Athenian victory, and his patriotic subject, coupled with the fact that the Spartans had expelled him on the ground that 'new songs dishonoured the ancient Muse', may have helped to secure his success at the Panathenaia. But however skilful Athenian choruses were in adapting themselves to the new music, both the style and the music were criticised. Our two chief sources for this criticism are comedy and Plato, but if it is right to see an early reaction to Melanippides in Sophocles' *Thamyras*, it is earlier than either. Comedy is evidence of the interest of the mass of the Athenian public in the new music, but this is really not surprising since the same audience at the City Dionysia had watched the dithyrambs the day before they saw the first comedy produced at the festival, and a thousand of them had sung and danced in those dithyrambs. The whole history— Melanippides, Kinesias, Phrynis, Timotheos, Philoxenos—is given in a fragment of a comedy by Pherekrates called *Cheiron*. Cheiron was the wise Centaur who taught Achilles and Jason, so that moral education is a theme to be expected, and the new music is relevant, if only because half the dithyrambic choruses were composed of boys under eighteen. The fragment is a dialogue between two female figures, Justice and Poetry (or Music? Both names are used in introducing the fragment, which shows how closely they were connected in the Greek mind.) Poetry has been beaten up, and Justice wants to know the reason. The successive musicians with their twists and turns and modulations have taken all the stiffness out of her. Presumably Justice proposes punishment for the musicians and perhaps a more disciplined music for Poetry.[11]

Of the musicians Phrynis is named in Aristophanes' *Clouds* in 423. In the Old Education they were taught the ancestral strict music and beaten 'if they twisted any twist, the ugly twists of Phrynis' style they sing today'. This must have been shortly before Phrynis' defeat by Timotheos, when he had been known in Athens for more than twenty years. A Paestan vase of the mid-fourth century shows a scene from a comedy with the Athenian general Myronides dragging a frightened Phrynis off to punishment. The comedy must have been produced in Athens about a hundred years before; the scene showed military objection to the new 'undisciplined' music, and the theme was sufficiently universal to be revived a century later in South Italy. In the *Peace*, produced in 421, Aristophanes' hero sees on his way to heaven 'two or three souls of dithyrambic poets flying around, collecting some aerybreezeswimming preludes'. The monstrous adjective parodies the poetic style, and 'preludes' is a keyword for the new formlessness. And in 414, in the *Birds*, Kinesias, who is one of the mishandlers of Poetry in Pherekrates' list, demands wings in Cloudcuckooland so that he may 'fly up and get new airstruck and snowthrowing preludes from the clouds', and he claims that the tribes compete hotly for his services as a poet. The *Birds* also has a very beautiful adaptation of the new metric in the hoopoe's call, in which the different kinds of birds are summoned in different metres.[12]

In the *Republic* Plato passes in his discussion of educating the young soldiers from literature to music, and demands that there should be two harmonies, one 'imitating' the sounds of the brave man and one the sounds of temperate man; the flute is to be excluded as having the maximum number of tones; the lyre is kept, and thus the instruments of Apollo are preferred to the instruments of Marsyas. The criticism of Melanippides and his successors is clear. Then he goes on to rhythms, and says that he will leave Damon to decide what are the rhythms that belong to meanness and violence and madness and what to their opposites, and the section ends with the saying that 'good subject matter and good harmony and good rhythm accompany goodness of character'. The reverse naturally also follows, and Plato would regard the new music as born of and producing madness. It is tempting to connect the whole theory and not only the classification of rhythms with Damon, and twenty pages later he is mentioned again : 'a new form of music must be adopted with supreme caution as it endangers the whole state. For the forms of music are not changed without changing the laws and customs of the whole state, as Damon says and I believe ... this sort of lawlessness slips unnoticed into people's minds.' Other quotations from Damon agree and add a little; 'by singing and playing the lyre a boy strengthens not only courage and modesty but also justice', 'the sounds of continuous song mould new character in boys and adults', 'good song and dance make free and noble souls, and the opposite the reverse'. The image of 'moulding' in the second quotation takes us back to the Old Education in the *Clouds*, where the boys who are having the traditional education and avoiding the 'twists of Phrynis' are 'moulding a statue of Respect'. In the *Clouds* also Socrates shows knowledge of Damon's technical terminology for rhythms. Thus the theory that music is character-forming, and that musical education must be designed to mould the kind of citizen that is desired, goes back behind Plato to at least 423 and is part of the criticism of the new music.[13]

This much is firm ground. If we try to get further, the ground becomes extremely treacherous. Damon's father, Damonides, persuaded Pericles to introduce jury pay to counter the riches of Kimon, and was later ostracised; Damon was ostracised. Father and son both ostracised? Damon was taught by Pindar's teacher, and was a friend of Prodikos; he must have lived a very long time? Damon appeared in comedy as the wise Centaur who taught Pericles, but he put forward his theories in a speech to the Areiopagos, which Pericles had robbed of its powers. Probably it is impossible to reconcile all this now. Plato certainly conceived of Damon as living until at least 420, and this is compatible with his being born about 500, older than Pericles and old enough to be taught by Pindar's teacher. With such teaching he would naturally hate the new music, and he may even have made a speech to the Areiopagos before their curtailment by Pericles. His views would not necessarily be repugnant to Pericles, since they were aimed at instilling through music the same virtues that Pheidias was propounding through sculpture; on these civic needs Kimon and Pericles were not at variance, but politically when the split came father and son, Damonides and Damon, went with Pericles. This probably means that the son Damon was ostracised about 432 in the period of Pericles' unpopularity. This would not prevent the conservative political tract alluding to him when saying that the demos has destroyed music; he was a conservative musician even if he was ostracised as the friend of Pericles. Much of this is uncertain; what is important is to establish a line of conservative musical-educational criticism which runs from Pindar's teacher to Plato. With Plato it becomes a rigid censorship of music and poetry; it was left to the more realistic Aristotle to point out the therapeutic effects of wild music and to extend this observation to tragedy.[14]

One point in Plato's theory might have been fruitfully developed but apparently was not. Where Damon was interested in the effect of music, Plato held in addition that the moral character of music and poetry reflected the moral character of its author. Aristotle followed this up a little way when he said that after Homer poetry was divided according to the moral character of the poets; the more serious poets wrote first hymns and then tragedy and the more frivolous poets wrote first satire and then comedy. The whole question of the relationship of the product to the mind of the producer, which has bulked so large in modern literary criticism, was hardly explored, although Plato had provided the formula. The one problem connected with the personality of the poet which was live in the fifth century but had been reduced to a formula in the fourth was the question whether the poet worked by inspiration, genius, or craftsmanship. The theory that the poet was inspired by the Muse is very old, and Socrates only uses it in the *Apology* and *Ion* as a means of arriving at his desired conclusion that the poets have no knowledge about what they write; they are under the influence of inspiration. Demokritos, however, managed to unite inspiration and craftsmanship: 'Homer's divinely inspired genius carpentered a universe of widely ranging verses.' More commonly the untidy stormy genius is contrasted with the conscious, careful craftsman. One of the sayings of Sophocles shows that he felt this distinction between himself and Aeschylus: 'even if he does what is right, he does not know it'. And the association of actors and chorusmen which he formed is a sign of his conscious craftsmanship. At the end of the fifth century this contrast shows up again very clearly in the portraits of Aeschylus as a genius and Euripides as a craftsman which Aristophanes draws in the *Frogs.*[15]

If the poet is a craftsman, his works need the same kind of technical study and terminology as artefacts. So in the fifth century we find Damon discussing metrical quantity and giving names to different metres, and in the territory where poetry overlaps with rhetoric, Protagoras discussing morphology and syntax, and Prodikos the precise meanings of words, and in the *Frogs* a considerable technical terminology for drama. That, however, and its subsequent development in the fourth century must be reserved for the next chapter.[16]

Criticism of Homer started, as we have seen, with Xenophanes, who complained that Homer and Hesiod attributed every kind of mortal transgression to the gods. Defence of Homer was sometimes made in terms of allegory. In the fifth century Homeric texts also came in for discussion by the sophists who were interested in language or meaning, while the moral criticism started by Xenophanes was continued by those who were concerned with theology. Nonetheless Homer dominated the schools, and Nikias prepared his son for life by making him learn the *Iliad* and the *Odyssey* off by heart. The rhapsode Ion's account of the emotional effects of Homer on his audience suggests that the fifth-century rhapsode may have learnt a new emotional technique from the tragic actor. So for Plato in the early fourth century Homer has no knowledge because he operates by inspiration from the Muses, his gods are open to all the objections raised by Xenophanes, his heroes give way to unworthy displays of emotion which corrupt the young, and the epic, like drama and like painting, is only the copy of a copy of a copy. Aristotle restores epic, like drama, to its proper place as a beneficial force in society. His criticism is so obviously constructed as a parallel to his criticism of drama that the details are better left to the next chapter. The differences are length, diffuseness, primacy of narrative, metre, absence of music, dance, and spectacle, so that epic is a kind of slow-motion tragedy. He had also collected all the detailed objections to Homer, and explained them sometimes by local usage, sometimes by obsolete practice, sometimes by dialect, punctuation, accentuation, or by poetic use of language, so that we come with him to the beginning of modern commentaries.[17]

10 *Tragic Poets, Actors and Audiences*

Tragedy was produced in Athens itself at the Lenaia in January and at the City Dionysia in March. We know very little about tragedy at the Lenaia, and it is probable that it was only introduced about 440. If this is so, it is an indication of the increasing popularity of tragedy in the later fifth century. The increase continued: the demes began to build their own theatres, and tragedy was produced there at the Rural Dionysia in December; these were probably usually revivals of plays already produced in Athens. Plato in the early fourth century speaks of people running round to the different Dionysia to hear all the plays. We must, however, confine ourselves to the City Dionysia because only the plays produced there have survived.[1]

As our problem is the relation of society and culture, we have three main questions to which we have to try and find answers: first, who were the audiences and did they have any influence on the poets? And we should at the same time consider whether any of the officials involved in production had any influence on the poets. Secondly, what did the poets provide for society? And thirdly, what did the most articulate of the critics think about tragedy?

For the seating capacity of the theatre we have two wildly different estimates. Modern scholars assess it at 14,000, and Plato speaks of more than 30,000. Plato seems to be giving a round figure for the total citizen population, and we must therefore accept and interpret the smaller figure. It will be remembered that an allowance of a third of a drachma, called the *theorikon*, was made to Athenian citizens to allow them to attend the theatre, and Aristotle in one of his less sympathetic passages says that spectators are of two kinds, the free and educated, and the vulgar, composed of artisans and *thetes* (the lowest property class) and such like. This proves that the poorer citizens did take up their tickets, but on the other hand a number of texts show that the audience was not restricted to adult male citizens, although in their full numbers they would have filled a theatre of vastly larger size. Plato speaks of boys, women, and slaves among the audience; the appeal for applause at the end of Menander's plays includes boys and striplings, as well as men and old men, and two passages of Aristophanes imply the presence of women. The solution may be that the boys, women, and slaves used seats that had not been taken up by citizens. This is suggested by two passages in Theophrastos' *Characters*, probably referring to the late fourth century: in one an Athenian buys seats for foreigners, including a seat for himself in the price that he charges them, and on the next day sends his sons and their slave-tutor; in the other an Athenian waits until the seats are declared free by the managers and then takes his sons. Nevertheless, even if we suppose that a considerable proportion of the rich, the 1,000 of the top two property classes, bought extra seats for wives, mistresses, children, slaves, probably something like 12,000 seats were available for the rest.[2]

The numerous references, quotations, parodies, and criticisms of tragedy in the plays of the comic poets suggest that the audiences of tragedy were interested and engaged, and a number of stories bear this out. In 468, the first production of Sophocles, the audience was so engaged that the archon asked Kimon and his board of generals to act as judges (cf. below). In 467, when the messenger in Aeschylus' *Seven against Thebes* described the courage and wisdom of Amphiaraos, all looked at the Athenian statesman Aristeides. Two defeats of outstanding plays may perhaps be ascribed to audience participation, although this is not recorded. Euripides' *Trojan* trilogy with its fierce denunciation of the Greek heroes of the Trojan War as aggressors was produced in March 415, when the Athenians had just completed a peculiarly brutal operation against the island of Melos, and when they were planning the major aggressive expedition against Sicily, which was to sail that July. It is hard to regard the defeat of Euripides as other than political. The case of the defeat of Sophocles' *Oedipus Tyrannus* is more doubtful, but it is possible that the ancient audience saw in the plague and the demand to expel the murderer and in the quick-wittedness of Oidipous himself an allusion to Pericles in the first two years of the Peloponnesian war, and that Sophocles was caught by the resurgence of Pericles' popularity at the time of the play's production. Elaborate precautions were taken to ensure that the judges were not bribed in advance, and the five decisive votes were drawn by lot from the ten votes which they cast, but Plato at any rate is quite clear that they were swayed by the applause of the audience. In this sense the audience could influence the poet. He knew that they were engaged and would demonstrate their engagement.[3]

Soon after he took office at the end of June, the archon, the chief civil magistrate, who gave his name to the year, chose the three rich men (choregoi) to produce the choruses for the three tragic poets, whom he also chose, for the next Dionysia. What the poet showed to the archon we do not know; perhaps it was the prologue and a synopsis of the play. But the archon had a choice. We never hear of Aeschylus or Euripides being refused, but an archon once gave a production to a little-known tragedian called Gnesippos in preference to Sophocles. The date was sometime before 430, and we should dearly like to know the reason why. In 468 the archon had chosen Aeschylus, Sophocles, and an unknown as poets; tension was high, Aeschylus was committed to Pericles, and Sophocles, who was making his first appearance, was committed to Kimon, who had just returned with Theseus' bones from Skyros: the archon must have known perfectly well what the result would be, when he substituted Kimon and his generals for the usual judges. The three other cases where archon or choregos (or perhaps it would be truer to say archon and choregos) seem to have been specially concerned are the three unique cases where the poet dramatised a contemporary subject instead of a legendary subject: it is highly probable that Themistokles was archon when Phrynichos produced the *Capture of Miletos* in 492, and was choregos when Phrynichos produced the

Phoinissai (on the Persian War) in 476, and Pericles was choregos when Aeschylus produced the *Persians* in 472. All three plays favoured Themistokles' foreign policy, and Pericles was his political successor. What the choregos could do was to secure the best possible chorus and flute-player, to train them extensively and to dress them lavishly; he seems also to have been responsible for the mute attendants who accompanied the actors playing royal parts. All this contributed to the success of the play. Success was a good advertisement for him, which might, as we have seen, help him in public life and in the law-courts. The vast majority of Greek tragedies were non-political, or only political in the broadest sense, but in the instances that we have quoted (and still more for Euripides' Trojan trilogy) a politically sympathetic archon and choregos was highly desirable. It must always be remembered that this was a small open society and political sympathies were well known.[4]

Like other ancient professions, the profession of writing tragedies ran in families. Aeschylus had a son Euphorion, who was a tragic poet, and a son Euaion, who may have been a tragic poet and was almost certainly a tragic actor. Aeschylus' sister had a son Philokles; his son was Morsimos, who was the father of the elder Astydamas, and he in turn was the father of the younger Astydamas; they were all tragic poets and carry the line of Aeschylus down to the time of Aristotle. Sophocles had a son Iophon, who was a tragic poet, and a grandson Sophocles, who carried the art on into the fourth century. Euripides had a son who was a tragic actor and a son who was a tragic poet, and at least three other families of poets could be mentioned.[5]

Let us look for a moment at the actors. Originally the poet acted in his own plays and engaged his assistants. The poet was the actor, and so it is natural to find the sons of poets becoming actors. From about 450 acting became a profession, and actors became more and more professional in the fourth century. At the beginning when Sophocles made his association in honour of the Muses and when Euaion, son of Aeschylus, was acting for him, there can have been no social distinction between the poet and the actor. And in the fourth century the actor had his own prominence. Because they acted in the festivals of Dionysos, they were privileged persons and were granted freedom of travel and immunity from hostile action. These privileges were guaranteed by Delphi, probably from the early fourth century, and we find Athenian actors, both tragic and comic, negotiating Athenian business with Philip and Alexander of Macedon. The status of actors is a reminder that Greek drama was not commercial entertainment but a religious occasion, and the poets too must always have been conscious of this.[6]

Aeschylus was born at Eleusis in 525, and his family was noble. He fought in the Persian War at Marathon, Salamis, and Plataea. He visited Hiero, the tyrant of Syracuse in 470, and produced his *Persians* a second time there and also wrote a new play to celebrate the foundation of Hiero's new city of Aitna. He went to Sicily again after the production of the *Oresteia* in 458 and died there in 456. There is little enough information, but at least it tells us that he fought as a patriotic Athenian, and that he was towards the end of his life open to new influences from the West. Two other facts which give us an important clue have already been noted; Pericles was choregos when he produced the *Persians* in Athens in 472, and he was defeated by the young Sophocles when Kimon and his generals adjudged the competition in 468. We are concerned here not so much with the development of drama as an art form, which has been briefly sketched above, but with the impact of Aeschylean drama on the large audiences; that he used all the resources of masks, costumes, stage-machinery, music, dance, and language to 'knock his audience out' is well attested, but what was he trying to achieve?[7]

Primarily the *Iliad* and the *Odyssey*, which the Athenians heard recited at the Panathenaia, are straight human stories; the gods are there, they intervene, everything happens according to Zeus' plan, but what one remembers and what surely the Athenian audience remembered is the story of Achilles, Agamemnon, and Hektor or of Odysseus, Penelope, and the suitors, rather than either divine government or psychological motivation. Now that we know a little more about Stesichoros, the Western lyric poet who wrote in the first half of the sixth century and was well known in Athens, we can say that the narrative of sixth-century choral lyric as narrative differed very little from epic. His Herakles is a glorious strong man who steals Geryon's cattle without a question. But Pindar, who was seven years younger than Aeschylus, was worried by Herakles' violence and wrote a whole poem to justify it, the justification apparently being that Herakles finally ended up on Olympos. The important point is that the Persian War generation feels the need to justify its heroes and its gods.[8]

Aeschylus' earliest surviving play, the *Persians*, is perhaps easier for us to understand because it is not on a mythical theme. It was brilliant but not new to set the scene in Persia and have no Greek among the characters; Phrynichos had already done this in the *Phoinissai*. The Greeks are sufficiently praised in the dialogue with the Persian queen: 'No man's slave or subject are they', and in the messenger speech of the defeat at Salamis and the prophecy of the defeat at Plataea. Twice Aeschylus alludes to Themistokles: Athenian wealth depends on the silver at Laureion (and Themistokles had persuaded the Athenians to use a lucky strike to build warships), and Xerxes was tricked into fighting at Salamis by a Greek message (which had been sent by Themistokles). Twice also he alludes to Aristeides, Themistokles' partner in setting up the league of Greek states which became the Athenian empire; a minor action on the island of Psyttaleia, which was conducted by Aristeides, is given a whole section of the Salamis messenger speech, and the account of Dareios' acquisitions in the chorus after Dareios' appearance reads like a muster-list of the league. So far but only so far the *Persians* is a political play in the narrow sense.

Far more important is the way in which Aeschylus sees the whole story. The worried Persian elders at the beginning, the queen apprehensive because of her dream, are answered by the news of Salamis: they summon up the ghost of Dareios to help them, and the play culminates in the laments with Xerxes, who has caused the disaster. Dareios does two things besides prophesying the future. He puts Xerxes in the perspective of Persian history, and with all the majesty of a royal ghost, he announces that Zeus punishes the man who steps outside the proper bounds of human activity, as Xerxes had by trying to convert the land empire of the Persians into a sea empire. It is this divine retribution on human excess that Aeschylus is using all his art to put across to the Athenians.[9]

The same elements appear again on a larger scale in the *Oresteia*, which was produced in 458, four years after the Areiopagos had been reduced to a murder-court and four years after Athens had broken with Kimon's pro-Spartan policy and made an alliance with Argos. Again Aeschylus shows his approval: Agamemnon's palace is set in Argos instead of Mycenae so that in the third play Orestes can offer Athens alliance with the Argives in return for acquittal, and Athena sets up the Areiopagos as a murder-court to try Orestes. Thus both the Argive alliance and the Areiopagos are given a mythical sanction.[10]

The story begins with the night of the capture of Troy. Agamemnon returns with Kassandra, and both are murdered by Klytaimestra with the help of Aigisthos; in the second play Agamemnon's son Orestes returns from exile at Apollo's command to kill his mother and Aigisthos; in the third play he is chased by the Furies from Delphi to Athens, and they accuse him before the newly instituted murder-court; he is acquitted because the votes are equal, and they are persuaded to take up residence on the Areiopagos; thus the new court is given the very solemn sanction of these ancient deities, who avenge crime and can give material prosperity to the land where crime is avenged.

As in the *Persians*, the events are put into a historical perspective and shown to be the working out of a divine law, essentially the same divine law under which Xerxes suffered. If a man commits a crime of excess, Zeus sets him on a disaster course, and he learns modesty by suffering, or others learn by seeing him suffer. Paris committed the crime of stealing Helen, and Troy suffered. Agamemnon was right to punish Paris, but wrong to sacrifice his daughter Iphigeneia without even questioning the seer's advice to do this, wrong to punish Paris at such cost of innocent Trojan and Greek lives, wrong to bring back Kassandra, wrong to let himself be treated as a god on his return. Kassandra as a prophetess is used by Aeschylus to put in further background: Agamemnon's father Atreus had punished his brother Thyestes for seducing his wife and attempting to get his throne by serving Thyestes' children up to him for dinner, so that there was a curse on Atreus' son Agamemnon from Thyestes, a curse embodied in Thyestes' son Aigisthos, who moved in on Klytaimestra while Agamemnon was at Troy. Klytaimestra, when she had murdered Agamemnon and Kassandra, claimed that she embodied this curse, as well as avenging Iphigeneia.[11]

There is no doubt that Klytaimestra chose wrong. Agamemnon's decisions before going to Troy were much more difficult, but the first two choruses of the *Agamemnon* show that he bought the punishment of Paris at far too high a price. By sacrificing Iphigeneia he set the whole machinery of divine retribution in motion against himself. In the *Choephoroe* Orestes' decision to kill his mother was a yet more difficult choice; he was commanded to do it by Apollo and threatened with vengeance from his father if he abstained. But he had to make the choice himself, and by making it set the machinery of retribution by the Furies in motion against himself. This is what Athena has to resolve by the murder-trial in the third play the *Eumenides*. The final argument used by Apollo, and accepted by Athena in her speech when she casts her vote and thereby makes the votes equal for acquittal, is that the child is the child of the father alone, the mother only provides the place in which it grows; Orestes, therefore, is not a blood-relation of Klytaimestra, and so cannot justly be pursued by her Furies. This was the modern scientific view of procreation which can be found in the South-Italian doctor Alkmaion of Kroton and in Anaxagoras, so that at the crucial point Aeschylus makes Apollo base his case on science and so allows Athena to compare the two murders, the murder of the master of the house and the murder of his murderess. It is a final crucial decision. As Aeschylus has phrased this passage, it seems that he must have meant us to conclude that the jurors voted six to five against Orestes; Athena votes last, announcing the principle that equal votes acquit; then the votes are counted and found equal. Orestes is saved by an act of 'violent grace', which in fact reverses the mortal verdict.[12]

But this crucial decision too sets the machinery of retribution in motion. The Furies claim that they can ruin Athena's city and land, and Athena can blast the Furies with the thunderbolts of Zeus. Instead she offers them the benefit of a cult in Athens, which they accept. They are not only the automatic pursuers of those who murder their kin. In Hesiod and Homer crime entails famine and sterility in the land, particularly crime in the rulers. So the Furies can ruin Athens for an unjust decision, but installed near the just court they will bless Athens. In more modern terms (and this is the point of the song that they sing while Athena assembles the court) they stand against violence and for modesty and moderation, what Zeus stands for in the choruses of the *Agamemnon*. As in the *Persians*, the immediate political problems of the Argive alliance and the Areiopagos are only a small part of what Aeschylus is using the tremendous resources of his art to say. Far more important is the conception of how under Zeus the world works, the complicated concatenation of causes which press upon a man who makes an important decision and the inevitable reaction which his decision sets in motion, the need to walk cautiously when opposing views are strongly held, and the possibility, if a mortal can copy Athena, of reversing a decision beneficially.[13]

The *Oresteia* was produced in 458; Sophocles had been producing for ten years, and Euripides was to produce his first plays three years later in 455. Sophocles was twenty-nine years younger than Aeschylus, and Euripides was twelve years younger than Sophocles; together they dominated production until the last years of the fifth century, when they died within two years of each other. Technically they belong together and not with Aeschylus. However different they are, they have in common a shift of emphasis from the divine machinery and the long perspectives of Aeschylus to the human characters in their present situation, which entails increasing the spoken dialogue between characters at the expense of the sung choruses. The unit is now the single play and not the trilogy of three connected plays. (In the only connected trilogy after Aeschylus of which we can say anything, Euripides' Trojan trilogy, the connection is much looser than in the *Oresteia*, and the three plays are three disconnected but relevant chapters in the story of the Trojan war.)

Sophocles was born in 496. His father was a rich man, who owned industrial slaves. As a boy he lead the victory chorus after Salamis. He won his first tragic victory in 468, when Kimon and his board of strategoi did the judging. He was painted by Polygnotos, probably in the character of Thamyras, and his early plays seem to have inspired other pictures by Polygnotos. He also knew Ion of Chios, who again was attached to Kimon. He gave up acting about 450, and the association of trained actors and chorusmen which he founded probably belongs to this time. He was a conscious artist who thought that Aeschylus only succeeded by luck and that Euripides was a realist, whereas he drew the sort of characters one should draw and had developed the best style, the style 'with the most ethos' (Damon's word, and probably an approximation to Damon's thought). He was certainly elected strategos for the Samian war in 440. He may have held public office again as strategos, as chairman of the board who looked after the tribute from the empire, and as one of the ten special councillors appointed after the Sicilian disaster, but in all these cases it is possible that he has been confused with another Sophocles. He also held several minor priesthoods. One understands Ion's characterisation: 'he was like one of the Athenian nobles'.[14]

Euripides was quite different. His father must have been well-off, if he considered having the boy trained as an athlete; his connection with commerce may not have been entirely the invention of the comic poets. Euripides wrote in a cave on Salamis and is the first man we know to have had a library. The ancient authorities put in a school period with Archelaos, Anaxagoras, Protagoras, Prodikos, and Socrates. This is, of course, nonsense, but Euripides certainly quotes the views of Anaxagoras, Protagoras, and Prodikos. Protagoras is said to have read his book on the gods in Euripides' house. If he developed there the view that, though knowledge of the gods is impossible, belief in the gods is a human characteristic and the rules of ethical and political conduct sanctioned by that belief are to be respected as the work of ancient and wise lawgivers, he was putting forward a view which, with his relativism, would account for a great deal in

Euripides. The echoes of these three thinkers are clear enough in Euripides' plays, and the audience must have been expected to appreciate them. Euripides is said to have lent Socrates a text of Herakleitos, and Socrates is said to have enjoyed the plays of Euripides. According to the comic poets, writing in the years before and after 430, Socrates helped Euripides to compose his plays; what this probably means is that it was obvious to the general public that Euripides at that time was dealing with a moral problem that Socrates had brought into prominence. We have also noted already that Euripides was much more influenced by the modern musicians, particularly Timotheos, than Sophocles was.[15]

To see what these poets were saying to their audiences we can look at three different periods, the late forties when the struggle between Pericles and Thucydides son of Melesias had been decided in favour of Pericles, the beginning of the Peloponnesian War, and the last years of the Peloponnesian War just before the fall of Athens. Sophocles produced his *Antigone* in 442, but we do not know what other plays he produced with it. The ode which Sophocles wrote to Herodotos was written within a year of the production of the *Antigone* and may have been the acknowledgement of a debt. Herodotos has a story of a woman who was allowed to save either her brother or her husband or her son from death, and she chose her brother because he was irreplaceable. This may have turned Sophocles' mind to Antigone, who buried her brother in defiance of Kreon's orders. Certainly he remembered it when he wrote Antigone's last speech just before she is led off to be immured for her disobedience: at this lowest moment she says that she would not have defied Kreon to bury a husband or a son, but a brother was irreplaceable. In this speech and in the preceding lyric dialogue with the chorus Antigone is at her most human, a lonely girl taking refuge in the only intellectual argument she can find. Till then she has been proud in her lonely resolution to follow the law of the gods, which commands the burial of the dead.[16]

The play starts with Antigone proposing to her sister Ismene to bury their brother Polyneikes in spite of Kreon's decree. Ismene fails to dissuade her with the argument that women cannot fight with men. In the opening chorus the old Thebans sing of the enormous relief of the victory over Polyneikes and his Argive champions. Kreon enters and explains his decree that Polyneikes' body shall be left without burial. A guard arrives to tell that a layer of dust has been put over the body. Kreon immediately suspects a political plot. The chorus in the first stasimon sing of the wonders of civilisation, which may lead to bad but may lead to good, if associated with religion. Thus Sophocles gives Kreon's first reaction and their first reaction, before it is known who has defied him. The guard returns with Antigone, who maintains that she acted in obedience to the unwritten laws of the gods as overriding Kreon's decree. Ismene begs to share the guilt and is rejected by Antigone; she then pleads with Kreon to spare Antigone as his son's future wife. The chorus sing a thoroughly Aeschylean song: it is a law of the gods that no mortal excess escapes disaster. They think primarily of Antigone; the audience perhaps already think of Kreon. Kreon's son Haimon comes to plead for Antigone. For Kreon she is simply a traitor in the family. Haimon says that the city regards her as a heroine, and it might be wise to reflect. Kreon threatens to kill Antigone before Haimon's eyes and Haimon rushes off. The chorus put the responsibility for this quarrel on Eros. Then Antigone is led out and makes her last speech, and the chorus sing a song of consolation as she goes off stage. The aged seer Teiresias warns Kreon that the gods will punish him for not burying Polyneikes and for immuring Antigone: Kreon first accuses him of being bribed, and then reluctantly yields. The chorus prays to Dionysos for salvation. The messenger tells Kreon's wife Eurydike of the death of Antigone and Haimon. Kreon returns with Haimon's body to find that his wife has committed suicide. The chorus sum up: 'Wisdom is by far the first part of happiness. And there must be no irreverence towards the gods. Great words of the proud are punished by great blows. and teach wisdom in old age.'[17]

The summing-up is Aeschylean, like the chorus before the scene between Haimon and Kreon, but this is the framework: Sophocles shows what kind of people produce these results, and the two chief characters are defined by the other characters:

Antigone by the feminine Ismene, as well as by Kreon, and Kreon by Haimon and Teiresias, as well as by Antigone. The rightness and wrongness of Antigone and Kreon have been much debated, but the end of the play leaves no doubt of Sophocles' view: Antigone was right, but she had to be hard and lonely to run her course; Kreon was wrong, although he is given some quite respectable political sentiments. Primarily this is a conflict between rebellious idealism and authority, and Sophocles may have been thinking of the clash between the old families and Pericles when he chose this story to dramatise, or at least a member of the audience might have interpreted it in this way. It may be relevant that when he is arguing against Teiresias, Kreon quotes a very modern religious view, which Sophocles clearly brands as wrong by giving it to Kreon at this moment: 'You shall not bury him even if the eagles of Zeus carry his carrion up to the throne of Zeus, not even through fear of this pollution will I allow his burial. For I know well that no mortal is strong enough to pollute the gods.' The last sentence is an enlightened view, but by giving it to Kreon in this context Sophocles proclaims his religious conservatism, and when Sophocles lets his chorus attribute the growth of civilisation (very much like Protagoras) to the contriving of human skill, he also points out that respect for the gods is the only safeguard against disaster.[18]

In the *Oedipus Tyrannus* again, which was produced in the early years of the Peloponnesian War, probably in 429, the audience may have seen an allusion to Pericles, as I have noted: Pericles' family were connected with an ancient sacrilege, for which the Spartans demanded his expulsion just before the war, and in the play Delphi demands the expulsion of the 'pollution of the land', which turns out to be Oidipous. The plague in Thebes may have been introduced into the story by Sophocles, and in any case recalled the plague which struck Athens in the second year of the Peloponnesian War. Oidipous' reliance on his own intelligence to discover the truth is a very Periclean quality. At least it is fair to say that Sophocles has given the play enough contemporary colour for an audience and the judges to interpret it politically if they wanted to. Aeschylus' nephew, Philokles, who won the first prize, was perhaps a Periclean. As in the *Antigone*, Sophocles makes his own religious standpoint entirely clear. In a long scene of 350 lines, after Oidipous has accused Kreon of using Teiresias in a plot against his throne and has threatened him with death, Iokaste stops the quarrel and tries to calm Oidipous by telling him that no human has the gift of prophecy; Laios was to be killed by his child, but he was killed by robbers at a crossroads. This starts in Oidipous the memory that, after he had received the oracle at Delphi that he would marry his mother and kill his father, he had killed an old man at the crossroads. Arrangements are made to summon the survivor, and Iokaste again stresses the unreliability of prophecy. The chorus (and this song is their second stasimon, like the Aeschylean chorus in the *Antigone*) sing that it is the law of the gods that hybris is part of a tyrant's nature and leads to disaster; if injustice and irreverence is held in honour, 'why should I dance? ... Apollo is nowhere held in honour, and religion is gone.' It is true that Oidipous has behaved like a tyrant in his treatment of Kreon and was at least hasty in his action at the crossroads ('I killed the lot'), and that Iokaste has twice stated that prophecies are not fulfilled. The reaction of the chorus is so strong that many have felt (and the same feeling may well have been shared by some of the audience) that this is Sophocles commenting on contemporary Athens rather than the chorus commenting on what they have heard. Immediately after this chorus, when the Corinthian arrives as if in answer to Iokaste's prayer to Apollo, the truth begins to come out: Oidipous has indeed killed his father Laios and married his mother Iokaste. Iokaste commits suicide and Oidipous blinds himself. Unless the second stasimon is irrelevant as being entirely concerned with contemporary Athens and not with the play, it must give Sophocles' meaning. The gods can foresee and do foretell the future. What causes the future, is the working out of their laws, the Aeschylean laws. Oidipous comes to disaster because of his hybris, and Sophocles shows what sort of man could make this story come true. But Oidipous is guiltless of intentional patricide and incest because he did not know who his parents were.[19]

Oidipous did not know who his parents were. In the *Trachiniae*, which was probably written slightly earlier, Deianeira did not know that the love-charm with which she anointed Herakles' robe was a deadly poison. In the *Phaidra*, which seems also to have been written in the late thirties, Phaidra fell in love with her stepson Hippolytos and approached him through her nurse; she had the excuse that, because Theseus had gone to Hades, she thought he was dead. In each case the disastrous course is due to the makeup of the chief character, but in each case the chief character is innocent, because ignorant of an essential piece of information. This surely implies an interest in Athens at this time in the relation between knowledge and crime. Socrates equated virtue with knowledge and drew the conclusion that if you knew what was right you did it. On these terms Oidipous, Deianeira, and Phaidra would not have committed their crimes, if they had had the knowledge. Euripides quoted but rejected Socrates' conclusion (and this is what the comic poets meant when they very unfairly said that Socrates helped him with his plays): Media in 431 knows that she is committing a crime when she murders her children, and Phaidra in 428 puts the position in general terms: 'it is not lack of knowledge that leads to disaster. Many have good sense, you should look at it like this: we know and recognise the good, but we do not work it out, some because of laziness and some because of pleasure.'[20]

The Phaidra of Euripides' *Hippolytus* is the perfect refutation of the Socratic equation. She knows what is right, and she tries desperately to suppress her love and, when that fails, to starve herself to death. She is not strong enough to prevent the nurse extracting the truth from her and approaching Hippolytos. She overhears Hippolytos violently reject the approach and decides on suicide, leaving a letter implicating Hippolytos (her main reason, and it is difficult for us to find it satisfactory, is her desire to preserve her children's rights). Theseus returns, finds and believes the letter, and causes Hippolytos' death with the curse, which his father Poseidon fulfils. Hippolytos is brought on dying, and father and son are reconciled before he dies. On the human level Euripides has portrayed men 'as they are'; Phaidra had not the strength either to die or to survive in silence; the unheroic, realistic nurse suggested a way out which could only lead to disaster; Hippolytos, the dedicated hunter and athlete, like other careerists, has no time for women, and his violent expression of this is part of the reason for Phaidra writing the letter. Theseus asks no question before he curses. As in Sophocles, they are the people to make the story work, but each one is essential for the action: there is no dominant like Oidipous or dominant pair like Kreon and Antigone.[21]

The story is not an example of the divine law of the dangers of excess. But there are other levels besides the human level briefly described. The goddess Aphrodite, who speaks the prologue, is the embodiment of sexual desire, which dominates Phaidra, and the goddess Artemis, to whom Hippolytos prays at the beginning of the play and who reconciles him to his father at the end, is the embodiment of dedication to hunting, which dominates Hippolytos. (So later in the *Bacchae* Euripides used Dionysos as ecstasy.) On another level, which might perhaps be called Homeric, since it is very much what Xenophanes criticised, these gods are spiteful: Aphrodite punishes Hippolytos because Hippolytos does not honour her, and Artemis will avenge Hippolytos by shooting a favourite of Aphrodite. On another level still Euripides asserts the gods of cult: a cult of Aphrodite 'by Hippolytos' in Athens, and a cult of Hippolytos in Troizen. Finally, in their songs the choruses sing, more obviously than in Aeschylus or Sophocles, a different poetic language from the spoken language of the realistic characters, a decorated language of fantasy, 'the apple-tree, the singing, and the gold', and this too is a level that Euripides wants to assert. How the spectator interprets the play is his own affair, and the guide lines are less clear than in Sophocles or Aeschylus.[22]

Many of the same tendencies are clear in the *Phoenissae*, which was produced in 410. Euripides may have been inspired by a revival of Aeschylus' *Seven against Thebes*. In Aeschylus Eteokles is the patriotic defender of Thebes, who makes the fatal decision to fight his brother Polyneikes; the chorus sees it as the last of a series of fatal decisions starting with Laios' fatal decision to disregard the oracle and beget a child. Euripides' Eteokles is in love with power, and in pursuit of power ruins his whole family. This is the point: as in other late Euripidean plays, the *Bacchae*, the *Iphigenia in Aulis*, and the *Orestes*, the whole family is involved, and the whole family is shown. Oidipous and Iokaste have lived on in the palace. Iokaste has arranged a truce so that Polyneikes can parley with Eteokles; Polyneikes' claim to alternate rule is rejected by Eteokles. Kreon discusses strategy with Eteokles and receives Teiresias' advice that his son Menoikeus must be sacrificed to save Thebes; he tries to save his son, but his son commits suicide. A messenger brings the news that the brothers are to fight. Iokaste goes to them with Antigone (who was seen at the beginning of the play watching Polyneikes and his allies from the walls). They arrive as the brothers are dying, Iokaste commits suicide, and Antigone comes back with their bodies. She calls Oidipous out to say farewell to his wife and sons. Kreon banishes Oidipous and forbids the burial of Polyneikes. At the end Antigone leads Oidipous off.[23]

Thus the whole family is ruined by Eteokles' selfishness. Polyneikes is in the right but is prepared to sack Thebes to get his rights. Kreon is human in his attempt to save his son, but vengeful against Polyneikes and Oidipous. In contrast to them stand the youthful unselfishness and heroism of Antigone and Menoikeus and the aged dignity of Iokaste and Oidipous, who are in their different ways immensely moving. Each of them, and the paidagogos and Teiresias as well, has a part in moving the action forward, so that progression is the resultant of a number of minor but clearly distinct forces, and this must be part of what Euripides is saying.

The chorus are Phoenician women sent via Thebes as an offering to Apollo at Delphi. They are therefore both exotic and detached, yet sympathetic because they regard Io as a common ancestress to themselves and the Thebans. Even more than the Troizenian women of the *Hippolytus* they can naturally move in a world of decorative fantasy. But in this play some of the characters too move into this world in their long lyric passages, which reflect the new music, notably Antigone in the beginning when she sees the seven champions in their armour but also in her later lament and lyric dialogues with Oidipous.[24]

The play belongs to the unhappy political situation after the Sicilian disaster and the oligarchic revolution, which lasted from the spring of 411 to the summer of 410. We cannot be certain whether the play was produced in 411, 410, or 409; 410 is the most likely, but it does not very much matter, because in any of these years the whole situation, which is essentially a civil war between Polyneikes with his external allies and the uncompromising incumbent Eteokles, and the political debate between Polyneikes and Eteokles is terribly relevant. The debate is conducted in the terminology of the time, and Iokaste's summing up—ambition is extremely dangerous to its possessor; proportional equality is the safe basis for political and social relationships, as it is also the rule for the Seasons; why worship Tyranny when it may lead to defeat?—is strongly reminiscent of Protagoras. Here too, as in the *Trojan Women*, Euripides makes his political comment.[25]

The last two plays preserved of Sophocles, the *Philoctetes* produced in 409 and the *Oedipus Coloneus* produced posthumously in 401, also reflect the selfish and unscrupulous politics of the time in the Odysseus of the *Philoctetes* and the Kreon and Polyneikes of the *Oedipus Coloneus*, and this is part of what Sophocles has to say. The technique of drawing minor characters so as to display the major characters remains the same. The amount of lyric dialogue with one, or even two, actors singing is increased at the expense of choral lyric, but, unlike Euripides, Sophocles never abandons strophic correspondence. The gods are there, and still both foresee and foretell the future. But they are further removed from the chief characters than before. All we can say is that they turn a kindlier face on the chief character at the end: Elektra (the Sophoclean *Electra* was probably produced in 413) is liberated from oppression, Philoktetes will be healed and win glory at Troy, Oidipous becomes a Hero at Kolonos. The emphasis is on the chief character, who is on stage for nearly the whole of the play, an essentially noble character, warped by an intolerable event some years back (Elektra by the death of Agamemnon, Philoktetes by exposure on Lemnos, Oidipous by the deeds revealed in the *Oedipus Tyrannus*) and put through a series of confrontations with friends and foes, which arouse extreme emotions, but at the end reaching a new and more tolerable situation. In these plays Sophocles is saying that breed is invincible, but we have no knowledge of his other late plays.[26]

Criticism of drama runs parallel to criticism of painting and criticism of music and non-dramatic poetry, which we have already discussed. Sophocles committed himself to a technical view of poetry and to an educational view of poetry, as forming *ethos*, and so would seem to be in line with Damon's musical criticism, which certainly included sung poetry as well as music. Euripides in his view was a realist. All three views are found again in Aristophanes. The accident that Sophocles died only shortly before the *Frogs* was produced may account for the choice of Aeschylus rather than Sophocles as a foil to Euripides, but that choice also gave Aristophanes the chance of contrasting the poet of genius, Aeschylus, with the technician Euripides. Both poets accept the educational view of poetry, education both as character-forming (which goes back to the earlier *Clouds* and Damon) and as giving instruction (which reminds us of Nikias' view of Homer). Much of the detailed criticism is technical: heavy lines against light lines, technique and versification of prologues, technique of songs. Some of this certainly goes back to Protagoras. Predictably Aristophanes dislikes, or at any rate mercilessly parodies, the influence of the new music on Euripides and on the younger tragic poet Agathon (in the earlier *Thesmophoriazusae*). Euripides is a realist who lets every minor character prattle, whose heroes are beggars and cripples, and whose heroines are immoral women. The general attitude might very well be an elaboration of Sophocles' view, as we know it from his sayings and his practice.[27]

It is unfortunate that we cannot date Gorgias' few very interesting remarks more closely. His description of Aeschylus' *Seven against Thebes* as a drama 'full of Ares' is used by Aristophanes in the *Frogs*, and there is no reason why the rest should not belong to the late fifth century rather than the early fourth. Gorgias recognises that illusion is the purpose of tragedy: 'the man who is deceived is happier than the man who is not deceived, and the man who deceives is more just than the man who does not deceive'. He also very clearly states that poetry stirs emotion: 'the hearers are penetrated by a shudder full of fear, a pity full of tears, a yearning to grieve; words make the soul feel in itself the good and bad fortunes of others'. This is extended by a very interesting comparison with medicine. 'The power of the the word acts on the disposition of the soul as the disposition of drugs acts on the nature of the body. For as different drugs drive different juices out of the body, and some stop disease and others stop life, so some words give fear, some joy, some grief, some restore confidence, some by evil persuasion drug and bewitch the soul.'[28]

Plato's attitude to drama in the *Republic* has already been largely described in discussing his attitude to art and poetry. The main points are these. Characters in tragedy utter sentiments about the gods which are unsuitable for the young (this is the line of criticism which descends from Xenophanes). Tragedy is an illusion and therefore can give no knowledge of the truth, because it is the copy of a copy of a copy. Tragedy appeals to an inferior part of the soul, to the emotions rather than to the reason. The emotional appeal of tragedy, clearly stated by Gorgias, is a reason for banning it from the ideal city. In two points Plato goes beyond fifth-century theory; first, the position of drama, as of painting, on the lowest level of the scale of truth and reality, and secondly the view, which is closely parallel to the rhapsode Ion's account of his effect on his audience and to Damon's account of the effect of music, that the audience identifies with the actor and the actor identifies with the character, so that if the dramatist presents an undesirable character, the audience acquires those undesirable characteristics. Plato has a list of female characters undesirable from this point of view, which is very like similar lists of Euripides' heroines in the *Frogs*, and he stands in the line of criticism which we have traced from Damon's musical theory through Sophocles and Aristophanes.[29]

Plato did not change his general position; tragedy is excluded from the state in the *Laws*, as in the *Republic*. But in the *Phaedrus*, which was written between 360 and 350, he incidentally states a technical view of tragedy. Having argued that a speech must be an organic composition, he goes on to say that to know how to make rhetorical and emotional speeches is only to know the preliminaries of the tragic poet's art; the important thing is to know how to compose them into an organic whole. It is not chance that Aristotle joins in here. Aristotle was a member of the Academy at this time and may, as I suggested, have helped with the *Phaedrus,* and it is possible that Theodektes, who was both a tragic poet and a rhetorician, came over into the Academy at that time. We cannot argue, as we could with the artists, that the tragic poets in the fourth century had done anything to allay the fears of the philosophers. What little we know of fourth-century tragedy suggests long and exciting plays with hairbreadth escapes, violent incidents, and some-times nice discrimination of motives. Great characters, like Anti-gone or Oidipous, had given place to emotional characters, and choruses, which in the fifth century were often used to relate the particular action to universal laws, were no longer written for the particular play but were transferred from play to play. From 386 a fifth-century tragedy was revived every year at the City Dionysia, and in 341-39 (the only years for which we have evidence) the author was Euripides. Tragedy was still open to Plato's criticism, but Aristotle as a scientist must have thought that he ought to account for an extremely popular and flourish-ing phenomenon.[30]

The text of Aristotle's *Poetics,* as we have it, has grown with insertions and additions from the time of its conception in Aristotle's first period at the Academy (367-47) to his second Athenian residence (335-22). We are concerned briefly with the first part (ch. 1-6) in which he arrives at a definition of tragedy, and the second part (ch. 7-22), which may be called rules for writing a good tragedy. The third part, epic poetry and the principles of literary criticism, have been described in the last chapter.[31]

Aristotle reaches his definition by good Platonic methods. Tragedy is a form of *mimesis* (representation). The representa-tional arts are distinguished by means, objects, and manner. So a smaller group, tragedy, comedy, and epic, is formed, and from this he can proceed to the definition of tragedy, which immediately concerns him. On the way he asserts that *mimesis* and seeing *mimesis* produces learning as well as pleasure, and this disposes of Plato's objection that tragedy does not give knowledge. The objects represented are firmly said to be people better than ourselves, and this disposes of Plato's criticism that the heroes and heroines of tragedy are unworthy. On the way also he relates seriousness of subject matter to seriousness of character in the poets, as noted above, and introduces a summary history of tragedy. This is based on three ideas. First, it derives from records, presumably his own collection for the work called 'Productions' (*Didaskaliai*); and this is the beginning of historical literary scholarship. The other two ideas he took over from biology. A new literary form arises when someone improvises on an old literary form: this is, I think, derived from the idea of a plant or animal changing to deal with a special environment. 'Having been through many changes tragedy stopped when it had attained its own nature': this is clearly biological, and introduces the idea of growth to perfection into literary and art history, which has been difficult to dislodge.[32]

'Tragedy, then, is the representation of serious and complete action on a large scale in language differently decorated in different parts [explained as dialogue and song] with actors and no narrative, by pity and fear achieving the katharsis of such emotions.' Three elements in this definition do not derive from the previous discussion. The concept of a 'complete action' would be known to anyone familiar with the passage from the *Phaedrus* quoted above. The arousing of 'pity and fear' is already in Gorgias and is the assumption of Plato. But where Plato rejects tragedy as emotional, Aristotle accepts it as causing a katharsis. Discussion of katharsis has been endless because the fuller account that Aristotle promised is lost (perhaps with the second book of the *Poetics*). Here only two points can be made. First, the passage quoted above from Gorgias, in which he compares the action of words on the soul to the action of drugs on the body, is very near. 'Different drugs expel different juices from the body'; he might have gone on to say 'different words expel different emotions from the soul'. This passage may have prompted Aristotle to complete the parallel, which is what essentially he does here. Secondly, in the *Politics*, where he gives the cross-reference to the *Poetics*, he is discussing the therapeutic effect of wild flute-music: 'when they experience songs which have an orgiastic effect on the soul, they are put into the same sort of state if they had had doctoring and katharsis. The same thing will necessarily happen to those who are prone to pity or fear or are generally emotional; anyone who has an excess of any particular emotion finds katharsis and pleasurable relief.' Thus so far from making people more emotional, as Plato thought, seeing tragedy draws off the excess of emotion.[33]

The first part ends with some consequences drawn from this definition. Plot is primary. *Ethos* (here the quality in the speech which makes it possible to say the speaker is of such and such a kind) and *dianoia* (the rhetorical skill which adapts the speech to stir this or that emotion) are secondary, then vocabulary, then song, and finally spectacle, which does stir emotion but belongs to the mask-maker rather than the poet; Aristotle preferred reading his tragedies to seeing them.[34]

The second part starts with a definition of the good plot. It is an organic structure of necessary or probable incidents; we have discussed already the use of this word probable (*eikos*) as a law-court argument; Aristotle defines it as 'what happens for the most part'. 'Poetry is therefore more philosophical and more serious than history.' Here is the last attack on Plato's position, and it can be explained roughly like this. For Plato 'brave' and 'man' are Ideas, more real than the real world. They are copied by the brave action of Socrates, and the tragedian copies that. For Aristotle the historian is on the same bottom level as the tragedian in Plato, but the tragedian constructs his plot of incidents which it is necessary or probable that the brave (or whatever) man would perform, so that his plot is on the level of the universal Idea. He then individualises it by adding names (just as Socrates is the Idea 'brave man' individualised by matter), so that the resultant tragedy is in Platonic terms a copy of the Idea and not the copy of a copy.[35]

In what follows we can be brief. It must, I think, be kept in mind that these are rules for writing a tragedy and not a theory to explain all existing Greek tragedies. Aristotle has a few superb examples and makes his rules on them. It does not matter that all tragedies do not fit the rules or that one rule may be incompatible with another rule: either makes a good tragedy. The object is to stir pity and fear; sudden and unexpected but still probable incidents, like reversals and recognitions (the marks of the 'involved' tragedy) produce this effect: so do deaths, woundings or agonies on the stage. Pity and fear are only felt for unworthy sufferers like ourselves; the man whose fortune changes for the worse in an involved tragedy must not be excessively virtuous or excessively vicious but rather better than ourselves and the victim of a major error. He instances Oidipous, who had failed to recognise his father or his mother, and Thyestes, who failed to recognise that he was eating his children's flesh. The conception is carried over into the next chapter on the most pitiful and terrifying tragic deed: Euripides' Merope is going to kill her son and Iphigeneia is going to kill her brother, but they are prevented by recognition in the nick of time. It does not matter that this kind of play must end happily, whereas in discussing the ideal hero Aristotle has expressly said that the major error must involve him in disaster. Nor does it matter that the major error as defined does nothing to explain some of the most moving Greek tragedies, the *Oresteia* or the *Medea* or the *Bacchae*. These are rules for writing, not explanations of past practice. We need not follow him into further discussion of *ethos*, recognition scenes, complication and solution, dianoia, and vocabulary. He does not discuss choruses presumably because they were no longer written.[36]

Unfortunately we have no tragedy of his period or later, so that we cannot see how far his rules were drawn from contemporary practice, as well as from a few classical tragedies, or how far his rules were followed. But we have the comedy of Menander, and he was a pupil of Aristotle's successor Theophrastos.

11 *Comedy*

Comedy was produced at the same festivals in Athens as tragedy, and the audience was the same. The only difference was that comedy went back further than tragedy at the Lenaia and tragedy went back further than comedy at the City Dionysia; the first official production of comedy at the City Dionysia was in 486, and from that time the normal arrangement at both festivals was that five poets competed, each with one play, except for a short period in the Peloponnesian war when the number was reduced to three. The choice, production, and judging of comedy was done in the same way as for tragedy. Unfortunately we have no significant information about the archons who chose or the choregoi who produced comedy. One of Lysias' clients produced a comedy of Kephisodoros in 402 and spent 1,600 drachmai on it. He counted it to his credit to have put on a good show, but this is not politically significant in the way that Pericles' production of Aeschylus' *Persians* is significant. It is, however, worth noting that when Aristophanes produced the *Clouds* at the City Dionysia in 423, with its portrait of Socrates and the new education, Ameipsias produced the *Konnos*: Konnos was a lyre-singer who taught Socrates music, the chorus was composed of thinkers, and Socrates himself had a part. In 414 at the City Dionysia Aristophanes produced the *Birds*, in which the two Athenians build a city in the clouds to avoid the troubles of Athens, and Phrynichos produced the *Hermit*, who escaped his troubles by solitude. In 405 Aristophanes produced the *Frogs* with its contest of Aeschylus and Euripides, and Phrynichos produced the

Muses, in which Sophocles was mentioned. In these three years the archon chose two plays of similar subject, and it seems likely that this was his taste.[1]

It would be more interesting if we knew something about the archons who chose and the choregoi who produced the political plays. It is true that the *Knights*, which has the most concentrated attack on Kleon, was produced in 424 at the Lenaia, the winter festival when there were few foreigners in Athens, but the *Peace* in 421 was produced at the City Dionysia; it must have been accepted when the war was still on and Kleon was still alive, although it was not produced until a week or so before the treaty between the Athenians and Peloponnesians was signed. In 426 Aristophanes produced the *Babylonians* at the City Dionysia, and we are told that he attacked the elected officials, the officials chosen by lot, and Kleon; he himself says that Kleon dragged him before the council and slandered him. What exactly this means we do not know, but we hear of laws passed on other occasions to prevent comic poets from direct and open attacks on particular persons. Comedy was evidently regarded as a serious force in politics, and if during the Peloponnesian war the political plays of Aristophanes plead for peace, one reason why choregoi could be found may be that the richest men, from whom they were drawn, suffered most from the war both in damage to their property in Attica and in extra expense in military service, equipping triremes, and war-tax. The archon chose the play, but the archon had also to know that he could find a choregos willing to produce. It is not entirely easy to reconcile this willingness with the view of the conservative tract that comedy attacks the rich and noble and influential and only attacks the poor when they meddle in politics or try to get the better of the common people. This view implies that the success of comedy depends on its appeal to the popular audience and the influence that they exert on the judges.[2]

Comedy was willingly produced by the rich and sometimes followed their political line, but comedy also attacked the rich. To understand this we need to define more clearly the nature of fifth-century comedy, which is known as Old Comedy; how it develops through Middle Comedy to the New Comedy of

Menander, which is the recognisable ancestor of modern social comedy, will concern us later. If comedy originated at the Lenaia, it originated at the winter festival of Dionysos, when the primary concern was releasing the fruitful earth from the bonds of winter, and it is possible that the releasing of Hera by Hephaistos under the influence of Dionysos is the archetypal story of comedy. In early fertility festivals abuse of various kinds plays an important part. Abuse of the good forces may cause them to do their work; abuse of the bad forces may diminish their powers; abuse of the spectators may free the atmosphere of the festival so that the rites can achieve their object. It is from these ideas that the costumed dances which precede comedy arise, and survivals of these ideas can be seen in comedy itself. The costume of comedy, which survives from the dances, is itself abusive: gods, heroes, and men wear the same ugly masks, padded stomachs, and enlarged genitals. We have therefore to distinguish various different kinds of abuse, which all have the sanction of religion. In one sense the poet abuses the characters by putting them on the stage in this shape. When Dionysos is shown on the stage as an incompetent oarsman and a coward, as he is in Eupolis' *Commanders* and Aristophanes' *Frogs*, this may be a remnant of abusing the god to make him act. When Kleon is put on the stage as a Paphlagonian slave in Aristophanes' *Knights*, this is abuse of an evil power to make it go away. Telekleides in *Hesiod and his companions* said that Pericles was in love with a Corinthian hetaira, and Pherekrates in an unknown play said that Alkibiades was every woman's man before he was a man; these statements may or may not be true; they are quite harmless survivals of comedy's licence to abuse the spectators. They would not deter any rich men from producing the plays, but the conservative tract could call them attacks on the rich if it suited the argument.[3]

Probably the ancient audience was adept at distinguishing between these different kinds of abuse, but quite often the comic poet tells them when he is serious. Here the convention is quite different from tragedy. The audience is frequently addressed directly, and either a character or the chorus can tell them directly the poet's intentions. It is very likely that this convention comes from pre-comedy but we have not the evidence to know. What is certain is that it antedates Aristophanes. The *Odysseus and his companions* of Kratinos was probably produced before 435; the chorus enters singing: 'Silence, now everyone silence. All of the tale you shall hear. Ithake is our homeland, and we sail with goodly Odysseus.' The prologue of tragedy also has to give the exposition, but it is done by soliloquy or dialogue without explicit address to the spectators. In Aristophanes, particularly in the early plays, the spectators are directly addressed: 'Do you want me to tell the story to the spectators?', says Demosthenes in the *Knights*.[4]

There is a special place for the poet to announce his serious views (though he may use other places too). This is the Parabasis. Generally about the middle of the play the chorus, instead of dancing round the orchestra, turn towards the audience and recite a long stretch of recitative anapaests about the poet. The opening formula is clearest in a fragment of the comic poet Plato: 'If I had not been constrained by you, sirs, to turn in this direction, I would not have come forward to speak these words.' The anapaests are the beginning of a formal system; they are followed by a strophe, a longish section of recitative trochaics, an antistrophe, and a second section of recitative trochaics of the same length as the first, but after the anapaests the chorus normally sing or recite in character about themselves. It is worth looking briefly at the opening anapaests of the parabasis in Aristophanes. In the *Acharnians* he claims that he stops the Athenians from being deceived by the flattering speeches of foreign ambassadors: 'so let Kleon do his worst against me'. In the *Knights* he chides the Athenian audiences with being unfaithful to comic poets when they grow old. The *Clouds* is a special case: the opening part of the parabasis is in a different metre and belongs to the second edition of the play, which on its first production had only won the third prize. He claims the superiority of this intellectual comedy, coming after his attacks on Kleon in his prime, whereas his rivals go on attacking Hyperbolos. In the *Wasps* and the *Peace* he claims that he has been a kind of Herakles fighting the monster Kleon. In the later plays the parabasis is either reduced or absent, and this is one of the changes of form which must be discussed later. But the demand for peace, external and internal, which is the real centre of the attacks on Kleon (in the *Wasps* the old juror who delights in condemning people in the courts is called Love-Kleon, and the play is a plea for internal peace) goes on in the *Birds*, *Lysistrata*, *Frogs*, and *Ecclesiazusae*. It is the plea for internal peace implied by the comparison of the old and new education in the *Clouds* and the comparison of Aeschylus and Euripides in the *Frogs* which gives these plays also a consistent serious purpose. This purpose was acceptable to the rich choregoi and was also acceptable to the large number of countrymen in the audience, particularly when they had to desert their farms for military service and suffered damage from the annual Spartan invasion of Attica. The city people who profited from war and internal trouble had to be won by the sheer fantasy, boisterousness, and ribaldry of comedy.[5]

Aristophanes again and again speaks of other comic poets, in the *Knights* pleading for kindness towards their old age (but Kratinos at least needed no sympathy as he defeated Aristophanes at the City Dionysia a year later) and (more often) praising his own comedy as more intelligent than theirs. The other comic poets did the same. Kratinos called Aristophanes 'oversubtle, pursuer of maxims, Euripides-Aristophaniser', and told the audience to wake up after listening to the chatter of one-day poets. Eupolis claimed to be part author of Aristophanes' *Knights*, criticised his statue of Peace in the *Peace*, and told the Athenians to listen to homegrown poets, probably also a hit at Aristophanes, whose father had land in Aigina, perhaps as an Athenian settler.[6]

Old Comedy is so loosely knit that the many short fragments which survive from lost plays do not give any idea of what the outlines of the plays may have been, and even the few longer fragments on papyrus are far less indicative of structure than similar lengths of New Comedy or tragedy. The other poets of Old Comedy may therefore have been more different from Aristophanes than the fragments suggest. The fragments do, however, show that the range of subject matter and the wealth of detailed allusion to philosophy, science, and poetry, which makes us rate the intelligence of Aristophanes' audience so high, was not confined to Aristophanes. They show also that the major enemies of the comic poets were largely the same and that the same people were subjected to what we have called harmless abuse by a number of comic poets.[7]

A summary of Aristophanes' references to Euripides runs: 'Over a hundred references to Euripides in nine plays; nearly thirty references to characters or events; extensive paratragedy in *Acharnians* and *Peace*; two comedies (*Frogs* and *Thesmophoriazusae*) largely concerned with Euripides.' We cannot make any such statistics for the other poets, but we have some evidence. Plays with titles like *Hesiod and his companions* (Telekleides), *Archilochos and his companions* (Kratinos), *Tragoidoi*, *Muses* (Phrynichos), *Properties*, *Poets* (Plato) seem from their titles to have dealt with poetry, and the fragments prove it. Kratinos' *Seriphians* parodies Euripides' *Diktys*; Eupolis' *Commanders* quoted Sophocles' *Tereus*; Strattis' *Phoinissai* parodied the beginning of Euripides' *Hypsipyle*; in a line like 'I built the art up high and handed it on', spoken by Aeschylus in a play of Pherekrates, we hear a pre-echo of the *Frogs*.[8]

For musicians we have already quoted Pherekrates' account of the havoc wrought by modern music and Plato's description of Damon as the wise Centaur who taught Pericles. Eupolis has a reference to the sloppy singing of paians, which recalls the *Clouds*. We have also mentioned the various plays in which Socrates occurred with his music-master Konnos or as assisting Euripides to write his plays. Eupolis' attack on Athenians who wore female dress to sing in the rites of the Thracian goddess Kottyto is perhaps political rather than musical criticism as Alkibiades is involved, but in the same play he speaks scornfully of the long preludes of dithyrambs, just like Aristophanes. On scientists and sophists the *Clouds* is a mine of information and for us most interesting testimony of what the audience was expected to know about recent theory. The *Panoptai* (all-seers) of Kratinos, which mentioned the physical theories of Hippon of Rhegion, and the *Flatterers* of Eupolis, which showed the sophists assembled in Kallias' house and included Protagoras among them, must have been plays of the same kind.[9]

Three figures stand out among the politicians, Pericles, Kleon, and Hyperbolos. We have no complete play from Pericles' lifetime, but what we know of Kratinos' *Dionysalexandros* and *Cheirones*, which were written at the beginning of the Peloponnesian War, suggests that they were intended to damage Pericles as a warmonger. To call him 'the son of Kronos and Revolution, and the greatest of tyrants' is damaging, whereas to continue that this new Zeus had 'as his Hera, Aspasia, bitch-faced concubine, child of Lust' is merely funny. Aristophanes' persistent attacks on Kleon from his early *Babylonians* to the time of Kleon's death (and beyond) are damaging, and he was joined by Hermippos, Eupolis, and Plato. Hyperbolos the lampmaker, who succeeded Kleon as leader of the popular party, was attacked from his entrance into politics till his ostracism by Kratinos, Hermippos, Aristophanes, Eupolis, Plato, and Leukon, and when Aristophanes says that he despises all the poets who rush to attack Hyperbolos, he is not inspired by any love of Hyperbolos; he is commending his own originality and claiming that he attacked a more dangerous enemy in Kleon. On our evidence the poets of Old Comedy took a common line in attacking the more advanced politicians partly for their use of the law-courts to injure innocent citizens but still more for their war policy. But other prominent figures like the seer Lampon, the conservative Nikias, Peisander, Antiphon, and the young Alkibiades, are represented as gluttonous, miserly, cowardly or debauched, because it is the normal licence of comedy to represent people so and no damage is felt or intended. It is only towards the end of the century that Alkibiades became dangerous, and then Eupolis' picture of him taking parts in the rites of Kottyto probably is meant to damage, and Aristophanes is serious when he makes Dionysos ask both Aeschylus and Euripides for their advice on what to do with Alkibiades.[10]

The poet of Old Comedy has serious advice to give, a conservative line in politics and education, which it is believed will bring external and internal peace. It is widely palatable because it is wrapped up in the peculiar, fantastic, satirical, obscene, lyrical form of Old Comedy. This form we can see gradually changing through the plays of Aristophanes, and we have to assume that there was a similar change in the other poets too.

Let us look for a moment at the beginning and the end of the development. The *Acharnians*, produced in 425, is a serious plea for peace against the war policy of Kleon. The old countryman comes to the Assembly to put the question about making peace. He is put off by two farcical deputations, from Persia and from Thrace. Between them he sends a man to Sparta to buy a bottle of peace. The man comes back chased by the chorus of furious old Acharnians, who have had their vines ruined by Spartan invasions. The old countryman celebrates the Rural Dionysia. Then there is a long, formally constructed battle-scene, in which the old countryman declares his reasons for making a private peace; to do this he borrows rags from Euripides so that he can be as persuasive as one of Euripides' beggar heroes. Half of the Acharnians are convinced; the other half summon the general Lamachos, who enters in full armour and is defeated in argument by the old countryman (his name we learn in the battle scene is Dikaiopolis, 'Just in his city'). The whole chorus is now convinced and sing the parabasis. Dikaiopolis opens his market to enemy traders from Megara and Boeotia, and sells an informer to the Boeotian in return for an eel. Dikaiopolis is summoned to the pitcher festival and Lamachos to war. Side by side one prepares his basket of food and the other arms. Lamachos comes back wounded, and Dikaiopolis reels back supported by two hetairai, and the chorus sing a victory song.[11]

The formal elements are the opening chorus, the battle-scene or agon, and the parabasis. The agon in its strictest shape consists of sung strophe, longer recitative, sung antistrophe and then corresponding recitative. The parabasis has the same structure with a long stretch of recitative anapaests in front of it, in which, as we have said, the chorus speaks for the poet. The prologue and the parts between and after these formal elements consist of iambic scenes and choral strophes or odes. The opening chorus, the agon, and the final chorus which concludes the play come from the predramatic dances, which bequeath to comedy choruses of animals, birds, fat men, fat women, and mythical beings like Titans. The iambic scenes were probably modelled on the iambic scenes of tragedy. The parabasis may have been a new element when comedy became official, modelled on the older agon.

The *Acharnians* was produced in 425. In the *Birds* of 414 the anapaests of the parabasis are not about the poet but about the birds themselves, and in all the later fifth-century plays the parabasis is either without the anapaestic section or without half of the succeeding section. In the two fourth-century comedies, *Ecclesiazusae* and *Plutus*, the parabasis is completely absent. The agon survives, but in the two fourth-century plays has only half its full structure. The opening chorus and the closing chorus survive to the end, but in the *Plutus* the closing chorus is reduced to two lines of instruction to dance out after the speakers. After the opening chorus the *Ecclesiazusae* only has two choral odes, one between scenes and the other at the beginning of the half-agon, and there are two places where a note in the manuscript suggests that an interlude (not written for the play but taken from elsewhere) was performed, and the *Plutus* has no special odes after the opening chorus but six notes for interludes. Thus we can see two main changes: first, the gradual suppression of the parabasis and the agon, and secondly, as in fourth-century tragedy, the substitution of interludes for specially written choruses. The first change meant that, like tragedy, comedy became a succession of dialogue scenes, but the metres included iambic tetrameters as well as iambic trimeters and trochaic tetrameters, and there is some evidence in the fragments of fourth-century comedy for solos in recitative or lyric by actors. As for the second change, we do not know whether the singing of interludes was universal in fourth-century tragedy or whether the opening chorus was always or sometimes still written for the play, but in comedy we have traces of special opening choruses until quite late in the fourth century, and in Menander the arrival of the chorus to sing the first interlude is marked by a formula, 'Let us get out of the way; I see some drunks coming'.[12]

Old Comedy had a special form which enshrined traditional elements. Through the latter part of the fifth century and into the first quarter of the fourth we can see it gradually breaking up and changing into a shape resembling the structure of modern comedy. The question which we have now to ask is how far the content changed with the form. The mixture of characters from mythology, known Athenian personages, fictional characters continues; the costume remains unchanged until Menander's time, but new masks are introduced for new types of character. Certainly the new theatre of Lykourgos, which was built about ten years before the first plays of Menander, had three stage doors and wings, and it is possible that an earlier wooden stage building already had this shape. This gave a long narrow stage so that attention was concentrated on the action rather than on the dancing, but what was more important for the development towards realistic drama, the three doors could represent three different houses (or two houses and a shrine), whereas Old Comedy had made use of the single door used for tragedy. In the *Acharnians* the single door was the entrance to Dikaiopolis' house, Euripides' house and Lamachos' house, and still in the *Ecclesiazusae* part of the fun of the conclusion comes from the girl and the old woman using the same door to the distress of the young man. Probably the side doors had to be introduced when the poets started writing about identical twins: confusion of place would have made confusion of persons intolerable.[13]

The realism of social comedy was reached slowly. It is clear from Plato, Isocrates, and Aristotle that in the middle of the fourth century comedy was still regarded as a serious political force. Isocrates says that no one has freedom of speech except the comic poets and they publish the city's mistakes to the rest of the Greeks. Aristotle in the *Rhetoric* puts the same view more succinctly: 'comic poets speak evil and publish it'. Plato in the *Laws* will not allow any comic poet to ridicule any of the citizen's 'either in word or in likeness, either in anger or without anger'. The distinction between word and likeness is a distinction between indirect ridicule in the words of another character and direct ridicule by bringing the man to be ridiculed on the stage. The second distinction between 'in anger' and 'without anger' is very much the same as the distinction between harmful and harmless abuse which we drew for comedy of the fifth century. Titles like *Kinesias* (Strattis) and *Dionysios* (Euboulos) show that politicians were still put on the stage in the early fourth century. The two men are connected in fact, because Kinesias, the lyric poet ridiculed in the fifth century by Aristophanes, in 393 proposed a decree honouring Dionysios I the tyrant of Syracuse at a time when the Athenian general Konon sent an embassy to Dionysios to ask him for an alliance. Later the comic poet Mnesimachos named a play after Philip of Macedon, and the fragments show that it was an attack on his imperialism. In general, it looks as if the comic poets in the early fourth century were critical of a forward policy which involved Athens in continual wars, as they had been in the fifth century; after the rise of Philip of Macedon they seem to have divided into pro-Macedonian and anti-Macedonian, as the Athenians themselves were divided. All through the period and on into the earlier plays of Menander himself there is plenty of evidence for what we have called harmless abuse.[14]

It is true that the fragments of Strattis' *Kinesias* also criticise Kinesias' poetry and that in Ephippos' *Homoioi* someone hopes that his worst enemy may have to learn the drama of Dionysios: Dionysios was also a writer of tragedy and was awarded a victory in the Athenian competition in the year that he died. But the political objections to Kinesias and Dionysios outweighed the aesthetic objections, and serious literary criticism is now the province of the philosophers and not of the comic poets. The battle over the new education is over, and though the philosophers are good for harmless abuse, they are treated more kindly than the earlier sophists. The range is considerable: the audience are expected to recognise allusions to the Cynics, the Megarian eristic philosophers, Aristippos of Cyrene, and Herakleides Pontikos, as well as to the Pythagoreans and Plato. A number of allusions can be quoted to particular dialogues of Plato, and a fragment of Epikrates describes the pupils in the Academy discussing the classification of the pumpkin in the presence of a Sicilian doctor and Plato himself. This is valuable evidence of the date when the Academy took up biological classification, as well as of the interest in this move outside the Academy. In general the philosophers are funny because they are not interested in pleasure and they are apt to be unpractical in ordinary life, but the old charge continues that the philosophers teach rhetoric and so train the young for making money out of politics.[15]

Nothing that we have seen so far shows the change towards social comedy, and yet Aristotle in the *Poetics* quotes a comedy as his evidence for the universality of poetry against the particularity of history. 'In the case of comedy this has become clear; for they put together the plot of probable incidents and add chance names.' We cannot tell whether this note on comedy was part of the original draft written before 347 or added after Aristotle returned to Athens in 335. On either view it implies a comedy of ordinary life with fictional characters well before Menander's first production. This was not the only kind of comedy. Besides the plays we have noticed which introduced historical characters, Aristotle himself mentions a mythological comedy in which Orestes and Aigisthos became friends 'and nobody was killed by anybody'. Mythological comedy has a long history, which goes back to Epicharmos' plays about Odysseus, Herakles, and Prometheus and to Kratinos' *Odysseus and his companions*. In the first half of the fourth century something between a third and a half of the dated plays have mythological titles, but between 350 and 320 the proportion falls to a tenth. Titles of course, cannot show that the whole play is a parody of mythology: in Aristophanes' *Plutus* Ploutos is the only mythological character. On the other hand Strattis' *Phoinissai* certainly had a parody of the debate between Iokaste and her two sons in Euripides' *Phoenissae* and opened with a parody of the beginning of Euripides' *Hypsipyle*, which probably belonged to the same trilogy. The formula is clear from a single fragment, 'I want to give you both some wise advice. When you boil beans, do not pour myrrh on them.' Euripides' Iokaste had said: 'I want to give you both some wise advice. When a friend is angry with a friend and meets him face to face, he should only consider why he has come, and forget entirely former wrongs.' The mythological hero takes off the magnificent costume of tragedy and puts on the padded obscene comic costume and with it the earthy realistic world of comedy, but his name and the occasional parody of the original or quotation of the original keep the connection alive in the mind of the audience. It seems a possibility that parody of tragedy brought into comedy situations, which then became part of the stock in trade of non-mythological comedy, in particular love-affairs and intriguing slaves from late Euripides. Then in the second half of the fourth century the mythological connection was faded out.[16]

Another source of fictional stock characters, which are implied by Aristotle's chance names and probable incidents, is their historical prototypes in Athens. Aristotle defines the universal as the performance of a certain kind of action by a certain kind of man, and thus presupposes stock characters. Lamachos in the *Acharnians* is the ancestor of the braggart soldier of later comedy; he was an Athenian general who was killed in the Sicilian expedition. Timon of Athens was alive at the time of the *Birds*, and he is the ancestor of the misanthropic old man of later comedy. In the early fourth century, and very occasionally before, plays are named after hetairai, and some of them were certainly historical hetairai, so that here again the historical figure probably precedes the fictional figure. It is of course true that comedy's way of seeing is caricature, and therefore a historical figure on the comic stage includes a strong element of fiction: the Aristophanic portraits of Kleon and Socrates make that clear. The point here is that figures prominent in society once transposed into comedy could form the models of later fictional characters. The condition probably is that they must not be too unique or tied too closely to unique events; thus Lamachos and Timon qualify, Kleon and Socrates do not. The stock characters belong to private life rather than to public life: the braggart soldier, though by definition the member of an army, only appears in civilian surroundings. He, the greedy hetaira, and the misanthropic father, to whom we can add the intriguing slave, the impecunious hanger-on, the loquacious cook, and the shameless pimp as well-attested types of fourth-century comedy, are in Aristotle's terms people of a certain kind, who, because they are of that kind, perform a corresponding kind of action. The plot constructed of such actions is essentially a story of private lives. The fantastic element of Old Comedy has to a large extent gone with the special choruses; the serious criticism of Old Comedy has become marginal. What remains is on the one side the central optimism of comedy: whatever the obstacles on the way, the ending is happy and often a marriage; this is the legacy of the story pattern based on the old ritual meant to ensure fertility. On the other side comedy is by derivation abuse, and therefore the stock characters are caricatured and the traditional costume fits in with this.[17]

This picture of fourth-century comedy before Menander is

reconstructed from the surviving fragments and from the few remarks in Aristotle about the comedy of his own day. If we had some surviving plays, particularly of the period immediately before Menander's first production in 321, we should be able to tell how far the characters were being given more sympathetic treatment in spite of the tradition of caricature and in spite of the costume.

It is worth noting a single point which is firmly established. Terracotta statuettes of comic slaves dated before 350 parade large sexual organs; similar statuettes of 330 show sexual organs of normal size; in Menander's time slaves wear chitons which come down to the middle of their thighs and conceal their sex. In general it is true to say that Menander's actors looked like the Athenians of his day, and the essential step (by whatever official arrangement and whoever, poet or politician, was responsible) was to give all male characters a chiton which concealed instead of revealing their sex. But the statuettes of 330 show that the movement towards decency, and therefore the movement away from caricature, had begun well before Menander.[18]

Menander takes us outside our period, but we may glance at him for a moment. The costume has changed. The form has become fixed with five acts and four choral interludes, for which the poet composed neither the words nor the music. The shape is standardised with an opening prologue, a climax in the fourth act, and a fifth act to bring the story to rest. The stories all come under the head of overcoming obstacles in the way of conjugal felicity, but Menander manages to find an immense variety of obstacles and an immense variety of ways to overcome them. A great deal both in characters and in situations is derived from preceding comedy or tragedy. What is new is the prevailing sympathy with which the characters are treated, even and most remarkably the traditionally unsympathetic characters. The rich hetaira may be wholly concerned with achieving a marriage for her younger orphan friend, the braggart soldier may be revealed as an unselfish lover, the misanthropic old man has retired from the world because the values of the world are corrupt. The new form which Menander gave to comedy can be called social comedy, and as such has survived to our own day.[19]

12 *Geographers, Doctors and Historians*

We are apt to think of geography, medicine, and history as three very different activities with three very different sorts of practitioners, but the historian Herodotos drew enormously on the geographers and was to some extent influenced by medical writing, the interaction between geographers and medical writers is demonstrable, and the historian Thucydides was probably influenced by the doctors. Our neat specialisations do not fit the ancient world: we have already noticed that Empedokles and Diogenes of Apollonia were both philosophers and doctors, and that the philosopher rhetorician Gorgias was the brother of a doctor. Geographical description and medical thought spill over into works which are essentially different in kind, what we should naturally class as philosophy as well as what we class as history. This chapter is not concerned with the Greek achievement in geography or medicine but with the kind of thinking that the geographers and doctors gave to other practitioners and particularly to the historians. Then we have to sketch what the historians actually did. Finally we have to see whether we can trace primarily in the doctors and historians but also in the philosophers a method or arguing about physical and psychological unknowns which, while it has not the certainty of mathematical argument (to be discussed in the next chapter), is nevertheless capable of being applied with a certain amount of rigour.[1]

One obvious distinction between geographers, doctors, and historians on the one hand and all the writers that we have discussed up to now is that they are far more dependent than the rest on written words reaching a reading public. The poets have their public performances, and parts of their works are sung afterwards in symposia; inscribed poetry is displayed in a public place on dedications or grave monuments. Political and law-court speeches are made in public. The sophists often came to a city on public business, then gave lectures, were on display in the houses of the rich, and were seen in the Agora. In the fourth century the philosophers and rhetoricians had their schools. In the late fifth century the book-trade had evidently come into existence, and from that time onwards publication is no problem. For the earlier period we can only state the little evidence that we have.[2]

The sixth-century geographer and genealogist, Hekataios of Miletos, is called by Herodotos 'the logopoios'. The similar word 'logographos' is used later in the meaning of writer of speeches for others to deliver. Here logos must rather mean 'accounts', but the whole word does probably imply a writer and therefore a book. Herodotos could consult this book, and fragments of it survived. We hear that Herakleitos of Ephesos deposited his book in the temple of Artemis, and this may not have been an isolated case. In the Augustan period Dionysios of Halikarnassos says that the local historians who were predecessors and contemporaries of Thucydides (and he includes Hekataios among them) all had the same object, to bring to the general knowledge of the public the written records that they found preserved in temples or in secular buildings, in the form in which they found them. Taken literally, this is obviously untrue since we find no such quotation of records, but it may preserve a memory that the early historians actually deposited their histories in temples where they could be consulted and copied. What we can put on the demand side is the interest in geography shown by Athenian audiences in the early fifth century: the description of the places to be visited by Triptolemos in Sophocles' play of 468, and the wanderings of Io in the *Prometheus Bound* and of Herakles in the *Prometheus Unbound* of Aeschylus, written probably in 457.[3]

The doctors are in a rather different position, because, where there was an established medical school, this was a natural place for their writings to be kept and a natural place for those who needed them to go and consult them. Particularly one would expect to find the purely technical treatises here, the accounts of cases and the accounts of particular diseases; more general treatises must have circulated like other books, and the travels of the doctors themselves must have helped the circulation. The best known schools were in Kos and Knidos; the school in Kroton was probably closely related to the Pythagorean community there. The famous Hippokrates of Kos was born about 460 and belongs to a family which can be traced back for four generations. His great uncle made a dedication on the Akropolis at Athens about 500, and he himself is said to have visited Macedonia, Persia, and Athens. Like other professions, medicine evidently ran in families, but Hippokrates might also take pupils at a fee, as Plato says in the *Protagoras*. Herodotos provides good early evidence about another doctor who travelled, Demokedes of Kroton. His father Kalliphon (according to another source) came from Knidos, and this may link the schools of Kroton and Knidos in the mid-sixth century. Demokedes quarrelled with his father and went to Aigina. In the first year he showed his superiority to all the other doctors, although he had no instruments (they had presumably remained with his father). The next year the Aiginetans hired him publicly for 6,000 drachmai, and the following year the Athenians hired him publicly for 10,000 drachmai. (We need not follow his further adventures with Polykrates and Dareios of Persia.) This is interesting evidence for a doctor appointed by the state by the side of doctors practising on their own. The rate of pay (over thirty drachmai a day in Athens) puts him right out of the range of ordinary wage-earners and more into the class of the sophists.[4]

Drama tells us a little about the ordinary Athenian's interest in doctors and medicine. In Aristophanes' *Clouds* Socrates mixes his fine thought with the kindred air, and this is probably an allusion to the equation of air and mind in Diogenes of Apollonia; in the *Frogs* Euripides describes in medical terms how he had to treat tragedy when he inherited from Aeschylus: 'she was all swollen up, and I dried her by giving her a decoction, and then I built her up again with monodies'. The tragic poets also used medicine as a source of imagery and had extremely accurate descriptions of diseased and deranged states, particularly Philoktetes' diseased foot in Sophocles' play and Agave's madness and awakening in *Bacchae*.[5]

We have already mentioned that Herodotos was in Athens in 442 when Sophocles wrote an ode to him. Shortly afterwards he went to the new colony, Thourioi, in South Italy. He is said to have lectured in Athens in 445/4 and to have received ten talents, an excessively large sum. Thucydides heard him and burst into tears, which Herodotos took as a compliment. We can, therefore, accept that Herodotos, like a sophist, gave lectures: this made him known, and conceivably copies were made of the text of the lectures. Sophocles used the story of Dareios and Intaphernes' wife for the *Antigone*, but this does not tell us much about the progress of the history since we should expect in any case that Herodotos had collected his Eastern material before he came to Athens. The latest date that he mentions is the execution of the Spartan heralds in 430; this adds a further chapter to a story in the VIIth book and was presumably inserted when the news reached him. We have no knowledge that he ever came back to Athens from the West, but there are two indications that his book was known in Athens by 425: Aristophanes parodies the beginning of the 1st book in the *Acharnians*, and Euripides refers to Scythian burial customs in the *Kresphontes*. It does therefore seem likely that a copy or copies got back to Athens very soon after he had completed his work.[6]

About the circulation of Thucydides' work we know even less than we do about Herodotos. He had the advantage of being an Athenian of prominent family, related both to Kimon and to Thucydides, son of Melesias. His wealth came from the right to work gold mines in Thrace opposite Thasos. He was strategos in 424 and was exiled for failing to prevent Brasidas' capture of Amphipolis. He spent his exile 'with the Peloponnesians', probably in Sicily as well as in the Peloponnese, and possibly at the end with Archelaos of Macedon, and returned to Athens in 404. He began to write at the beginning of the Peloponnesian war in 431 and reaches a preliminary conclusion with the truce of 421. He then starts again with a new prologue, which was not written until 404. This suggests that his account of the first ten years of the war was released as a separate work, but the text which has come down to us is evidently based on a copy which Thucydides edited later, since the passage on Archelaos in Book II cannot have been written before 413 at the earliest and the evaluation of Pericles' policy in the same book was not written until after 404. The second part of the history (from 421) presents a curious problem: it stops in 411, and therefore we must assume that Thucydides had not gone any further when he died. But it falls into two distinct pieces; in the account of the Melian attack and of the Sicilian expedition the speeches are highly polished and purport to be the words used by the speaker, as in the account of the first ten years of the war, but in the rest of the second part, both before the Melian attack and after the Sicilian expedition, the speeches are merely reported summaries. The conclusion seems inevitable that the attack on Melos and the Sicilian expedition were written up for separate publication, and as the Sicilian expedition has its own prologue, they must have been separate publications. I say 'publications', but these two sections are on a scale compatible with recitation, and it remains a possibility that Thucydides, however scornful he may be of 'ephemeral contest-pieces', did give public recitations like Herodotos, and this was one of the means by which historians became known.[7]

In different ways the historians were affected by the work of the geographers and doctors. We know least about the geographers, and our best guides to their work are the long accounts in Herodotos of the lands and customs of non-Greek peoples. From the seventh century and increasingly in the sixth the Greeks had come into contact by trade and exploration with non-Greek people in the hinterland of their colonies and settlements and on the shores of the Mediterranean and its adjacent seas. Greeks were intelligent and inquisitive: it was useful to know about the people with whom they traded, and amusing to know about their customs, buildings, and animals. The comparison of different customs led to the appreciation that they were all man-made, and so to the intellectually very fruitful contrast between artificial *nomos* and permanent *physis*, which we have already discussed. There was competition in this reporting: Hekataios begins, 'I write this as it seems to me to be true; for the reports of the Greeks are many and ridiculous, as they appear to me.' And

Herodotos, discussing the flooding of the Nile, first says that he could not find any explanation by asking the Egyptians and then continues, 'Certain Greeks, wanting a reputation for wisdom, gave three explanations of this water, two of which I do not think worth mentioning, except just to indicate their existence ... the third explanation is the most elegant and the furthest from the truth.' We know that the three Greeks were Thales, Hekataios, and Anaxagoras. But, of course, for all his independence Herodotos does use his predecessors, and his long descriptions of the lands and customs of Egyptians, Babylonians, Scythians, and others are indebted to them not only for matter but also for the form of the report. Two points may be noted here before leaving the geographers, first the development of the map, and secondly the very simple style which marks their descriptions.[8]

We have already spoken of Anaximander's sixth-century map of a round earth encircled by a circular ocean and divided into four quarters. Much detail was put in by Hekataios, and it was probably his map that Aristagoras took with him at the end of the century when he tried to persuade the Spartan king to aid the Ionian revolt against Persia. He had 'a bronze tablet on which the circuit of the whole earth was engraved and every sea and all the rivers', and he pointed out the Ionians and all the tributary nations of the Persian empire on this map. Herodotos laughs at the idea of the circular ocean and at the symmetry which makes Asia plus Africa the same size as Europe. He conceives of an Asia with two peninsulas, Asia Minor and Africa. What happens beyond India he does not know, but from his knowledge of sea-voyages he can sketch in the coast from the Black Sea to beyond the straits of Gibraltar, and he knows about the Red Sea. He thinks that Asia is smaller than Europe, largely because he does not know anything about the north of Europe and has grave doubts about the existence of a surrounding sea. What is interesting is not what he gets wrong but that he breaks up the earlier geometrical scheme to accommodate his more recent information. Aristophanes includes a map of the world in the think-shop of Socrates in the *Clouds*, as a known part of higher education.[9]

The style of the geographer's description is extremely simple and may abandon grammar in listing points. Herodotos' description of the hippopotamus is generally supposed to be a direct transcription of Hekataios. It runs: 'It is four-footed, cloven-hoofed, hooves of an ox, snub-nosed, having the mane of a horse, showing tusks, tail, and voice of a horse, size as big as the biggest ox.' This is the inventory style of the Pylos tablets which list decorated chairs and footstools nearly a thousand years earlier, and the same style is found 150 years later when Theophrastos describes roses. Herodotos admits it into his history because it is the proper style for this particular job.[10]

The same style is found in the doctors' accounts of their cases: 'The Klazomenian, who lay sick by the well of Phrynichides, was attacked by fever. He suffered in head, neck, loins from the beginning. Soon deafness. Sleep was absent. Strong fever attacked. Hypochondrium was swollen, not excessively. Distension. Dry tongue. On the fourth day he was delirious at night. On the fifth, painfully.' These are the notes of a doctor on his case. Presumably he kept them for reference, and they were preserved in the school library for future doctors to use. The style is recognisably the same as in the description of the hippopotamus. Here too it is entirely adequate for its purpose. These texts show that the doctors based their practice on a careful record of detailed observations on particular cases. It is, however, in their more theoretical writings that they link up with the historians and philosophers. Three, which were probably written in the fifth century, particularly concern us: *Airs, waters, places* (abbreviated as *Airs*), *Sacred disease*, and *Ancient medicine*. *Airs* begins with the statement that the true doctor must know the effect of different seasons, different winds, and different kinds of water, 'so that when one comes to a city of which one is ignorant one must work out its position, how it lies with regard to the winds and to the rising of the sun'. We are promised a kind of ecology for the travelling doctor (like Demokedes or Hippokrates himself), and it is this that connects this treatise with the geographers and Herodotos.[11]

But before pursuing this, let us note how the doctor with his detailed records of cases, his knowledge of the external physical things which affect the human body (and, as we shall see, the human mind), was regarded by ethical philosophers. In one of his discussions of education the Platonic Socrates defines learning as 'tending the soul', and the word 'tending' is the normal word for treatment by a doctor. In the *Gorgias* he says that there are four arts which work for the good of the body and for the good of the soul, gymnastics, medicine, law-giving, justice; 'medicine has considered both the nature of the patient and the reason for what it is doing and can give an account of each of these'. Thus medicine as practised is an example of the kind of art which the statesman ought to have. Later in the *Phaedrus* he develops the same sort of comparison to embrace his new view of the true orator, who must know how to treat different kinds of soul; Hippokrates can diagnose whether what he wants to treat is simple or multiple and what its simple or multiple capabilities are of affecting something else or being affected by something else. This is in fact how *Ancient medicine* defines the doctor's task with the actual example of cheese and its different effects on differently constituted people. But the point is that Plato saw medicine as a successful art for tending bodies, for which he wanted a parallel art for treating souls, and medicine continues to hold the same special place in Aristotle's ethical thought.[12]

Herodotos touches *Airs* at a number of points and *Sacred disease* once. *Airs* divides the world into Asia and Europe and describes the effect of climate and landscape on the populations of each. This is the division given by Hekataios with Africa as part of Asia. Both *Airs* and Herodotos speak of Scythia as the coldest part of Europe, of the frightening women in Scythia, and of the impotence of some Scythian men, who are called *Enarees*. Herodotos says that they attribute this impotence to the anger of Aphrodite of Askalon, whose temple they raided. *Airs* gives a medical explanation for the disease, and says that this disease is no more or less divine than any other; each has its own nature and none arises without nature. This is very like the beginning of *Sacred disease* (which is possibly by the same author): 'It does not seem to me any more divine or sacred than the other diseases, but the rest have a nature from which they arise and so has this, but men think it divine because of their ignorance.' The sacred disease is epilepsy but includes also certain forms of madness. The author goes on to attribute it to a hereditary mischance to the brain in the womb; this causes the brain to contain moisture in-

stead of dry air, which produces sanity and wisdom. In identify-
ing air and mind and locating mind in the brain and in making
the veins the system of transmission to the brain, *Sacred disease*
is very close to Diogenes of Apollonia, of whom we have already
spoken. Herodotos speaks of the sacred disease in connection with
Kambyses, king of Persia: 'These acts of madness Kambyses performed against his family, whether because of (the vengeance of
the Egyptian god) Apis or in the normal way that evils befall
men. For Kambyses is said to have had from birth a great disease,
which some call the sacred disease. There is nothing strange in a
man with a great disease of the body being unhealthy in mind
too.' Herodotos certainly must know some account of the sacred
disease very like the one which we have.[13]

At the very end of the history Herodotos gives an ecological
account of the Persian defeat. Long ago Artembares had proposed
to Cyrus the conquest of Asia. Cyrus told the Persians to go
ahead if they were prepared to be subjects instead of rulers; 'soft
men grow out of soft lands. The same land cannot produce won-
derful fruit and warriors.' This doctrine is spelt out in *Airs*. 'The
part of the land that lies between the hot and the cold, this is
very fruitful and very well treed ... but the brave and the endur-
ing and the spirited would not arise in such a nature, whether of
a native or of an alien.' This is exactly what Cyrus fears in
Herodotos. 'Such a nature' (*physis*) means here a human body
living in these conditions, and the terminology gives first the
intimate connection between the equability of the climate (*physis*)
and the equability of the inhabitants, but also asks for the other
term, *nomos*. This comes a little later: 'for these reasons, it seems
to me, Asiatics are unwarlike and also because of their institutions
(*nomoi*). For the greatest part of Asia is ruled by kings.... All
the Greeks or non-Greeks in Asia who are not under a despot
but are independent and work for themselves are the most warlike of all.' He goes back to this point again when he writes of
Europeans. The frequent changes of climate engender 'the wild
and the unsociable and the spirited.... Therefore the Europeans
are more warlike, and also because of their institutions (*nomoi*)
because they are not ruled by a king.' In this writer there is no
question of *nomos* being weak because it is man-made; it is a

force which can act with or against *physis*.[14]

Herodotos owes a great deal to the geographers and a certain amount to the doctors who came nearest in outlook to the geographers. Two other thinkers who came close to this kind of observational science were in Athens when Herodotos was, Anaxagoras and Protagoras. Anaxagoras' demonstration that the one-horned ram had a curiously formed skull is entirely in tune with Ionian science, and we know that Herodotos quoted his explanation of the Nile flood. Protagoras' perception of the barrenness of fierce beasts and the prolific offspring of weak beasts also belongs here and again is quoted by Herodotos. The influence of what we may call in general Ionian science was very strong, and his use of the story about Cyrus as a conclusion shows that he still believed that physical surroundings were one important factor in character at the time that he finished his history. But it is at least a possible theory that what excited Herodotos in Athens was not primarily more Ionian science but the recitations of Homer at the Panathenaia and the performances of tragedy. What the *Iliad* gave him was a method of telling a complicated story. The main story line of the *Iliad* is the wrath of Achilles against Agamemnon, which turns into the wrath of Achilles against Hektor and finally ends with the reconciliation between Achilles and Priam. This story is a framework for a great deal more about the main heroes of the Trojan war and about events connected with them, which in some cases happened both before and after the short stretch of the Trojan war which is the subject of the *Iliad*. The *Iliad* may also be termed a moral story: moral failures by Agamemnon, Achilles, and Hektor cause their disasters, and a great effort of will by Achilles leads to reconciliation at the end. This sequence is in some sense 'the will of Zeus'; it is the way in which the gods allow human affairs to work. Thus the *Iliad* provided an example of a great story which allowed many digressions, a story which ultimately depended on human character but with the gods in the background. Tragedy takes stories which are similar to the main story line of the *Iliad* and concentrates them in a few dramatic moments; its influence on Herodotos is clearest in the moments of decision like the council of Xerxes before his expedition, where not only the shape and the imagery but even the rhythms seem to come from tragedy and more particularly from Sophocles.[15]

Let us look at Herodotos' programme and very briefly at its execution. He begins that he wants to preserve the past and the great deeds of Greeks and non-Greeks, particularly the reason for their fighting each other. This is the good Homeric idea of song preserving 'the fames of heroes'. He then disposes of the mythical past history told by Persians and Phoenicians and defines his task: 'Having pointed out the man whom I know to have been the first aggressor against the Greeks, I will go forward in my story, treating the small and great towns of men. For the formerly great have mostly become small, and the great of today were small before. Knowing therefore that human prosperity never remains in the same place, I will recall both alike. Kroisos was a Lydian.' The beginning of this sentence recalls the beginning of the *Odyssey*, 'Sing of a versatile man, who saw the towns of many men and learnt their mind'. Here the man is instead an aggressor, and the towns, or rather the countries, which are geographically described are partly those of the aggressors and partly those which are attacked: Lydia and Persia on the one hand, Babylonia, Egypt, Scythia on the other. The fragility of human prosperity is associated with the towns, but it belongs still more to the aggressors. Herodotos, probably unhistorically, sends the Athenian Solon to warn Kroisos of this fragility, but Kroisos, who was bound to suffer for a murder in an earlier generation, was misled by an oracle to attack Cyrus of Persia. In his defeat and on his funeral pyre he remembered Solon, and Cyrus saved him to become his own wise adviser. We need not follow the story through Kambyses and Dareios. The final great moment of decision is the decision of Xerxes to bridge the Hellespont and attack Greece. Xerxes at the beginning did not want to go. He was overpersuaded by his cousin Mardonios, and even at this stage a prophecy by the exiled Athenian Onomakritos that a Persian would yoke the Hellespont played a part. At the next council Artabanos, Xerxes' uncle, playing the part of the wise adviser, argued strongly against the expedition (in a speech reminiscent of the *Antigone*). Xerxes decided to march, but in the night changed his mind. He then had a dream telling him to march, which he disregarded and cancelled the expedition. The dream returned the next night, and Xerxes then persuaded Artabanos to take his place and the dream visited him too. Artabanos advised Xerxes to make the expedition 'since there is a divine impulse and the Greeks, as it seems, are being attacked by destruction from heaven'. It is the classic case of the doctrine stated in the *Antigone*: 'evil seems good to the man whose wits god brings to infatuation'. It is the moral of the *Iliad* and it is the moral of Aeschylus' *Persians*. Man makes the first step but then it is too late for him to turn back because the gods push him on. This thread runs right through the history from the aggression of Kroisos to the aggression of Xerxes. It is a major part of the story because the Persian empire was ruled by a king. On the other side are the Greeks, treacherous, patriotic, and brave, and their back history too is brought in as occasion permits. Herodotos does not treat their customs as fully as those of the non-Greeks because they are known. He would probably agree with *Airs* that the frequent changes of climate made them fierce, quarrelsome, and spirited; but he only gives us the influence of climate as a contributory cause of the Persian defeat: they became soft because they lived soft.[16]

Herodotos may have felt at the end of his life that Athens, like Persia before, was running on a danger course. Such a moral story has been seen in Thucydides' history, the tragedy of Athens, starting with the Periclean dream of the Funeral speech and ending, as was clearly intended, with the fall of Athens in 404. The divine background is of course lacking; Thucydides does not think, at any rate explicitly, that the gods punish aggression; Herodotos refers Kroisos' fall to a transgression generations before, and a dream sent by the gods is a decisive element in Xerxes' resolve to attack Greece; this kind of causation does not appear in Thucydides. We do not know how the war would appear if he had written it up to the end in its final form, but we have two pointers to his latest thought. The dialogue between the Athenians and Melians assumes that the Spartans will treat the Athenians mercifully in the case of defeat, and this is likely to have been written after the actual defeat, when the Spartans resisted the Corinthian and Boeotian demand to destroy Athens.

The Melian dialogue describes Athenian imperialism at its most realistic: the Melians have suggested that their just claims will give them the help of the gods; the Athenians answer: 'The gods, as we believe, and men, as we see, always by a necessity of their nature rule whatever they conquer. We neither made this law nor are the first to take advantage of its establishment. It was in existence when we received it, and we shall leave it behind us to exist for ever. We are taking advantage of it, because we know that you and anyone else who had the same power as us would do the same. And therefore we naturally are not afraid of any reverse from heaven.' It has been pointed out that in a rather similar exposition of the rationale of empire in 431 the Athenians made the significant addition that they are worthy of praise for using their power with extreme moderation. The omission of this is the measure of the difference that Thucydides saw between the Athens of 431 and the Athens of 416: in 416 naked aggression, just before Athens embarked on the more disastrous aggression of the Sicilian expedition. The other significant late passage is the obituary of Pericles. His successors, who ruined Athens, were only interested in their private ambitions and their private gains, but Pericles, besides his superiority in position and intellect, was incorruptible and so could lead Athens as free men should be led; he did not have to flatter them, he could resist them if it was necessary. So incorruptibility and the moral power that it gave were in Thucydides' final analysis a real force, which at the beginning kept Athens safe; and disaster came, as for instance in Euripides' *Phoenissae*, from the selfishness of lesser men, which added up to naked but incompetent aggression. Herodotos makes us think of Sophocles, but Thucydides makes us think of late Euripides. It is also true that the finished version of the history has well-spaced dramatic moments, roughly one for each year of the war: the funeral speech, the plague, the debate on Mytilene, the attack on Pylos, the Melian dialogue, and the debates before the expedition to Sicily. This is essentially tragic technique.[17]

Thucydides certainly owes much to tragedy and epic in shaping his work so as to have the maximum force on his readers. We can see this, but he himself, like Herodotos, gives quite a different account of his intentions. He will be satisfied if his account is judged useful by those who may want a clear account of what happened and what is likely, given human nature, to recur in a similar form: 'it is composed to be a treasure for ever rather than a contest-piece for ephemeral hearing'. What he means by 'clear account', he has explained just before: in the speeches, while keeping the general tenor of what was actually said, he has made the speakers say what he thought the particular situation required; for the events of the war he has sifted the often conflicting accounts of eyewitnesses and reached as far as possible an accurate account.[18]

A treasure is something that can be used in the future, and Thucydides' history is useful because the universality of human nature makes events recur in a similar form. He is not far from the Aristotelian definition of universal: 'a certain kind of man acts or speaks probably or necessarily in a certain way'. He does not have any grand cyclical view of history. He means more simply that, if your present situation reminds you of a Thucydidean situation, his careful analysis of his situation may help you to understand the likeness and the differences in your situation. He has at least three other references to the universality of human nature. One is the Athenian statement in the Melian dialogue: 'men, as we see, always by a necessity in their nature rule whatever they conquer.' Another is in the analysis of revolution, which follows the account of the revolution in Corcyra: 'many evils befell the cities in revolution, evils that happen and will always happen as long as human nature is the same, more disturbed or less or different in form, according as the circumstances in each case vary.' In both these the universal is the effects caused by certain psychological forces in human nature.[19]

His statement about the usefulness of the history is often compared to his very similarly phrased statement about the plague: 'I will show those features the consideration of which would cause a man with this foreknowledge to recognise it, if it befell again.' The parallel has suggested that Thucydides was largely influenced by the doctors and wrote his Peloponnesian war as a sort of case history. The plague was an evil which 'befell' human bodies and would have similar recognisable effects another time because of the universal constitution of human bodies; revolution is an evil which 'befell' human souls and would have similar effects another time because of the universal constitution of human souls. Thucydides does seem to imply this parallelism, but what primarily interests him is the reaction of human minds to particular situations. His account of Greek history down to the Persian wars (to which we shall return) has two leading ideas, the desire of the strong to dominate and the fear of domination on the part of the weak. So also after he has defined his aim of being useful, he distinguishes between the causes of the Peloponnesian war and the truest reason, which was that the size of the Athenian empire frightened the Spartans and so they necessarily went to war. He picks this up again after his account of the causes of war, which are a series of incidents between 445 and 431: 'the Spartans were afraid that the Athenians would become even more powerful.' Then he recounts the growth of Athenian power from 480 to 431; the Spartans did not move because they were slow, but finally they found it intolerable and decided 'to attack and destroy this might'. This is all history in outline. In the detailed year by year account of the Peloponnesian war the power theme recurs, for instance in Pericles' speech early in the war, in Kleon's speech in the Mytilene debate, and in the Melian dialogue, and in Thucydides' own analysis of revolution. It is perhaps equally important to note that the shifts in the war are normally initiated by debates, usually with pairs of speeches delivered by men of different kinds, very often one an aggressor and one a non-aggressor. We have to ask how far this very personal view of history is influenced by the doctors, and it is natural to ask first what the ancient *Life* of Thucydides tells us.[20]

The ancient *Life* says nothing about the doctors, but gives us Antiphon and Anaxagoras as his teachers and Gorgias and Prodikos as influences on style. The extreme precision of Thucydides' terminology clearly shows the influence of Prodikos, and the antithetic parallel phrases of Gorgias are given a highly idiosyncratic twist by Thucydides. The power-fear theme which dominates the history is closely akin to the jungle-law interpretation of the *physis-nomos* contrast, as we have already shown;

it is possible that the ancient commentators thought of Antiphon in connection with this, but they may merely have taken their cue from Thucydides' praise of Antiphon as the back-room boy of the oligarchic revolution in 411. The mention of Anaxagoras is surprising unless it is merely a confused memory of the fact that the elder Thucydides, son of Melesias, prosecuted Anaxagoras. There is another intriguing possibility. The late historian Diodoros preserves a cosmogony which leads into an account of the origin and growth of civilisation. It is generally agreed that it goes back to a fifth-century source, and both Demokritos and Anaxagoras have been suggested. Diodoros at one point says that 'Euripides, the disciple of Anaxagoras', agrees with this account, and there are at least six points of contact with known doctrines of Anaxagoras. In this account the earliest men were at war with beasts; they learnt to help each other by expedience and collected together out of fear. Whether this goes back to Anaxagoras himself or not, one can very well imagine that it inspired Thucydides to continue the power-fear story down into early Greek history as a prelude to the Peloponnesian war.[21]

When, however, we seek a source for the psychological terminology used by Thucydides, it is tempting to look to the doctors. A detailed recent study notes particularly his use of abstract nouns in -sis and of neuter adjectives made into substantives by the addition of the definite article. The latter is for our immediate purpose the more profitable to examine. Thucydides has some interesting uses. 'The inactive is not preserved unless it is combined with the energetic'; here the two neuters are a shorthand for inactive men and energetic men. 'The prudent was a cover-name for the cowardly', 'the result of this was the eager of those addicted to conquest', 'while congratulating you on the innocent, we do not envy you the mad'; here the neuter adjective is in each case a mental quality. This is of course one particular subdivision of the very general Greek usage of the substantive-adjective. Nor is it confined to Thucydides and the doctors; it is found in Gorgias and Euripides and has a great future in Plato. But, because we know no earlier example of the brave, the spirited etc., the parallel with Airs may nevertheless be significant.[22]

In the description of Asiatics quoted above neuter substantised adjectives are used both for mental qualities '*the brave*' etc. and for temperature '*the hot* and *the cold*', and the juxtaposition not only means that the temperature had an effect on the mental qualities, but possibly also suggests that the writer thought of both as being in some sense material. The writer of *Ancient Medicine*, who is much more interested in food than in temperature as the cause of sickness and health, uses the same kind of terminology for elements in the human body: 'the first doctors did not think that *the dry* or *the wet* or *the hot* or *the cold* or any of these things damage a man, but that *the strong* of each thing and *the stronger* than human nature, which human nature cannot master, hurts a man'. The doctors whom the writer of *Ancient Medicine* rejects take the hot and the cold and the dry and the wet as determining the health of the human body, just as *Airs* takes them as determining mental qualities, so that we have here the sort of parallelism between mental and physical reactions to knowable elements which Thucydides seems to imply. We can then at least say that Thucydides' approach to history is closely in line with the doctor's views of human minds and bodies.[23]

A little more can be extracted from a consideration of the terminology. The hot and the cold etc., which are so firmly rejected by *Ancient Medicine*, are found as constituents of the universe in Anaxagoras and Empedokles, who was himself a doctor, and probably earlier still in Anaximander, so that it is a reasonable assumption that they come into medicine from physical philosophy. Earlier than that in Homer and the Mycenaean tablets the substantised neuter adjective seems to have been used of something material like 'rose-oil' or 'the people's land'. This material sense always to a certain extent remains: 'the hot' is active hot material in the world or in the body, and 'the brave' (possibly first introduced in *Airs*) is active brave stuff in the mind. Later still, when Plato uses 'the just' for abstract Justice, the kind of verbs which are used for men 'partaking of *the just*' or 'having *the just* in them' shows that this material sense of *the just* is not wholly lost. This too makes the parallelism of mind and body easier to assert.[24]

The other kind of word which Thucydides uses notably often in describing the actions of the mind is the noun ending in -*sis*. This is a noun formed by adding -*sis* to a verbal stem, so that it essentially means the process denoted by the verb. Some of them are old, but both the numbers of different words and the numbers of occurrences per page explode in the fifth century. Homer has forty words of this form, Thucydides has 196; they occur on an average once every 14 pages in Homer, once every 4 pages in Aeschylus, over once a page in Thucydides, and more than three times a page in the early Hippocratic writings. Just because the *sis*-noun is a noun, it may be convenient for use in a sentence which would be encumbered by the corresponding verb. (Our nouns ending in -*ing* can be used as a translation.) *Airs*, explaining that even temperature produces even temperament, says: 'For *shattering* of the mind and strong *changing* of the body do not occur, from which....' The use of the noun emphasises the process as distinct from the agents, and it is the process which the author regards as responsible. So in Thucydides 'the *taking* of Plemmyrion damaged the Athenian force worst' is an effective sentence; but '*perceiving* soon supervened' has little to commend it over 'they were quickly perceived', and we can here speak of an affectation of scientific style. In very many places verbs could be substituted for *sis*-nouns; where this is easy, the use of the noun is a mannerism; where it is difficult, the use of the noun is a justifiable aid to expression. But the *sis*-noun can also be used to express something concrete which is achieved by the process: '*ploughing*' in Homer means 'arable land', and '*seeing*' in Thucydides once means the concrete appearance of a man in moonlight. More interesting are the places where the process is spoken of almost as if it were a person. The sentence above, 'the *taking* of Plemmyrion *damaged* ...', is a very mild instance. This use is particularly clear with *physis*, which we translate nature (or in this use Nature) but which is a *sis*-noun meaning 'begetting' or 'growing', according as it is felt as coming from the active or the passive sense of the verb. When Thucydides writes 'Human nature is eager to act energetically', this is not simply another way of saying 'men'; it carries the further implication that because they have grown as men, they will act like all other men in a given situation. In the Melian dialogue 'the human (neuter adjective) rules whatever it conquers because of necessary *physis*'. The Greek word for 'because of' is normally used of human agents, so that this is nature with a capital N; it is 'necessary' because there is no avoiding its operations: Nature compels the stronger to exploit the weaker. In the doctors *physis* is more often the constitution of human bodies than the constitution of human minds, but may still be almost personified: 'Medicine has found compulsions which force Nature to disclose her secrets without harm.' This picture in Hippokrates' *Art* is of an interrogation by Medicine of Nature, and it is a convenient shorthand for saying that doctors can use the experimental technique to diagnose what is wrong with their patients. As the use of Medicine here shows, this personification of abstracts is not confined to *sis*-nouns, and its origin lies way back with such impressive figures as Justice and Infatuation in Homer and Hesiod. They have their counterpart in the personification of art, particularly on the vases of the late fifth century— Health, for instance, is represented as a woman among the Hesperides when those nymphs are visited by Herakles. Thus it was very easy for Plato to use this terminology too when speaking of his Forms; if he speaks of Justice instead of the Just, he thinks to a certain extent of Justice as a goddess, and in this terminology men do not 'partake of the Just' but 'imitate Justice' or 'reach out for Justice'.[25]

The development of terminology, of which a part has been sketched above, is not only an aid to description, which is the chief reason why an accurate but at the same time pliable terminology is needed by the geographers, doctors, and historians, but also an aid to argument, to which we can now turn. In this chapter we are primarily concerned with arguments which establish the nature of the unknown from a consideration of the known, and the possibility of this is stated by several different authors. Anaxagoras' formulation is the most concise: 'what appears (gives) sight of the unclear'. Herodotos conjectures that the course of the Nile, which he only partly knows, is a southern complement to the course of the Danube, which he claims to know; he says that he is 'using what is clear as a token for the unknown'.

235

Thucydides says that it is impossible to get clarity about past history; one uses 'tokens' and 'the most conspicuous signs'. The same principle is asserted by the doctors. *Ancient Medicine* says, 'you should learn these things from what appears outside'; the attraction of moisture by the bladder, the head, and the womb is explained by the behaviour of the cupping-glass and of the mouth sucking liquid through a tube. The interrogation quoted above from the *Art* is another application : by causing discharges from the body, the doctor has visible 'tokens' to inform him about parts that cannot be seen. By the fifth century, therefore, the principle is applied in a number of different ways to very differing material, and something like a vocabulary has developed: seen, unseen, clear, signs, tokens.[26]

The vocabulary tells us a little about the origins of this kind of argument. The words translated 'signs' and 'tokens' or words deriving from the same roots are used very early for omens and portents sent by the gods, which the Greeks believed were significant and capable of interpretation by experts. The method of the seers is now applied to different subject matter with different assumptions. We can see two steps in the transition. Herakleitos in the late sixth century says : 'the lord whose oracle is in Delphi neither speaks nor conceals but gives signs'. Probably the interpretation of oracles is adduced as a parallel to Herakleitos' own method. In the early fifth century the doctor Alkmaion of Kroton began his book : 'concerning the unseen, the mortal, the gods have clarity, but to men the use of tokens (is given?)'; the text is not entirely clear, but Alkmaion certainly contrasted the clarity of divine knowledge with human knowledge based on tokens.[27]

Two other outside influences have to be considered. In *Ancient Medicine* the argument is not from known signs to the unknown that they signify but from the known behaviour of cupping glasses to the unknown behaviour of similarly shaped organs in the body. This is what Homer does with his elaborate similes : he makes a working model of the heroic situation which he wants to illustrate. The battle between the Greeks and Trojans sways this way and that, and it is desperately important for the Trojans to break through to the ships and for the Greeks to prevent it.

Homer compares the trembling of the balance as the woman weighs her wool, and this too is desperately important, because her work is what keeps her and her children alive.[28]

The other outside influence is argument in the law-courts. In the trial in Aeschylus' *Eumenides*, produced in 458, Athena tells the contending parties to summon 'testimonies and tokens', and at least from this time onwards the word translated 'tokens' is constantly used in law-court speeches. 'Tokens' belong both to scientific and to legal argument. 'Testimonies' are taken over from legal into scientific argument. Herodotos says that 'hot winds provide the first and greatest testimony that it is not even probable that the Nile flows from snow', and Thucydides calls the presence of Carian equipment in graves excavated on Delos 'testimony' that Carians occupied the islands in early times. But the most interesting word shared by the orators and the scientists is 'probable' (*eikos*). We have noticed already that the Sicilian rhetoricians in the second quarter of the fifth century used this idea of probability to give a logical reconstruction of events, wherever possible based on the character of their clients, and that juries came to accept this rather than the simple statement of oath or witnesses. For Herodotos it is not even *probable* that the Nile flows from snow. For Thucydides 'Minos put down piracy, as was *probable*, so that his revenues would come in better'. In *Airs* it is *probable* that the rich sacrifice more to the gods and the poor less. Probability is very much a key word of the second half of the fifth century, and Thucydides uses a noun from the same root to describe Themistokles as the best judge of probability, the best forecaster of future events. Certainly the orators gave the word a great fillip, but in the interconnected Greek world they need not necessarily have originated it.[29]

Aristotle defines the probable as that which happens for the most part among things that could happen otherwise. This means that people or things of like constitution behave similarly in similar conditions, which is the basic assumption of the doctors and the historians. Signs, working models, and experiments are applications of this assumption to find out unknown or unseen processes. Let us examine a few examples of each. Xenophanes wants to establish the general rule that man makes god in his own image: the signs are that Homer and Hesiod attribute human failings to the gods, that Thracians worship red-haired gods and that Ethiopians worship black gods, and then he adds a different kind of sign, which we may term an experiment: if animals could paint and sculpt, they would paint and sculpt gods of the same form as themselves. From the doctors we have already quoted the passage in *Art* where discharges are used as signs of the hidden condition of the body. Here too the signs are partly unforced and partly forced by the doctor; in the latter case again we can speak of experiment. Diogenes of Apollonia uses the fact that breath and perception are lost to animals at death as 'great signs' that air is both the principle of life and intelligence. Herodotos' argument against Anaxagoras' view that the Nile flows from snow is a series of signs: the winds are hot, there is no rain or ice, the men are black because of the heat, the birds do not migrate, but the cranes migrate there from the cold of Scythia. Thucydides uses a number of interesting signs in reconstructing the early history of Greece. The Carian equipment in the tombs on Delos has already been mentioned. The prevalence of piracy before Minos is established by the fact that piracy is still considered respectable in some parts and that it was considered respectable by Homer. Land-raiding before Minos is established by the survival of the practice in some parts of Greece and by the custom of wearing arms habitually. The more luxurious dress of the Athenians, which survived until the Persian war period, is evidence of post-Minoan civilisation. Then Thucydides gives yet another inset example to establish the general rule that survivals are a reliable guide to earlier Greek practice, the Greeks used to wear loincloths at the Olympic games; the Spartans first started naked athletics, but there are still non-Greeks who wear loincloths for boxing and wrestling. Thus early Greek history is reconstructed from many signs of different kinds, and it all adds up to a *probable* account, which exhibits the main human drives, desire to dominate and fear of domination. The argument from signs is what Aristotle calls induction, and he says that only enumeration of all the instances can make induction a conclusive argument. This is true, and probably from the time of the doctors with their case-histories the need for a multiplicity of signs rather than one significant sign become more apparent.[30]

We have noticed as special cases of the use of signs Xenophanes' construction of the animal gods worshipped by animals and the discharges specially induced by the doctors. In both cases the signs are specially constructed by the investigator to suit his purpose. They are not isolated. In *Airs* the 'token' that frozen water has lost its purest part is an experiment: freeze some water and then melt it again quickly, and it will be found to have lost some of its volume. In *Sacred Disease* the disease can be shown to be due to moisture in the brain by splitting the skull of a diseased goat. It is curious how often these experiments are phrased in the form: if you do such and such, you will find such and such. They are in fact constructions rather than experiments, and Aristotle expresses grave doubts about them. But when he speaks of Anaxagoras as proving the corporeality of air by twisting wineskins and catching air in pipettes, these are presumably experiments that Anaxagoras performed. Plato expresses himself scornfully in the *Republic* of musicians who try to distinguish differences of tone by ear and in the *Timaeus* of those who try to distinguish differences of colour by eye. We have here the old distinction, which goes back to Alkmaion and Xenophones, between the clarity which is available only to the gods and the probable account which man can achieve. Physical experiments for Plato are a vain attempt to reach divine clarity, but constructions, embodying as much knowledge as exists, may be a valid and probable account of subjects beyond human knowledge. So in the *Timaeus* he prefaces his account of the creation of the world: 'If we are incapable of giving a completely consistent and detailed account of many things, such as the gods and the origin of all, do not be surprised. But if we provide the most probable possible account, you must be satisfied, remembering that I the speaker and you the judges are human beings and therefore cannot ask for anything further, if we receive this probable account of these things.' The divine planner is a fact for Plato, and the myth of the creation is a construction to show how he probably worked. Similarly in the *Phaedo* the myth of the after-life of the soul in Hades is followed by the statement: 'it is wrong for any sensible man to assert that my account is true; but, since the soul manifestly is immortal, it is right and a risk worth taking to suppose that this, or some such account as this, about our souls and their dwelling is true'. These two instances are what are called technically Platonic myths, but he does also use the experiment-construction formula elsewhere, and he has some particularly striking constructions to illustrate the working of the soul. 'Let us mould an image of the soul in language', says Socrates in the *Republic*, when he likens the tripartite soul to a man, a lion, and a many-headed hydra in a human envelope. Or in the *Phaedrus* 'Let it be like the united powers of a pair of winged horses and a charioteer'. Or in the *Laws* 'Let us think that each one of us is a puppet made by god'. In all these the opening phrase shows that Plato is going to construct a model in quite different material to give a probable account of the behaviour of the soul.[31]

The construction as used by Plato is a kind of working model, but it is an imaginary working model. Neither the construction in the *Republic* nor the chariot with winged horses in the *Phaedrus* ever existed outside the imagination. Comprehension of the *Phaedrus* is, of course, assisted by the winged horses of art and particularly by pictures of Herakles' drive to heaven. But when Homer compares the swaying battle-line to the woman weighing her wool, or when the author of *Ancient Medicine* uses the action of cupping glasses to explain the action of similarly shaped organs in the body, the appeal for confirmation is to know everyday reality. The physical theories of the early Greek philosophers, where and in so far as they are not based on some modification of the very old idea of a world-being or a world-god, are mostly based on a comparison with something in the everyday world, like the Homeric simile. Here we can only mention a very few fifth-century examples. Empedokles compares the action of breathing to the action of a pipette and the action of the seeing eye to the action of a storm lantern. It does not matter in the least that his physical theories are entirely wrong in the modern view. What is interesting is his selection of well-known objects to explain his theories and his very careful cross-referencing at a number of points from the pipette and the

lantern to breathing and the eye. The model is the more satisfactory because it has detailed as well as general agreement with
the original.[32]

It would be interesting to know whether Anaxagoras and the
atomists quoted a mechanical model for the rotary motion which
they both assumed in the creation of the universe. In Anaxagoras
Mind started the rotation which separated off the opposites, hot
and cold, thin and thick etc., by its violence and speed. He also
speaks of the present rotation of 'the stars, the sun, the moon, the
lower air, and the upper air, which are being separated off'.
Perhaps he took the rotation of the stars as his model for a
rotation which was much faster and more violent. But he may
have thought of some kind of sorting machine. Demokritos thinks
of a whirlpool in which the atoms circle and collide so that they
are separated off, like to like. He illustrates 'like to like' by seeds
which are being sieved and pebbles on the beach. The pebbles
should presumably be thought of as deposited by the whirlpool,
and the seeds are sorted by the rotary action of a sieve. It is
probably this kind of sorting that Anaxagoras also had in mind.[33]

Plato also uses the working model for his rather different purposes. An excellent instance is the comparison of poetic inspiration to magnetic force in the *Ion*. The Muse inspires the poet,
the poet inspires the rhapsode, the rhapsode inspires the spectator, just as the magnet attracts an iron ring and the iron ring
attracts another iron ring and so on. The common term here is
the force which goes out from the source and holds the whole
series together, but decreases the further it gets from its starting
point. In the *Politicus* (or *Statesman*) Plato examines the art of
weaving to demonstrate the nature of the art of statesmanship,
and he calls this method the use of *paradeigmata*. The *paradeigma* is a pattern, an original from which copies are made, so
that by the use of this word Plato means that the working model
is completely known and on its pattern the unknown is constructed.
It is in reverse relationship to the *eikon* (likeness), which is the
word that he uses for the winged chariot team of the *Phaedrus*;
that for him is an inferior copy of the original. In the *Politicus*
he says that he is seeking the smallest *paradeigma* which has the
same kind of activity as politics. He first divides all artefacts into

constructive and defensive, and then subdivides defensive artefacts again and again, until he comes down to clothes; weaving
is the art of making clothes. This process of subdivision, called
diairesis, is highly technical and will concern us in the next
chapter. Weaving is then shown in a long discussion to have two
chief characteristics: it is the summit of a hierarchy of minor arts
which only exist to serve it (spinning, carding, loom-making,
shuttle-making etc.), and it is the art of combining two different
elements of opposed characteristics, the strong warp and the weak
woof, into a new whole. In the same way the political art is shown
to be the summit of a hierarchy of minor arts (manufacturing,
mining, agriculture, merchants, heralds, soldiers, educators), and
its function is a similar combination of the warlike and peaceful
elements of the state into a harmonious whole. To make these
two points Plato's *paradeigma* is perfect. The comparison of
weaving to statesmanship was already in existence. In Aristophanes' *Lysistrata* the government of the Athenian empire is
compared to the carding, spinning, and weaving of wool, whether
Aristophanes invented the image or borrowed it from one of the
sophists. What Plato is doing, is to choose the most suitable
working-model from a number of available images, then treat it
in his own technical manner, and then treat the subject under
discussion in the same way with constant cross-references to the
paradeigma.[34]

The three kinds of argument that we have been discussing
are closely connected. They all rest on the assumption that there
is a useful parallel between the visible and known and the invisible
and unknown, whether the known is a set of signs or a working-
model or a construction. In the fifth century the Greeks seem
to have used the same terminology for them all and accorded
them much the same value. But the use of a terminology at all
is a step towards trying to control the validity of these arguments, and as we have seen, in the fourth century Plato and
Aristotle demanded considerable rigour.

13 *Mathematicians, Astronomers and Philosophers*

The main purpose of this chapter is to suggest that mathematics was a kind of ideal to which other thinkers, whether they were proficient in mathematics or not, wanted to make their thinking approximate. Mathematics in ancient Greece was primarily geometry, and was closely linked with astronomy. At least from the fifth century the astronomers were concerned with describing in geometric terms the courses which the stars must pursue to account for their appearances in the heavenly sphere. But at the beginning, in the late seventh and early sixth century, Thales and Anaximander of Miletos were practical men. They knew of Babylonian observations: Thales could foretell an eclipse (probably he knew that the eclipse would occur in a given year and recognised it when it came, so that he could warn the fighting troops not to panic); Anaximander took over the Babylonian sundial. Thales also encouraged navigation by the Little Bear. Which of them introduced the idea of the Zodiac is not clear. Anaximander conceived a rather complicated model of the heavens. Thales also measured the height of the pyramids and the distance of a ship from land, which probably meant that he had arrived at the theory of similar triangles.[1]

The second great impulse came from the Pythagoreans. Pythagoras himself migrated from Samos to Kroton in 530. It is impossible to distinguish between the thought of Pythagoras himself and his early followers, but we can regard as early

Pythagorean the discovery that the chief musical intervals can be expressed in simple numerical ratios between the first four integers, the belief that in some sense things were numbers, the proof that the square on the hypotenuse of a right-angled triangle is equal to the sum of the squares on the other two sides, and a very individual astronomical picture in which the earth, counter-earth, sun, moon, five planets, and the fixed stars revolved round a central fire (counter-earth was added to make the number up to the holy Pythagorean number of Ten). The Pythagoreans lived in communities, which seem to have been ascetic, aristocratic, and politically influential. They flourished in several cities in South Italy in the fifth and fourth centuries. As communities concerned with mathematics, astronomy, and philosophy, they were the ancestors and models of the schools of Plato and Aristotle. For the Pythagoreans too, as for Thales and Anaximander, mathematics were a part of philosophy, although perhaps a controlling part.[2]

Let us look a little further at the personalities of the classical period, particularly when we know that they visited or lived in Athens. The philosophers Anaxagoras and Demokritos and the sophists Hippias and Antiphon were all concerned with mathematical problems. Whether Socrates was, depends on the credence that we give to the picture in the *Clouds*, where Socrates examines 'the paths and circuits of the moon' and draws diagrams with a compass in the dust. Whether this is true of Socrates or not, it at least shows that the audience had some awareness of astronomical problems and mathematical procedure. Far more important, as showing the influence of mathematics on philosophy, were Parmenides, Zeno, and Melissos. Parmenides of Elea in South Italy was a rich aristocrat, who built a shrine to his Pythagorean teacher; he also made laws for his city. Zeno, also a Pythagorean, was his pupil. They came to Athens to see the Panathenaia while Socrates was still young, presumably about 450. Melissos of Samos was an admiral and defeated the Athenian fleet under Pericles in 441/0. He is called a pupil of Parmenides, but this may only mean that he read Parmenides, which he certainly must have done.[3]

Then we come to the few 'pure' mathematicians and

astronomers of whom we know anything. Hippokrates of Chios was a merchant who was attacked by pirates and lost everything; he came to Athens to go to law with the pirates, and while he was waiting for the suit to be tried visited 'the philosophers', and became highly proficient in geometry. We do not know who 'the philosophers' were. It is natural to think of Meton, who, like Hippokrates, was interested in squaring the circle. He also is rather more than a name. He was an Athenian and a pupil of a metic Phaeinos, who observed the solstice from Mount Lykabettos. He organised the Athenian calendar, and also built a fountain house. At the time of the Sicilian expedition he burnt his house down and then pleaded poverty to prevent his son serving as captain of a trireme. He also appears in comedy. In 427 somebody in Aristophanes' *Banqueters* says, 'Is this a polos, whereby in Kolonos they examine the heavenly bodies here and the slants here?'. Meton lived in Kolonos; the polos may have been a hemisphere marked with the ecliptic (the slants). In the *Birds* in 414 Meton visits Cloudcuckooland and offers to plan the air with his instruments, so that they will have a square town in a circular heaven with radial roads from a central agora. From the fourth century we have Plato's portrait of Theaitetos. The dialogue called after him purports to be a record of a conversation between Theodoros, Theaitetos, and Socrates, which took place shortly before Socrates' death in 399 but was only written up on Theaitetos' death in 369. Theodoros of Cyrene was himself a distinguished mathematician, said to be a Pythagorean, who had important theories about irrational numbers. He apparently visited Athens fairly often; Theaitetos was his pupil, and developed the theory of irrationals further. His father was a rich man, but Theaitetos' inheritance was squandered by his guardians. What this means we do not know; possibly Theaitetos was serving as a hoplite when he died. Plato's unique eulogy may very well indicate that he was working in the Academy. The most distinguished mathematician and astronomer at the Academy was Eudoxos of Knidos, who practised observational astronomy but also had a theory of concentric spheres to account for the apparent motions of the sun, moon, and planets, and in mathematics he made a new theory of proportion which was applicable to commensurable and incommensurable magnitudes alike. At first sight he seems to be what we should call a pure mathematician and astronomer, but then we are told that he studied medicine with Philistion in Sicily and, presumably as a result of his work in the Academy, gave laws to his own city. And of course the Academy itself is proof that even in the specialist fourth century very different disciplines could and did live together.[4]

What mathematics and astronomy had to give, apart from their own discoveries in their own fields, was first a vision of a world where shapes were clear and precise, and where truth, if it could be discovered, was universally valid, and secondly a method of arguing, which, because it was precise and universally valid, was regarded as an ideal to which arguments on other kinds of subject-matter should approximate as far as possible. It is this influence of mathematical argument on other kinds of thinking which particularly concerns us.

A link between the kinds of argument discussed in the last chapter and mathematical argument is given by what we may call proportional argument. Proportional argument is a working model expressed in the terms of a mathematical proportion. Already in Homer Nausikaa and her maidens are compared to Artemis and her nymphs: Artemis is the tallest of all but they are all beautiful; so Nausikaa shone out among her attendants. This is a normal working-model simile, but it is very easy to express it as a proportion: as Artemis is to her nymphs, so Nausikaa was to her maidens. Thus proportional thinking was a mode of Greek thought long before Pythagoras discovered the numerical ratio between the musical intervals and the existence of the geometric mean ($a:b::b:c$). Nevertheless the fact that the fragments of Herakleitos (to whom Pythagoras' work was known) can very often be reduced to the pattern $a:b::b:c$ suggests that he is trying to give his comparisons the cogency of a geometric proof. A simple example is: 'man is called childish by god, as child is by man'. The common term is man; the object is to show that divine intelligence is as far above ordinary human intelligence as ordinary human intelligence is above the intelligence of a child. The relationship between child and man is known and defines the relationship between man and god.[5]

But four-term and three-term proportions are found fairly commonly in treatises by the doctors which can probably be ascribed to the fifth century. In *Ancient Medicine* a rather difficult sentence reads: 'if one were to consider the diet of the sick against the diet of the healthy, he would find the diet of animals not more harmful compared with the diet of the healthy'. He is talking about dieting the sick, and the known relationship is the cooked food of the healthy compared with the raw food of animals; sick men need food milder in the same proportion. In Plato the proportional argument is extremely common and has some interesting extensions. In the *Gorgias* an elaborate proportion is constructed to discover the nature of rhetoric. As soul is to body, so is politics, which covers lawgiving and justice, to the nameless art which covers gymnastic and medicine. Each of the four is imitated by a 'flattery': sophistry, rhetoric, cosmetics, cookery. This is expressly stated as a geometric proportion: 'I want to say, like the geometers, that as cosmetics is to gymnastic, so is sophistic to lawgiving, and as cooking is to medicine, so is rhetoric to justice.' Plato emphasises the geometrical nature of his demonstration of the nature of rhetoric, and we should perhaps recognise a new impulse from fourth-century mathematics here.[6]

The whole of the *Republic* is built on the proportion: 'as large letters are to small letters, so is the city to the single man', and therefore if justice can be discovered in the city, it can be pinpointed in the man. In the sixth and seventh books three great interconnected proportions, the Sun, the Line, and the Cave, are designed to show the nature of the Idea of the Good and how we can apprehend it. In the first the word 'proportionate' is used: 'the sun is the offspring of the good, which it begat proportionate to itself—what the good is in the mental sphere in relation to mind and the things known, that the sun is in the visible sphere in relation to sight and the things seen.' In the second proportion he actually makes the geometrical construction: 'Take a line cut in two unequal sections, and cut each section again in the same proportion.' The original line is divided into things seen and things known. The longer the section the more clearly the things in that section are apprehended. The shortest section contains reflections, the second section things seen, the third section mathematical ideas, and the fourth section pure ideas apprehended through dialectic by mind. The last are the clearest and truest, and the diagram fixes this clarity and truth because we know how unclear and deceptive reflections of things seen can be, and by construction the relation of things seen to things reflected is the same as the relation of all things known to all things seen and as the relation of the pure ideas to the mathematical ideas. One other point is inherent in the construction: the second section, things seen, is the same length as the third section, mathematical ideas. The reason is not so much that they both have the same clarity as that the mathematician, particularly the geometer, uses things seen, visible circles etc., as symbols of the perfect circles etc. about which he argues.[7]

The Greek for proportion is *logos* and for proportionate is *analogos*, from which we derive analogy, the word that Aristotle uses for this kind of argument. The argument seems the more cogent because from the time of Anaximander Greeks had been finding proportions in the world, particularly in the relation of the seasons to the year and of days and nights to the seasons, but also as we have seen, in musical intervals and in the balance between hot and cold etc. in the body, and between rich and poor in the state. When Aristotle says that 'sight in the body equals intuition in the soul', he is simply recalling the proportion in the *Republic*, but he goes on to give a four-term proportion to illustrate the distribution of honours in the state. The kind of state determines the standard used; the amount of honour given to the citizens is proportionate to where they rank on that standard. Aristotle also finds analogy useful in scientific classification for defining the relationship between living things which are not species of the same genus: 'I mean bird differs from bird by quantity or excellence (for one is long-winged and another short-winged), but fish are linked to birds by analogy (the scale is to the fish, as the feather to the bird).'[8]

We reach a similar goal (classification of nature) by starting off from Plato's Line in another direction. In describing the fourth section of the line, Plato describes the mind using the hypotheses of the mathematical sciences as rungs of a ladder to climb up to the beginning of all, and then having touched it and holding on to the things that hold on to it, descending to an end. In so far as this is not a mystical experience, it does imply a kind of family tree of Ideas, the less general depending on the more general. The Line itself is a small scale example: the most general 'things apprehended' is divided into 'things apprehended with the eye' and 'things apprehended with (reflections etc.) the mind', and each of these is again subdivided into more specialised classes of things apprehended. In the *Phaedrus* he is rather clearer: he speaks of collecting the many scattered things into a single Idea, and then cutting this up into Forms according to the natural joints; this second process is called diairesis. The process is shown in operation when he defines *himatia* (garments) and weaving in the *Statesman*. Artefacts are divided into creative and defensive, the defensive are divided into medicine and shields, and it takes eight more subdivisions to arrive at a definition of himatia as defensive coverings made out of hairs twisted together. The method seems to be founded on a geometrical figure like the Line, and the terminology comes from geometry—'dividing, cutting, section, invisible'. Here the original line representing artefacts is divided in half, the left half is bisected again, the left half of that is bisected again and so on. A complete definition of himation would include the names of all the left halves ending with 'defensive artefact': Plato's brief definition gives the first stage 'defensive', one intermediate stage 'coverings', and the two last stages 'made of hairs' and 'twisted together'. The object is to attain a definition, and though it is a lengthy and laborious process, Aristotle grants that it has two chief advantages; nothing is left out and the concepts are easily arranged in the right order from the most general to the particular.[9]

This Platonic exercise of diairesis or dichotomy (cutting things in two) has three further points of interest. In the first place the Ideas which are so arranged in a hierarchy of decreasing generality are on the way to becoming logical universals; they are losing or have already lost the kind of reality which they had when Plato spoke of them as if they were goddesses (feminine abstracts) or things (neuter adjectives used as substantives). This is clear in the passages quoted from the earlier *Phaedrus* and *Republic*, and there are traces earlier still. Probably Plato never completely thought himself out of his earlier way of thinking: the superior reality of Justice and the Good was far too important to be abandoned. But the dichotomies pointed the way towards Aristotelian logic, and this is the second point of interest: any three successive steps in a Platonic dichotomy can be recast into an Aristotelian syllogism of the first figure. The last three steps of the dichotomy quoted from the *Statesman* are 1. coverings with holes, *coverings without holes*, 2. things made of fibres, *things made of hair*, 3. things made of hair glued together, *things made of hair twisted together (himatia)*. As an Aristotelian syllogism, this would read: if things made of hair are coverings without holes, and if himatia are things made of hair, then himatia are coverings without holes. If these steps are seen in their proper Platonic shape as a line continually bisected, then the truth of the syllogism is obvious because the longer section of the line (1) contains the two shorter sections (2 and 3), and it is probably right to suppose that Aristotle derived the syllogism from geometrical figures of this kind.[10]

If, however, instead of taking one half only of each bisection, both halves are taken, as in the Line in the *Republic*, which produces a classification of things apprehended into four classes grouped into two pairs, dichotomy can be used to produce a classification. In the passage from the comic poet Epikrates in which the pupils of the Academy are discussing the classification of a pumpkin, Plato tells them to go on with their diairesis. There is, therefore, no doubt that dichotomy was used for classification in Plato's time. It showed the possibility of a classification into genera, sub-genera, species, and sub-species. Aristotle saw the obvious objection that each natural genus has many differentiae and not two only. Aristotle proposed a freer classification in the *Parts of Animals*. There genera are distinguished from each other by the fact that the likenesses between them only rest on analogy, and within each genus the species are distinguished by quantitative differences in bodily attributes, such as size, hardness, roughness etc., as for instance the long-winged and short-winged birds quoted above. Aristotle was a good observer, and his observation showed him that Plato's rigid geometrical classification would not work, and so he loosened up the framework to fit the variety of natural objects, not natural objects only, since the same kind of classification is used for mimetic arts at the beginning of the *Poetics*.[11]

In the types of argument that we have been examining, the words, or in the case of the syllogism the propositions, are tied together on a straight line, and it is the relative lengths of the segments of the line which validate the argument. The argument is true in so far as it is justifiably reduced to a mathematical diagram. The further question is whether certain other kinds of argument in Greek philosophy were borrowed from the mathematicians and were felt the more valid because of the certainty of mathematical proof. The material is extremely difficult, and only a brief sketch can be attempted here. What we should most like to be able to say is that in the fifth century some philosophers, particularly Parmenides and his successors, argued as mathematicians argued. But we have lost early mathematics, and it is only when we come to Plato that we are on safe ground. We have however a proof of the theorem that the three angles of a triangle add up to two right angles which is ascribed to the Pythagoreans by Aristotle's pupil Eudemos and is quoted by Aristotle himself. It shows both how such a demonstration was conducted and how Aristotle fitted it into a syllogism.

In the *Prior Analytics* Aristotle discusses some of the difficulties of fitting a proof into syllogistic form. In the instance given above—if things made of hair (B) are coverings without holes (A), and if himatia (C) are things made of hair (B), then himatia (C) are coverings without holes (A)—all the terms—A, B, C—are nouns. But, says Aristotle, if we want to prove that 'every triangle is two right angles', we can put the conclusion in this form—every C (triangle) is A (two right angles)—but we cannot find a noun B for the two premises; we have to substitute a *logos* for B—a proposition. The proposition in this case is given in the *Metaphysics*: 'the angles about a point on a straight line are equal to two right angles'. This proposition seems to Aristotle to do the same job as the middle term B of the syllogism: if B is A, and if C is B, then C is A. In the mathematical proof B is the way in which we get from the triangle to the two right angles; we show by construction that the three angles of a triangle are equal to the angles about a point. The proof in the *Metaphysics* is a shorthand version of the proof ascribed by Eudemos to the Pythagoreans. 'Let ABC be a triangle and through A draw DE parallel to BC. Since BC and DE are parallel and the alternate angles are equal, the angle DAB equals ABC and EAC equals ACB. Add the angle BAC. Then the angles DAB, BAC, CAE, that is the angles DAB, BAE, that is two right angles are equal to the three angles of the triangle ABC.' It is the last sentence which brings in Aristotle's middle term B; because the three angles of the triangle are shown to be equal to the angles about a point, they can be shown to be equal to two right angles.

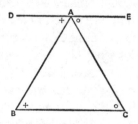

In the *Metaphysics* Aristotle uses the proof as a demonstration that mathematical constructions actualise what is potentially present. The result is that mathematical argument is deductive argument, and for that reason it can be put in syllogistic form: it does not bring new knowledge but by the construction (here the drawing of the parallel) makes clear a piece of knowledge which was already implicit in the original conception. What Aristotle does not say, is that the construction is accepted because it brings into the problem (in addition to B) another piece of knowledge which the solver already possesses, that when two parallel lines are joined by a straight line the alternate angles are equal.[12]

What this example shows is that mathematical argument is deductive, that it proceeds by a construction which brings in a previously proved proposition, and that it is universally valid.

Parmenides uses 'Being' very much in the sense that the mathematicians say that a triangle *is* or that a triangle *is* equal to two right angles. He means by Being something with universal validity. And he argues about it deductively. 'On this road to truth there are many signs that Being is unborn and indestructible. For it is whole and unmoving and unending. It was not nor shall it be. For it is now, whole, one, continuous.' The 'signs' of Parmenides have nothing to do with the signs of induction or experiment. They are given in the two sentences beginning with 'for', and the argument (like a mathematical argument) is a deduction from the properties which Parmenides attributes to Being—whole in the sense of unmoving, and whole in the sense of continuous in time. He goes on: 'For what birth will you seek for it? How, from whence grown? I will not allow you to think or say "from not-being". For it must not be said or thought that it is not.' Here he posits his opponent's view that Being had an origin, and shows that this leads to the absurdity of saying that Being arose from not-being. Again this seems to be a mathematical argument—to assume the contrary of the proposition to be proved and to demonstrate that it leads to something known to be untrue. This *reductio ad absurdum* is well known as a method of proof in later Greek mathematics, but we have no evidence earlier than Parmenides. My feeling is that it is more likely that Parmenides got it from the Pythagorean mathematicians than that the later mathematicians took it from Parmenides.[13]

The very difficult arguments of Parmenides' pupil Zeno are all based on this method of assuming his opponent's position and showing to what contradictions it leads. Melissos of Samos, who is called a pupil of Parmenides, defends unitary Being in the Parmenidean sense by assuming that Being is plural and then showing that this conflicts with the evidence of the senses, which he establishes by an induction. Thus he uses induction within the framework of a *reductio ad absurdum*. The argument is (1) if many things are said to *be*, they ought to *be* in the Parmenidean sense, (1a) if the elements and metals and the opposites (hot and cold etc.) *are*, they ought to be permanent and unchanging in the Parmenidean sense, but (2) we observe that water becomes earth, iron rusts, and the hot becomes cold. The second proposition established by induction contradicts the first, and a plurality of being in the Parmenidean sense is impossible.[14]

The method of using induction within the framework of a *reductio ad absurdum* is found again in Plato. In the first book of the *Republic* Socrates accepts his opponent's position that justice is to benefit friends and harm foes. He takes the second part, harming foes: (1) Horses become worse as horses by being harmed, dogs become worse as dogs by being harmed, men become worse as men by being harmed. Becoming worse as men means becoming more unjust. (Thus induction establishes that men who are harmed become more unjust.) (2) Musicians cannot by musicianship make men unmusical, horsemen cannot by horsemanship make men incapable as riders, just men cannot by justice make men unjust. (Again the conclusion is established by induction.) (3) Heat does not cool, dryness does not moisten, the good does not harm but the opposite of good harms. The just man is good; therefore he cannot harm either a friend or anyone else. The opponent's position is accepted, three propositions are established by induction. The first is extended by what seems to us a very doubtful equation of 'worse as men' with 'more unjust', but the equation is accepted without question: it is previous knowledge like the knowledge that, when two parallel lines are joined by a straight line, the alternate angles are equal, which was assumed in the proof that the three angles of a triangle add up to two right angles. Here 'harm' is defined as harming the particular excellence of the thing harmed (hence my translation 'as horses' etc.); justice is accepted as a human excellence, therefore a man harmed becomes more unjust. The same previous knowledge (the just man is good) is used to extend the third proposition from 'the good does not harm' to 'the just does not harm'. I have called the three arguments inductions. In the simplest form the first would run: harm is a sign that horse A is lacking the excellence of a horse, so also horses B, C, D ..., therefore all harmed horses lack the excellence of a horse. Socrates leaves us to supply these stages and simply gives the conclusion followed by the same conclusion for dogs and men. The second and third arguments are similarly summary. By using this summary form Socrates can build them into his *reductio ad absurdum*, and so give them in appearance the certainty of a mathematical argument.[15]

In the *Meno* Plato expressly says that he is proceeding like a mathematician in discussing whether virtue can be taught. Socrates says that he wants to use a hypothesis for the discussion. He illustrates what he means: if a geometer is asked whether a triangle of this area will go into this circle, he starts with a useful hypothesis; if the area in the form of a rectangle is applied to the diameter of the circle, it will either fall short of the diameter or not; the area can only be inscribed in the circle in the form of a triangle if in rectangular form it does so fall short. The hypothesis here is a construction which shows whether the original question should be answered in the affirmative or negative. Socrates then proposes as a hypothesis that, if virtue can be taught, it must be a kind of knowledge, so that the next question is whether virtue is a kind of knowledge. He then takes another hypothesis that virtue is good, and goes on to prove that only knowledge is good and therefore virtue is a kind of knowledge. We need not pursue the argument further. In each case the hypothesis is a substitution for a term in the original proposition, rectangle for triangle, knowledge for teachable, good for virtue; the substitution gets the argument going, and then it is possible to put back the original term.[16]

In the *Republic* hypothesis is used more generally for the unquestioned assumptions of mathematics 'like odd and even, the figures, and the three kinds of angles', and it is these hypotheses which are used by dialectic as steps in the ladder up to the Idea of the good. But in the *Phaedo* Plato uses hypothesis in the more restricted sense of the *Meno*, though without reference to mathematics. Socrates has just expressed his disappointment with the physics of Anaxagoras, which failed to provide him with the kind of final cause that he required. He decided to abandon physics for *logoi*: 'I made my hypothesis whatever *logos* seemed to me strongest, and I set down as true whatever agrees with it and as false whatever disagrees with it.' So in the present case his hypothesis is the existence of Ideas (the beautiful etc.), and he will show from it the immortality of the soul. He develops the hypothesis in the form 'it is because of beauty that the beautiful is beautiful etc. etc.'. He then makes a very significant extension that not only can opposites themselves (i.e. Ideas) not admit their opposite (hot cannot admit cold), but also some physical things cannot admit the opposite quality (fire is so essentially hot that it cannot admit cold). He calls this a new 'safety', which certainly means a new hypothesis, or rather an extension of the original hypothesis, and it is this that proves for him the immortality of the soul: the opposites are life and death, and the soul is so bound up with life that it cannot admit death. The original hypothesis is supported by a number of examples—greatness, smallness, multitude, as well as beauty—and the special things of the new hypothesis are not only fire and snow but also all odd numbers, which refuse to admit evenness, and all even numbers, which refuse to admit oddness. The hypotheses are used as a framework for what are essentially inductions. What the procedure has in common with the procedure in the *Meno* is that it starts from an agreed truth which at first sight has no connection with the proposition to be proved.[17]

In one way or another the arguments which we have been looking at in this chapter are connected with mathematics. This influence of mathematics on other kinds of thinking has at least three causes. First, the mathematicians were not, as now, a race apart; they lived in the small Greek cities and had both an intellectual and practical life outside mathematics. Secondly, the Greeks saw things clear and sharp, and so their pictures for the earth or the sky were simple mathematical shapes. Thirdly, whether they were thinking about the physical world or the human body or the human mind, they felt an increasing need to make their thought cogent, and the mathematicians produced models for cogent arguments.

14 *Conclusion*

Classical Athens was a small city, Attica was a tiny country, and the Mediterranean was a small sea. By modern standards, in spite of the absence of modern transport, communications were easy. This is the first and most obvious fact to be appreciated if we are to try to estimate the relation between culture and society. During the fifth century Athens was the centre of the Greek world, and the Athenian fleet made sea-communications safe. Athens had the money, the imperial law-courts, the buildings, the festivals, the games, the trainers, and the intellectual life to attract foreigners. And there is no doubt that they came. To quote the most obvious names, the philosopher Anaxagoras came from Klazomenai, the sophist Protagoras from Abdera, the painter Polygnotos from Thasos, the poet Pindar from Thebes, the mathematical astronomer Eudoxos from Knidos, the doctor Hippokrates from Kos, and the athlete Phayllos from Kroton. Athenian society was therefore open to non-Athenian culture: communications may have been easier and the attractions stronger in imperial Athens, but Athens was already an intellectual capital before the Persian wars and it remained an intellectual capital all through the fourth century, as, for instance, the list of Plato's pupils shows.[1]

The physical arrangement of the city and the organisation of Greek life helped the dissemination of culture. Everyone found his way to the Agora, and the Stoai were comfortable places to talk. The area and the population were small enough for foreigners and notables to be seen and recognised. There were many other meeting places: gymnasia, palaistrai, baths, shops—not only barbers' shops but the shops of any craftsman where the customers waited and talked while the work was done—and lastly private houses and their symposia. The Assembly was probably only open to foreigners when they came as delegates from their own cities, but this is how many of the sophists and rhetoricians came, and their appearance in the Assembly made them known so that they would be recognised in the Agora. Then the festivals were open to foreigners in three ways. They could come as visitors, they could come as delegates from their cities, they could come as competitors: we do not know whether Parmenides and Zeno of Elea visited the Panathenaia as visitors or as delegates; we do know that the lyric poet Timotheos of Miletos won a victory at the Panathenaia by defeating another foreigner Phrynis of Mytilene.[2]

Athenian society was an open society, and foreign experts were welcome. Before we can ask what was the range of that welcome and whether it affected their expertise, we shall have to consider Athenian society itself, what were its components and how high were the barriers between them. At first sight it looks like a stratified society. The citizens were divided into 500-bushel men, knights, hoplites, thetes, and were clearly marked off from resident aliens and slaves. We seem to have six very firmly defined classes. But examination shows that the boundaries were much more fluid in practice than they appear in theory. Legally they exist: each of the six classes has its own duties and its own rights. Resident aliens and slaves can only go to law if a patron takes up their case, and they have practically no political rights. Certain offices are reserved to the top two classes of citizens, and others to the top three. But in practice it is possible for a slave to become a freedman and even a citizen: the banker Pasion is not unique, though parallels were probably rare. The resident alien could become a citizen, and the rich resident alien like Kephalos moved in the highest Athenian society. Poorer citizens worked side by side with resident aliens and slaves on the land, in the mines, on buildings, on sculpture, and in the potteries. Pericles, who was very rich, and Socrates, who belonged to the hoplite class, both talked philosophy with Simon the cobbler.

Leagros, the aristocratic athlete and later general, lived in the Kerameikos and seems to have known the potters socially as well as professionally. Legally Athens had six classes, but practically and to a large extent socially there were imperceptible gradations from the poorest slave to the few very rich at the top. The conservative tract is surely right in connecting this social structure with the commercial, industrial, and naval needs of imperial Athens. One result was the legal protection and opportunity for self-government given to resident aliens and slaves. Another was the political and legal system—the government of Athens by a mass-meeting of all the citizens, the wide diffusion and the rigorous audit of offices, the quantity of litigation and the large juries appointed to deal with it, and as a result a very wide spread of political knowledge.[3]

But what was the effect of this political and social structure on culture? Or, to return to the definitions of the first chapter, what was the effect of such a society on the creative artists and thinkers? A number of effects can be suggested, and it is not easy to put them in a logical order. But patronage is a possible starting point. If we think of the political and legal struggles of the rich from the time of Kimon, then we see at once that their needs called the sophists and the rhetoricians into existence and produced political theory as a kind of background. The patronage of the rich Kallias and his like gave Protagoras, Hippias, and their like a means of existence. But what is admirable and goes far beyond the immediate needs of the patron, is the width of knowledge shown by the sophists. This kind of patronage was not only interested in immediate results, and if we include the association between Pericles and Anaxagoras the practical result would have to be reckoned a loss, since the trial of Anaxagoras was an attempt to discredit Pericles.[4]

Another kind of patronage is patronage of art and literature. Here again politics are involved in various ways. The Stoa Poikile and the Theseion were propaganda for the kind of democracy and the kind of policy in which Kimon believed, and the Parthenon was propaganda for the kind of democracy in which Pericles believed. But little compulsion was exercised on the artist since Pheidias seems to have moved from Kimon to

Pericles. What was achieved as a sideline was a fantastic education of public taste, partly because of the number of craftsmen employed, partly because these superb works of sculpture and painting were always open to the public. And there is a further difference between Kimon's buildings and Pericles' buildings. Pericles' buildings (and later buildings) were approved by the Assembly; he may have proposed them and chosen the artist, but the mass of Athenian citizens had to approve the expenditure of public money.[5]

The most individual form of poetic patronage was the liturgy. Undoubtedly the rich man who undertook the bulk of the expenditure for producing tragedy, comedy, or dithyramb had a political reason. A successful production advertised him and was a service to the people, which would be remembered to his credit in a lawsuit. But again the evidence for compulsion on the poet is minimal: the one case is the appointment of Kimon and his generals to judge the tragedies in 468, when Sophocles first produced, and that was the decision of the archon. Officially it was the archon who chose the rich man for the poet, and the archon who drew lots for the judges, and the applause of the audience had some effect on the judges. The goodwill of the rich man was important to secure a good production, but the goodwill of the audience secured victory. A sideline of this system, the training of choruses, must in fact have added considerably to the technical appreciation of the audiences. At every City Dionysia there were 1,000 trained chorusmen, who, having competed in the dithyrambs written by the most advanced lyric poets, presumably watched the tragedies and comedies. We have also to remember all the other festivals public and private at which choruses performed. The number of ex-chorusmen cannot be assessed, but it is fair to suggest that a considerable proportion of the audiences of tragedy and comedy must themselves at some time have sung in a chorus (quite apart from their experience in the symposion) and so had technical knowledge of what was being done.[6]

One other form of patronage affects art rather than poetry. Religious patronage is general Greek rather than democratic Athenian. Politics only comes in with cases like the Parthenon.

The whole of Greek life is dominated by religion, and for every occasion the gods have to have their offerings. Birth, manhood, marriage, childbirth, every success public or private, commercial, political, or athletic, health, sickness, and death demand an offering to the gods. The size of the occasion and the wealth of the person decide whether the offering is a shrine, a statue, a relief, or a vase. Thus there was a continuous demand for the whole range of Greek art, from the cheapest to the most expensive, for patrons from the whole range of society, all of whom were exposed to the great public painting and sculpture of Athens, so that their patronage was intelligent.[7]

Athenian society was competitive. A great many contracts, and probably much more than we know, were awarded by public competition. The most valuable contract for the potters was the contract to make the 1,300 prize-amphorai for the Panathenaic games, and this was awarded by competition. The making of statues was sometimes open to competition; we know, for instance, that Paionios won the contract for the akroteria of one pediment of the temple of Zeus at Olympia, and this procedure may have been usual for public buildings. Dithyramb, tragedy, and comedy were all produced competitively. Music of different kinds was produced competitively at the Panathenaia. Reciters of Homer competed at the Panathenaia. Thucydides' phrase that his history was not a contest-piece implies that recital of history could be competitive. Probably there were contests at which prose, whether history, oratory, philosophy, or literary criticism, could be performed, as well as poetry. No doubt such competitiveness gave rise to as much injustice and heartbreak as it does today. An obvious sign is the firm assertion of worth and innovation, coupled usually with contempt for contemporaries and predecessors, which we have noted in such different kinds of artists as the potter-painter Euthymides, the painters Apollodoros, Zeuxis, Parrhasios, and Euphranor, the lyric poets Pindar, Bacchylides, and Timotheos, the tragic poet Sophocles, the comic poet Aristophanes, the geographer Hekataios, the historians Herodotos and Thucydides, and the doctor who wrote *Ancient Medicine*. As far as we can judge from what survives, there is no sign that competition in classical Athens produced shoddy work; it is, I think, arguable that it may have made for intelligibility; the judges liked what they understood.[8]

We can then ask where the creators belonged in this Athenian society. The first and partial answer is that there was an inner society of intellectuals who grouped themselves round the rich. This helps to explain the fact that we have noticed again and again, the interpenetration of art, poetry, drama, oratory, philosophy, mathematics, medicine, geography, and history. Plato gives a picture of this, and there is no reason to doubt its accuracy: Socrates meets a number of sophists at Kallias' house in the *Protagoras*, the *Symposion* brings together Socrates, a tragic poet, a comic poet, a doctor, and a young politician. Such anecdotes as we have illustrate this further. Sophocles, the painter Polygnotos, the philosopher poet Archelaos, the poet, dramatist, philosopher, anecdotalist Ion from Chios group themselves round Kimon, and slightly later Sophocles is associated with the historian Herodotos. Pericles is associated with the philosopher Anaxagoras and with Damon the theorist of music, metre, and education. Euripides had Protagoras reading aloud in his house and lent his copy of Herakleitos to Socrates. Examples could be multiplied, but this is enough evidence of a society in which the creators met, and which prevented them from becoming overspecialised in the modern sense and compelled them to be aware of each other's thinking.[9]

Within this society there were enclaves of various kinds, but they were in one way or another open enclaves. We have noticed what we may call family businesses in pottery, in medicine, in tragedy: we know less about comedy, but Aristophanes had two sons who are known as comic poets in the fourth century. The tragic and comic poets no doubt inherited the family manuscripts, and the family name no doubt helped them when they asked the archon to produce their plays. Sophocles' Association in honour of the Muses may have been a gathering of actors and chorusmen, who gathered to sacrifice to the Muses and hold symposia to discuss dramatic problems, but we must admit that we have no hard knowledge about it. The doctors' schools were certainly professional, but the great doctors travelled and published in a form that was generally intelligible. The potters were professionals; the family businesses had a strong individuality and probably had their secret formulae. But they were wide open to influences from outside—from patrons, from bronzeworkers and stone sculptors, who lived and worked in the immediate neighbourhood, and from the great painters. In the art world particularly we have evidence for imperceptible gradations from the humblest craftsmen to the greatest painters, sculptors and architects. The Pythagorean communities are said to have been secret. They do not strictly concern us because they were not Athenian, but they may have been a model for the Academy. What is clear about them is that secrecy did not prevent them having a considerable influence on local politics, and their philosophical and mathematical doctrines were widely known outside. The Athenian schools of the fourth century, which centred round Plato, Isokrates, and later Aristotle, certainly represented an advance towards professional research institutes. But Isokrates' school was tiny, Plato's school and still more Aristotle's were multidiscipline; all of them took foreigners as well as Athenians, and all of them took from and fed back into public life. Enclaves existed as a necessary means of research, but they were open enclaves.[10]

The openness and viability of Athenian society may help to explain the speed of progress. One of the questions propounded in the first chapter was how quickly new ideas were accepted and how strong was the opposition to them. What we see, is astonishingly rapid advance all round. In politics we can also see the opposition, and we must admit that the in-fighting was pretty dirty on both sides during the period between the Persian wars and the Peloponnesian war, when the full democracy was being established. But the new ideas were put into practice without a civil war, and political theory was formulated to correspond to them. Civil war only broke out under the rule of the Thirty Tyrants imposed by Sparta in 404, and the restored democracy proclaimed an amnesty and took as its watchword *homonoia*, Concord.[11]

It is perfectly true that we can trace a line of conservative criticism of poetry, drama, music, and art from before the middle of the fifth century to Plato. We know it from the fragments of

Damon and from Attic comedy. But how much did it effect? The lyric poet Timotheos was heartbroken at his defeat, but with Euripides to console him he won a victory at the Panathenaia very soon afterwards. The conservative Sophocles won eighteen first prizes at the City Dionysia, and the modernist Euripides only won five. But Euripides was never refused a production, and the later plays of Sophocles clearly show the influence of the new music. What I have called the Late Classical style in art of the mid-fourth century, may be as much a natural swing as a reaction to Plato's criticism. As far as freedom of thought is concerned, the trials of Protagoras, Anaxagoras, and Socrates cannot be reckoned as opposition to new ideas because their main purpose was clearly political. Similarly the various attacks on comic poets were political and had remarkably little effect. Opposition was ineffective against the drive of highly competitive poets, artists, and thinkers, striving to defeat their rivals before engaged and intelligent audiences, whether the smaller picked audiences of intellectual society or the larger mixed audiences of festivals, law-courts, and Assembly.[12]

The audience wanted what was new, provided that they could understand it. Reverence for the beauty of old poetry or art was not common. Old religious images might be preserved because they were venerable, and venerability accounts for the archaic Athena on coins and Panathenaic vases. The Persian wars were a splendid recent memory, particularly in bad times. The age of heroes was a noble past, and its traditions were collected by the mythographers but the artists and tragic poets modernised it. Homer was still recited at the Panathenaia; he survived because he was venerable, and the reciters were modern in technique. The old songs survived in the schools and in symposia, but the schools had nothing to do with progress, and on the evidence of comedy it was the old men who demanded the old songs in the symposia while their sons insisted on modernity. Probably the first clear sign of reverence for the past is the revival of one fifth-century tragedy at each competition after 386. After that many signs of looking backwards appear, of which the Late Classical style may be one, but by then the historical scholarship of the Hellenistic age was not far away.[13]

A small city with many meeting places, an open society, a viable social structure, intelligent patronage, educated audiences, the spirit of competition, these are the things that classical Athens offered to artists, poets, and thinkers, and they are partly responsible for the flowering of culture. But classical Athens is the heir of archaic Athens or rather to archaic Greece, and we have to look there for further clues. First let us recall very briefly what we have said about religion and what we have said about Homer. Both provide a static and a dynamic element. By the static element in religion I mean the simple fact that ritual, prayer, sacrifice, and dedications take care of the life of the ancient Greek from birth to death. Many occasions which for us involve individual decisions and worry can be met by religious formulae which are well-known or easily discoverable. The operations prescribed are often beautiful and mind-filling, such as dedication of beautiful objects or the performance of choral dances. They are a kind of beautiful drill which tranquillises the mind so that it is the freer for bold speculation. By the dynamic element in religion I do not mean theology; I regard theology as a speculative enterprise of thought which has remarkably little to do with religion in the sense that I have been using the word, although conflict was always possible and became actual, when politics was involved. I mean here much more simply the use of omens and the like to interpret the future, which was dynamic because the Greeks brilliantly transferred the method to the interpretation of the physical world by induction.[14]

The static element in Homer is his world of gods and heroes. They may be criticised by Xenophanes and later Plato, they may be reinterpreted by Aeschylus, Sophocles, and Euripides, they may be parodied by the comic poets. Everyone knew them from childhood. Partly they represent the glorious past. But still more they are a set of knowns so that no one can doubt what the criticism or reinterpretation means, what new values are being established. Greek tragedy could have invented its plots; by using the epic as its source, it freed the audience to concentrate on what was essentially being said—they came with a knowledge of who the characters were and what would probably happen to them. And, far more generally, the epic stories were a set of paradigms to which reference could be made in many situations.[15]

Two dynamic elements in Homer have concerned us frequently through this book and need only be mentioned here—the Homeric simile as the model for the working-model comparisons of the philosophers and the doctors, and the personified feminine abstracts, which may have or approximate to the status of a goddess. Parallel to the feminine abstract, but still awaiting development, was the neuter adjective with the definite article, which in Homer denotes a thing and maintained some of its material quality even when later it is used for an abstract. But words belong in sentences, and sentences are shaped to express thought.[16]

Sentence-structure in Homer has come a long way from the sentence-structure of the Mycenaean tablets and has a long way further to go before reaching the complication that we have seen in Lysias and Demosthenes. Here I want to notice two types which both have a great future. Greek had two particles, *men* and *de*, which can be laboriously translated 'on the one hand' and 'on the other hand'. *Men* does not occur on the Mycenaean tablets, but of course that does not prove that it did not already exist. *De* is found and means, as often later, 'but' or 'and'. It is the use of *men* in the first sentence which makes us translate *de* 'on the other hand' when it introduces the second sentence. This is fully developed in Homer: 'Nine days (*men*) the arrows of Apollo went through the host, on the tenth (*de*) Achilles summoned the army to a meeting.' The particles make the two sentences into a contrasting pair, and the language has provided a very simple method for people who habitually see and think in this simple pattern, to express the contrast. Later authors like Gorgias and Isokrates, as we have seen, immensely elaborate this kind of paired sentence, but basically they preserve the same simple pattern.[17]

In the complicated sentences of Lysias and Demosthenes a single fact is stated and all the other statements in the sentence are related to this main statement as conditions, causes, results, or attendant circumstance. The sentence expresses the relations of a number of statements to a single statement of fact. It is a system with its relations expressed, and an indispensable tool for advanced thought. Homer only has the germ of this, and we can feel behind him a stage (actually visible in the Mycenaean tablets) where main sentences could be made to express conditions, results, and the rest, by prefixing a particle or by altering the mood of the verb, but were not tied together into systems. Chryses' prayer to Apollo shows the system in the making: 'if ever I roofed a temple to your pleasure, fulfil this prayer, may the Greeks pay for my tears'. The condition 'if ...' is phrased as a subordinate clause, but the prayer is hung on as another main sentence, shown to be a prayer by the mood of the verb, which we translate 'may'. But this example shows that the language had already the potentiality to form new patterns, when such were needed, to express a new kind of reality.[18]

I think that here we are near an idea which may help us to understand, even if it does not explain, the speed with which the Greeks were able to move forward in thought, poetry, and art. As a first formulation, to explain reality the Greeks chose some simple form, developed it and complicated it so that it contained more of reality as they now saw it, and then dropped it in favour of a new simple form, with which the process was repeated.

What distinguishes Greek art from Mycenaean art is a new precision of shape and new simple geometrical patterns. The concentric circles which decorate a tenth-century Attic vase (*fig. 1*) form a simple rational pattern: they contrast with an equally rational triglyph pattern between them and with the surrounding black glaze. But this simplest schematisation of reality does not satisfy for long. By 740 (*fig. 2*) the vase is covered all over by a system of geometric patterns and includes now vegetable ornament, animals, and even humans. This is too complicated, and the interest shifts to the humans. In the seventh century a new simple, and conventional formula is devised for the human figure. It is developed to include all sorts of detail and by 490 has become complicated again (*fig. 3*). A new shift of interest makes the artist want to include the third dimension, depth, and so a new formula is devised (*fig. 4*), the figure with one stiff leg and one free leg and swinging hips. Depth also enters painting, piecemeal. Here I suspect that a false step was taken (*fig. 5*): Polygnotos divided up the depth by a number of wavy lines representing hills, on which figures could stand or sit, and which could mask the lower parts of their bodies. This was too complicated and too restricted in its applications. About 430 Agatharchos invented a new formula: the figures are put on a stage with a perspective backcloth, and this formula lasted into the Hellenistic age (*fig. 6*).[19]

I have traced this example through, because in it the sequence —simple form, complication, new simple form—can be seen repeating itself. But we have had a number of other examples in the course of this book. Take, for instance, the development of lyric metre, remembering that the metre regulates the dance as well as the tune and the words. The earliest songs are simple systems of identical lines with sections of the song marked off by lines which are shorter than the normal by one syllable. Then we find in Alkman in the seventh century very shapely repeating stanzas, clearly divided into three parts which are different from each other in metre but still very simple. Then in the early sixth century Stesichoros introduces the more complicated triad form, each triad consisting of identical strophe and antistrophe and variant epode. The triad continues, but the metre becomes immensely more complicated with Pindar in the early fifth century. Then the new music introduces the long free preludes, and this is the model for Timotheos to abandon the triad form altogether, so that the whole song becomes a long complex of free verse. This, as far as we know, is an end, and later lyric poetry reverts to older simpler forms. Or take the development of drama. We can imagine a very simple form for Thespis- spoken prologue, sung chorus, messenger speech, sung lament. This is built up into the immense complication of the Aeschylean connected trilogy. With classical tragedy the unit is the single play, the choral odes are shorter and simpler, the emphasis has switched to the actors. It is probable that in the fourth century the choruses were reduced to irrelevant interludes. In comedy we can trace the same sort of change, and there we have the final step in the five-act social comedy of Menander, which can legitimately be called a new form. Or to take a quite different case, in the sixth century Anaximander's map was as simple as the design on a geometric vase, a circle with a cross in it, and we can trace two subsequent stages of complication to bring it nearer to reality, Hekataios' map at the end of the sixth century and Herodotos' map in the middle of the fifth. Aristotle unwittingly announces the rule for this kind of development when he writes at the beginning of the *Poetics*: 'let us start like nature with what is first'; what is first for him is the general class of 'imitations' to which the poetic arts with which he is concerned belong. The Greek sees or makes a simple and intelligible general form first, and then elaborates it to bring it closer to reality.[20]

Contrasting pairs, of which the *men* ... *de* sentence is one expression, are an extraordinarily fruitful simple form of this kind. A recent study has called the use of contrasting pairs Polarity as distinct from Analogy, by which is meant what we have called the use of working models. Analogy also uses pairs, but the relation between them is likeness and not contrast. Homer already has both early short comparisons and late long similes. In the fifth century Empedokles ties model and original together at more points in his use of the pipette to illustrate breathing. Finally, in Plato's use of paradeigmata—e.g. weaving and statesmanship in the *Statesman*—the cross-referencing is very detailed, and one feels that the form has become so complicated that its further usefulness is doubtful.[21]

Contrasting pairs we have met again and again. Let us note first one line of development which starts with the early Pythagoreans. They regarded as first principles ten sets of contrasting pairs arranged in two columns, so that the members of each column were felt to be cognate to each other as well as paired against the other column. One column has as its members limit, odd, one, right, male, still, straight, light, good, square; the other column contained unlimited, even, many, left, female, moving, crooked, dark, bad, oblong. If we take from the first column limit, one, still, and oppose them to their opposites in the other column, unlimited, many, moving, we have something very like Being on the one side opposed to Becoming on the other, as conceived by Parmenides. The Parmenidean concept of eternal, valid Being opposed to Becoming is taken over by Plato as the eternal and real Ideas opposed to the changing and unreal world of the senses. But then as we have seen, Plato complicates the simple contrast: the Ideas are placed in a hierarchy, first in the *Republic*, and then in the dichotomies of the later dialogues. The principle of contrasting pairs continues to operate both in the *Republic* and in the dichotomies, but the final result is unwieldy, undermines the reality of the Ideas, and is faulty as a system of classification. Aristotle brilliantly breaks off three sections of the dichotomised line to invent a new fruitful shape, the logical syllogism with major premiss, minor premiss, and conclusion, and loosens up the system to produce a classification which corresponds to reality.[22]

The physical philosophers also used contrasting pairs, probably from the time of Anaximander: the hot and the cold, the dry and the wet etc. We have seen them also in the geographers, doctors, and historians, and have noted how pairs of mental qualities, the brave and the cowardly, the fierce and the mild developed alongside them and to some extent even out of them. Here I only want to recall briefly the *nomos-physis* contrast, which dominated much of fifth-century thought. We do not know who invented it. On the one hand many indications showed that *nomos* was man-made and artificial. Customs differed irreconcilably from country to country. The laws passed by a democratic government changed from day to day. The gods were shown not to be responsible for physical events (such as weather and disease). Gods, laws, and customs fell under *nomos*. To this instability could be opposed the indubitable reality of *physis*, the physical world including man as a physical animal. The observable law of the physical world is jungle-law, and that is the way to behave. But aggression is both uncomfortable for the many weak and may become impossible for the strong few, unless they have overwhelming strength. So the contrast has to be rethought. Rather outside the main battle the author of *Airs* sees *nomos*, here political organisation, as a force which may act either with or against physical environment (*physis*) in determining human behaviour. Various rescue operations are conducted to save the reality of the gods; the most satisfactory is perhaps the view that piety is of such long standing that it can be regarded as *physis* rather than *nomos*. *Nomos* in its political meaning is subdivided into ancestral customs, international law (these two Aristotle calls 'natural justice', *physis*), criminal law, and executive decrees, each of which have a different validity. Most drastically Plato turns the contrast on its head by asserting the superior reality of the conceptual world of Ideas, which he calls *physis*, and the instability of the physical world. The *nomos-physis* contrast was a useful way of looking at the mid-fifth-century situation; seen in these terms, the situation gave rise to strenuous thought, which produced new solutions, and they in fact destroyed the original contrast.[23]

Let us look finally at another story which we may call 'from creation to history'. 'First Chaos was born and then Earth ... and Tartara ... and Eros. From Chaos Erebos and black Night were born. From Night Aither and Day were born. Earth bore first starry Heaven ... and she bore the long Mountains ... and she gave birth to Sea. Then bedded with Heaven, she bore Ocean etc.... After them as youngest Kronos was born.' The story was continued with the pedigree of the gods. It is a magnificent piece of systematisation by Hesiod in the eighth century. What interests us here is that he in no way distinguishes between Night bearing Day, Earth bearing Mountains, Earth bearing the personal god Kronos. He has his one model (human procreation) and he uses it both for his cosmogony and for his theogony. He probably did think of Night, Day, Earth, Heaven, and Ocean as personal, but Chaos, Erebos, and Mountains are in the neuter gender. In the sixth century the Milesians take up cosmogony, and they still think of an ensoulled world-being, as the original substance: Thales takes Water, so far depersonalising the Homeric-Hesiodic Ocean, Anaximander takes the Unlimited, and Anaximenes takes Air. They speak of them as gods in hymn-style, but for the creation of the physical world instead of pro-creation they use analogies from everyday life, what we have called working-models—which naturally leads to a mechanistic view of the universe. Anaximenes equated Air with divine mind and with human mind. This produces the very fruitful macrocosm-microcosm analogy and leads, because the mind of the divine planner and craftsman is modelled on the mind of the human planner and craftsman, to the Forethought of god and the principle of balance in Protagoras and to teleology in Diogenes of Apollonia and later in Plato and Aristotle. That is one line.[24]

Rather before the middle of the fifth century the rise of human civilisation was added to cosmogony. In the *Protagoras* myth balanced power is the model for the creation of animals, e.g. strong animals are slow, and the weak animals are swift. Men are then given different arts and crafts, but they are all given justice and respect, so that they can live together and ward off the animals. The jungle-law operates, but civilisation is a defence against it. The myth probably ended in a justification of Athenian democracy. Protagoras seems to have defined King-ship, Oligarchy, Democracy and Tyranny; Plato added Timo-cracy in the *Republic* and arranged the constitutions in a logical sequence of degradation; but in later life, as we have seen, he increased the number and rearranged them in chronological order with some of the stages tied to history. It is an interesting case of historical reality breaking a preconceived pattern.[25]

The jungle-law pattern also dominates the rise of civilisation attributed to Anaxagoras. Thucydides took it over and made it the nerve both of his summary of early history and of his history of Peloponnesian war. Here the pattern is applied firmly to historical reality, with perhaps the sole exception of the unique and in-corruptible Pericles. I have called the principle the jungle-law, and certainly this is one way in which the Greeks saw it. But it was of very wide application. In the cosmogonies the opposites are separated out from the mass by whatever mechanical analogy the particular thinker adopts. In their comparatively pure state the opposites are at war with one another, but the war may be controlled by proportions, by a planning divinity, or whatever. The doctors take the analogy over to explain health and sickness, whether they use hot and cold or, as in *Ancient Medicine*, the strong as their principle. *Airs* sees environment and institutions as producing by their interaction strong men and weak men. The rhetoricians found their case on *eikos*, the predictability of human behaviour, and particularly the probability that the strong man will exploit the weak man.[26]

What we see in the fifth century is a veritable explosion of this idea of probability (*eikos*) with the strong exploiting the weak as one model. The physical world and human behaviour both work on the principle of probability. (For Parmenides and Plato the polarity principle counters with the Necessity of Being and the Ideas as a contrast to probability in the world of the senses.) But the idea of probability has further implications. If you are moving towards or have reached this concept of general predictability, it means that you have ceased to see things or events as isolated units of equal significance; you have come to see them as interconnected, and you are, perhaps now primarily, interested in the relation between them rather than in the things or events in themselves. This needs the complicated sentence (instead of a string of main sentences) to express it in prose and some representation of three-dimensional space for expression in art.

The progress was swift and the development far more complicated than we can now see. The poets, artists, and thinkers were extremely intelligent and highly competitive. The audiences were receptive and demanded intelligibility. I think it helps to understand them if we think of them as choosing simple forms and gradually developing them to include more reality, and then when necessary starting again with a new simple form. Perhaps the landscape and light of Greece provide some analogy. Everything is defined; the mountains have sharp outlines, and even the sea is marked off by jagged islands. These are the simple forms. For the two hours after dawn and two hours before dusk the detail stands out in incredibly bright colours. This is reality complicating the clear shapes. For the Greek the pattern is beautiful in its symmetry and proportions, and reality ought to be like that. But reality is too exciting to be left alone, and honest inquiry shows that it will not fit the pattern. So, ever optimistic, the Greek makes a new pattern to fit the new view of reality.

Notes

Abbreviations used for titles of Journals

A.A.   Archäologischer Anzeiger
A.J.A. American Journal of Archaeology
A.J.P. American Journal of Philology
B.I.C.S. Bulletin of the Institute of Classical Studies
B.S.A. Annual of the British School at Athens
C.Q.   Classical Quarterly
C.R.   Classical Review
G.R.B.S. Greek, Roman, and Byzantine Studies
R.E.G. Revue des Etudes Grecques
T.A.P.A. Transactions of the American Philological Association

Notes to 2. *The Greek Achievement*

1 Cf. in general my *Mycenae to Homer*, London and New York 1964, chs. 1-4, with bibliography.

2 *Mycenae to Homer*, ch. 5; V. Desborough, *The Last Mycenaeans*, Oxford 1964.

3 *Mycenae to Homer*, ch. 7, and p. 292f.; cf. also E. Aronson in J. W. Atkinson, *Motives in Fantasy, Action and Society*, New York 1958, 544.

4 *Mycenae to Homer*, ch. 6; Dietrich, *B.I.C.S.* 17, 1970, 16.

5 J. L. Benson, *Horse, Bird and Man*, Amherst 1970; B. Schweitzer, *Greek Geometric Style*, London 1972, 26, 36; N. Himmelmann-Wildschütz, *Abhandlungen der Mainzer Akademie*, 1968, 290; *Mycenae to Homer*, 137ff., 325. For Keos see the annual accounts from 1960 in *Archaeological Reports* and *A.J.A.* Hero cults in Athens, H. A. Thompson, *A.A.*, 1961, 225; *Annals of Athens University*, 1963-4, 283f.

6 Cf. W. J. Verdenius, *Homer the Educator of the Greeks*, Royal

Netherlands Academy 1970.

7 *Iliad* 12, 432; *Mycenae to Homer*, 224ff.; *Greek Art and Literature, 700-530 B.C.* (abbreviated below as *G.A.L.*), 82ff.; G. E. R. Lloyd, *Polarity and Analogy*, Cambridge 1966, 183ff.

8 *G.A.L.* 84f., 97; *Journal of the Warburg and Courtauld Institutes*, 17, 1954, 14f.; Lloyd, *op. cit.*, 203 (on Hesiod).

9 C. Roebuck, *The Muses at Work*, Cambridge (Mass.) 1969 (abbreviated below as Roebuck) is excellent on technology and has good bibliography; 118f. pottery (J. V. Noble), 96f. stone-carving (B. S. Ridgway).

10 Roebuck 6of. (D. K. Hill), 108ff. (Ridgway).

11 Cog-wheels: *Archaeological Reports*, 1964-5, 19; S. Dakaris, *Antike Kunst*, Beiheft 1, 35. Astrological machine: D. Price, *Scientific American*, June 1959, 60; *U.S. National Museum Bulletin*, 218, 81ff. Archimedes: Cicero, *Republic*, 1, 14. Plato, *Republic*, 10, 617a. Cf. also P. M. Schuhl, *Fabulation Platonicienne*, 82ff., 105.

12 *Mycenae to Homer*, 214ff.; A. Snodgrass, *Early Greek Armour and Weapons*, Edinburgh 1964; *J.H.S.* 85, 1965, 110ff.

13 Attic oil was widely exported from the late eighth century (E. Brann, *Agora* VIII, 32), but Solon gave a new impulse; cf. A. French, *Growth of the Athenian Economy*, London 1964. Ram and trireme: Roebuck 176 (L. Casson). Thucydides, I, 13-14.

14 Roebuck 213ff. (C. Roebuck).

15 L. H. Jeffery, *Local Scripts of Archaic Greece*, Oxford 1961; E. Brann, *Hesperia* 30, 1961, 146.

16 On all this cf. E. G. Turner, *Athenian Books in the fifth and fourth centuries B.C.*, London 1952; R. Pfeiffer, *History of Classical Scholarship*, 25ff. Stesichoros, D. L. Page, *Lyrica Graeca Selecta*, 263ff.

17 Herakleitos, Diogenes Laertius, ix, 6; Protagoras, Diogenes Laertius, ix, 54; satyr-play vase, Naples 3240, Webster, *Greek Theatre Production*, pl. 8; relief of comic poet, Lyme Hall, Stockport, *Greek Theatre Production*, pl. 16.

18 Isokrates, *Antidosis*, 193, *Panathenaicus*, 233. Vases: H. R. Immerwahr in *Classical, Mediaeval, and Renaissance Studies in honor of B. L. Ullman*, 1, Rome 1964, 17ff. Euripides: library, *Vita* 5. Text of Herakleitos, Diogenes Laertius, II, 22. Eupolis, fr. 304K. Euthydemos: Xenophon, *Mem.*, IV, ii, 1.

19 Plato, *Phaedo* 97c; Plutarch, *Nicias*, 23, 2; Plato, *Apology*, 26d. Aristophanes, *Frogs* 1114.

20 Much of what follows will be found in Aristotle, *Constitution of the Athenians*, chs. 6-8 (on date cf. J. Keany, *Historia* 19, 1970, 327). Cf. also C. Hignett, *History of the Athenian Constitution*, Oxford 1952; V. Ehrenberg, *Solon to Socrates*, London 1968, 48ff.

21 Aristotle, *Constitution of Athens*, chs. 20-2, 26-7, 29-41; also Hignett, see n. 20; Ehrenberg, 78ff.

22 Aristotle, *Constitution of Athens*, 4; text of earliest laws, Tod, *Greek Historical Inscriptions*, 1, no. 87; R. J. Bonner and G. Smith, *Administration of Justice from Homer to Aristotle*, Chicago 1930-8; M. Ostwald, *Nomos and the beginnings of Greek democracy*, Oxford 1969; R. S. Stroud, *Drakon's Law of Homicide*, Berkeley 1968.

23 Cf. below pp. 120ff.

24 Cf. below p. 146ff. Town planning: R. E. Wycherley, *How the Greeks built cities*, London 1969, ch. 7. Siting: R. D. Martienssen, *Idea of Space in Greek Architecture*, Johannesburg 1956. Hippodamos: Wycherley, *Historia* 13, 1964, 135.

25 Cf. *Mycenae to Homer*, 202ff.; *C.Q.*, 32, 1939, 166. N. Himmelmann-Wildschutz, *Abhandlung der Mainzer Akademie*, 1968, 340. Cf. particularly G. M. A. Richter, *Handbook of Greek Art*, 2nd ed., London 1969, figs. 409-10; J. D. Beazley and B. Ashmole, *Greek Sculpture and Painting*, Cambridge 1966, figs. 2 and 3.

26 Cf. *G.A.L.*, 41ff., 79ff.; Richter, *Handbook*, figs. 412-31; 53-8, 63-86; Beazley and Ashmole, figs. 14-44.

27 J. White, *Perspective in Ancient Drawing and Painting*, London 1956; G. M. A. Richter, *Perspective in Greek and Roman Art*, London 1970. *G.A.L.*, fig. 13. Richter, *Handbook*, figs. 452-8; Beazley and Ashmole, figs. 45, 55-62 (folds).

28 Cf. Richter, *Handbook*, figs. 87, 117, 129, 133, 196; Beazley and Ashmole, figs. 56, 63, 75, 79, 87, 126, 128, 130.

29 Cf. Richter, *Perspective*, figs. 98-104, 111, 137-40; White, *Perspective*, pls. 3-5.

30 Richter, *Handbook*, fig. 464; Beazley and Ashmole, fig. 82.

31 White, *Perspective*, 43ff., and pl. 6; Richter, *Perspective*, fig. 159; Richter, *Handbook*, fig. 396; Beazley and Ashmole, figs. 108, 142; A. Rumpf, *J.H.S.*, 67, 1949, 13ff.

32 Rumpf, *op. cit.*, 10ff.; *J.D.A.I.*, 49, 1934, 6ff.; Webster, *Everyday Life in Classical Athens*, London 1969, figs. 39, 82, 89; Richter, *Handbook*, fig. 463, 395.

33 Cf. my *Greek Chorus*, London 1970, 84ff., 95ff.; A. M. Dale, *Collected Papers*, Cambridge, 40ff.

34 *Greek Chorus*, 132f., 151f.; A. W. Pickard-Cambridge, *Dithyramb etc.*, 2nd ed., Oxford 1966, 38ff.

35 Pickard-Cambridge, *Dithyramb etc.*, 2nd ed., 80ff., 128, 152ff.; *G.A.L.*, 62f., 69f.; *Greek Chorus*, 110ff.

36 On production cf. my *Greek Theatre Production*, 2nd ed., London 1970, 5, 173; *Everyday Life in Classical Athens*, 90f. On Aeschylus, C. J. Herington, *The Author of the Prometheus Bound*, Austin 1970, ch. 3.

37 Cf. my *Introduction to Sophocles*, 2nd ed., London 1969, 206f.

38 Cf. my *Tragedies of Euripides*, 1967, particularly ch. vi.

39 Pickard-Cambridge, *Dithyramb etc.*, 2nd ed., 159ff.

40 G. G. A. Murray, *Aristophanes*, Oxford 1933.
41 Webster, *Studies in Later Greek Comedy*, 2nd ed., Manchester 1970, chs. III and IV.
42 *G.A.L.*, 83f., 86; W. K. C. Guthrie, *History of Greek Philosophy*, I, Cambridge 1962 (abbreviated below as Guthrie), 45ff., 72ff.; G. E. R. Lloyd, *Polarity and Analogy*, Cambridge 1966 (abbreviated below as Lloyd), 233f., 306f.
43 Anaximenes, *G.A.L.*, 39, 89; Guthrie, I, 131; Lloyd, 235.
44 *G.A.L.*, 40, 91; Guthrie, I, 181ff.; Lloyd, 86. H. Thesleff, *Scripta Instituti Donneriani Aboensis* 5, 1970, 77.
45 *G.A.L.*, 92f., 94; *Acta Congressus Madvigiani*, II, 38ff. Guthrie, I, 360ff., 403ff.; II, 1ff., 80, 101f.; Lloyd, 105ff.
46 L. Pearson, *Early Ionian Historians*, Oxford 1939.
47 Plato, *Protagoras*, 320d, cf. Herodotos iii, 108; Aesch. *PV* 436; Soph. *Ant.* 332; Eur. *Suppl.* 201; Kritias 25B; Diodoros I, 7-8. Guthrie, III, 262; J. S. Morrison, *C.Q.*, 35, 1962, 1; G. Vlastos, *A.J.P.*, 67, 51.
48 *G.A.L.*, 96; Guthrie, III, 269, 274, 378.
49 Alkmaion of Kroton: Guthrie, I, 341ff.; *On the Sacred Disease*; *Ancient Medicine*, W. H. S. Jones, Loeb Classical Library.
50 H. A. Immerwahr, *Form and Thought in Herodotos*, Cleveland 1966.
51 J. H. Finley, *Thucydides*, Cambridge (Mass.) 1942 (1963).

Notes to 3. *Attica and its Population*

1 Pseudo-Xenophon, *Poroi*, chs. I, III, V.
2 The evidence from Menander is given in *Rylands Bulletin*, 45, 1962, 237ff. Cf. also *Studies in Later Greek Comedy*, 190.
3 On the following sections see in general my *Everyday Life in Classical Athens*, ch. I, with bibliography; J. Travlos, *Poleodomike Exelixis ton Athenon*, Athens 1960, 5ff. (abbreviated below as Travlos); Pausanias, Bk. I.
4 Cf. Travlos, particularly ch. III.
5 Travlos, 71f.
6 Travlos, 65, 68, 69, 81; *Everyday Life in Classical Athens*, 28.
7 A. H. M. Jones, *Athenian Democracy*, Oxford 1957, 76f. (abbreviated below as Jones); N. G. L. Hammond, *History of Greece to 322 B.C.*, Oxford 1959, 528.
8 The low figure: Jones, 77ff. (cf. P. Bicknell, *Mnemosyne*, 1968, 74). Thucydides, VII, 27, 5; Pseudo-Xenophon, *Poroi*, IV, 25. Cf. also G. E. M. de Ste Croix, *C.R.*, 71, 1957, 56.
9 Nikias: Pseudo-Xenophon, *Poroi*, IV, 14. Auction prices: W. K. Pritchett, *Hesperia*, 22, 1953, 242ff.; 25, 1966, 277ff. Lysias: *Or.*, XII, 8, 19. Demosthenes, *Or.*, XXVII, 9.

10 On slaves in Old Comedy, V. Ehrenberg, *People of Aristophanes*, 2nd ed., Oxford 1951, 165ff. In Menander's *Dyskolos* the rich man Kallippides has Getas, Pyrrhias, Donax; Plangon appears to be a free girl who is his wife's servant; others presumably are left at home; the miserly Knemon has the old woman, Simike; the poor Gorgias has Daos.

11 In all this I have followed Jones' analysis, 79ff. Wages: Jones 143, n. 86.

12 War tax on property: Jones 83ff.

13 Jones, 85ff. Isaeus, VIII, 35; *Hesperia*, 25, 1966, 277; Pseudo-Xenophon, *Poroi*, IV, 14; Lysias, XIX, 45, Demosthenes, XXXVII, 9-11 (cf. Jones 15).

14. Jones, 90. Tod, *Greek Historical Inscriptions*, II, 100, metics enfranchised in 403 B.C. Plato, *Republic* I; Lysias, XII, 4, 8, 11, 19.

15 Jones, 14, 87. Demosthenes XXXVI, 5, 11, 43, 47; XLV, 71, 85; LII, 13. R. Bogaert, *Banques et Banquiers*, Leyden 1968.

16 Lysias, XXX, 2, 27; Aristophanes, *Frogs*, 1506. Lysias XIII, 6, 18, 64, 67. Tod, *Greek Historical Inscriptions*, I, no. 86. Andokides fr. 4; Aristophanes, *Knights* 1303, *Clouds* 1065, *Peace* 682; Plutarch, *Nic.* 11, *Alc.* 13; Thucydides, VIII, 73, 3.

17 Cf. below ch. 7. Hyperbolos: Eupolis fr. 364 (Kock, Edmonds).

18 Erechtheion: Roebuck, *Muses at Work*, 26; J. J. Pollitt, *The Art of Greece*, 118f. Mines: Xenophon, *Poroi*, IV, 22; Demosthenes, XLII, 20. Prices: Xenophon, *Mem.* II, v, 2; *Hesperia* 25, 1966, 277f. Pseudo-Xenophon, *Constitution of Athens*, i, 10.

19 Jones, 33, 55-7, Lysias, XXI, 2-5. Pickard-Cambridge, *Dithyramb etc.*, 2nd ed., ch. II. J. K. Davies, *J.H.S.* 87, 1967, 33. Cf. Plutarch, *Nic.* III, 2.

20 *Everyday Life in Classical Athens*, ch. 3; R. E. Wycherley, *The Athenian Agora*, III, Princeton 1957; *Greece and Rome*, 3, 1956, 2, Plutarch, *Nic.* 30. On barbers' shops cf. Menander *Samia*, 510 with Colin Austin's note.

21 Plutarch, *Nic.* 12. D. B. Thompson, *Archaeology*, 13, 1960, 234; Diogenes Laertius, II, xiii, 122. Xenophon, *Mem.* IV, ii, 1.

22 Stoa of Herms: *Everyday Life in Classical Athens*, 63; *Greek Chorus*, 93. Stoa Poikile: R. E. Wycherley, *Phoenix*, 7, 1953, 20; L. H. Jeffery, *B.S.A.*, 60, 1965, 50. Stoa of Zeus: R. E. Wycherley, *Greece and Rome* 8, 1961, 158. Royal Stoa: *A.J.A.*, 75, 1971, 213.

23 R. E. Wycherley, *Greece and Rome*, 8, 1961, 152ff.; 9, 1962, 2ff. *Everyday Life in Classical Athens*, 49f. J. Delorme, *Gymnasion*, Paris 1960. R. Ginouvés, *Balaneutike*, Paris 1962. Isaios V, 22; VI, 33. M. K. Donaldson, *Hesperia*, 24, 1965, 77.

24 Plutarch, *Phocion*, 4; *Themistocles* 2. Fordyce Mitchel, *Lykourgan Athens*, Cincinnati 1970, 38.

25 Pseudo-Xenophon, *Constitution of Athens*, i, 13, ii, 10.

26 *Everyday Life in Classical Athens*, ch. 2. W. K. Lacey, *The Family in Classical Greece*, London 1968, particularly chapters IV-VII.
27 Simon the cobbler, see above n. 21. Plato, *Protagoras*, 314d.
28 Lacey, chs. VI, VII. G. de Ste Croix, *C.R.*, 20, 1970, 274.
29 Comedy situations: cf. *Studies in Later Greek Comedy*, 77; Menander, *Arrhephoros, Synaristosai, Epitrepontes, Dyskolos*. Xenophon, *Symp.*, VIII, 3.
30 *Potter and Patron*, London 1972, chs. XVI, XVII.
31 Isaios VI, 19. Cf. Demosthenes, LIX, 18. Habrotonon in Menander's *Epitrepontes*. Xenophon, *Symp.* II, i, 11, 15; III, 1; VII, 2; VIII, 2.
32 *Studies in Later Greek Comedy*, 22, 63. Plutarch, *Pericles*, 24, 32, 37.
33 Lacey, 100, 282. Demosthenes, LIX, 38, 50, 72, 89. Menander, *Perikeiromene, Sikyonios, Synaristosai*.
34 Xenophon, *Symp.* I, II, III, VII. Xenophon, *Oeconomicus*, viii, 13. Plato, *Symposium* 173e.
35 *Everyday Life in Classical Athens*, 43; *Greek Chorus*, 64, 72, 84, 104, 194.
36 Aristophanes, fr. 223K; *Clouds*, 1354ff.
37 Cf. above n. 6. E. T. Vermeule, *Antike Kunst* 8, 1965, 34; *Potter and Patron*, ch. II.

Notes to 4. *Education*

1 H. I. Marrou, *History of Education in Antiquity*, London 1956 (abbreviated below as Marrou) particularly 36ff.; K. J. Dover, *Aristophanes Clouds*, Oxford 1968, lviii-lxiv.
2 Marrou, 26ff.; Dover, *op. cit.*, lxiv-vi; *B.I.C.S.*, 11, 1964, 31ff.; G. Devereux, *C.Q.*, 20, 1970, 17ff.; *Symbolae Osloenses*, 42, 1967, 69ff. (much the most satisfactory treatment).
3 Plato, *Protagoras*, 325c-326c.
4 Plato, *Republic*, 377c.
5 Earliest inscriptions, above ch. 2, n. 15. Alphabets: E. Brann, Hesperia, 30, 1961, 63. Aristeides: Plutarch, *Aristides*, VII. Comedy: Kratinos, fr. 122K; Aristophanes, *Knights* 188.
6 Aristophanes, *Clouds*, 964f. (*Kometai*, cf. Isocrates, VII, 46). Herodotus, VI, 27, 2. Plutarch, *Themistocles*, x. Archaeological Reports, 1958, 3. Wycherley, *Greece and Rome* 9, 1962, 9. Military training figures: Jones 82.
7 Munich 2421, *ARV*, 2nd ed., 23/7.
8 *Potter and Patron*, chs. II, XVIII. The scenes with book-rolls are discussed and illustrated by H. R. Immerwahr in *Studies in honor of B. Ullman*, Rome 1964, 17.
9 Vases cf. preceding note. Plato, *Republic*, 377-92. Homer: Xenophon, *Symposium*, III, 5; Plutarch, *Alcibiades*, VII. Cf. also Verdenius, cited ch. 2, n. 6.

NOTES

10 Aristophanes, *Clouds*, 961-1104 (with Dover's commentary).
11 Simonides, *PMG*, 542; Plato, *Protagoras*, 339a.
12 Aristophanes, *Clouds*, 878; Plutarch, *Demosthenes*, 5.
13 Xenophon, *Eq.*, II, 2; Plutarch, *Nicias* 5.
14 Pamphilos, Pliny *NH*, 35, 76. Pasion, see above ch. 3, n. 15.
15 *Potter and Patron* ch. I, and cf. above ch. 3, n. 31. Demosthenes, LIX, 18. Xenophon, *Symposium*, II, III, VII, IX. *Potter and Patron*, ch. XVI. Elpinike: Naples 3232, *ARV*, 2nd ed., 1032/61.
16 The Sophists: Marrou, 48ff.; Guthrie, 261ff.; Pfeiffer, *History of Classical Scholarship*, 30ff.
17 On dating of Protagoras, J. A. Davison, *C.Q.*, 3, 1953, 33ff.
18 Plato, *Protagoras*, 314d (ch. 3, n. 27); *Gorgias*, 447a; *Republic*, 328b; *Euthydemos*, 271-3; *Lysis*, 203-4.
19 Plato, *Protagoras*, 315a, 311c; Diogenes Laertius, IX, 52; *Hippias Major*, 282b-e.
20 Plato, *Hippias Minor*, 368b; *Cratylus*, 384b; Aristotle, *Rhetoric* 1415b16; *Hippias Major*, 282e.
21 Cf. above ch. 3, n. 21.
22 *Clouds*, cf. Dover. *op. cit.*, xxxii ff. Plato, *Protagoras*, 320d (myth), 314c (Hippias). C. Segal, *Rh.Mus.*, 113, 1970, 152 (Protagoras and Aristophanes).
23 Plato, *Phaedo*, 96a, *Apology*, 19d. Xenophon, *Mem.* I, ii, 15.
24 *Life of Sophocles*, 6, cf. my *Introduction to Sophocles*, 198, 205f.
25 Pythagorean communities: G. S. Kirk and J. E. Raven, *The Presocratic Philosophers*, Cambridge 1957, 217ff. Archytas, H. Diels and W. Kranz, *Die Fragmente der Vorsokratiker*, Berlin 1934, no. 47. Plato, *Letter VII*, 327c.
26 R. E. Wycherley, *Greece and Rome* 9, 1962, 2. The house: Plutarch, *Moralia*, 603b, cf. Jones 89, 151. Speusippos: Athenaeus, 279e, 547d (Lykon), 548a (Plato).
27 Plato, *Republic*, 523-535a, 537b-c, 539-540c.
28 Marrou 63ff.; C. B. Armstrong, *Proc. Leeds Philosophical Society*, 1953, 89ff. Renehan, *G.R.B.S.*, 11, 1970, 219. Plutarch, *Moralia*, 1126c; *Dion: Phocion*, 4, 14, 18, 27, 29-30; P. M. Schuhl, *R.E.G.*, 59, 1946, 46. *Later Greek Comedy*, 51 on Ephippos 14K. Fordyce Mitchel, *Lykourgan Athens*, Cincinnati 1970, 11, 18, 22.
29 Cf. my *Art and Literature in fourth-century Athens*, 47, 51ff., 58f. (abbreviated below *A.A.L.*).
30 Marrou 79ff. Demosthenes: Plutarch, *Isocrates*, 837. Isocrates, XV, 87, 224.
31 Isocrates, XIII, 1-13; XV, 261-9, cf. XII, 26-9. Plato, *Phaedrus*, 278e. *A.A.L.* 11ff., 58.
32 Isocrates, XV, 180-5; XIII, 16-18.
33 Isocrates, XV, 276; IV, 171, cf. *Ep.* I, 9; XII, 200ff., 231ff., 262ff.

Notes to 5. *Religion*

1 On Greek religion in general M. P. Nilsson, *Geschichte der Religion*, Munich 1941; *Greek Piety*, Oxford 1948; W. K. C. Guthrie, *The Greeks and their Gods*, London 1950; P. E. Corbett, Greek Temples and Greek Worshippers, *B.I.C.S.*, 17, 1970, 149. On Attic cults, L. Deubner, *Attische Feste*, Berlin 1932 (abbreviated below as Deubner); a brief account in *Everyday Life in Classical Athens*, 81f.

2 *Mycenae to Homer*, 142f. Athenian priestly families: Deubner, 46, 71, 69 (cf. also 19, 214); Herodotus, v, 61.

3 Haloa: Deubner, 60ff. Rural Dionysia: Deubner, 134ff.; Pickard-Cambridge, *Festivals*, 2nd ed., 42ff.; Aristophanes, *Acharnians*, 201, 241ff. Lenaia: Deubner, 123ff.; Pickard-Cambridge, *Festivals*, 25ff.; *Dithyramb etc.*, 2nd ed., 144f., 154.

4 The Vases: Deubner, 127ff.; Pickard-Cambridge, *Festivals*, 30ff.; *Greek Chorus*, 81f.; *Potter and Patron*, ch. IX. Anthesteria: Deubner 93ff.; Pickard-Cambridge, *Festivals*, 1ff.; G. van Hoorn, *Choes and Anthesteria*, Leyden 1951; K. Friis Johansen, *Acta Archaeologica*, 38, 1967, 175ff.; E. Simon, *Die Götter der Griechen*, Munich 1969, 275ff.

5 City Dionysia: Deubner, 138ff.; Pickard-Cambridge, *Festivals*, 57ff.

6 Thargelia: Deubner, 179ff.; Pickard-Cambridge, *Dithyramb etc.*, 37; Mitsos, *Athens Annals of Archaeology*, 3, 1970, 393. Kallynteria and Plynteria: Deubner, 17ff. Arrhetophoria: Deubner, 9ff. Skirophoria: Deubner, 40ff. Dipolieia: Deubner, 158. Kronia: Deubner 152.

7 Deubner, 22; C. J. Herington, *Athena Parthenos and Athena Polias*, Manchester 1955; H. A. Thompson, *Archäologische Anzeiger*, 1961, 225.

8 Deubner, 91, 69ff.; G. E. Mylonas, *Eleusis and the Eleusinian Mysteries*, Princeton 1961.

9 Deubner, 50ff., 198ff., 142ff.; B. Jordan, *A.J.A.*, 75, 1971, 205.

10 Cf. ch. 3 and n. 19.

11 Deubner, 224; 219 (cf. Plato, *Republic*, 328a), 214, 228, 174, 204; 226.

12 Linear B tablets, *Mycenae to Homer*, 109. Sophocles and Plato, cf. above pp. 72-3; the Muses were also honoured in schools, Deubner, 217. Actors etc.: *Art and Literature in fourth-century Athens*, 30, 110. Chalkeia: Deubner, 35. Hephaistia: Deubner, 212. Promethia: Deubner, 211. Hermaia: Deubner, 217; *Potter and Patron*, ch. IX. Elaphebolia: Deubner, 205.

13 Apatouria: Deubner, 232. Brauronia: Deubner, 207; *Potter and Patron*, ch. XX, 2. Genesia: Deubner, 229; F. Jacoby, *J.H.S.*, 64, 1944, 37. Diasia: Deubner, 155.

14 On oracles cf. H. W. Parke, *Greek Oracles*, London 1967. Sicilian expedition: Plutarch, *Nicias* XIII. Nikias, Plutarch, *Nicias*, IV. Theo-

phrastus, *Characters*, XVI, 11. For a poor interpreter of dreams cf. Plutarch, *Aristides*, XXVII. Pericles, Plutarch, *Pericles*, VI, 1.

15 Deme Mysteries cf. above n. 2. Demosthenes, *De Corona*, 259. Theophrastos, *Characters*, XVI, 12. Euripides, *Hippolytus* 71ff. Cf. A. J. Festugière, *Personal Religion among the Greeks*, Berkeley 1954.

16 Telesinos: A. E. Raubitschek, *Dedications from the Athenian Acropolis*, Princeton 1949, no. 40. Kallias: Raubitschek, nos. 21, 164. Vases: *Potter and Patron*, chs. I and II. Statues and reliefs: Raubitschek, *passim*.

17 Herodotus V, 62, 3. Alkibiades: Thucydides, VI, 16; Plutarch, *Alcibiades*, XI, XII. Nikias: Plutarch, *Nicias*, III, 4.

18 Plutarch, *Nicias*, III, 1-2. Political tract cf. ch. III n. 25. Pseudo-Xenophon, *Constitution of the Athenians*, I, 13. Plutarch, *Cimon*, V, 2 (bridle); X; XIII, 7 (beautification of Athens); VIII, 6, cf. Pausanias I, 17. Theseus: K. Schefold, *Museum Helveticum* 3, 1946, 60; *Potter and Patron* ch. V.

19 Plutarch, *Pericles*, XI, 4 (cf. Thucydides II, 38, 1); XII, 2-4; Thucydides II, 41, 1.

20 Plutarch, *Pericles*, XXXI-II, Pheidias, Anaxagoras, Aspasia; Pheidias: E. B. Harrison, *Hesperia*, 35, 1966, 132, Anaxagoras: cf. J. A. Davison, *C.Q.* 3, 1953, 43; H. T. Wade-Gery, *Essays in Greek History*, Oxford 1958, 258f. Protagoras, Diogenes Laertius 9, 54, cf. J. A. Davison, *op. cit.*, 35; J. S. Morrison, *C.Q.*, 35, 1942, 1ff. Plutarch, *Alcibiades*, XIX-XXII; Thucydides, VI, 28f. Juries: Jones, 123f. with notes. Socrates, cf. above ch. 4; Plato, *Apology*, 18b, 19c.

21 Cf. above ch. 2, pp. 10ff. for references.

22 Cf. above ch. 2. *Iliad*, 14, 246. W. Jaeger, *The Theology of the Early Greek Philosophers*, Oxford 1947.

23 *Mycenae to Homer*, 297; P. Walcot, *Hesiod and the Near East*, Cardiff 1966, 37. Solon, 1 D.

24 Aeschylus, *Eumenides* 640ff. Pindar, e.g. *Nemean* V, 14; *Olympian* I, 32. Xenophanes, particularly frs. 169-175, Kirk and Raven; Xenophanes and Aeschylus, C. J. Herington, *The Author of the Prometheus Bound*, Austin 1970, 92. Plato, *Republic*, II and III.

25 Plato, *Phaedo* 97-8. Protagoras, cf. above ch. 2. Diogenes of Apollonia, Kirk and Raven, 604; Diels-Kranz, B 3; Jaeger, *Theology*, 167. Xenophon, *Memorabilia* IV, iii, 3; I, iv, 5. Development of Civilisation, cf. above ch. 2, n. 47.

26 Geographers cf. above ch. 2, n. 46. Political Nomos, cf. above ch. 2, n. 22.

27 Kritias, Diels-Kranz, B 25.

28 Prodikos, Diels-Kranz, B 5. Plato, *Protagoras*, 326c. Xenophon, *Memorabilia*, I, iv, 16. Demokritos, Diels-Kranz, B 30.

29 Euripides cf. above ch. 2, n. 38. The myth of metals: Plato, *Republic*, 414-5. Jungle-law: particularly 358. The poets: 363. Mystery sects:

363-4. Censorship of myths: 379-83. Teleological universe: cf. above n. 25. Plato, *Laws*, 903; *Timaeus* 33, 45, 77. Cf. W. Theiler, *Teleologische Naturbetrachtung* 75f. Criticism of materialistic philosophers: *Laws*, 889f.

30 Heavenly bodies: *Laws*, 898f.

31 The gods: *Laws*, 920, 774, 945, 671, 844.

Notes to 6. *Political and Legal Life*

1 Cf. above ch. 2.

2 Ostracism cf. above ch. 2 and G. R. Stanton, *J.H.S.*, 90, 1970, 180. Population, ch. 3. Men on service: Aristotle, *Constitution of Athens*, 24, 3; Jones, 7ff.

3 Aristophanes, *Wasps*, 230; *Knights*, 255f. Population over 30, cf. Jones 82f. Demosthenes, xxii, 47f. Cf. Jones 36f., 123f. On mechanical devices to prevent corruption: J. D. Bishop, *J.H.S.* 90, 1970, 1, and works there cited, particularly Aristotle, *Constitution of Athens*, 63-6.

4 Aristotle, *Constitution of Athens*, 21, 3; 45-9. A. W. Gomme, *History*, 1951, 16ff. Jones, 105f.

5 Aristotle, *Constitution of Athens*, 43, 1; 61. Jones 49, 99f., 126-9.

6 Aristotle, *Constitution of Athens*, 47-8, 50-60, 61-2. Jones 47f., 101ff. Intake, reckoned on the graph, Jones, 82. Demosthenes, xxi, 111; xix, 154 was Councillor in 349-8 and 347-6 B.C. Socrates, Plato, *Apology* 32b.

7 Pay: Jones, 5. Fordyce Mitchel, *Lykourgan Athens*, Cincinnati 1970, 40. Procedure: Jones, 108ff.

8 J. L. Hammond, *History of Greece*, Oxford 1959 (abbreviated below as Hammond), 287; W. G. Forrest, *C.Q.*, 10, 1960, 232ff. Kimon: Plutarch, *Cimon*, partic. chs. x, xiii. Areiopagos: Aristotle, *Constitution of the Athenians*, 8; 23; 25. Aristeides: Aristotle, *Constitution of Athens*, 23-4.

9 Aristotle, *loc. cit.*; Forrest *loc. cit.* Skyros: Smart, *J.H.S.* 87, 1967, 136. Cf. above ch. 5, p. 90.

10 Pericles and Kimon: Aristotle, *Constitution of Athens*, 27. Thucydides, son of Melesias: Plutarch, *Pericles*, 11; Wade-Gery, *Essays in Greek History*, 243. Pericles' generalships: Jones, 126f.

11 Funeral speech: Thucydides, II, 37, 1-2; 40, 2; 41, 1; 37, 3. F. Jacoby, *J.H.S.* 64, 1944, 36; *C.Q.* 38, 1944, 65.

12 Thucydides, II, 65, 8-9.

13 Herodotus, III, 80-2; J. S. Morrison, *C.Q.* 35, 1942, 1f.; J. de Romilly, *R.E.G.* 72, 1959, 81.

14 Protagoras, cf. ch. 4, p. 71; ch. 5, pp. 95ff. Plato, *Theaetetus*, 167; *Protagoras*, 322, 324, 326. Morrison, *loc. cit.*; G. B. Kerferd, *Durham*

University Journal, 1949, 21ff.; *J.H.S.* 73, 1953, 42ff.; M. Gagarin, *T.A.P.A.* 100, 1969, 133.

15 Xenophon, *Constitution of Athens*, particularly ch. I. Cf. above chs. 3, pp. 47, 51. H. Frisch, *Pseudo-Xenophon: la constitution d'Athènes*, Copenhagen, 1942; J. de Romilly, *R.P.*, 36, 1962, 225; G. E. M. de Ste Croix, *C.Q.* 11, 1961, 278.

16 Thucydides, II, 65, 10. Kleon: Thucydides III, 36, 6; Aristotle, *Constitution of the Athenians*, 28, 3; Aristophanes, *Knights*, partic. 40ff., 75ff.; *Acharnians*, 6, 377; *Wasps*, 292, 596.

17 The revolution of 411: Hammond, 443ff.; M. Cary, *J.H.S.* 72, 1952, 56; Thucydides VIII, 97, 2. The revolution of 404: Hammond, 403ff; K. Hannestad, *Die 30 Tyranner*, Copenhagen 1950. Hignett, 285.

18 Thucydides VIII, 1. Guthrie, 285; W. Aly, *Philologus Supplement*, 1928, 104f.; G. B. Kerferd, *C.P.S.*, 1958, 27; J. S. Morrison, *Phronesis*, 8, 1963, 35. Antiphon, Diels-Kranz, B 61, 44, cf. also C 1 on giving testimony.

19 Cf. above ch. 5, p. 97. Thrasymachos: Plato, *Rep.* 338e; G. B. Kerferd, *Durham University Journal*, 1947, 19f. Thucydides, I, 4; II, 63, 2; III, 37, 2; V, 105; III, 82, 2. Plato, *Gorgias* 484a.

20 Restoration: Hammond, 446ff. Revision of laws: Jones, 52, 122.

21 Lysias II 18, cf. 63. Homonoia: Lysias XXV, 20; Andocides, *Mysteries*, 76; Lysias XVIII, 37; Isocrates XVIII, 27, 44; VII, 69. The Laws: Isocrates XX, 10; Demosthenes XXIV, 5 (cf. XXI, 150, 188); XXIV, 210; XXI, 48 (cf. XXII 57; XIII, 17). Pseudo-Demosthenes XXV, 11, 15-16, 20.

22 Isocrates VII, 26 (cf. Demosthenes X, 45). Demosthenes XXIV, 37; XIV, 14 (cf. II, 30). Demosthenes XIX, 99 (cf. XX, 16, 108). Demosthenes VIII, 69, 72 (cf. XVIII, 246). The rich: Lysias XX, 23; XXV, 13; XXI, 13; XVIII, 20; XIX, 62.

23 Selfish politicians: Lysias XVIII, 16; XXVII, 2, 10; XXVIII, 13; Isocrates VIII, 124-131; VII, 54; Demosthenes XXIII, 207-9. Poor and rich: Isokrates, XV, 142, 160, 164.

24 Cf. above ch. 4, 73. Socrates, cf. particularly Plato, *Apology*, 29d (cf. *Gorgias*, 464); 21b-23c; 31-2; *Crito*, 50.

25 Plato, *Letter* VII, 325-9

26 Plato, *Republic*, 336-67; 369-70; 433. Decline of constitutions: *Republic* 544-69.

27 Plato, *Politicus*, 294, 297, 300-3; *Laws* 697-700. J. B. Skemp, *Plato's Statesman*, 43f., 59. In the *Critias* the Ideal State is put into prehistory.

28 Plato, *Laws*, 744c (wealth), 850 (resident aliens), 756 (council), 752 (guardians of the law), 765 (minister of education), 961 (nocturnal council). Glenn R. Morrow, *Plato's Cretan City*, Princeton 1960.

29 Aristotle, *Politics* 1285b30, 1288a8 (kingship), 1281-2 (amateur judgment), 1295a25 (middle class), 1328b39 (restriction of citizenship).

Fordyce Mitchel, *Lykourgan Athens*, Cincinnati 1970, 40.

30 Kimon: Plutarch, *Cimon* XVI, 8. Pericles: Plutarch, *Pericles*, VIII; Eupolis, fr. 94K. Cf. in general, W. Aly, *Philologus Supplementband*, 1928. Sophocles, *Ant.*, 683ff., *El.*, 516ff.; cf. my *Introduction to Sophocles*, 148ff.

31 Cf. F. Solmsen, *Antiphonstudien*, 1931, particularly 17, 31, 44f., 53. Degradation: Thucydides, III, 82.

32 A. *Eum.* 429f.; 614ff. Aristophanes, *Wasps*, particularly 951ff. Solmsen, *op. cit.*, particularly 26ff.

33 L. Radermacher, *Artium Scriptores*, Vienna 1951, has an extremely useful collection of texts. Korax, Teisias: cf. particularly Cicero, *Brutus* 12, 46; Aristotle, *Rhetoric*, 1402a17; Plato, *Phaedrus*, 273A; Plutarch, *Moralia* 835D; Protagoras, Diogenes Laertius 9, 51. Thrasymachos: Aristotle, *Rhetoric* 1404a12. Gorgias: Diodorus, 12, 53, 4.

34 Aristophanes, fr. 198K; Pausanias, VI, xvii, 8. Aristophanes, *Knights*, 1378, cf. Plutarch, *Nicias* XI, *Alcibiades* XIII.

35 Antiphon, V, 26-7.

36 Gorgias quoted by Dionysius of Halicarnassus, *De Demosthene*, 127. Isocrates, cf. above 4, p. 76; *Art and Literature in fourth-century Athens*, 12f.

37 Lysias XII, 13-15. Aristophanes, *Knights*, 1378, quoted above. Demosthenes, XVIII, 257-66. Cf. *Art and Literature in fourth-century Athens*, 74f. H. and A. Thornton, *Time and Style*, London 1962.

38 Compare Lysias XII, 42-61 with Demosthenes, XVIII, 258-64; Aeschines, III, 171f.; I. Bruns, *Das literarische Porträt*, 552. *Art and Literature in fourth-century Athens*, 21, 98. S. Usher, *Eranos*, 63, 1965, 99.

39 Cf. above pp. 76 and 75. Plato, *Phaedrus*, 246b, 266d, 268d, 271d. Aristotle, *Rhetoric*, 1355b8; 1378a31; 1389a2; 1397a7; 1409b1; 1414a30. *Art and Literature in fourth-century Athens*, 57ff., 75ff.

Notes to 7. *Potters and Patrons*

1 My *Potter and Patron in Classical Athens*, London 1972, contains the detail used in this chapter (it is referred to here as *P and P*). Schools: above ch. 4, p. 61f. Cults: above ch. 5, 82-3, 86, 89. Development of painting: above ch. 2, 21-5.

2 Family workshops: *P and P*, ch. 1, above, ch. 4, 65f. Slaves and resident aliens, above ch. 3, 37. Numbers, collaboration etc.: *P and P*, ch. 1. Plaques: e.g. *ABV* 352; Rumpf, *Malerei und Zeichnung*, 74, 78, cf. also below p. 148 Black-glaze, plain ware: B. A. Sparkes and L. Talcott, *The Athenian Agora* XII.

3 *P and P*, ch. 1. Epiktetos plate: *ARV*, 2nd ed., 78/102. Statues:

A. E. Raubitschek, *Dedications from the Athenian Acropolis*, nos. 178, 197. Hyperbolos, cf. above ch. 3, n. 17. Euthymides: cf. above ch. IV, 61; *P and P*, ch. II. Hydria: *ARV* 33/8. Mixing-bowls: *ARV* 1619/3 bis; 14/2.

4 *P and P*, ch. XX. Export classes: cf. also J. Boardman, *The Greeks Overseas*, 212; R. Eismann, *A.J.A.* 74, 1970, 193. Douris school cup, cf. above ch. 4, p. 62. Etruscan inscription: *Notizie degli Scavi*, 1934, 378, fig. 32; *ARV* 969/66. LE inscriptions: D. A. Amyx, *Hesperia* 27, 1958, pl. 53a-e, h; red-figure hydriai, above n. 3 and ch. 4, p. 61. Vassallaggi: Archaeological Reports, 1963-4, 43. Pindar, fr. 124 (Snell).

5 Taranto: F. G. Lo Porto, *Atti Societa Magna Grecia*, 8, 1967, 46ff.; *ABV* 369/113; 195/2-5. Gela: J. D. Beazley, *J.H.S.* 68, 1948, 26. Exekias: *ABV* 146/20. Cup in Boeotia: *ABV* 51/2.

6 *P and P*, ch. XX, 2. Brauron: cf. above ch. 5, p. 86. L. Kahil, *Antike Kunst* Beiheft 1; *Antike Kunst* 8, 1965, 20. *ARV*, Index of proveniences, s.v. Brauron.

7 *B.S.A.*, 57, 1962, 88. Cf. *P and P*, ch. XX, 2.

8 Asopodoros: *Archaiologikon Deltion*, 1927-8, 91; *ARV* 447/274. White lekythoi: *ARV* 1687. Subjects on vases in tombs: *P and P*, ch. XX, 2. Boreas and Oreithyia: *P and P*, ch. XIX; Herodotus VII, 189. Bronze hydria: *Art and Literature in fourth-century Athens*, 105; *Ephemeris Archaiologike*, 1950-1, 80.

9 Prize-amphorai: Beazley, *DBV*, 88. Non-prize amphorai: *P and P*, chs. II, III, IV, X. Acropolis jugs: *ARV* 1211, 1518, 1597; J. R. Green, *Hesperia*, 31, 1962, 82. Loutrophoroi: *P and P*, ch. VII; E. B. Harrison, *A.J.A.*, 71, 1967, 57; R. E. Wycherley, *Phoenix*, 24, 1970, 293. Anthesteria: above, ch. 5, p. 82. Choes: G. van Hoorn, *Choes and Anthesteria*.

10 Cult scenes: *P and P*, ch. X. Mixing-bowl: *ARV* 1028/15; *P and P*, p. 50, fig. 3.

11 Prices: *P and P*, ch. XX; D. A. Amyx, *Hesperia* 27, 1958, 287.

12 Smikros, cf. above n. 3. Anakreon: *ARV* 185/32. Cf. *P and P*, chs. II, VIII; *The Greek Chorus*, 83f.

13 Cf. above notes 3, 4 and 10. Athlete vases: *P and P*, chs. II, XI, XV. Euphronios: *ARV* 13/1; Noble, *Techniques*, fig. 152. Phintias: ARV 24/11. Nikias: *ARV* 1333/1. Pseudo-Xenophon, cf. above ch. 3, p. 51.

14 *P and P*, chs. IV, XIV. Leagros: *ARV* 16/17, cf. M. Robertson, *C.Q.* 19, 1969, 210, 218. The large cup: *ARV* 882/35.

15 *P and P*, chs. XIV, XV, XVI, XVII. Cf. also above ch. 2, 53. The figures are based on *ABV* and *ARV*.

16 *P and P*, ch. XIX. Thigh-shield (epinetron or onos): *ARV* 1250/34.

17 *P and P*, ch. XIX. A. G. Ward, *The Quest for Theseus*, New York 1971; *Everyday Life in Classical Athens*, ch. V; K. Friis Johansen,

Thésée et la danse à Délos, Copenhagen 1945; K. Schefold, *Museum Helveticum*, 3, 60; F. Jacoby, *C.Q.*, 41, 1947, 6 n. 6. Early cup: *ARV* 108/27.

18 Epilykos cup: *ARV* 83/14. Kroisos amphora: *ARV* 238/1. The Alkmaionid Kroisos, statue from Anavysos, Athens, National Museum, 3851; C. W. Eliot, *Historia*, 16, 1967, 279. Bacchylides III. Apollo temple: Herodotus, 5, 62. Athenian Treasury: G. M. A. Richter, *Sculpture and Sculptors of the Greeks*, 126.

19 Theseus, 460-50. B.C. Cf. above ch. 6, n. 18; below ch. 8, n. 5. *Prometheus Pyrkaeus*: *ARV* 1153/13; 1046/10; J. D. Beazley, *A.J.A.*, 43, 1939, 618; 44, 1940, 212.

20 Euripides *Aigeus*, cf. my *Tragedies of Euripides*, 77ff.; *Antiquité Classique*, 34, 1965, 519; B. B. Shefton, *A.J.A.*, 60, 1956, 159; the series starts with *ARV* 1023/148.

21 On representations of drama see *P and P*, ch. V; BICS, Supplt 20, 1967; A. D. Trendall-T. B. L. Webster, *Illustrations of Ancient Drama*, London 1971. Plato, *Symposium*, 173a. Sophocles, cf. above ch. 4, p. 72. Representations of Dithyramb: Froning, *Dithyrambos und Vasenmalerei*, Würzburg 1971.

22 For the names cf. *ABV* 664, *ARV* 1559; Fluck and Robinson, *Greek Love Names*, Baltimore 1937, 66.

Notes to 8. *Architects, Sculptors and Painters*

1 J. A. Bundgaard, *Mnesicles*, Copenhagen 1957. Roebuck, 5ff., particularly 26ff. (R. Scranton); J. J. Pollitt, *The Art of Greece*, 119f. (abbreviated below as Pollitt).

2 Erechtheion: Roebuck, Pollitt, *loc. cit.* Parthenon: *ibid.* Nike balustrade: Rhys Carpenter, *Sculpture of the Nike Temple Parapet*; E. B. Harrison, *Hesperia*, 29, 1960, 373. Grave-reliefs: J. Frel, *Les Sculptures Attiques anonymes*, Prague 1969; *Athens, Annals of Archaeology* III, 1970, 368ff.

3 Erechtheion: Roebuck, Pollitt, *loc. cit.* Incised cups: H. A. Thompson ap. B. Sparkes and L. Talcott, *The Athenian Agora* XII, 22. Praxiteles: Pollitt, 175. Painted grave-stelai: G. M. A. Richter, *Archaic Gravestones of Attica*, London 1961, figs. 138-40, 159-60, 167 (cf. A. Rumpf, *Malerei und Zeichnung*, 74-5, 78). Pollitt, 172, 176.

4 Kimon and Pericles: cf. above ch. 5, 90-1; 6, 142-3.

5 Pollitt, 106. The vases: *P and P*, ch. V; B. B. Shefton, *Hesperia* 31, 1965, 365; D. von Bothmer, *Amazons in Greek Art*, Oxford 1957, 161.

6 Pollitt, 113; *Everyday Life in Classical Athens*, 121ff.; B. Ashmole and N. Yalouris, *Olympia*, London 1967. Mikon's statue: Pausanias,

VI, vi, 1. Kimon's sons: Plutarch, *Cimon*, ch. XVI. Alkmaionidai, above ch. 5, 89. Pheidias, above ch. 5, 91.

7 Pollitt 76. Cf. E. Kluwe, *Wissentschaftliche ZeitschriftRostock*, 17, 1968, 677.

8 Pollitt 96, 106, 107. *P and P*, ch. V; von Bothmer, *loc. cit.* E. Vanderpool, *Hesperia* 35, 1966, 93. R. E. Wycherley, *Phoenix* 7, 1953, 20f. Polygnotos and Sophocles, cf. my *Sophocles* 9, 201. On his art, cf. above ch. 2, p. 24. Oinoe: L. H. Jeffery, *B.S.A.* 60, 1965, 42ff. Cf. E. Simon, *A.J.A.* 67, 1963, 54.

9 The Parthenon: *Everyday Life in Classical Athens*, 135ff.; P. E. Corbett, *The Sculpture of the Parthenon*, London 1959; C. J. Herington, *Athena Polias and Athena Parthenos*, Manchester 1955; E. B. Harrison, *A.J.A.* 71, 1967, 27 (east pediment); *Hesperia* 35, 1966, 107 (the shield of the cult-statue).

10 Hephaisteion: H. A. Thompson, *A.J.A.* 66, 1962, 339. Erechtheion: *A.J.A.* 74, 1970, 204. Nike Temple: *A.J.A.* 74, 1970, 201. Cf. also G. Lippold, *Griechische Plastik*, 193-4.

11 Pollitt 172f.; *Art and Literature in fourth-century Athens*, 48f.

12 Euphranor: see n. 11. The revolution, cf. ch. 2, p. 23ff. Euthymides: *ARV* 26/1.

13 Sentence structure: cf. above ch. 6, p. 125.

14 Cf. *C.Q.* 33, 1939, 166ff. for further references. Euripides, *Helen* 71-3; *Hecuba*, 807 (cf. Plato, *Rep.* 598c etc.); *Oidipous*, *P.Oxy.* 2459; cf. also *Phoenissae*, 161ff. Cf. S. Barlow, *Imagery of Euripides*, London 1971. *Skenographia* and *Skiagraphia* cf. above pp. 24-5. Xenophon *Mem.*, III, 10. Pliny, *NH*, XXXV, 29; Rumpf, *J.H.S.* 67, 1947, 14; Pollitt, 228.

15 Pollitt, 109, 212, 89. On the dating Rumpf, *op. cit.*, 13.

16 Hippodamos: Pollitt 240. Cf. above p. 21. Apollodoros: Pollitt, 112. Zeuxis: Pollitt, 154; Aristides, II, 521 (Dindorf). Parrhasios: Athenaeus XII, 543E-F.

17 Cf. above ch. 2, p. 23ff. Pheidias: Pollitt, 73. Aristotle: *Poetics* 1450a27 cf. 1448a5.

18 Xenophon, Mem., III, 10; Pollitt, 160. Zeuxis' Helen: Pollitt, 156, cf. Plato, *Rep.* 472d. Facial expression: Pollitt, 96, 158. Zeuxis: Pliny, *NH* XXXV, 66; Tzetzes, *Chil.* VIII, 390. Parrhasios: Seneca, *Controv.* X, 34; Pliny, *NH*, XXXV, 71; Gow-Page, *Garland of Philip*, 3875-80; Pliny, *NH*, XXXV, cf. A. Rumpf, *A.J.A.* 55, 1951, 7.

19 Plato and Greek art: R. G. Steven, *C.Q.* 27, 1933, 149f.; Webster, *Symbolae Osloenses* 29, 1952, 8. Couches: cf. above ch. 2 notes 27, 29. *Republic*, 579e, 598a. Agatharchos and Alkibiades: Pollitt, 110. Irrational part of the soul: *Republic*, 602d-603a; 386-9; 401b.

20 Euripides: cf. my *Tragedies of Euripides*, 283ff. Zeuxis' Eros: Scholiast to Aristophanes, *Acharnians*, 991. Meidias painter, e.g. *ARV* 1313, British Museum E 224, *Everyday Life in Classical Athens*,

fig. 52. Prodikos *apud* Xenophon, *Mem.* II 1, 21. Sophocles, *Philoctetes*, 1420. Herakles' driving to heaven, *ARV* 1186, Munich 2360. Plato, *Phaedrus* 247c. Praxiteles: *Everyday Life in Classical Athens*, 176.

21 Pamphilos: Pollitt, 162f.: date, Aristophanes, *Plutus*, 385 with scholiast, cf. also above ch. 4, n. 14. Euphranor: Pollitt, 173. Hephaistos: Dio Chrysostom 37, 43. Vases: e.g. *Art and Literature in fourth-century Athens*, pl. 10, British Museum F 68, E 227.

22 Plato, *Gorgias*, 503e. *Phaedrus*, 264c. *Laws*, 668-9. *Philebus*, 64e.

23 Plato and Aristotle, cf. *Art and Literature in fourth-century Athens*, 52ff. Organic composition etc.: 1450b21. *Mimesis: Poetics*, 1448b5. Pausias: Pollitt, 170f.

24 Polygnotos: *Poetics*, 1448a5. Zeuxis: 1450a26. Pauson: 1448a6. Problems and Solutions: 1460b8.

Notes to 9. *Poets and their Patrons*

1 Cf. above, school, p. 62, symposion, p. 55, festivals, p. 80ff., contests, p. 81ff., dedications, p. 88, works of art, p. 156. City Dionysia, p. 82.

2 Apollodoros, etc., above p. 156. Exekias: *ABV* 143/1 and 13. Melanthios: Pollitt, 96; Plutarch, *Cimon* 4. Mnesiades: above ch. 7, n. 3. Hegelochos: Raubitschek, *Dedications*, no. 121. Antilochos: Peek, *Griechische Versinschriften*, no. 44. Poteidaia: Tod, *Greek Historical Inscriptions*, no. 59. Cf. R. Lattimore, *Themes in Greek and Latin Epitaphs*, Urbana 1962.

3 Epic in education, ch. 4, n. 9. The Panathenaia: ch. 5, n. 7. Theseid: ch. 7. Rhapsode: *ARV* 183/5, British Museum E 270, *Everyday Life in Classical Athens*, fig. 38. Plato, *Ion* 530d, 531a, 535b-e (cf. *Laws* 658d).

4 Cf. above ch. 3, p. 55f. Attic skolia: C. M. Bowra, *Greek Lyric Poetry*, Oxford 1961, 373ff.; V. Ehrenberg, *Wiener Studien*, 69, 1956, 57.

5 Melanthios cf. above n. 2. Archelaos: Plutarch, *Cimon* 4; Guthrie, II, 329; F. Jacoby, *C.Q.* 41, 1947, 9f. Ion of Chios: F. Jacoby, *loc. cit.*, 1f.; T. B. L. Webster, *Hermes* 71, 1936, 263; symposion song, Athenaeus 11, 463a. Sophocles: Hephaestion 1, 5; Plutarch, *Moralia*, 785b.

6 Panathenaic victories mentioned, Pindar, *O* VII, 82; IX, 88; XIII, 38; *N* IV, 19. *Greek Chorus*, 86; A. M. Dale, *Collected Papers*, 52ff.

7 On *Nemean* 2, H. Fränkel, *Dichtung und Philosophie*, 236, n. 9. Alkibiades: D. L. Page, *Poetae Melici Graeci*, no. 755. Phayllos: cf. above ch. 7, p. 138. Menandros: *Nemean* 5, 49. Melesias: *Nemean* 4, 93; 6, 65; *Olympian* VIII, 54. On dating and the tone see H. T. Wade-Gery, *Essays in Greek History*, Oxford 1958, 247ff., 264.

(C. M. Bowra, *Pindar*, 409, 412 dates *Nemean* 6 later but the grounds are not compelling.)

8 Narrative poems: A. E. Harvey, *C.Q.* 15, 1955, 172. Dithyramb: *Greek Chorus* 90ff., 102f., A. W. Pickard-Cambridge, *Dithyramb, Tragedy and Comedy*, 2nd ed., 15ff. Pindar, fr. 75-7, Snell.

9 Melanippides: cf. above p. 26; *Greek Chorus*, 132; Pickard-Cambridge, *op. cit.*, 39ff. Myron's group: J. D. Beazley and B. Ashmole, *Greek Sculpture and Painting*, figs. 73-4, cf. J. Boardman, *J.H.S.* 76, 1956, 18f., Froning (cited above ch. 7, n. 21). The satyrs: Page, *Poetae Melici Graeci*, no. 708; *Greek Chorus*, 133. Thamyras: cf. my *Sophocles*, 200ff.

10 Timotheos, *Greek Chorus*, 153ff.; Pickard-Cambridge, *op. cit.*, 48ff. Page, *Poetae Melici Graeci*, Nos. 796 and 791, 28-34, 140-61.

11 The Spartans, Timotheos, *op. cit.*, 206ff. Pherekrates: Pickard-Cambridge, *op. cit.*, 39ff.; I. Düring, *Eranos*, 43, 1945, 176ff.

12 Aristophanes, *Clouds*, 968. Paestan vase: A. D. Trendall, *Phlyax Vases*, 2nd ed., 43, no. 58. Aristophanes, *Peace*, 829ff. *Birds* 1383, 1403; 227ff.

13 Plato, *Republic*, 399a-400e; 424c-d. Damon, Diels-Kranz, B 4, 7, 6. Aristophanes, *Clouds*, 968, 995, 638.

14 Plutarch, *Pericles*, IX, with Aristotle, *Constitution of Athens*, XXVII. Plato, *Laches*, 180d, 197b. Plutarch, *Pericles*, 4. Damon, Diels-Kranz, A 2. Political Tract, above p. 51. Aristotle, *Politics*, 1341b32-1342a15. Cf. U. von Wilamowitz-Moellendorff, *Griechische Verskunst*, Berlin 1921, 59ff.; E. Ryffel, *Museum Helveticum* 4, 1947, 23; A. E. Raubitschek, *Classica et Mediaevalia*, 16, 1955, 78; W. D. Anderson, *T.A.P.A.* 86, 1955, 88; R. P. Winnington-Ingram, *Lustrum*, 3, 1958, 51ff.

15 Plato, *Republic*, 400d-e; Aristotle, *Poetics*, 1448b24-1449a6. Plato, *Apology*, 22a-c; *Ion*, 533d-535a. Cf. *C.Q.* 32, 1939, 173ff. Demokritos, Diels-Kranz, B 21. Sophocles: Athenaeus 1, 22a. The association: above ch. 4, p. 72. Aristophanes, *Frogs*, 814ff.

16 Protagoras and Prodikos, cf. above ch. 4, p. 71. Pfeiffer, *History of Classical Scholarship*, 32ff., 37ff.

17 Xenophanes, cf. above ch. 5, 96ff. Allegory: Pfeiffer, *op. cit.*, 9, 35. The schools: above ch. 4, p. 62. Plato, *Ion*, 533d-535a; *Republic* 377d-396e, 598d-601a, 603c-608a; Pfeiffer, *op. cit.*, 58ff. Aristotle, *Poetics*, particularly chapters 23-6; Pfeiffer, *op. cit.*, 69ff.

Notes to 10. *Tragic Poets, Actors and Audiences*

1 Cf. above pp. 81ff. Deme-theatres: A. W. Pickard-Cambridge, *Dramatic Festivals of Athens*, 2nd ed., 46ff.; my *Griechische Bühnenaltertumer*, 20; Plato, *Republic*, 475d.

2 A. W. Pickard-Cambridge, *Dramatic Festivals of Athens*, 268. Plato, *Symposium*, 175e. *Theorikon*, above p. 48. Aristotle, *Politics*, 1342a. Plato, *Gorgias*, 502, cf. *Laws*, 817c. Menander, *Samia*, 733f. Aristophanes, *Peace*, 962f.; *Frogs*, 1050f. Theophrastus, *Characters*, IX, XXX.

3 References in comedy, R. Harriott, *B.I.C.S.* 9, 1962, 1ff. Plutarch, *Cimon*, VIII; *Aristides*, III. *Oedipus Tyrannus*, second argument. Trojan trilogy: cf. *Tragedies of Euripides*, 28, 165. The judges: Pickard-Cambridge, *op. cit.*, 97.

4 Cf. above p. 48; *Everyday Life in Classical Athens*, 96; Pickard-Cambridge, *op. cit.*, 84ff. Gnesippos, Cratinus fr. 15K. Kimon, cf. above n. 3, and pp. 90ff. Phrynichos: Pickard-Cambridge, *Dithyramb etc.*, 64.

5 A. E. Haigh, *Tragic Drama of the Greeks*, 413ff. Euaion, cf. my *Sophocles*, 203ff.

6 Cf. Pickard-Cambridge, *Festivals*, 286; *Art and Literature in fourth-century Athens*, 30, III.

7 Cf. the *Life of Aeschylus*, which has been handed down with the manuscripts, and above p. 27ff.

8 Stesichoros cf. above p. 165 n. 14. Eupolis, fr. 361K. Pindar, fr. 169, Snell. *Everyday Life in Classical Athens*, 101f.; 105f.

9 *Persians* 242, 386ff., 816ff. Political allusions: 238, 253, 447, 865. Dareios 759ff.

10 On political references in this and other plays, see A. J. Podlecki, *Political Background of Aeschylean Tragedy*, Ann Arbor, 1966.

11 Paris: *Ag.* 6of., 362ff. Iphigeneia: 205ff. Cost of life: 110ff., 429ff. Treated as a god: 921ff. Atreus, Thyestes, Aigisthos: 1096ff., 1217ff. Klytaimestra: 1414ff., 1497.

12 Klytaimestra: *Agamemnon*, 1505. Agamemnon: 205ff., 110ff., 429ff. Orestes: *Choephoroe*, 269ff., 924, 1048. Apollo's argument: *Eumenides*, 658ff., 734ff., cf. C. J. Herington, *J.H.S.* 87, 1967, 81. Alkmaion. Diels-Kranz, A 13 (?). Anaxagoras: Diels-Kranz, A 107. The voting: *Eumenides* 735, 741-2, 752-3. Violent grace: *Agamemnon*, 182-3.

13 *Eumenides* 780ff., 827; 804, 834, 854ff.; 490ff.

14 Cf. the *Life of Sophocles* which has been handed down with the manuscripts. My *Sophocles*, 1ff., 191, 198ff. Kimon: above p. 180. Polygnotos, above p. 150. Ion, above p. 167. Damon, above p. 175. Public office: cf. L. Woodbury, *Phoenix*, 1970, 209.

15 Cf. the *Life of Euripides*, handed down with manuscripts, and *Life* by Satyros (*Studi Classici e Orientali*, 13, 1965); P. T. Stevens, *J.H.S.* 86, 1956, 87; my *Tragedies of Euripides*, 20ff. Anaxagoras, particularly *Trojan Women*, 886. Prodikos: *Bacchae*, 275f. Protagoras: *Supplices*, 195ff., 403ff.; *Hecuba*, 798ff.; *Phoen.*, 535ff.; *Bacch.*, 200f. Timotheos: cf. above p. 172.

16 Sophocles and Herodotus, cf. above p. 167; my *Sophocles*, 10, 53.

The story: *Herodotus*, III, 119. *Antigone*, 905ff.

17 The wonders of civilisation: *Antigone*, 332ff. The Aeschylean song: 582ff., particularly 604-25. The summing up: *Antigone*, 1348-53.

18 Pollution: *Antigone*, 1039-1044. Contrast Euripides, *Hercules Furens*, 1232.

19 Pollution: *Oedipus Tyrannus*, 96-8. Plague: *O.T.* 27ff., 168ff. The long scene: *O.T.* 512-862. Second stasimon: 863ff., particularly 895, 909, cf. G. H. Gellie, *A.J.P.* 85, 1964, 113; J. S. Kamerbeek, *Sophocles: Oedipus Tyrannus*, Leiden 1967.

20 *Trachiniae*, *Phaidra* cf. my *Sophocles*, 4, 195f. Euripides and Socrates: B. Snell, *Scenes from Greek Drama*, 59ff. Euripides, *Medea*, 1078; *Hippolytus*, 377ff.

21 Cf. *Tragedies of Euripides*, 64ff., 71ff.

22 Epic level: *Hippolytus* 21, 1420. Cult: *Hippolytus* 32, 1423. Choruses: particularly 123ff., 732.

23 Cf. *Tragedies of Euripides*, 215ff. Aeschylus, *Seven against Thebes*, 1ff., 677ff., 742ff.

24 The Chorus: *Phoenissae*, 203ff., 248, 638ff., 784ff., 1019ff. Antigone: *Phoenissae*, 103ff., 1485ff., 1710ff. *The Greek Chorus*, 168f., 210f.

25. Cf. above ch. 6, 113ff. *Phoenissae*, 446ff., 528ff. Cf. J. de Romilly, *Revue de Philologie*, 39, 1965, 28. Protagoras, above ch. 4, p. 71.

26 Cf. my *Sophocles* 41f., 83ff.

27 Cf. above ch. 8. p. 158ff.; 9, p. 174ff. Sophocles: cf. above p. 188. Aristophanes: genius and technician, *Frogs*, 814ff. Educational view: *Frogs*, 1009ff. Technical: *Frogs*, 1378ff., 1119f., 1261ff. Protagoras: Segal, *Rheinisches Museum*, 113, 1970, 158. Agathon: *Thesmophoriazusae*, 95ff. Realism: *Acharnians*, 410ff.; *Frogs*, 946ff., 1043f., 1079ff.

28 Gorgias. *VS* fr. 23 (cf. *Dissoi Logoi* 3, 10), 24; *Helen*, 9, 14; *Frogs*, 1021.

29 Cf. above ch. 8, p. 158f.; 9, p. 174ff. *Republic*, 280a, 381d, 383b; 598d; 605a; 607a; 395d-e, cf. *Frogs*, 1043, 1080.

30 *Laws*, 817c. *Phaedrus*, 264c, 268c. Cf. above ch. 6, p. 126. Fourth-century tragedy: *Athenian Art and Literature in the fourth century B.C.*, 62ff.; B. Snell, *Szenen aus griechischen Dramen*, 164.

31 Cf. *Athenian Art and Literature in the fourth century B.C.*, 54ff.; D. W. Lucas, *Aristotle Poetics*, Oxford 1968.

32 Mimesis: *Poetics* 4. 1448b4. People better than ourselves: 2. 1448a16. History of tragedy: 4. 1448b20, 1449a14.

33 6. 1449b24. *Politics*, 1342a9.

34 *Poetics*, 6. 1449b25-1450b20.

35 7. 1450b21. *eikos*: cf. above ch. 6, 122f. History: 9. 1451b5.

36 10.-11. 1451a36. 13. 1452b14. Oidipous: 1453a11. 14. 1453b1.

Notes to 11. *Comedy*

1 On festivals, production etc. cf. above p. 179ff. Lysias, XXI, 4. *Clouds* etc. Production information is given in the hypothesis preceding the text. Fragments of lost plays in T. Kock, *Comicorum Atticorum Fragmenta.*

2 *Babylonians*: see *Acharnians* 377, and scholiast (Kock, i, p. 407). Laws: V. Ehrenberg, *The People of Aristophanes*, 25f. The conservative tract: Pseudo-Xenophon, *Constitution of the Athenians*, II, 18.

3 Cf. above p. 81. Hera and Hephaistos: Pickard-Cambridge, *Dithyramb, etc.*, 171ff. Costume: Pickard-Cambridge, *op. cit.*, 169ff.; *Greek Theatre Production* 28ff., 55ff. Eupolis: fr. 250, 254; *P.Oxy.* 2740. Aristophanes, *Frogs*, 199ff., 296f. *Knights*, 43ff., 230ff. Telekleides: fr. 17. Pherekrates: fr. 155.

4 Kratinos: fr. 144. Aristophanes, *Knights*, 36, cf. *Wasps*, 54; *Peace*, 50, *Birds*, 30. Ehrenberg, *op. cit.*, 28.

5 Outside the parabasis, Aristophanes, *Acharnians* 377, 496. Parabasis: Pickard-Cambridge, *Dithyramb, etc.*, 142, 148, 160ff., 197ff.; G. M. Sifakis, *Parabasis and Animal Choruses*, London 1971. Plato, fr. 92. Formal system: cf. above p. 26. Aristophanes, *Acharnians* 626ff.; *Knights*, 507ff.; *Clouds*, 518ff.; *Wasps*, 1015ff.; *Peace*, 729ff.

6 Aristophanes, *Knights*, 517ff.; *Clouds*, 518ff.; *Wasps*, 1023ff.; *Peace*, 736ff. Aegina: cf. Ehrenberg, *op. cit.* 20. Kratinos, fr. 307, 306, cf. 237. Eupolis, fr. 78, 54 (cf. Plato, fr. 81), 357.

7 For the range of comedy cf. above chs. 3, n. 16, 17, 36; 4, n. 5, 6, 10, 22; 5, n. 3; 6, n. 3, 16, 30, 32, 34; 8, n. 21; 9, n. 11-14; 10, n. 2-4, 26.

8 R. Harriott, *B.I.C.S.* 9, 1962, 1; P. Walcot, *Greece and Rome* 18, 1971, 35. Kratinos, *P.Oxy.* 2742; Eupolis, *P.Oxy.* 2740; Strattis, *P.Oxy.* 2742; Pherekrates, fr. 94, cf. *Frogs*, 1004.

9 Phrekrates, fr. 145; Plato, fr. 191. Eupolis, *P.Oxy.* 2738, cf. *Clouds*, 966ff. Konnos: Phrynichos, Ameipsias. Socrates and Euripides: Kallias, fr. 12; Telekleides, fr. 39-40. Kottyto: Eupolis, Kock p. 273. Kratinos, fr. 154-5. Eupolis, fr. 146-7.

10 Kratinos, *Dionysalexandros*, J. U. Powell, *New Chapters*, iii, 160; *Cheirones*, fr. 240-1. Kleon: Hermippos, fr. 42; Eupolis, fr. 282; Plato, fr. 107. Hyperbolos: Kratinos, fr. 196, 262; Hermippos, fr. 8; Eupolis, fr. 181-90, *P.Oxy.* 2741; Plato, fr. 187; Leukon, fr. 1; Aristophanes, *Clouds*, 551, etc. Lampon: Kratinos, fr. 57-8, 62; Kallias, fr. 14; Eupolis, fr. 297, etc. Nikias: Eupolis, fr. 181; Telekleides fr. 41; Aristophanes, *Knights* 358, etc. Peisander: Hermippos fr. 9; Eupolis fr. 31, 182; Phrynichos, fr. 20; Aristophanes, fr. 81, etc. Antiphon: Plato, fr. 103; Aristophanes, *Wasps* 1301. Alkibiades: Pherekrates, fr. 155; Eupolis, fr. 158; Aristophanes, fr. 198, *Acharnians*

716, *Wasps*, 44; contrast *Frogs*, 1422; Eupolis, Kock, p. 273.

11 On the *Acharnians* see A. M. Dale, *Collected Papers*, 281.

12 On the structure and its change cf. Pickard-Cambridge, *Dithyramb, etc.*, 194ff.; T. Gelzer, *Der epirrhematische Agon bei Aristophanes*, Munich 1960, 228ff.; G. M. Sifakis, *op. cit.* On fourth-century metres and choruses cf. Webster, *Studies in Later Greek Comedy* (abbreviated *LGC*), 59ff.

13 Cf. *LGC* 13, 68; *Rylands Bulletin* 42, 1960, 509; A. M. Dale, *Collected Papers*, 110ff.

14 Isokrates, VIII, 14; Aristotle, *Rhetoric*, 1384b10; Plato, *Laws*, 935e. Kinesias' decree, Tod, *Greek Historical Inscriptions*, no. 108. On political references and harmless abuse, *LGC* 23ff., 36ff.

15 Kinesias: Strattis, fr. 15: cf. earlier Aristophanes, *Birds*, 1372ff., etc. Dionysios: Ephippos, fr. 16. Philosophers: *LGC*, 34ff., 50ff. Epikrates, fr. 11.

16 Aristotle, *Poetics*, 1451b11, cf. above, 201f. Mythological comedy: *Poetics*, 1453a36; *LGC* 16ff., 82ff. Strattis: fr. 45, with Euripides, *Phoen.* 460-4; *P.Oxy.* 2742, fr. 1, 12, with Euripides, fr. 752N.

17 Lamachos: cf. above, p. 210. Timon: *Birds*, 1549, etc. Hetairai, etc. *LGC*, 22ff., 49, 63ff., 74ff.

18 Compare, for instance, Pickard-Cambridge, *Festivals*, figs. 78, 102, 125. Cf. *B.I.C.S.*, Supplement, no. 23, 1969, 6.

19 Menander: *LGC* 184ff. Hetairai, *Samia, Eunouchos*; soldier, *Perikeiromene, Misoumenos*; old man, *Dyskolos*.

Notes to 12. *Geographers, Doctors, and Historians*

1 Cf. above ch. 2, p. 32ff.

2 The Sophists: cf. above ch. IV, p. 68f. The book: cf., above ch. II, p. 17.

3 Hekataios: cf. L. Pearson, *Early Ionian Historians*, Oxford 1939, 25ff. Dionysios of Halikarnassos, *Thucydides*, 5. Sophocles, fr. 598P. Aeschylus *Prometheus Bound*, 707ff., 790ff., 829ff.; *Prometheus Unbound*, fr. 195-9N.

4 In general see W. H. S. Jones, *Hippocrates*, Loeb Classical Library, which contains all the texts quoted below; L. Edelstein, *Die Sammlung der hippocratischen Schriften*, Berlin 1931; I. M. Lonie, *C.Q.* 15, 1965, 1ff.; E. Berger, *Der Basler Artzt-relief*, Mainz 1970. Dedication: Pfuhl, *Malerei und Zeichnung*, fig. 485. Plato, *Protagoras*, 311b. Demokedes: Herodotus, III, 131.

5 Aristophanes, *Clouds*, 230; *Frogs*, 939; cf. V. Ehrenberg, *The People of Aristophanes*, 246, 280f. Tragedy: cf. J. Dumortier, *Le Vocabulaire médicale d'Eschyle*, 1935; N. E. Collinge, *B.I.C.S.* 9, 1962, 43ff.; Devereux, *J.H.S.* 90, 1970, 35.

6 Sophocles' ode: cf. above pp. 167, 189. The lectures: H. R. Immerwahr, *Form and Thought in Herodotus*, Cleveland 1966, 7ff.; C. W. Fornara, *Herodotus*, Oxford 1971, 46 n. 17. Sophocles: cf. above p. 189. Spartan heralds: VII, 137, cf. also IX, 73, 3, which cannot be earlier (cf. Fornara, 43). Aristophanes, *Acharnians*, 524ff. Euripides, fr. 449N, cf. R. Browning, *C.R.* 11, 1961, 201.

7 Thucydides' pedigree: H. T. Wade-Gery, *Essays in Greek History*, 246ff. Amphipolis: Thucydides, IV, 104. His exile: V, 26, and the ancient *Life*, 24, with Thucydides II, 100. Beginning: I, 1. Second prologue: V, 25. Archelaos: II, 100. Pericles: II, 65. Melian attack: V, 84-116. Sicilian expedition: VI and VII. 'Ephemeral contest-pieces': I, 22, 4. Unity: J. de Romilly, *Thucydides and Athenian Imperialism*, 344ff.

8 *Nomos* and *Physis*: above pp. 96, 114. Hekataios, fr. 1. The Nile: Herodotus, II, 19-26. Report form: cf. Immerwahr, *op. cit.*, 317ff.

9 Anaximander's map: above ch. II, pp. 31, 32. Aristagoras: Herodotus, V, 49. Herodotus: IV, 36ff.; cf. Immerwahr, *op. cit.*, 315f. Aristophanes, *Clouds*, 206ff.

10 Herodotus, II, 71. Cf. H. Fränkel, *Wege und Formen*, 61f.; H. Thesleff, *Arctos*, 4, 1966, 98. Pylos tablets: Tn series.

11 *Epidemics*, I, 10: cf. Thesleff, *op. cit.*, 108. *Airs*, I.

12 Plato, *Laches*, 185e; *Gorgias*, 464b, 500e; *Phaedrus*, 270c-d, *Ancient Medicine* 20. Aristotle, *Ethics*, I, 4, cf. W. Jaeger, *J.H.S.* 77, 1957, 55; L. Edelstein, *Bulletin of the History of Medicine*, 26, 1952, 299.

13 *Airs*, XII (Asia includes Egypt and Libya). Scythia: *Airs*, 19 with Herodotus IV, 28; *Airs*, 17, with Herodotus, IV, 117; *Airs*, 22 with Herodotus, I, 105; IV, 67. *Sacred Disease*, I; 5; 6; 16, Diogenes of Apollonia, cf. Kirk and Raven, 440f. Herodotus, III, 33.

14 Herodotus, IX, 122. *Airs* 12; 16; 23. On *nomos* and *physis*, cf. above p. 114.

15 Anaxagoras: cf. above p. 87. Protagoras: cf. above p. 115. Homer: Immerwahr, *op. cit.*, 11, 73, 263, 311; Fornara, *op. cit.*, 35. Tragedy: Immerwahr, *op. cit.*, 69, 181, 243, 276, 311. Sophocles: *Ant.*, 710ff., is picked up by Herodotus, VII, 10.

16 Herodotus, I, 1; 5. Kroisos and Solon: I, 29, 34, 86. Xerxes: VIII, 5-18, cf. *Antigone*, 620; Aeschylus, *Persians*, 739ff.

17 Cornford, *Thucydides Mythistoricus*, Cambridge 1907; J. H. Finley, *Thucydides*, Cambridge, Mass. 1942, 321ff. Melian dialogue: V, 85ff. particularly 91; 104-5, contrast I, 76, cf. J. de Romilly, *Thucydides and Athenian Imperialism*, Oxford 1963, 296. Pericles: II, 65. Euripides, *Phoenissae*, cf. above p. 195. Dramatic moments: funeral speech, II, 34ff.; plague, II, 47ff. Mytilene, III, 36ff. Pylos, IV, 9ff. Melos, V, 85ff.; Sicily, VI, 8ff.

18 I, 22. Cf. particularly H. Hudson-Williams, *C.Q.* 42, 1948, 79; A. Parry, *B.I.C.S.*, 16, 1969, 108.

19 Aristotle, *Poetics*, 1451b8, cf. above p. 201. Thucydides, V, 105; III, 82, 2 (cf. I, 76, 3).

20 II, 48, 3. Early Greek History: I, 2-19: cf. J. de Romilly, *Histoire et Raison*, Paris, 1956, 240ff. Power/Fear theme: I, 23, 5; 88; 118, cf. also I, 76; III, 37; V, 105; III, 82. Thucydides and the doctors: C. N. Cochrane, *Thucydides and the Science of History*, Oxford 1929; Finley, *op. cit.*, 68f.; Parry, *op. cit.*

21 *Vita Marcellina*, 22, 36. Prodikos and Gorgias, cf. above pp. 70f., 122f. Jungle-law, above pp. 97, 114ff. Antiphon, above p. 114. Diodoros I, 7-8; Diels-Kranz, 68B5, 1; Kirk and Raven, 403. I owe the suggestion of Anaxagoras to a paper given by Professor E. R. Dodds in 1951.

22 P. Huart, *Le Vocabulaire de l'analyse psychologique dans l'oeuvre de Thucydide*, Paris 1968, 21ff. and in general B. Snell, *Discovery of the Mind*, 228ff. Thucydides, II, 63, 3; III, 82, 4, 8; V, 105. Gorgias, fr. 6; Euripides, *Orestes* 1180, etc. (Cf. *J.H.S.* 77, 1957, 149ff.)

23 *Airs*, XII, cf. above p. 225. *Ancient Medicine*, XIV.

24 Anaxagoras, Kirk and Raven, 368, no. 496. Empedokles, Kirk and Raven, 329. Anaximander, Kirk and Raven, 114. Homer, *Odyssey*, 14, 12. Mycenaean tablets: Ventris and Chadwick, *Documents in Mycenaean Greek*, 325f. Plato, cf. D. Ross, *Plato's Theory of Ideas*, 228.

25 Jens Holt, *Les noms d'action à sis*, Aarhus, 1941; R. Browning, *Philologus* 102, 1958, 60. *Airs* XVI. Thucydides VII, 24, 3 (cf. III, 82, 6); II, 4, 4 (cf. II, 50, 2); Homer, *Odyssey* 9, 134; Thucydides, VII, 44, 2 *Physis*: Thucydides, III, 45, 7; V, 105, 2. Hippocrates, *Art*, XIII. Homer, *Iliad* 19, 91; Hesiod, *Erga* 256. Vases: *Art and literature in fourth-century Athens*, 40f. Plato, cf. D. Ross, *Plato's Theory of Ideas*, 228.

26 Cf. H. Diller, *Hermes* 67, 1932, 31; Lloyd, *Polarity*, 333. Anaxagoras, Kirk and Raven, no. 537. Herodotus, II, 33. Thucydides, I, 1, 2-3; 21, 2. *Ancient Medicine* XXII. *Art* XIII.

27 'Signs', cf. e.g. *Iliad* 2, 308; 'tokens', e.g. *Iliad* I, 525. Cf. Lloyd, *Polarity*, 425. Herakleitos, Kirk and Raven, no. 247.

28 *Ancient Medicine* XXII. *Iliad*, 12, 432, cf. above ch. 2, n. 7.

29 Aeschylus, *Eumenides*, 485. Cf. H. Thesleff, *Arctos*, 4, 1966, 96ff. Herodotus, II, 22, 2; Thucydides, I, 8, 1. *eikos* cf above ch. 6, p. 122ff. Thucydides, I, 4, 1. *Airs*, XXII. Thucydides, I, 138.

30 Aristotle, *Rhetoric*, 1357a34. Xenophanes, Kirk and Raven, nos. 169-72. Hippocrates, *Art* XIII. Diogenes, Kirk and Raven, no. 605. Herodotus, II, 22. Thucydides, I, 5-6; cf. J. de Romilly, *Histoire et Raison*, 240ff.; N. Hammond, *C.Q.* 2, 1952, 127ff. Aristotle, *Prior Analytics*, 68b27.

31 Xenophanes, Kirk and Raven, no. 172; Hippocrates, *Art*, XIII. *Airs*, VIII; *Sacred Disease*, XIV. Aristotle, Generation of Animals, 765a21.

Lloyd, *Polarity*, 73, 351. Anaxagoras, Kirk and Raven, no. 498.
Plato, *Republic*, 531a-b; *Timaeus*, 68d. Alkmaion, Kirk and Raven,
no. 285; Xenophanes, nos. 189-90. Plato, *Timaeus*, 29c, cf.
28c; *Phaedo*, 114d; Frutiger, *Les Mythes de Platon*, Paris 1930, 38ff.
Republic, 588b; *Phaedrus*, 246a; *Laws*, 644d; cf. *Theaetetus*, 191c,
197d.
32 Herakles' drive to heaven, cf. *Art and literature in fourth-century
Athens*, 41, pl. 4a. Homer, *Iliad*, 12, 432. *Ancient Medicine*, XXII.
Physical Theories, cf. above ch. 2, p. 30f. Empedocles, Kirk and
Raven, no. 453; Diels-Kranz, B 100, 84. (For the pipette, cf. *C.V.A.*
Robinson 3, pl. 3.)
33 Anaxagoras, Kirk and Raven, nos. 503-5. Demokritos, Kirk and
Raven, nos. 562, 569.
34 Plato, *Ion* 533d, cf. above p. 165. *Politicus* 277-end. Cf. J. B.
Skemp, *Plato's Statesman*; Aristophanes, *Lysistrata*, 573ff.

Notes to 13. *Mathematicians, Astronomers, and Philosophers*

1 In addition to G. S. Kirk and J. E. Raven, *The Presocratic Philosophers*, I have found most useful O. Neugebauer, *The Exact
Sciences in Antiquity*, Oxford 1957; T. L. Heath, *A Manual of
Greek Mathematics*, Oxford 1931; I. Thomas, *Greek Mathematical
Works*, Loeb Classical Library, 1939; E. Schrödinger, *Nature and
the Greeks*, Cambridge 1954; K. von Fritz, *Archiv für Begriffs-
geschichte*, I, 13ff.; C. H. Kahn, *J.H.S.* 90, 1970, 99. These are
quoted below by the name of the author. Some further references are
given above ch. 2, 30ff. Thales: Kirk and Raven, 74ff.; von Fritz,
77; Kahn, 115; Heath 81. Anaximader, Kirk and Raven, 99ff.; Kahn
101ff.
2 Pythagoras: Kirk and Raven, 217, 236ff., 257f.; Heath, 121f.; Thomas,
66f., 172; Schrödinger, 43; von Fritz, 80. Pythagorean communities:
Kirk and Raven, 219ff.
3 Anaxagoras: Kirk and Raven, 391, Heath, 113. Demokritos: Kirk
and Raven, 404; Heath, 115; Thomas, 228. Hippias: Heath, 120,
Thomas, 336. Antiphon: Heath, 122, Thomas, 310. Socrates: Aristophanes, *Clouds*, 171-5. Parmenides, Zeno: Kirk and Raven, 264.
Melissos: Kirk and Raven, 298.
4 Hippokrates: Heath, 121, Thomas, 234, von Fritz, 91. Meton: Kahn,
111, 114; Plutarch, *Nicias*, 13; Comedy, Phrynichos, fr. 21K (the
fountain); Aristophanes, *Banqueters*, ap. Kahn, 114; *Birds*, 997ff., cf.
R. E. Wycherley, *C.Q.* 31, 1937, 22. Theaitetos and Theodoros:
above, ch. 4, p. 68; Plato, *Theaetetus*, 142-3, 147c; Heath, 132ff.;
Thomas, 378f. Eudoxos: above, ch. IV, p. 74; Neugebauer, 153;
Heath 187; Thomas 408.
5 Homer, *Odyssey*, 6, 101; cf. *Iliad*, 8, 13-16; 9, 496-8. Pythagoras, cf.

above, n. 1. Herakleitos, cf. Hermann Fränkel, *A.J.P.* 59, 1938, 309f.; *Wege und Formen*, 253f., 265; Diels-Kranz, no. B 79.

6 *Ancient Medicine*, ch. VIII, cf. also IX, XV; cf. O. Regenbogen, *Quellen u. Studien zur Geschichte der Mathematik*, B, 1, 1931, 131ff.; P. Grenet, *L'Analogie dans Platon*, 253. Plato: *Gorgias* 464b, 465b, cf. P. M. Schuhl, *Fabulation Platonicienne*, 41ff.

7 Plato, *Republic* 368d; the Sun, 506e, particularly 508b-c; the Line, 509d; the Cave, 514a. Grenet, *op. cit.*, 120ff., 171ff.; D. Ross, *Plato's Theory of Ideas*, 39f.

8 Proportions in the world: e.g. Anaximander, Kirk and Raven, no. 112; Pythagoras, cf. above; Herakleitos, Kirk and Raven, nos. 220-1; Alkmaion, Kirk and Raven, no. 286; Euripides, *Phoenissae*, 535; Plato, *Philebus* 30. Aristotle, *Nicomachean Ethics*, 1096b28; 1131a28ff. *Parts of Animals*, 644a17.

9 Plato, *Republic* 511b; *Phaedrus* 265c; *Politicus* 279c; Aristotle, *Posterior Analytics*, 96b25.

10 Goddesses, etc.: cf. above ch. 12, p. 235. *Phaedrus*, 265c; *Republic*, 511b, earlier *Euthyphro*, 12; *Phaedo*, 104a. The syllogism: Aristotle, *Prior Analytics*, 25b37, with Ross *ad loc.*; Einarson, *A.J.P.* 57, 1936, 155. Plato, *Politicus* 279d7-e6.

11 Plato, *Republic*, 509d. Epikrates, above p. 213. Aristotle's objection: *Parts of Animals*, 643b10; Classification: 644a12. *Poetics*, 1447a13.

12 Pythagorean proof: Heath, 94; Thomas, 178. Aristotle, *Prior Analytics*, 48a31-9, cf. Ross, *ad loc.* The syllogism above p. 250 from Plato, *Politicus*. *Metaphysics* 1051a22-23.

13 Parmenides, Kirk and Raven, no. 347. Cf. F. M. Cornford, *Principium Sapientiae*, 118.

14 Zeno, Kirk and Raven 288ff.; cf. H. Fränkel, *A.J.P.* 53, 1942, 1ff., 193ff.; *Wege und Formen*, 198. Melissos: Kirk and Raven, no. 392.

15 Plato, *Republic* 335a-e.

16 Plato, *Meno*, 86e-89c; cf. Thomas, 395; Heath, 178; R. Robinson, *Plato's Earlier Dialectic*, Oxford 1953, 114ff.

17 Plato, *Republic*, 510-511b; cf. above p. 249. *Phaedo*, 97a, 100a-c, 103c, 105b-d. Robinson, *op. cit.*, 123ff.

Notes to 14. *Conclusion*

1 Cf. ch. 3.

2 Cf. ch. 3; ch. 4, 68ff.; ch. 9.

3 Cf. ch. 3; 6, 7. Conservative tract; above p. 112.

4 Kallias, ch. 4, 69ff. Anaxagoras, ch. 5, p. 92.

5 Art, cf. above ch. 8, 148f.

6 Cf. ch. 3, p. 48; ch. 10, p. 182; ch. 9, p. 203.

7 Cf. ch. 5.
8 Cf. ch. 7, p. 129; ch. 9, p. 163; ch. 10, p. 181; ch. 11, p. 203. Assertions: pp. 154, 156, 188, 206, 221, 230.
9 Sophocles etc.: p. 166f. Pericles etc.: pp. 91, 175f. Euripides etc.: p. 188f.
10 Families: pp. 65, 182, 219. Sophocles: p. 72. Pythagorean Communities: p. 244. Athenian schools: p. 73ff.
11 Politics, ch. 6, p. 108ff.
12 Conservative criticism: ch. 9, p. 173; ch. 10, p. 197. Trials: ch. 5, p. 91.
13 Archaism in art: *Everyday Life in Classical Athens*, 158. Panathenaia: ch. 9, p. 165. Symposion songs: ch. 3, p. 55.
14 Religion: ch. 5, p. 88. Omens: ch. 5, p. 87; ch. 12, p. 236.
15 Homer: ch. 2, p. 11.
16 Similes: ch. 2, p. 11; ch. 12, p. 236. Abstracts: ch. 2, p. 12; ch. 12, p. 232.
17 Sentence-structure: ch. 6, p. 123ff. Homer, *Iliad*, I, 53-4. Mycenaean tablets: M. Ventris and J. Chadwick, *Documents in Mycenaean Greek*, 256, no. 140.
18 Homer, *Iliad*, I, 39-41. Mycenaean tablets: Ventris and Chadwick, 257, no. 257.
19 Art: ch. 2, p. 21; ch. 8, p. 154ff.
20 Lyric metre: ch. 2, p. 26; ch. 9, p. 168ff. Drama: ch. 2, p. 27ff.; ch. 10, p. 187; ch. 11, pp. 210ff, 216ff. Maps: ch. 12, p. 222. *Poetics*, 1447a 12.
21 G. E. R. Lloyd, *Polarity and Analogy*; ch. 12, p. 240.
22 Pythagoreans: Kirk and Raven, no. 289. Parmanides, Plato, Aristotle: ch. 13, p. 253ff.
23 Anaximander etc.: ch. 12, p. 233. Physis Nomos: ch. 2, p. 21; ch. 5, p. 96ff.; ch. 6, p. 144; *Airs*, ch. 12, p. 225. Aristotle, *Nicomachean Ethics*, 1134b 18.
24 Hesiod, *Theogeny*, 116ff. Milesians: ch. 2, p. 30. Protagoras etc., ch. 5, p. 95.
25 Protagoras: ch. 6, p. 111. Plate: ch. 6, p. 118; *Republic*, 544; *Politicus*, 291, 301; *Laws*, 697, 698; *Critias*.
26 Anaxagoras and Thucydides: ch. 12, p. 232. Doctors: ch. 12, p. 223. Rhetoricians: ch. 6, p. 122.

Select Bibliography

General

A. Lesky, *History of Greek Literature*, London 1966
N. G. L. Hammond, *History of Greece to 322 B.C.*, Oxford 1967
V. Ehrenberg, *From Solon to Socrates*, London 1968
W. Jaeger, *Paideia*, Oxford 1947
T. B. L. Webster, *From Mycenae to Homer*, London and New York 1964
    Greek Art and Literature, 700-530 B.C., London 1959
    Art and Literature in fourth-century Athens, London 1956, New York 1969
    Everyday Life in Classical Athens, London 1969

Athens: Topography and Society

J. Travlos, *Poleodomike Exelixis ton Athenon*, Athens 1960
R. E. Wycherley, *The Athenian Agora*, III, Princeton 1957
H. A. Thompson, *The Athenian Agora*, Princeton 1962
A. H. M. Jones, *Athenian Democracy*, Oxford 1957
A. E. Zimmern, *The Greek Commonwealth*, Oxford 1922
W. K. Lacey, *The Family in Classical Greece*, London 1968
A. French, *Growth of the Athenian Economy*, London 1964
C. Roebuck, *The Muses at Work*, Cambridge (Mass.) 1969

Education

M. P. Nilsson, *Geschichte der Griechischen Religion*, Munich 1941
W. K. C. Guthrie, *The Greeks and their Gods*, London 1950
M. P. Nilsson, *Greek Piety*, Oxford 1948
A. J. Festugiere, *Personal Religion among the Greeks*, Berkeley 1954

300

L. Deubner, *Attische Feste*, Berlin 1932
C. J. Herington, *Athena Parthenos and Athena Polias*, Manchester 1955
G. E. Mylonas, *Eleusis and the Eleusinian Mysteries*, Princeton 1961
H. W. Parke, *Greek Oracles*, London 1967
A. E. Raubitschek, *Dedications from the Athenian Acropolis*, Princeton 1949

Politics, Law, Rhetoric

V. Ehrenberg, *The Greek State*, Oxford 1960
C. Hignett, *History of the Athenian Constitution*, London 1969
M. Ostwald, *Nomos and the Beginnings of Athenian Democracy*, London 1969
R. J. Bonner and G. Smith, *Administration of Justice from Homer to Aristotle*, Chicago 1930-38
A. R. W. Harrison, *The Law of Athens: the Family and Property*, Oxford 1968
W. Jaeger, *Demosthenes: the Origin and Growth of his Policy*, Cambridge 1938
R. C. Jebb, *The Attic Orators from Antiphon to Isaeus*, London 1893
G. A. Kennedy, *The Art of Persuasion in Greece*, Princeton 1963
J. D. Denniston, *Greek Prose Style*, Oxford 1952

Attic Vases

J. D. Beazley, *Attic Black-figure Vase Painters*, Oxford 1956 (=*ABV*)
 Development of Attic Black-figure, Berkeley 1951 (=*DBF*)
 Attic Red-figure Vase Painters, Oxford 1963 (=*ARV*)
T. B. L. Webster, *Potter and Patron*, London 1972 (=*P and P*)
E. J. Fluck and D. M. Robinson, *Greek Love Names*, Baltimore 1937

Art and Architecture

R. E. Wycherley, *How the Greeks Built Cities*, London 1969
A. W. Lawrence, *Greek Architecture*, Harmondsworth 1967
J. A. Bundgaard, *Mnesicles*, Copenhagen 1957
J. J. Pollitt, *The Art of Greece*, Englewood Cliffs 1965
G. M. A. Richter, *Handbook of Greek Art*, London 1969
J. D. Beazley and B. Ashmole, *Greek Sculpture and Painting*, Cambridge 1966
J. Barron, *Greek Sculpture*, London 1965
B. Ashmole and N. Yalouris, *Olympia*, Phaidon 1967

SELECT BIBLIOGRAPHY

P. E. Corbett, *The Sculpture of the Parthenon*, London 1959
M. Robertson, *Greek Painting*, Geneva 1959
G. M. A. Richter, *Perspective in Greek and Roman Art*, London 1970

Poetry, Music, and Criticism

C. M. Bowra, *Greek Lyric Poetry*, Oxford 1961
  Pindar, Oxford 1964
A. W. Pickard-Cambridge, *Dithyramb, Tragedy and Comedy*, Oxford 1962
T. B. L. Webster, *The Greek Chorus*, London 1970
R. Harriott, *Poetry and Criticism before Plato*, London 1969
J. W. H. Atkins, *Literary Criticism in Antiquity*, London 1952
G. M. A. Grube, *The Greek and Roman Critics*, London 1965
R. Pfeiffer, *History of Classical Scholarship*, Oxford 1968

Drama

A. W. Pickard-Cambridge, *Dramatic Festivals of Athens*, Oxford 1968
T. B. L. Webster, *Greek Theatre Production*, London 1970
A. D. Trendall and T. B. L. Webster, *Illustrations of Greek Drama*, London 1971
B. Snell, *Scenes from Attic Drama*, Berkeley 1965
G. G. A. Murray, *Aeschylus, the Creator of Tragedy*, Oxford 1940
C. J. Herington, *The Author of the Prometheus Bound*, Austin 1970
A. J. Podlecki, *Political Background of Aeschylean Tragedy*, Ann Arbor 1966
G. M. Kirkwood, *A Study of Sophoclean Drama*, Ithaca 1958
T. B. L. Webster, *Introduction to Sophocles*, London 1969
  Tragedies of Euripides, London 1967
D. J. Conacher, *Euripidean Drama*, Toronto 1967
S. A. Barlow, *Imagery of Euripides*, London 1971
A. W. Pickard-Cambridge, *Dithyramb, Tragedy and Comedy*, Oxford 1962
G. M. Sifakis, *Parabasis and Animal Choruses*, London 1971
C. H. Dearden, *The Stage of Aristophanes*, London
G. G. A. Murray, *Aristophanes*, Oxford 1933
V. Ehrenberg, *The People of Aristophanes*, Oxford 1951
T. B. L. Webster, *Studies in Later Greek Comedy*, Manchester 1970

Historians

L. Pearson, *Early Ionian Historians*, Oxford 1939
J. L. Myres, *Herodotus: Father of History*, Oxford 1953
H. A. Immerwahr, *Form and Thought in Herodotus*, Cleveland 1966
C. W. Fornara, *Herodotus*, Oxford 1971
F. M. Cornford, *Thucydides Mythistoricus*, Cambridge 1907
C. N. Cochrane, *Thucydides and the Science of History*, Oxford 1923
J. H. Finley, *Thucydides*, Cambridge (Mass.) 1942
J. de Romilly, *Thucydides and Athenian Imperialism*, Oxford 1942
H. D. Westlake, *Individuals in Thucydides*, Cambridge 1968

Scientists and Mathematicians

B. Farrington, *Science in Antiquity*, London 1969
J. O. Thompson, *A History of Ancient Geography*, Cambridge 1948
H. E. Sigerist, *A History of Medicine*, New York 1961
W. H. S. Jones, *Philosophy and Medicine in Ancient Greece*, Baltimore 1946
O. Neugebauer, *The Exact Sciences in Antiquity*, Oxford 1957
T. L. Heath, *A Manual of Greek Mathematics*, Oxford 1931
D. R. Dicks, *Early Greek Astronomy to Aristotle*, London 1970

Philosophy

W. K. C. Guthrie, *History of Greek Philosophy*, Cambridge 1962
B. Snell, *Discovery of the Mind*, Oxford 1950
G. E. R. Lloyd, *Polarity and Analogy*, Cambridge 1966
H. Diels and W. Kranz, *Die Fragmente der Vorsokratiker*, Berlin 1954
G. S. Kirk and J. E. Raven, *The Presocratic Philosophers*, Oxford 1947
W. D. Ross, *Plato's Theory of Ideas*, Oxford 1951
R. Robinson, *Plato's Earlier Dialectic*, Oxford 1953
J. Stenzel, *Plato's Method of Dialectic*, Oxford 1939
G. E. R. Lloyd, *Aristotle: the Growth and Structure of his Thought*, Cambridge 1968
D. J. Allan, *The Philosophy of Aristotle*, Oxford 1971

Index

INDEX